The Ultimate PMP®
Exam Prep Guide

Wes Balakian, PMP
Timothy S. Bergmann, PMP

Foreword

Welcome to the Ultimate PMP® Exam Prep Guide. We are honored and pleased that you have chosen the Ultimate PMP® Exam Prep Guide as your roadmap for achieving your PMP® credential.

In 1996, Hillary Clinton wrote the book It Takes a Village… This book validates that concept. It certainly took a "village" of TSI contributors to complete this Exam Prep Guide. This has been a team effort to complete the book and validate the concepts contained within. We have every confidence that this product will serve you well in preparing to pass the PMP® Exam.

This is the third book published since 2005 in a series of books and products that are part of TSI's Ultimate Project Management Series™. Please look for other titles and other products at your local bookstore, on Amazon.com and through our Web site: www.truesolutions.com.

As authors, we wo76uld like to thank our list of contributors who helped bring this book into being and who made individual contributions to the book.

Many thanks to participants past and present, including::

- Lorry Balakian
- Sharron Frohner, PMP
- Carole Evans, PMP
- Daron Miller

- Christy MacLennan
- Willis Thomas, PMP
- Darrell Stiffler, PMP
- Natalie Nix (Introduction photos in chapters 5, 8, 29, 38 and 49)

We wish each of you good reading and good luck on your PMP Exam.

Cheers,

Wes Balakian, PMP
CEO, True Solutions Inc.

Timothy S. Bergmann, PMP
CLO, True Solutions Inc.

Ultimate PMP® or CAPM® Exam Prep Course (Instructor-led)

Pass on Your FIRST Try!

Less than .01% of the students who complete our Ultimate PMP® /CAPM® Exam Prep Course have taken us up on this guarantee. Our goal is obviously to ensure that you pass the PMP®/CAPM® Exam on your FIRST attempt – and we are extremely effective at helping you accomplish this. But if you have successfully completed the entire TSI Class and passed our final exam with a 75 or above, and you take the PMP®/CAPM® Exam no sooner than 7 days and within 2 months (60 days) of completing our Ultimate PMP®/CAPM® Exam Prep Course and do not pass,

TSI will provide you with the following support:
FREE Evaluation of your exam results to uncover subject matter weaknesses
FREE one-on-one guidance from a senior TSI Instructor
FREE re-registration in a scheduled TSI Ultimate PMP®/CAPM® Exam Prep Course *
TSI will pay the exam re-take fee (PMI member rate) after your second attempt to pass the PMP®
Exam

*Student Must do the following or the guarantee outlined above will not be honored:
Notify TSI in writing within thirty (30) days of failing the exam, Review the TSI Materials, Read the PMBOK completely
Access the TSI 200 question bank and Score 75% or better. Can not miss more than two (2) consecutive hours of class time.
If you fail the exam and choose to retake our Ultimate PMP/CAPM Exam Prep Course, the course you retake must be based on the same edition of the PMBOK Guide as your original course.

Ultimate PMP® Exam Prep Course (5-Day Instructor-Led) First Pass Guarantee

Less than .01 percent of the students who completed our 5-day Instructor-Led Ultimate PMP® Exam Prep Course have taken us up on this guarantee. Our goal is to obviously ensure that you pass the PMP® Exam on your FIRST attempt, and we are extremely effective at helping you accomplish this. But if you successfully completed the entire TSI class, passed our final exam with a 75 or above, and you take the PMP® Exam no sooner than 7 days and within 2 months (60 days) of completing our Ultimate PMP® Exam Prep Course and do not pass, TSI will provide you with the following support:

• FREE evaluation of your exam results to uncover subject matter weaknesses

• FREE one-on-one guidance from a senior TSI instructor

• FREE re-registration in a scheduled TSI Ultimate PMP® Exam Prep course

• TSI will pay the exam re-take fee for your second attempt to pass the PMP Exam

Students must notify TSI in writing within 30 days of failing the exam, or the guarantee outlined above will not be honored.

If you fail the exam and choose to retake our Ultimate PMP® Exam Prep course, the course you retake must be based on the same edition of the PMBOK® Guide as your original course.

The First Pass Guarantee only applies to Instructor-Led classes.

This page intentionally blank.

Table of Contents

Lesson 1 27

Your ULTIMATE PMP Exam Prep Guide 27

How the Ultimate PMP Exam Prep Guide Gets You Ready to Pass............................. 28

Ultimate PMP Exam Prep Guide Format 29

Before You Begin 33

Lesson 2 35

Project Management Fundamentals 35

How the PMBOK® Guide Applies Processes.. 36

What defines a Project?... 36

Definition of Project Management 38

Interpersonal Skills.. 42

Project Life Cycle 44

Organizational Process Assets 47

Enterprise Environmental Factors... 47

Stakeholders 48

Project Management Office (PMO).. 48

Must Know Concepts 49

Additional Reading 49

Lesson Quiz 50

Lesson 3 53

Mastering the PMBOK® Guide 53

PMBOK® Guide Purpose and Content Structure.. 54

Project Management Processes 55

Project Management Process Groups 55

Knowledge Areas 58

Must Know Concepts 61

Additional Reading 61

Lesson Quiz 62

Lesson 4 63

Initiating Process Group **63**

    Initiating Tasks 64

    Knowledge Requirements 65

Lesson 5 .... **67**

Develop Project Charter **67**

    Process Elements 69

    Process Documents 70

    Process Tasks 72

    Think About It 72

    Must Know Concepts 73

    Additional Reading 73

    Lesson Quiz 74

Lesson 6 .... **77**

Identify Stakeholders **77**

    Process Elements 79

    Process Documents 80

    Process Tasks 81

    Think About It 81

    Must Know Concepts 81

    Additional Reading 82

    Lesson Quiz 83

Lesson 7 .... **85**

Planning Process Group **85**

    Planning Tasks 86

    Knowledge Requirements 87

    Knowledge Check 87

    Knowledge Check 88

Lesson 8 .... **89**

Plan Stakeholder Management **89**

    Process Elements 90

    Process Documents 91

Process Tasks 93

Think About It 93

Must Know Concepts 93

Additional Reading 93

Lesson Quiz 94

Lesson 9 .... **95**

Plan Communications Management **95**

Communication Skills 96

Communications Interference 97

Communication Channels 97

Process Elements 98

Process Documents 99

Process Tasks 101

Think About It 101

Must Know Concepts 101

Additional Reading 102

Lesson Quiz 103

Lesson 10 .... **105**

Plan Scope Management **105**

Process Elements 106

Process Documents 107

Process Tasks 109

Think About It 109

Must Know Concepts 109

Additional Reading 110

Lesson Quiz 110

Lesson 11 .... **113**

Collect Requirements **113**

Process Elements 114

Process Documents 116

Process Tasks 118

Think About It 118

Must Know Concepts 118

Additional Reading 119

Lesson Quiz 120

Lesson 12 123

Define Scope 123

Process Elements 124

Process Documents 125

Process Tasks 127

Think About It 127

Must Know Concepts 127

Additional Reading 128

Lesson Quiz 128

Lesson 13 129

Create WBS 129

Process Elements 131

Process Documents 132

Process Tasks 133

Think About It 133

Must Know Concepts 133

Additional Reading 134

Lesson Quiz 134

Lesson 14 137

Plan Schedule Management 137

Process Elements 138

Process Documents 139

Process Tasks 141

Think About It 141

Must Know Concepts 141

Additional Reading 142

Lesson Quiz 142

Lesson 15 143

Define Activities **143**

    Process Elements 144

    Process Documents 145

    Process Tasks 147

    Think About It 147

    Must Know Concepts 147

    Additional Reading 148

    Lesson Quiz 148

Lesson 16 .... **151**

Sequence Activities **151**

    Process Elements 152

    Process Documents 154

    Precedence Diagramming Method (PDM) 154

    PDM Conventions 155

    Applying Leads and Lags 156

    Process Tasks 157

    Think About It 158

    Must Know Concepts 158

    Additional Reading 159

    Lesson Quiz 160

Lesson 17 .... **163**

Estimate Activity Resources **163**

    Process Elements 164

    Process Documents 165

    Process Tasks 167

    Think About It 167

    Must Know Concepts 168

    Additional Reading 168

    Lesson Quiz 169

Lesson 18 .... **171**

Estimate Activity Durations **171**

    Process Elements 172

Process Documents 174

Process Tasks 174

Think About It 175

Must Know Concepts 175

Additional Reading 176

Lesson Quiz 177

Lesson 19 .... **179**

Develop Schedule **179**

Creating a Project Schedule 180

Tools to Compress a Project Schedule 180

Process Elements 181

Process Documents 183

Process Tasks 184

Think About It 184

Must Know Concepts 185

Additional Reading 186

Lesson Quiz 187

Lesson 20 .... **189**

Plan Human Resource Management **189**

Organizational Theory 190

Process Elements 192

Process Documents 193

Process Tasks 195

Think About It 195

Must Know Concepts 196

Additional Reading 196

Lesson Quiz 197

Lesson 21 .... **199**

Plan Cost Management **199**

Process Elements 200

Process Documents 201

Process Tasks 203

Think About It 203

Must Know Concepts 203

Additional Reading 204

Lesson Quiz 204

Lesson 22 207

Estimate Costs 207

Process Elements 210

Process Documents 212

Process Tasks 213

Think About It 213

Must Know Concepts 213

Additional Reading 214

Lesson Quiz 215

Lesson 23 217

Plan Procurement Management 217

Types of Contracts 219

Process Elements 220

Process Documents 222

Process Tasks 223

Think About It 223

Must Know Concepts 223

Additional Reading 224

Lesson Quiz 224

Lesson 24 225

Determine Budget 225

Process Elements 226

Process Documents 228

Process Tasks 228

Think About It 229

Must Know Concepts 229

Additional Reading 229

Lesson Quiz 230

Lesson 25 231

Plan Quality Management 231

    Process Elements 234

    Process Documents 235

    Process Tasks 237

    Think About It 237

    Must Know Concepts 237

    Additional Reading 238

    Lesson Quiz 238

Lesson 26 239

Plan Risk Management 239

    Process Elements 240

    Process Documents 241

    Process Tasks 244

    Think About It 244

    Must Know Concepts 245

    Additional Reading 245

    Lesson Quiz 246

Lesson 27 247

Identify Risks 247

    Identify Risks Fundamentals 248

    Process Elements 249

    Process Documents 251

    Think About It 252

    Must Know Concepts 253

    Additional Reading 253

    Lesson Quiz 254

Lesson 28 255

Perform Qualitative Risk Analysis 255

    Risk Probability/Impact (P-I) Matrix 256

    Process Elements 257

Process Documents 258

Process Tasks 258

Think About It 258

Must Know Concepts 259

Additional Reading 259

Lesson Quiz 260

Lesson 29 .... **263**

Perform Quantitative Risk Analysis **263**

Quantitative Risk Analysis Tools 264

Modeling Techniques 264

Data Gathering and Representation Techniques 265

Process Elements 265

Process Documents 266

Process Tasks 266

Think About It 267

Must Know Concepts 267

Additional Reading 268

Lesson Quiz 269

Lesson 30 .... **271**

Plan Risk Responses **271**

Risk Response Options 272

Strategies for Negative Risks or Threats 272

Strategies for Positive Risks or Opportunities 273

Process Elements 273

Process Documents 274

Process Tasks 275

Think About It 275

Must Know Concepts 275

Additional Reading 276

Lesson Quiz 277

Lesson 31 .... **279**

Develop Project Management Plan **279**

Process Elements 280

Process Documents 281

Process Tasks 282

Think About It 282

Must Know Concepts 282

Additional Reading 283

Lesson Quiz 284

Lesson 32 .... **287**

Executing Process Group **287**

Executing Tasks 288

Knowledge Requirements 288

Process Group Interactions 289

Knowledge Check 290

Lesson 33 .... **291**

Direct and Manage Project Work **291**

Conflict Management 292

The 'Seven Sources of Conflict' in Project Environments 292

Process Elements 295

Process Documents 296

Process Tasks 298

Think About It 298

Must Know Concepts 298

Additional Reading 299

Lesson Quiz 300

Lesson 34 .... **303**

Acquire Project Team **303**

Process Elements 304

Process Documents 305

Process Tasks 305

Think About it 306

Must Know Concepts 307

Additional Reading 307

Lesson Quiz 308

Lesson 35 .... **309**

Develop Project Team **309**

Motivation Theories 310

Process Elements 311

Process Tasks 313

Think About It 313

Must Know Concepts 313

Additional Reading 314

Lesson Quiz 315

Lesson 36 .... **317**

Manage Project Team **317**

Process Elements 318

Process Documents 319

Process Tasks 319

Think About It 320

Must Know Concepts 320

Additional Reading 321

Lesson Quiz 321

Lesson 37 .... **323**

Manage Communications **323**

Process Elements 324

Process Documents 325

Process Tasks 325

Think About It 326

Must Know Concepts 326

Additional Reading 327

Lesson Quiz 328

Lesson 38 .... **329**

Manage Stakeholder Engagement **329**

Process Elements 330

Process Documents 331

Process Tasks 333

Think About It 333

Must Know Concepts 333

Additional Reading 333

Lesson Quiz 334

Lesson 39 .... **335**

Perform Quality Assurance **335**

Process Elements 336

Process Documents 337

Process Tasks 339

Think About It 339

Must Know Concepts 339

Additional Reading 340

Lesson Quiz 340

Lesson 40 .... **341**

Conduct Procurements **341**

Process Elements 342

Process Documents 344

Process Tasks 345

Think About It 345

Must Know Concepts 345

Additional Reading 346

Lesson Quiz 346

Lesson 41 .... **347**

Monitoring & Controlling Process Group **347**

Monitoring and Controlling Tasks 348

Knowledge Requirements 349

Process Group Interactions 350

Knowledge Check 350

Lesson 42 .... **351**

Control Scope 351

    Process Elements 352

    Process Documents 353

    Process Tasks 355

    Think About It 355

    Must Know Concepts 355

    Additional Reading 356

    Lesson Quiz 356

Lesson 43 357

Control Schedule 357

    Process Elements 358

    Process Documents 360

    Process Tasks 361

    Think About It 361

    Must Know Concepts 361

    Additional Reading 362

    Lesson Quiz 362

Lesson 44 365

Control Costs 365

    Variance Formulas 367

    Process Elements 369

    Process Tasks 370

    Earned Value Application 370

    Must Know Concepts 373

    Additional Reading 374

    Lesson Quiz 375

Lesson 45 377

Control Communications 377

    Process Elements 378

    Process Documents 379

    Process Tasks 382

    Think About It 382

Must Know Concepts 383

Additional Reading 383

Lesson Quiz 384

Lesson 46 .... **385**

Control Stakeholder Engagement **385**

Process Elements 386

Process Documents 387

Process Tasks 387

Think About It 388

Must Know Concepts 388

Additional Reading 388

Lesson Quiz 389

Lesson 47 .... **391**

Control Risks **391**

Process Elements 392

Process Documents 393

Process Tasks 395

Think About It 395

Must Know Concepts 395

Additional Reading 396

Lesson Quiz 396

Lesson 48 .... **399**

Control Procurements **399**

Process Elements 400

Process Documents 402

Process Tasks 402

Think About It 403

Must Know Concepts 403

Additional Reading 404

Lesson Quiz 404

Lesson 49 .... **407**

Control Quality **407**

    Common Quality Tools 409

    Process Control Charts 409

    Process Elements 410

    Process Documents 411

    Process Tasks 412

    Think About It 412

    Must Know Concepts 412

    Additional Reading 413

    Lesson Quiz 414

Lesson 50 ....**415**

Validate Scope **415**

    Process Elements 416

    Process Documents 417

    Process Tasks 419

    Think About It 419

    Must Know Concepts 419

    Additional Reading 419

    Lesson Quiz 420

Lesson 51 ....**421**

Monitor & Control Project Work **421**

    Process Elements 422

    Process Documents 423

    Process Tasks 423

    Think About It 424

    Must Know Concepts 425

    Additional Reading 425

    Lesson Quiz 426

Lesson 52 ....**427**

Perform Integrated Change Control **427**

    Process Elements 428

    Process Documents 429

Process Tasks 432

Think About It 432

Must Know Concepts 433

Additional Reading 433

Lesson Quiz 434

Lesson 53 .... **435**

Closing Process Group **435**

Closing Tasks 436

Knowledge Requirements 437

Lesson 54 .... **439**

Close Procurements **439**

Process Elements 441

Process Documents 441

Process Tasks 442

Think About It 442

Must Know Concepts 443

Additional Reading 443

Lesson Quiz 444

Lesson 55 .... **445**

Close Project or Phase **445**

Process Elements 446

Process Tasks 449

Think About It 449

Must Know Concepts 450

Additional Reading 450

Lesson Quiz 451

Lesson 56 .... **453**

Mastering the PMP Exam **453**

The Science of Answering MCQ Exam Questions 454

Additional Reading 461

Appendix A **463**

Lesson Quiz Solutions 463

Appendix B 495

Rapid Review Sheets 495

    Lesson 2 – Fundamentals 495

    Lesson 3 – Mastering the PMBOK® Guide 496

    Lesson 4 – Initiating Process Group 497

    Lesson 5 – Develop Project Charter 498

    Lesson 6 – Identify Stakeholders 499

    Lesson 7 – Planning Process Group 500

    Lesson 8 – Plan Stakeholder Management 501

    Lesson 9 – Plan Communications Management 502

    Lesson 10 – Plan Scope Management 503

    Lesson 11 – Collect Requirements 504

    Lesson 12 – Define Scope 505

    Lesson 13 – Create WBS 506

    Lesson 14 – Plan Schedule Management 507

    Lesson 15 – Define Activities 508

    Lesson 16 – Sequence Activities 509

    Lesson 17 – Estimate Activity Resources 511

    Lesson 18 – Estimate Activity Durations 512

    Lesson 19 – Develop Schedule 514

    Lesson 20 – Plan Human Resource Management 517

    Lesson 21 – Plan Cost Management 518

    Lesson 22 – Estimate Costs 519

    Lesson 23 – Plan Procurement Management 520

    Lesson 24 – Determine Budget 521

    Lesson 25 – Plan Quality Management 522

    Lesson 26 – Plan Risk Management 523

    Lesson 27 – Identify Risks 524

    Lesson 28 – Perform Qualitative Risk Analysis 526

    Lesson 29 – Perform Quantitative Risk Analysis 527

    Lesson 30 – Plan Risk Responses 528

    Lesson 31 – Develop Project Management Plan 529

Lesson 32 – Executing Process Group 530

Lesson 33 – Direct & Manage Project Work 531

Lesson 34 – Acquire Project Team 532

Lesson 35 – Develop Project Team 533

Lesson 36 – Manage Project Team 534

Lesson 37 – Manage Communications 535

Lesson 38 – Manage Stakeholder Engagement 536

Lesson 39 – Perform Quality Assurance 537

Lesson 40 – Conduct Procurements 538

Lesson 41 – Monitoring and Controlling Process Group 539

Lesson 42 – Control Scope 540

Lesson 43 – Control Schedule 541

Lesson 44 – Control Costs 542

Lesson 45 – Control Communications 544

Lesson 46 – Control Stakeholder Engagement 545

Lesson 47 – Control Risks 546

Lesson 48 – Control Procurements 547

Lesson 49 – Control Quality 548

Lesson 50 – Validate Scope 549

Lesson 51 – Monitor and Control Project Work 550

Lesson 52 – Perform Integrated Change Control 551

Lesson 53 – Closing Process Group 552

Lesson 54 – Close Procurements 553

Lesson 55 – Close Project or Phase 554

Appendix C **555**

Additional Examples & Supplemental Materials **555**

This page intentionally blank

This page intentionally blank.

Lesson 1
Your ULTIMATE PMP Exam Prep Guide

Objectives

At the end of this lesson, you will be able to:

- Understand how this book is organized
- Understand how the Ultimate PMP Exam Prep Guide gets you ready to pass the PMP Exam

Process Locator for the PMBOK® Guide

	Initiating	Planning	Executing	M&C	Closing
Integration					
Scope					
Time					
Cost		Contains General Management Information that is applicable to all areas of the PMBOK® Guide and applies to project management in general			
Quality					
Human Resource					
Communications					
Risk					
Procurement					
Stakeholder					

Congratulations on your initiative to begin the Project Management Professional (PMP) certification process!

We are honored that you have chosen the *Ultimate PMP Exam Prep Guide* as your roadmap to achieve your Project Management Professional (PMP®) credential. This product will serve you well in preparing you to pass the PMP Exam.

In this lesson, we will familiarize you with this Guide. You will begin learning how to use the Guide to prepare for your PMP Exam. Ultimate PMP Exam Prep Guide incorporates many exercises to involve all of your learning senses. These exercises were carefully designed to ensure full synthesis of your learning abilities without having to spend hours with tedious memorization or endless flashcard drills. We suggest that you simply progress through this Guide and follow the instructions as they are presented. When you have worked your way completely through this Guide, you will have a much better grasp of the materials required to pass your PMP Exam.

Throughout the *Ultimate PMP Exam Prep Guide* we will direct you to read excerpts from the *Project Management Body of Knowledge (PMBOK® Guide) Fifth Edition*. These readings are essential to your understanding and knowledge transfer prior to attempting the PMP Exam. This book has pages marked *"This page intentionally blank"* that you can use to write on and keep notes.

How the Ultimate PMP Exam Prep Guide Gets You Ready to Pass

Ultimate PMP Exam Prep Guide prepares you to pass the PMP Exam by developing all the knowledge competencies you need to fully understand exam questions and recognize preferred answers. In addition to mastering the project management learning material, in Lesson 56 you will learn about multiple choice questions and the science behind answering these questions.

Please follow your Guide faithfully from start to finish and you will be assured of mastering all of the knowledge-based material needed to pass the PMP Exam. Your Ultimate PMP Exam Prep Guide employs adult learning techniques to ensure that you learn and understand the material.

- Information is presented in smaller, bite-sized portions. You will not be forced to labor with large blocks of complicated material.
- Effective repetition is used throughout the Guide. Embrace this as it will help in your learning.
- Personal reflection exercises are incorporated to help you understand how the information is applied in real-world project environments.
- Writing exercises are incorporated. Writing the material provides an extended dimension to your learning.
- To help you develop an effective mindset for the exam, much of the material is presented as if you are already a certified PMP.
- To help you better understand how the information is applied in real-world project environments, exercises and lessons learned narratives are included in the materials.
- Many training organizations present the PMP Exam materials in the same order as the PMBOK Guide. In order to facilitate your understanding of the material, we present the processes in a logical sequence like you would use these processes on a typical project. This helps your understanding of process flows throughout the project life cycle.

- Strong visual imagery helps ensure effective recall of information on exam day. Graphics are included in every chapter of this Guide. Additionally, visual review exercises are incorporated to enhance your learning.
- Sample questions are incorporated at the end of each lesson. This helps reinforce understanding of the material. Detailed answers are provided for each question.
- Comprehensive information about the PMP Exam is presented at the beginning of each process group throughout the Guide.
- Exam Tips are provided throughout the book along with an exam day checklist in the "Exam Preparation" chapter.

Ultimate PMP Exam Prep Guide Format

The Ultimate PMP Exam Prep Guide presents the needed information in a series of short lessons to facilitate your learning experience. No lesson in this guide is intended to take more than one hour to read, do the recommended reading, work the exercises, perform the knowledge check and finish that lesson. This allows the reader to proceed at his or her own pace and study as they have time.

At the beginning of every lesson there is a graphic advising the reader of the lesson number, the name of the lesson – and what parts of the PMBOK Guide the lesson refers to. A graphical grid shows what knowledge area and process group the lesson will be referring to.

Examples of these elements are shown below:

Example Lesson 5

Develop Project Charter

Objectives
At the end of this lesson, you will be able to:
- Describe the purpose of the Develop Project Charter process
- Describe the Inputs, Tools and Techniques, and Outputs of the
- Develop Project Charter Process
- List the key items that should be included in a Project Charter

Example Process Locator for the PMBOK® Guide

	Initiating	Planning	Executing	M&C	Closing
Integration					
Scope					
Time					
Cost					
Quality					
Human Resource					
Communications					
Risk					
Procurement					
Stakeholder					

Most lessons follow the introduction with a narrative describing the process or process group. After the reader has read the narrative describing the knowledge elements associated with that lesson, then in process related lessons a description of the process inputs, tools and techniques and outputs will be shown. The process elements are exposed in a narrative and a graphic format.

An example process graphic is shown below.

Develop Project Charter
This process formally sanctions a new project

Inputs	Tools and Techniques	Outputs
• Project Statement of Work (SOW)	• Expert Judgment	• Project Charter
• Business Case	• Facilitation Techniques	
• Agreements		*TSI* Study Aid
• Enterprise Environmental Factors		This chart is part of the study aid poster series available at: *www.TrueSolutions.com*
• Organizational Process Assets		

Figure x.1. Process Elements within the Develop Project Charter process

Most processes have specific defined outputs. These outputs are almost always a document of some sort. After we have discussed the process elements, we will look towards the practical application of the process by exposing the types of documents that would be expected and showing a sample of a document template for that process.

An example template is shown below (in highly reduced format).

True Solutions, Inc.
Project Management Template
Version 2: Project Charter Template

TSI

Project Charter

Project Name:	
Prepared by:	
Date:	
Project purpose:	Identify the customers who are to receive and benefit from the product developed by the project and the need the product is intended to meet (either as a problem to solve or as an opportunity to exploit)
Planned Objectives:	Identify what product or service is to be delivered at the end of the project, and at any interim delivery points. Describe the product sufficiently to enable the project team to create it, and for agreement to be reached at product delivery time that the product has been correctly produced
High level project description:	Briefly explain the requirements for the project and a description of the project to afford an understanding of known needs and tasks to accomplish project
High level product description:	Briefly identify major deliverables to be created by this project
Planned schedule:	Identify what milestones will be a key factor to reach to project objectives
Initial budget:	Use a Rough Order of Magnitude estimate to show budget requirements
Program or Portfolio Links:	Identify how the project links to the work of the organization and any programs being managed in the organization
Assignment of Project Manager, responsibility and authority	Often the Project Manager will have already been decided before hand or during the charter. Identify who the Project Manager is and what their responsibility is during the project and what authority level they have (decision making, budget, approving, etc.)
Name and Title of Sponsor:	Identify who the project sponsor is (persons or groups) and explain what their authority will be within the project
Other:	Identify and explain any other matters that are important for the initiation and conduct of the project. Focus on charter issues of importance between the project sponsor and the project manager. This section is not for describing the project plan
Approval:	Sponsor: Date:

TSI   Application Aid

This form is available
individually or as
part of a set at:
www.TrueSolutions.com

Following the exposition of process documents, most chapters will then discuss typical tasks associated with performing the process.

A "Think About It" exercise may follow the process task discussion. The Think About It exercises come in several versions. You may find a Lessons Learned discussion for your knowledge and enjoyment, you may find questions to answer, and you may find items to check off. Each will help you better understand the information that you have just read.

Every lesson contains a section of "Must Know Concepts". This is a list of elements from the lesson that are essential knowledge for your PMP Exam study. The Must Know Concepts are ranked in order of importance. There is a graphic associated with Must Knows that also indicates importance for the reader.

Every lesson ends with a knowledge check. This usually consists of 3-5 multiple choice questions. Explanations are found in the back of the Ultimate PMP Exam Prep Guide in Appendix A.

Before You Begin

Study Tip

Create Your Own PMP Exam Prep War Room

Preparing to pass your PMP Exam is a project in itself. Consider setting up your own project war room to create a dedicated space for working through your preparation activities. A quiet space where you can work undisturbed is best. You will need comfortable seating, desk space and wall space to display key information. An online computer will be helpful to access the Project Management Institute website, Prometric website or other websites for applying, scheduling and gathering information.

Many experts suggest low volume classical music to enhance your learning ability. You may wish to include this as a feature in your PMP Exam Prep war room.

As a final note, this Study Tip depiction will be used throughout the book when the author wants to call your attention to an important piece of information.

End of Lesson 1

This page intentionally blank.

Lesson 2
Project Management Fundamentals

Objectives

At the end of this lesson, you will be able to:

- Understand the definition of a project
- Understand the definition of project management
- Understand the role of the project manager
- Understand how constraints and external factors influence projects

Process Locator for the PMBOK® Guide

	Initiating	Planning	Executing	M&C	Closing
Integration					
Scope					
Time					
Cost					
Quality		Contains General Management Information that is applicable to all areas of the PMBOK® Guide and applies to project management in general			
Human Resource					
Communications					
Risk					
Procurement					
Stakeholder					

This chapter will discuss a basic diagram of project management as a whole to educate the student on the minimum required to manage a project.

In this chapter, we will explore some basic information about project management. We will provide basic definitions of projects and project management, discuss organizations and cultural affect on projects and their chances for success.

How the PMBOK® Guide Applies Processes

The PMBOK® Guide defines material and processes that are "Generally recognized as good practices" for project management. In the PMBOK® Guide, 47 processes have been defined. Will the project manager use each and every one of these processes on every project? The answer to this question is a resounding "maybe".

PMBOK® Guide stresses that there is no specific fixed way that a project must be managed. The project manager must choose which processes, and in what order the processes are performed, based on the needs of the specific project.

Many companies' project life cycles define specific subsets of processes that should be performed based on the size and complexity of the project. PMI specifies that the project manager must choose which processes are appropriate for the project, but each of the 5 process groups must be performed in each project phase.

We encourage the project manager to look at the 47 processes as a checklist. As we delve further into this information, we will discuss the concept that each of the 5 process groups must be performed in each phase of the project. Since we are using all of the process groups, it provides some logic that each of the 47 processes might be addressed in each phase of the project as well. While the project manager and project team may not fully perform and address each process in each phase, if the project manager uses the processes as a checklist, then there is a lesser chance that items will be missed on the project. Refer to your TSI Project Management Process Poster #1; reference the Process Knowledge Areas Table.

What defines a Project?

The definition of a project has three parts. A project is temporary, it is unique and it is progressive.

Temporary
The project must have a specific beginning date and a specific end date. It is a temporary endeavor undertaken to perform a specific set of objectives. The project is usually undertaken to create something.

A project is not an ongoing operation. While the project may fulfill the strategic plan of the organization and via the temporary endeavor, sustain the organizational entity, a project is not an operation.

Even though a project is a temporary experience – there is no specific timeframe associated with projects. Whether the project is 2 days long or 2 years long, if it is a temporary endeavor and has a defined scope, then it is a project.

Unique

The project is undertaken to perform a specific set of objectives. A project is usually performed to create something, usually a specific unique product or service. Sometimes a project is a temporary endeavor executed for a specific purpose; i.e. Sarbanes-Oxley projects that many companies recently performed. Projects focus on creating deliverables.

Progressive

The project is progressive – or more accurately stated, it is progressively elaborated. What do we mean by progressively elaborated? The definition or scope of the project is progressive. At the beginning of the project the project manager and stakeholders will have a high level idea of the scope of the project (work to be performed) and the scope of the product (configuration or requirements definition). As the project progresses the definition is progressively detailed. In the planning portion of the project, the project manager and stakeholders learn more about the project and product, and record the details into a scope and requirements document. In the executing and during monitoring and controlling, the stakeholders learn more and modify the project and product description in order to ensure that the end product meets needs.

This progressive elaboration can be closely compared to the "Plan-Do-Check-Act cycle" defined by Deming as a quality process. In the Plan portion – you obviously plan and document your intent. Details are documented as they are available and finalized. In the "Do" portion – you do the planned work, create the planned product. In the "Check-Act" portion of the project you make sure you are creating what you defined – and take corrective action if you are not on the right path. Combined with interpersonal skills that project managers must have and use in order to be successful, progressive elaboration is a powerful tool that facilitates project successes.

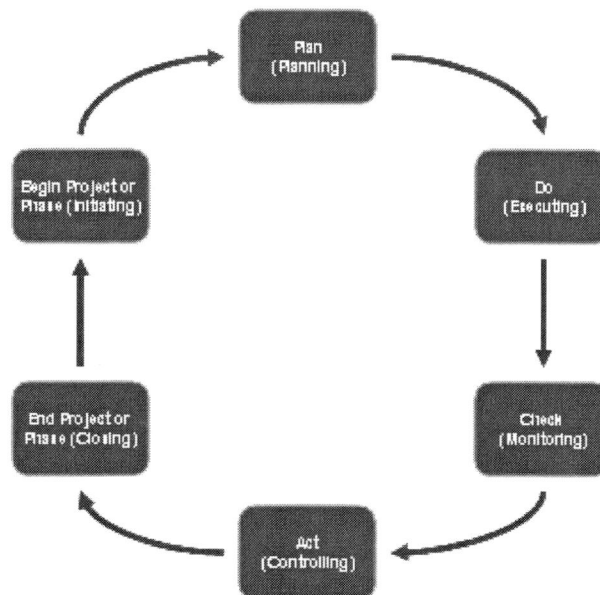

Figure 2.1 Plan-Do-Check-Act Cycle

Definition of Project Management

Project management is "the application of knowledge, skills, tools and techniques to project activities in order to meet project requirements".

This is the best definition of project management. This is how PMI defines project management in the PMBOK® Guide on p.5.

There are a few other definitions of project management that can also be considered. One simple definition of project management is "the management of competing project demands". Competing demands are most often defined as the project constraints that make up the "triple constraint". In addition, there are several other project elements that fall into this category; the triple constraint is most often defined as:

- Scope (Work)
- Time (Schedule)
- Cost (Budget)

Other project constraints or demands include:

- Risk
- Quality
- Resources

The "triple-triple constraint" is depicted in the illustration below.

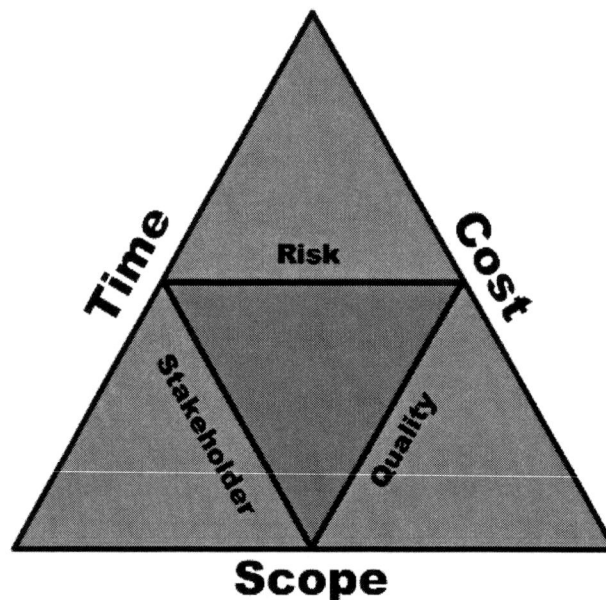

Figure 2.2 Triple Constraint

In addition to the concept of managing constraints, an additional vision of project success is emerging. This concept of success includes management of all of the constraint factors and providing value to the business.

Projects, Programs and Portfolios

Projects, Programs and Portfolios interact to manage the overall resource use and work outputs of the organization. In order to understand these three related, yet very different entities, we first need to understand their definitions at a high level. (We previously covered the definition of a project).

Programs

Programs are simply a group of projects that are managed together in a unified way. An example of a program could be the development of a new subdivision. The development company may have individual projects for installing the infrastructure (streets, drainage, sewer), surveying and sub-dividing the property, developing home plans, setting up a sales process, creating park spaces and perhaps designing and building a community center. Multiple projects that all roll up into one program: the "XYZ Subdivision."

Program Management

When projects are rolled together to create a program, a higher form of management takes place. Program management involves managing the multiple projects in order to achieve the objectives and planned benefits of the overall program. While the individual project objectives contribute to this overall benefit, the individual project outcomes are lessened in focus, with the overall focus remaining on the overall or program benefit.

Portfolio Management

A portfolio is a collection of projects or programs or other work within the enterprise. Portfolio management is intended to maximize the benefits from these projects and programs to the enterprise.

The primary purpose of Project Portfolio Management is an approach that is used in conjunction with other project management techniques. Project Portfolio Management is a method for selecting which projects should be undertaken and which should be shelved or discarded. The selection process is usually based on benefit, profitability and affordability of the proposed project. It can be simply a method of matching business need to available resources to determine project approval.

Figure 2.3 Portfolio Management Alignment

Projects, Programs and Portfolios interact on a constant basis within the enterprise. There are many interactions that occur between the Project and the Program. The successful alignment of the required Programs, Projects and Operational Work within the organization facilitates overall business success. Failure to consider all the required elements and the available resources often leads to over-allocation of resources, difficult or impossible working conditions and project, program or business failure.

The diagram following shows the high-level relationships between Portfolio Management, Program Management and Project Management.

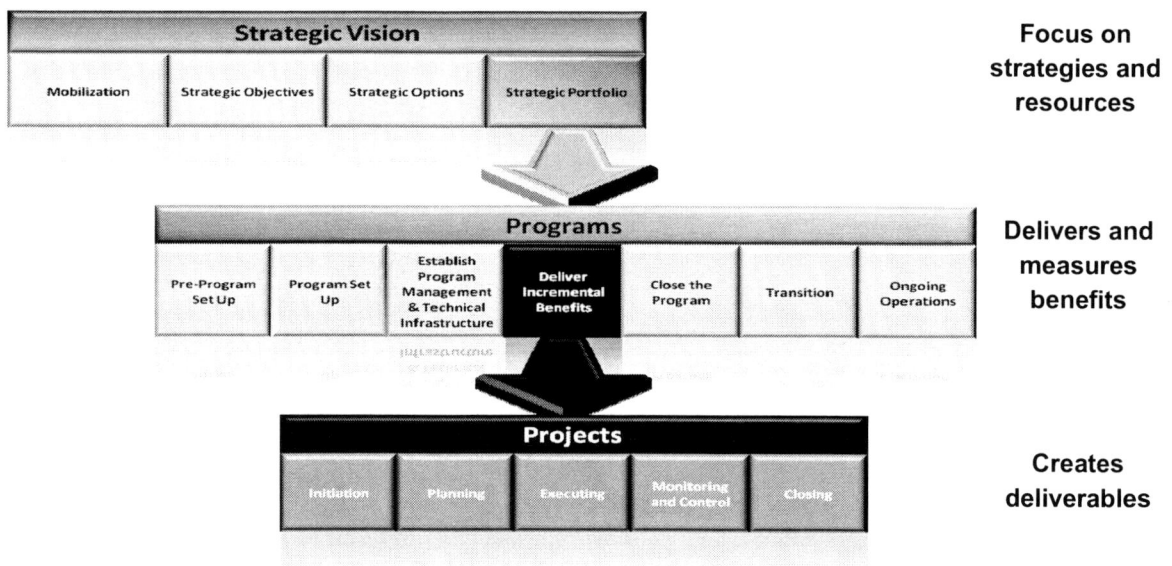

Figure 2.4 Portfolio, Program and Project Management Relationships

Other Areas of Project Interaction

When managing a project, the project manager will have many other interactions to be concerned with. In most organizations, the project manager will interact with many departments or groups. Some examples of these are:

- Operations Groups: Operations management is an area that is technically considered outside of project management. But many times, the project manager (or project coordinator) finds themselves working in an operations group and reporting to a functional/operations manager. The project manager or coordinator must work within the defined role and responsibility and interact with and accommodate operations needs.

- The Project Management Office (PMO): Project methodologies and processes are often defined by the organizational PMO. Projects within the organization are sometimes authorized by the PMO and their progress is sometimes monitored by the PMO.

- Strategic Planning departments: Projects are intended to be performed to meet the strategic objectives of the organization. While the strategies are decided at the executive and portfolio management level, the project manager and team will often interact with and respond to the strategy team.

- Other departments and organizations: Depending on what type of organization the project manager finds themselves working in, their role and level of authority may vary widely. In most cases, the project manager and project will have stakeholders based in multiple company departments.

Providing Business Value

Each business defines what items are defined as "valuable" for that organization or enterprise. As stated previously in this book, it is the main objective of a project to create a deliverable. When that deliverable is completed, it is transitioned to a program manager or an operations manager for benefits measurement and realization. The overriding goal of projects, along with programs and the overall portfolio, is to provide some form of value to the business.

Business value can be tangible elements, like: cash, income or stockholder equity. Value can also be less tangible elements like: goodwill, brand recognition, or public benefit. In some cases value can be derived for internal process improvement or efficiencies.

Competencies Required to be a Successful Project Manager

The main role of the project manager is to integrate all of the pieces and parts and elements associated with the project scope and product scope to successfully meet the business need. As the project integrator, the project manager has to have a wide knowledge base in order to be effective. The project manager has to have some areas of specific knowledge and capabilities or skills:

- **Knowledge** - of project management and general management

- **Performance** – ability to accomplish assigned role
- **Personal** - skills enabling communications and interaction with stakeholders

Project Management Knowledge

The project manager must have project management knowledge and experience to draw on. This experience base will contribute largely to the ability to make decisions based on project management situations.

In addition to general and experience based project management knowledge, the project manager who is taking the PMP Exam needs to have knowledge of specific knowledge contained in the PMBOK® Guide. The PMBOK® Guide specifies 10 Knowledge areas and 47 specific project processes contained in 5 process groups to be used to manage the project. Each process has inputs, tools and techniques and outputs to be used for project management. The successful project manager needs to be fully knowledgeable in this area and fully knowledgeable in using these processes.

General Management Knowledge

The project manager must be able to manage the business environment and the people involved in the project order to manage the project. Projects are a portion of the overall work portfolio of the organization and are executed in order to meet organizational objectives. General management includes knowledge elements like finance and budgeting, human resource processes, regulations and procedures, conflict management and other general business knowledge areas.

Interpersonal Skills

The project manager must be able to manage project communications and interactions among the people involved in the project order to manage the project. In order to accomplish this, project managers must have expert interpersonal skills.

The needed interpersonal skills that are cited in the PMBOK® Guide Fifth Edition are:

- Communicating
- Leadership
- Team Building
- Motivation
- Influencing
- Decision Making
- Political and cultural awareness
- Negotiation
- Trust Building
- Conflict Management
- Coaching

Communicating

Communicating is the most important skill that a project manager can have. In my opinion it is not overstated to say that if you are a good communicator, then you have the potential to be a good project manager. Conversely, if you are a poor communicator, if the skill does not "flow" from you – then you need to work on this skill in order to foster success. A poor communicator will almost always be a poor project manager.

Leadership

It may come as a surprise to some that the project management position is considered to be a leadership position. The project manager is expected to do more than just "manage" within the environment. The project manager is expected to lead the project team to fulfill the needs of the enterprise.

Leading includes establishing direction, aligning people in the organization to achieve goals and motivating the people to reach these goals.

Team Building

In order to achieve better levels of performance from the team, the leader must encourage the team to work together. Team Building is often done in conjunction with the process of "Develop Project Team". Team Building can include team building activities and common interpersonal interactions.

Motivation

In order to achieve better levels of performance from the team, the leader must motivate the team. Motivation requires encouragement, gaining buy-in for the goals and objectives and energizing the team to meet those goals.

Influencing the Organization

Influencing the Organization is an important interpersonal skill used by the project manager. Simply stated, influencing the organization is gaining buy-in and support from the organization for the project that you are executing. All of the preceding interpersonal skills will contribute to your ability to influence the organization.

Decision Making

Part of the role of the project manager is to make decisions. Decision styles tend to fall into one of four categories, such as: Command, Consult, Consensus or Chance.

Political and Cultural Awareness

Internal and external factors that affect the project make up the project environment. These cultural, economic, societal, religious (and other) factors that form the project environment influence the outcome of the project.

The project manager must understand the social and cultural environment that they are working in. In addition, the project manager should understand what affects the outcome of the project will have on society and the culture that the project is being executed in. In order to understand cultural and social implications, the project manager may need knowledge of religious, ethnic, economic, demographic, education and other aspects of the people/culture/environment that the project is being executed in.

Negotiating

The main definition for negotiating is to reach an agreement. *The goal of negotiating is to reach a fair and reasonable decision and to establish a positive relationship with the other parties while negotiating.*

A negotiator tries to reach a fair and reasonable resolution to whatever situation exists. The project manager should establish rules for conflict management up front when initiating and planning the project. If no rules exist, then open conflict can punctuate an otherwise successful project and ruin chances for success.

Trust Building

Progress is often lacking when trust is also not present. It is imperative that the project manager establish a trusting relationship between themselves and their project team and stakeholders. Without trust, every communication is colored with a potentially negative perception.

Conflict Management

Throughout the project, the project manager will experience a need to negotiate and to resolve minor and sometimes major conflicts. The project manager should know conflict management techniques, such as Confronting, Collaborating, Smoothing, Forcing, Compromising or Withdrawing, as tools to facilitate conflict resolution.

Coaching

A good project manager is a good coach. A good coach knows when to encourage the team or team member and when to use a reprimand as a tool. Knowing the team and knowing the stakeholders is a key project success element.

Project Life Cycle

Another important concept to understand is the Project Life Cycle (PLC). The project life cycle is created by the performing organization. The project life cycle meets the needs for project management for the organization and meets specific requirements dictated by the specialized application areas in which the organization works.

In general, the PLC defines what phases are to be used in executing projects. The PLC defines what type of work is to be done in each phase. The PLC defines what types of roles and organizations are expected in each phase of the project. If there is a Project Management Office (PMO) within the performing organization, the PMO may be responsible for creating the project life cycle.

Project Phases

A phase is part of the defined project life cycle. Each phase creates one or more deliverables and ends with a review. A deliverable is defined as a tangible, verifiable work product. The end of phase review appraises the deliverable and makes the decision to proceed or cancel the project.

Phases are generally named for the type of work to be performed within the phase. For example, a Discovery Phase might be at the beginning of a project, intended to discover all the pertinent facts and define the project. A Design phase might follow the Discovery phase. The Design phase intended to complete all of the planning and definitions for the product of the project. A Development phase could follow, where work would be performed to create the product and finally, a Deployment phase might be the final phase in the life cycle to implement the product and turn it over to an operational group.

The end of phase review usually measures project performance to date. This review can also be called a <u>phase exit, a stage gate or a kill point</u>. The end of a phase is a logical point to stop the project if it is not proceeding as planned.

The PMBOK Guide does not specify what your phase has to contain, what naming convention to use or how many phases a project life cycle has to have. This will be defined by the performing organization based on the specialized application area that the project is being executed in.

Phases can be sequential or overlapping. Your specialized application need will determine which method is best for project management in your organization.

Sequential Phases

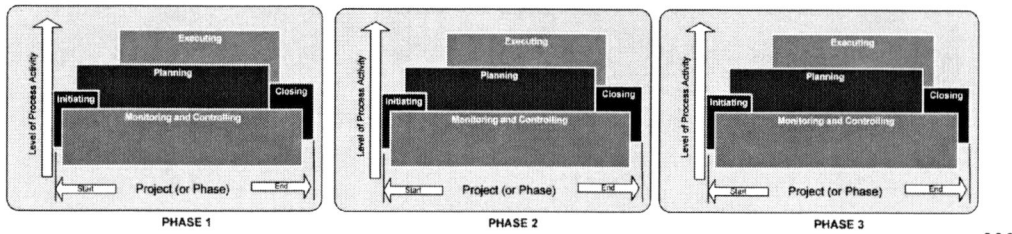

Overlapping Phases

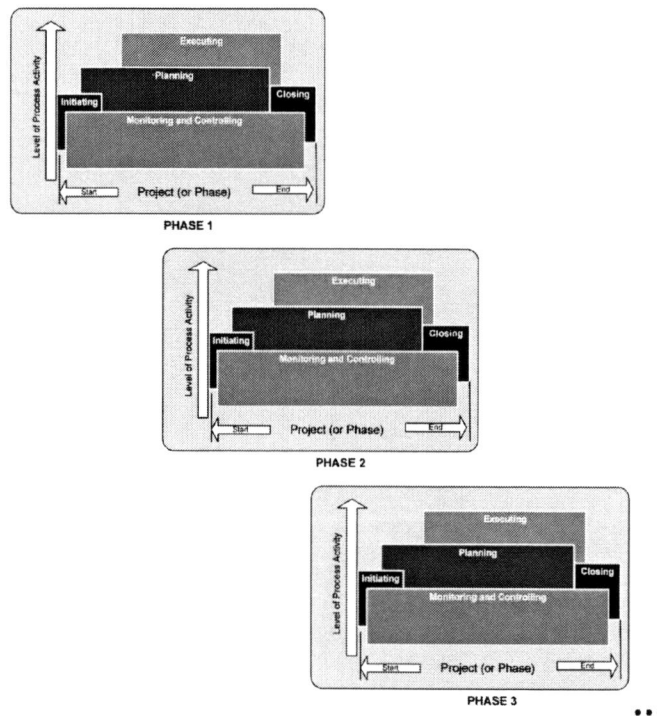

Figure 2.5 Sequential v. Overlapping Phases

How Organizations Influence a Project

Another important concept to understand is the how the organization affects projects and project management. Based on the organization's culture, the style of the organization and organization management, communications elements within the organization and the specific organization structure used, project management may be positively or negatively affected.

Elements of the organization culture, like, the leadership vision, mission and beliefs will provide an influence. Risk tolerance levels, cultural considerations such as being a fast, forward-thinking, flexible company versus being passive and reactive, will affect how the project is perceived and related to.

Communications factors such as the openness in the organization and available methods of communications will affect project management and potentially, project success. More will be discussed about communications models later in this book.

The organization structure itself, whether the project is performed in a Functional, Matrix or Projectized organization will influence project management. (This will be discussed later in our book in another chapter.)

Organizational Process Assets

Throughout the PMBOK Guide, you will see and use Organizational Process Assets as an important input to planning and executing the project. You will also see that Organizational Process Assets Updates are frequently cited as an output. So, it is important for you to understand this element.

Organizational Process Assets are processes, procedures, policies and the knowledge base that is present in and used by the performing entity to contribute to overall project management. These could be elements such as guidelines and criteria for performing project management, specific standards to be used, and templates or tools to use during project management.

As the project is executed, Organizational Process Assets include elements like change control procedures, financial controls and issue / defect management processes / policies. Processes, procedures and policies associated with risk management, quality management and work management overall, can also be included as part of Organizational Process Assets.

Updates to Organizational Process Assets are updates to records, processes, procedures or the corporate knowledge base.

Enterprise Environmental Factors

Along with Organizational Process Assets, Enterprise Environmental Factors are also often used as an input to many planning processes. In general, Enterprise Environmental Factors are the internal and external elements that may influence the organization and thereby affect the project.

Since this is an often used input, it is important to understand Enterprise Environmental Factors, which include:

- The organization's culture, structure and governance policies
- Geographic considerations
- Government regulation or industry standards
- Existing infrastructure
- Existing and available human resources
- Market conditions and condition of the industry your company is in
- Available enterprise tools, like a Project Management Information System (PMIS)
- Human Resources Personnel Records
- Configuration Management

Stakeholders

Stakeholders are the individuals and organizations that are participating in the project, or whose interests are being affected by the project.

Simply stated, stakeholders are anyone who has a viable interest in the project.

In an ideal world, all of the stakeholders for your project should be identified, considered, consulted, involved and apprised of project activities. In reality, many times your stakeholders will have individuals or groups who are working on their behalf. If you had to bring all of your stakeholders to each and every project meeting it would probably cause a long and arduous project. Using designated representatives will often provide adequate communications for defining and implementing the project.

You need to consider stakeholders that are apparent and some who might not be. Stakeholders that are close to the project and readily apparent include the project manager, project team members, sponsor, customer and end user. Stakeholders that might be a little further "removed" from the project include individuals and groups such as the executives in the organization, the board, other senior managers (think synergy), other departments and groups who might be able to use the product, vendors and suppliers and sometimes, the general public.

Your job as project manager is to communicate with your stakeholders about the project. In turn, the main role of the stakeholder is to communicate their objectives and expectations.

Project Management Office (PMO)

A Project Management Office (PMO) is an organizational structure intended to standardize project related processes and governance as well as to facilitate sharing of resources, methods, tools and techniques. There are three major PMO types listed in the PMBOK® Guide 5th Edition.

Type	Supportive	Controlling	Directive
Characteristics	A consultative organization providing templates, best practices, training and access to organizational process assets.	Provide support and require compliance to project management frameworks or methods. May create and require use of specific templates or tools.	Take control of projects by directly managing projects.
Control Provided by PMO	Low	Moderate	High

Project Life Cycles can be categorized as being predictive, iterative or adaptive. The type of project life cycle chosen should be based on the identified project requirements and need for flexibility. Characteristics are shown below:

Life Cycle Category	Predictive	Iterative/Incremental	Adaptive
Best Used When	Fully plan driven; define scope, schedule and costs in detailed documents early in the life cycle.	Project phases intentionally repeat activities from phase to phase. May change or improve initial products as project progresses.	Change driven or "agile" method. Use an iterative style but focus on short duration deliverables to be done in 2-4 week periods.
	The product to be delivered is well understood and project elements are definable and stable.	Moderate	High

The project team is intended to work together to execute the agreed upon project management plan to perform the work required to create the deliverables of the project.

Must Know Concepts

1. A project is a temporary endeavor undertaken to create a unique product, service or result. A project has a beginning and an end and is progressively elaborated.

2. Project management is the application of knowledge, skills, tools and techniques to project activities in order to meet project requirements.

3. A project manager must have several areas of skill and knowledge in order to manage projects successfully. These skills and knowledge are grouped into three categories: project management knowledge, performance ability and personal skills.

4. Portfolios are collections of projects, programs and other work in the organization.

5. Programs are made up of related projects that are managed in a unified manner to achieve planned benefits for the organization.

6. Projects should be organized in terms of phases or stages to form an overall project life cycle.

7. A stakeholder is anyone or any group that is actively involved in the project or whose interests may be affected (positively or negatively) by the project activities or outcome.

Additional Reading

- PMBOK® Guide Fifth Edition: Chapter 1 Introduction
- PMBOK® Guide Fifth Edition: Chapter 2 Project Life Cycle and Organizations

Lesson Quiz

Instructions: Circle the correct answer. Answer Key in Appendix A.

1. Which of these elements is not part of the definition of a project?

   A. Progressively planned
   B. Ongoing operation
   C. Temporary time period
   D. Produces a product or service

2. What is the best definition of project management?

   A. The application of knowledge and skills to project goals in order to complete the project
   B. The application of skills, tools and techniques, feelings and intuition to complete the project
   C. The application of knowledge, skills, tools and techniques to project activities in order to meet project requirements
   D. The application of knowledge, wisdom, art and science to project activities in order to meet project requirements

3. What is the main role of the project manager on the project?

   A. Manager
   B. Project leader
   C. Integrator
   D. Communicator

4. Which of these elements is not considered part of the "triple constraint"?

   A. Schedule
   B. Customer Satisfaction
   C. Budget
   D. Work to be performed

5. What is the primary role of stakeholders on the project?

   A. To provide input to the project manager
   B. To communicate with the project manager and other stakeholders
   C. To communicate among themselves in order to define requirements
   D. To communicate with the project manager when something goes wrong

6. A project can create all of these except a:

   A. Product or an enhancement of a product
   B. Service or capability to perform a service
   C. Improvement in an existing product or service
   D. Ongoing operational results

7. The project governance approach should be described in the Project Management Plan. Governance decisions that should be documented include all of the following except:

   A. The plan for controlling the project
   B. Escalation procedures
   C. Resources that are necessary
   D. General approach to completing the work

End of Lesson 2

This page intentionally blank.

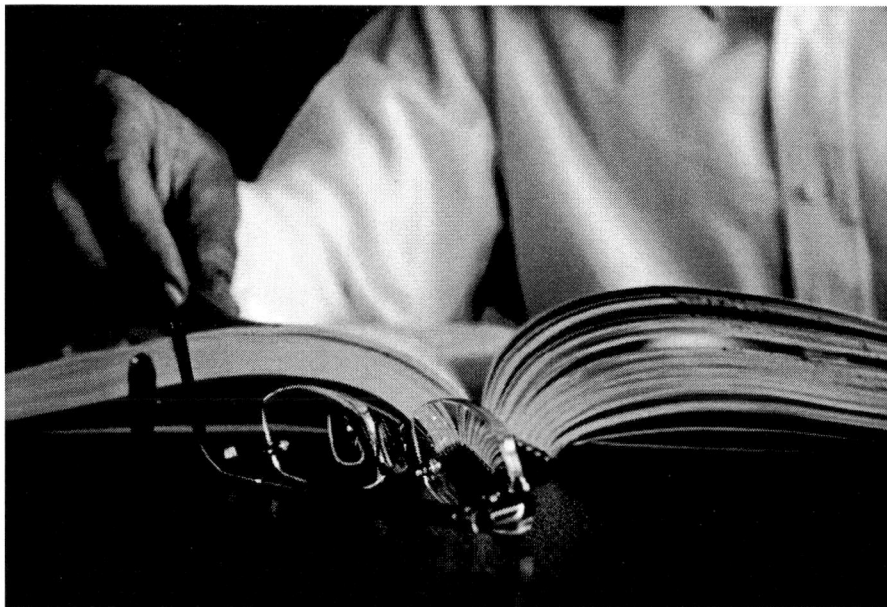

Lesson 3
Mastering the PMBOK® Guide

Objectives
7. At the end of this lesson, you will be able to:
8. Understand the purpose of the PMBOK® Guide
9. Understand the content structure of the PMBOK® Guide
10. Understand the application intent of project management processes and process groups
11. Understand the application intent of project management knowledge areas
12. Understand the application intent of Inputs, Tools & Techniques and Outputs associated with processes

Process Locator for the PMBOK® Guide

	Initiating	Planning	Executing	M&C	Closing
Integration					
Scope					
Time					
Cost					
Quality		Contains General Management Information that is applicable to all areas of the PMBOK® Guide and applies to project management in general			
Human Resource					
Communications					
Risk					
Procurement					
Stakeholder					

As a PMP candidate and eventually as a PMP, it is essential that you understand the intent, content and context of the PMBOK®

The PMBOK® Guide (A Guide to the Project Management Body of Knowledge; published by the Project Management Institute, PMI®) is the de-facto global standard for managing projects. In

September 1999, the PMBOK® Guide was formally adopted as an ANSI Standard. The PMBOK® Guide has been updated multiple times since being adopted; the current version is the *PMBOK® Guide Fifth Edition.*

Many exam questions are designed specifically to test your content knowledge of the PMBOK® Guide. However, the PMBOK® Guide is a reference standard, not a learning text. Therefore, the PMBOK® Guide can be difficult to quickly master. The PMBOK Guide® is not a methodology.

In this lesson, we will begin to master the PMBOK® Guide by developing a high level understanding of the intent, content and presentation structure. If you have purchased TSI's companion Project Management Process Poster Set, you can see the many processes, process groups and process flows illustrated in a full color graphics format.

Study Tip
To purchase TSI's exclusive companion Project Management Process Poster Set, please go to: www.truesolutions.com or call 866-770-0903. Since you have purchased this book, you are eligible to use coupon code "UPMGuide" to receive a 25% discount on your poster set.

PMBOK® Guide Purpose and Content Structure

The PMBOK® Guide defines material and processes that are generally recognized as good practices for project management that are applicable to most projects, most of the time.

It is important to understand that these generally accepted practices are not expected to be uniformly applied to all projects, all of the time. It should always be up to the project manager and project team to determine what is most appropriate for any given project. Generally, the level of project management effort should be sensibly proportional to the size and complexity of the project.

The PMBOK® Guide also provides a common vocabulary and understanding base for project management practitioners around the world.

The PMBOK® Guide organizes its content as an interrelated set of 47 well defined processes, further grouped into 5 progress groups and 10 knowledge areas.

The Process Groups are: Initiating, Planning, Executing, Monitoring & Controlling and Closing.

The 10 Knowledge Areas are: Project Integration Management, Project Scope Management, Project Time Management, Project Cost Management, Project Quality Management, Project Human Resource Management, Project Communications Management, Project Risk Management, Project Procurement Management and Project Stakeholder Management.

The content of the PMBOK Guide Fifth Edition compares very closely to the ISO 21500:2012 standard for project management published by the International Standards Organization. Both standards have comparable process groups, knowledge areas and processes.

Project Management Processes

Project management processes usually interact to affect the outcome of the project. Failure to take action in one area of the project will usually directly affect another area of the project. Project management involves managing competing demands. The project management processes defined by PMI in the PMBOK® Guide address a wide spectrum of project elements and serve as a framework for managing project demands.

- A process is defined as "a series of actions bringing about a pre-defined result".

- Project Management Processes describe, organize and complete the work required to complete the project scope.

Product Processes specify and create the product of the project. Product processes are generally defined as part of the project life cycle by the performing organization in order to meet specialized application needs.

Project management processes ensure that the project is managed in a logical and effective manner. Project management processes create a flow of actions and information through the project life cycle.

Product processes deal with the specification and creation of the product of the project. The unique product (project outcome) that is created will dictate the type of product oriented processes that are to be used. When performing project management, the project manager should have specialized application knowledge and skills appropriate to the industry and product that is being created.

The Ultimate PMP Exam Prep Guide and the PMBOK® Guide Fifth Edition, both focus on project management related processes and product-oriented processes. The one exception to this is reference to product definitions in Define Scope, and configuration management in Perform Integrated Change Control.

The PMP Exam will focus on project management related processes and actions.

Project Management Process Groups

Project process groups are literally groups of processes that are grouped together. The processes have some similarities to their outcomes. Process groups have clear dependencies and interactions. Process groups have a high degree of overlap and all process groups are performed in each phase of the project.

Usually the Inputs, Tools and Techniques and Outputs in a process group are complimentary and interactive with each other. There are 5 project management process groups.

- Initiating
- Planning
- Executing
- Monitoring and Controlling
- Closing

The process groups categorize their processes in relation to the naming convention for the process group.

Initiating *processes* are used at the beginning of a project or a phase of a project.

Planning *processes* are used to plan the project at the beginning of a project and are used to validate plans and re-plan portions of the project in subsequent phases. Planning processes are also re-used when a change is being made on the project to redefine whatever element requires change to ensure project success.

Executing *processes* are generally used to create deliverables for the project. Executing processes are used in each phase of the project. When using executing processes, the project manager and stakeholders will recognize change requirements; these recognized changes are fed into the next process group and its associated individual processes to manage change.

Monitoring and Controlling *processes* are used to ensure that changes are recognized as they occur and that changes that are needed to ensure project success are incorporated into the project definition through an approval process. Monitoring and Controlling processes check on progress and are intended to ensure that the project performs as planned and executes the planned work.

Closing *processes* are used to perform orderly closeout of a project or a phase of a project.

How the Project Life Cycle, Project Process Groups and Processes Work Together

If you view the overall project life cycle in an outline form you can clearly determine how the project management process groups and processes as defined in the PMBOK® Guide Fifth Edition will fit into your project life cycle.

The performing organization will define the project life cycle based on unique needs. This includes the overall definition, the phases and the activities that take place in the project environment for the organization.

PMI has defined process groups, processes and unique inputs, tools and techniques and outputs for each process.

<u>**Project Life Cycle**</u> (defined by the user organization)

- <u>Phases</u> (defined by the user organization; examples: Discover, Design, Develop)
    - ○ <u>Process Groups</u> (part of the PMI standard: Initiating, Planning, Executing, Monitoring and Controlling, Closing)
        - ▪ <u>Processes</u> (part of the PMI standard: 47 unique processes)
            - • <u>Inputs</u> (unique to a process)
            - • <u>Tools</u> and Techniques (unique to a process)
            - • <u>Outputs</u> (unique to a process)
                - ○ <u>Activities</u> (unique to the specialized application area)

It is absolutely critical that the reader understands how the PMI standard fits into the project life cycle of the performing organization. The PMI standard does not try to overpower the need of the organization; the PMI standard does not specify specific elements that have to occur to fulfill the project or activities that have to be performed. Rather, the PMI standard specifies a framework or process groups and processes along with recommendations for specific inputs, tools and outputs that can be used to guide the project to success.

A standard is defined as "a recommendation from a recognized body...defining guidelines and best practices...with which compliance is not necessary". This is a guideline, a recommendation on the best way to manage a project. You, as the reader, must know this body of information in order to pass the PMP exam.

In addition to the insertion of process groups and processes into the project life cycle, the reader needs to be aware of how the process groups themselves overlap and interact. The diagram below depicts that interaction.

Process Group Interaction

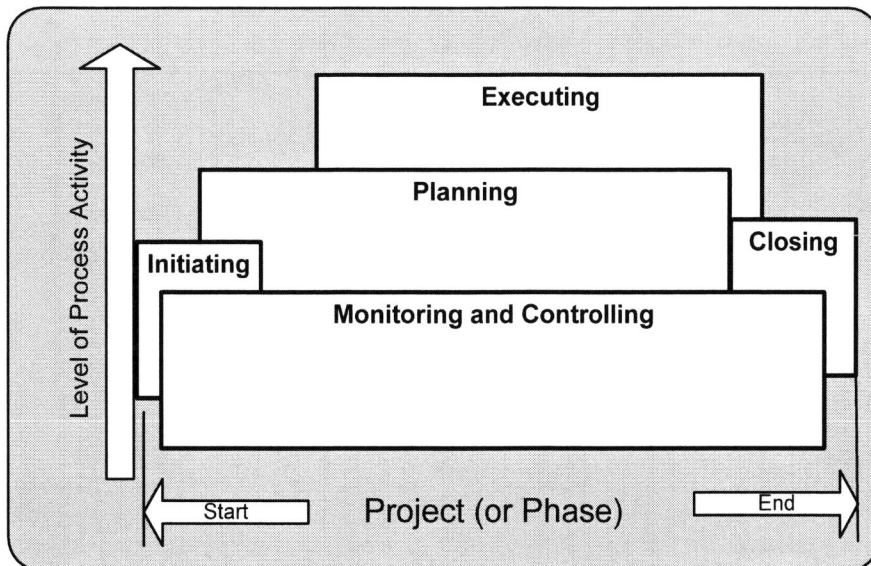

Figure 3.1 Process Group Interaction

To summarize the diagram (and to oversimplify the description), your project begins with the initiating processes that are resident in the Initiating Process Group and ends with the closing processes.

After initiating processes are used, the project manager would use the planning processes that are part of the Planning Process Group. The planning processes overlap with processes in the Initiating Process Group, the Executing Process Group and the Monitoring and Controlling Process Group. So, essentially, in the middle of a project, up to 45 processes could be performed by the project manager simultaneously.

As we go through all of the processes, these interactions and flows will become clearer to you.

Project Information Flow

Project management depends on the continual flow of information from the project manager and project team to the various stakeholders who have an interest in the project. There are several types of information categories defined in the PMBOK that the PMP aspirant needs to know and recognize for testing and real-world applications. These information types are used as both inputs and outputs in the processes defined in the PMBOK.

- **Work Performance Data**: This is the raw data and measurements identified during project execution processes. This raw data becomes an input to controlling processes.

- **Work Performance Information**: This is performance data collected during a controlling process that is analyzed and integrated to provide usable information used to predict status, forecasts or to justify change requests for the project.

- **Work Performance Reports**: This is data, usually derived from the Work Performance Information that is represented in some orderly format in a physical or electronic form to inform the project stakeholders. Work Performance Reports often take the form of status reports, information updates, electronic dashboards and other updates.

Knowledge Areas

Project Management Knowledge Areas consist of processes that are grouped together by their knowledge requirements. These processes usually interact with each other and have related Inputs, Tools and Techniques and Outputs. There are ten Knowledge Areas.

> **Project Management Knowledge Areas**
> - Project Integration Management
> - Project Scope Management
> - Project Time Management
> - Project Cost Management
> - Project Quality Management
> - Project Human Resource Management
> - Project Communications Management
> - Project Risk Management
> - Project Procurement Management
> - Project Stakeholder Management

Any given process is also part of a specific process group and project management knowledge area.

The table following – which is derived from page 61 of the *PMBOK® Guide Fifth Edition,* illustrates this dual relationship for individual processes.

Knowledge Areas	Project Management Process Groups				
	Initiating 2	Planning 24	Executing 8	Monitoring & Controlling 11	Closing 2
Project Integration Management	4.1 Develop Project Charter	4.2 Develop Project Management Plan	4.3 Direct & Manage Project Work	4.4 Monitor & Control Project Work 4.5 Perform Integrated Change Control	4.6 Close Project or Phase
Project Scope Management		5.1 Plan Scope Management 5.2 Collect Requirements 5.3 Define Scope 5.4 Create WBS		5.5 Validate Scope 5.6 Control Scope	
Project Time Management		6.1 Plan Schedule Management 6.2 Define Activities 6.3 Sequence Activities 6.4 Estimate Activity Resources 6.5 Estimate Activity Durations 6.6 Develop Schedule		6.7 Control Schedule	
Project Cost Management		7.1 Plan Cost Management 7.2 Estimate Costs 7.3 Determine Budget		7.4 Control Costs	
Project Quality Management		8.1 Plan Quality Management	8.2 Perform Quality Assurance	8.3 Control Quality	
Project Human Resource Management		9.1 Plan Human Resource Management	9.2 Acquire Project Team 9.3 Develop Project Team 9.4 Manage Project Team		
Project Communications Management		10.1 Plan Communications Management	10.2 Manage Communications	10.3 Control Communications	
Project Risk Management		11.1 Plan Risk Management 11.2 Identify Risks 11.3 Perform Qualitative Risk Analysis 11.4 Perform Quantitative Risk Analysis 11.5 Plan Risk Responses		11.6 Control Risks	
Project Procurement Management		12.1 Plan Procurement Management	12.2 Conduct Procurements	12.3 Control Procurements	12.4 Close Procurements
Project Stakeholder Management	13.1 Identify Stakeholders	13.2 Plan Stakeholder Management	13.3 Manage Stakeholder Engagement	13.4 Control Stakeholder Engagement	

Figure 3.2 Processes, Process Groups and Knowledge Areas

Must Know Concepts

1. The PMBOK® Guide identifies and describes generally recognized best practices that are applicable to most projects most of the time.

2. The level of project management effort should be sensibly proportional to the size and complexity of the project.

3. The PMBOK® Guide organizes its content as an interrelated set of 47 well defined processes, further grouped into 5 process groups and 10 knowledge areas.

4. The Process Groups are: Initiating, Planning, Executing, Monitoring & Controlling and Closing.

5. The 10 Knowledge Areas are: Project Integration Management, Project Scope Management, Project Time Management, Project Cost Management, Project Quality Management, Project Human Resource Management, Project Communications Management, Project Risk Management, Project Procurement Management and Project Stakeholder Management.

6. The relationship of project processes to specific project management knowledge areas and process groups is an important element to learn for the PMP Exam.

Additional Reading

- PMBOK® Guide Fifth Edition: Chapter 3.0 Project Management Processes for a Project

Lesson Quiz

Instructions: The actual PMP exam is done via computer. These questions are representative of what you will encounter. Circle the correct answer. Answer Key in Appendix A.

1. How many processes are defined in the PMBOK Guide Fifth Edition?

    A. 42
    B. 47
    C. 44
    D. 39

2. What portion of the project has the most overlapping number of processes?

    A. The portion when the project is initiated and planned
    B. The portion when the project is defining requirements
    C. The portion when the project work is being performed
    D. The portion when the project is being closed

3. Work performance information includes:

    A. Status of deliverables
    B. Physical or electronic representation of work performance
    C. Raw observations and measurements
    D. Status reports

End of Lesson 3

Lesson 4
Initiating Process Group

Objectives
At the end of this lesson, you will be able to:
- Understand what processes are used in the Initiating Process Group
- Understand the purpose for using Initiating processes for the project or project phase

Process Locator for the PMBOK® Guide

	Initiating	Planning	Executing	M&C	Closing
Integration					
Scope					
Time					
Cost					
Quality					
Human Resource					
Communications					
Risk					
Procurement					
Stakeholder					

The Initiating Process Group consists of two processes that are intended to begin a project or project phase.

The primary purpose that these Initiating processes are performed is to authorize the project (or phase) and to indentify the stakeholders that will be involved and interested in the project as it progresses. Initiating processes occur in the Integration Management knowledge area and the Stakeholder Management knowledge area of the *PMBOK® Guide Fifth Edition*.

An important part of the Initiating process group is the assignment of the project manager to the project and the PM's authority. This usually occurs during the authorization process of Develop Project Charter.

If there was a "keyword" that would characterize the Initiating Process Group, it might be "high-level". When a project is started, the sponsor, project manager and stakeholders have a high level view of the project; a vision of what is about to happen. There are usually not specific details available to define the complete project.

At the beginning of subsequent project phases, Initiating processes are used to confirm that the vision for the project is sound and that identified stakeholders still have a role on the project. In subsequent project phases, the Initiating processes will work in conjunction with the Closing processes as part of the Project Life Cycle review, stage gate or kill point decision. The Closing processes are used to review what happened in the phase that is ending; the Initiating processes will confirm that the project vision is sound, the business case is viable and the project manager who has been assigned can perform effectively on the subsequent phase.

In some cases, the Initiating processes may be performed by external organizational entities such as the portfolio manager or program manager. The PMBOK® Guide is very certain that the project begins when the Project Charter is issued. Prior to this issuance, there may be feasibility studies, business case development, project selection and preliminary resource assignments that take place.

When the project manager is assigned, his or her authority level should be defined. This may be included as part of the Project Charter, or prior to charter development.

Initiating Tasks

On your PMP Exam, you will encounter approximately many questions that will test your understanding of Initiating processes. These questions will generally focus on Initiating tasks. As a PMP or project manager initiating a project (or project phase), you may be required to:

1. Perform project assessment based on available information and meetings with the sponsor, customer, and other subject matter experts, in order to evaluate the feasibility of new products or services with the given assumptions and/or constraints.

2. Define the high-level scope of the project based on the business and compliance requirements, in order to meet the customer's project expectations.

3. Perform key stakeholder analysis using brainstorming, interviewing, and other data gathering techniques, in order to endure expectation alignment and gain support for the project.

4. Identify and document high level risks, assumptions and constraints based on current environment, historical data and/or expert judgment, in order to identify project limitations and propose an implementation approach.

5. Develop the project charter by further gathering and analyzing stakeholder requirements, in order to document project scope, milestones and deliverables.

6. Obtain approval for the project charter from the sponsor and customer (if required), in order to formalize the authority assigned to the project manager and gain commitment and acceptance for the project.

Knowledge Requirements

As a PMP applying Initiating processes in real-world projects, you will be required to possess in-depth knowledge in several project specific areas, as well as a broad knowledge of project management in general. The PMP Exam will test your understanding of these knowledge specifics.

By developing a familiarity with these knowledge specifics, you will better understand the context of many PMP Exam questions. As you progress through the Ultimate PMP Exam Prep Guide, you will see each of these areas mentioned. Please give some thought to each item as it relates to your own project management experiences with past and current projects.

Remember, the PMP or project manager is always required to have a very broad base of knowledge to work from. The project manager has to work across the entire organization spectrum in many cases to effectively perform project management.

As a PMP or project manager applying Initiating processes, you may be expected to have knowledge of:
- Cost-benefit analysis
- Business case development
- Project selection criteria
- Stakeholder identification techniques
- Risk identification techniques
- Elements of a Project Charter

In addition to specific knowledge requirements for Initiating the project, the project manager also has general knowledge requirements that will be used throughout the project:

- Active listening
- Conflict resolution techniques
- Data gathering techniques
- Facilitation techniques
- Leadership tools and techniques
- Oral and written communications techniques

- Knowledge of PMI's Code of Ethics and Professional Conduct
- Prioritization and time management techniques
- Team motivation methods
- Project management software
- Brainstorming techniques
- Cultural sensitivity and diversity awareness
- Decision making techniques
- Information management tools
- Negotiating techniques
- Targeting specific communications to the intended audience
- Presentation tools and techniques
- Stakeholder analysis techniques
- Relationship management

Study Tip

Read the *PMBOK® Guide Fifth Edition*

The information exposed in our Ultimate PMP Exam Prep Guide is often sufficient for you to pass your PMP Exam on the first try...without any other aids or tools.

However, since we are all interested in your success on the PMP Exam, we feel like it is imperative to remind you to read the PMBOK® Guide Fifth Edition. Throughout the Ultimate PMP Exam Prep Guide you will find references to the PMBOK and reading assignments.

In one of our classes, I was asked by a student: "If I just read one thing, would it be the PMBOK® Guide or the Ultimate PMP Exam Prep Guide?" I think the answer is not so simple. Like it has been stated above, we think that the Ultimate PMP Exam Prep Guide provides you with what you need – but why sell yourself short – or take unnecessary shortcuts. This is an important certification and an important step in your career. We recommend that you thoroughly read ***both*** documents.

Lesson 5
Develop Project Charter

Objectives

At the end of this lesson, you will be able to:

- Describe the purpose of the Develop Project Charter process
- Describe the Inputs, Tools and Techniques, and Outputs of the
- Develop Project Charter Process
- List the key items that should be included in a Project Charter

Process Locator for the PMBOK® Guide

	Initiating	Planning	Executing	M&C	Closing
Integration					
Scope					
Time					
Cost					
Quality					
Human Resource					
Communications					
Risk					
Procurement					
Stakeholder					

Choosing to undertake projects that are not mindfully justified up front can lead to non-efficient use of time and resources, and perhaps even project failure.

In today's increasingly competitive world, we must ensure that projects undertaken have value, provide efficiencies and meet the organizations strategic objectives. This requires solid planning, execution and control across the entire project life cycle.

But, even before we begin planning our projects, we must pay close attention to the very projects we choose to undertake. Good project management begins with good project selection.

If management chooses to undertake a project that is not aligned with the organization's strategic goals, or fails to thoroughly consider alternatives up front, then the ability to create real value from the project will be significantly handicapped. Choosing to undertake projects that are not mindfully justified up front can lead to non-efficient use of time and resources, and perhaps even project failure.

The Develop Project Charter process is intended to ensure that any project chartered and authorized by management is well thought-through and justified. With a solid beginning, any project has a greater probability of ultimate success.

Applying the Develop Project Charter process encourages management to thoroughly consider all high-level aspects of a proposed project, and then make an informed selection decision. The process suggests that management employ expert judgment and facilitations techniques to make good decisions and choose the "right" project. Typical facilitation techniques used to gather information could include: brainstorming, Delphi technique, problem solving techniques, meetings and facilitation. All of these methods are used here and in other processes to help collect information and document decision outcomes.

When using the Develop Project Charter process, the PMI process model assumes that any feasibility study or analysis to determine whether or not the project should be performed has already been completed. In practical application, a feasibility study or pre-analysis would be a separate process or a separate project that is completed prior to the authorization of the product creation project using Develop Project Charter.

When a project is selected, then the Develop Project Charter process suggests management prepare and issue a formal Project Charter that:

- Documents the preliminary characteristics of the project or a phase

- Authorizes the project

- Identifies/authorizes the project manager

A project sponsor or initiator authorizes the project by approving the Project Charter. This person should be at a level that is appropriate to fund the project. The project initiator may be the Project Management Office (PMO) or Portfolio Steering Committee.

Process Elements

The Develop Project Charter process has the following Inputs:

- Project Statement of Work (SOW) - Narrative description of the products/services to be delivered by the project

- Business Case - Describes the reason the project is worth investing in from the business standpoint

- Agreements – Contracts, Service Level Agreements or Memorandums of Understanding. Contracts are used for an external customer

- Enterprise Environmental Factors - Consideration factors such as; culture, industry standards, market conditions

- Organizational Process Assets - Consideration factors such as processes, procedures, templates, historical information and lessons learned

The Develop Project Charter process uses the following Tools & Techniques:

- Expert Judgment – Expert technical and/or managerial judgment (from any qualified source)

- Facilitation Techniques – Brainstorming, conflict resolutions and problem solving actions used to develop the project charter

The Develop Project Charter process has the following Output:

- Project Charter – High-level document that documents high level project definitions, authorizes the project and assigns/authorizes the project manager

Develop Project Charter		
This process formally sanctions a new project or authorizes a project to continue into the next phase		
Inputs	**Tools and Techniques**	**Outputs**
• Project Statement of Work (SOW) • Business Case • Agreements • Enterprise Environmental Factors • Organizational Process Assets	• Expert Judgment • Facilitation Techniques	• Project Charter TSI Study Aid This chart is part of the study aid poster series available at: www.TrueSolutions.com

Figure 5.1. Process Elements within the Develop Project Charter

Process Documents

The Project Charter documents the preliminary project information. As previously discussed, the Project Charter has one main outcome: to authorize the project to start. This authorization allows the project manager to begin the project and begin to use organizational resources. The Project Charter documents the initial vision of the project sponsor. This document can be very concise. Many Project Charter documents can be completed in one page.

Some of the elements that might be included in the Project Charter are:

- Project Name
- Project Purpose
- Measurable planned objectives
- High level description of the project requirements
- High level description of the product or service to be created by the project
- High level list of risks
- Planned summary milestone schedule
- Initial budget amount
- Stakeholder list
- Project approval requirements
- Description of how the project links to the organization work portfolio
- Assignment of a project manager,
- Name and title of person(s) authorizing the project
- Assumptions and constraints

For specific PMP exam guidance on the Project Charter document and its contents, please refer directly to the PMBOK® Guide Fifth Edition, section 4.1.

The following form reflects a template that can be used to record all of the preliminary project information and defines a Project Charter.

Project Charter

Project Name:	
Prepared by:	
Date:	
Project purpose:	*Identify the customers who are to receive and benefit from the product developed by the project and the need the product is intended to meet (either as a problem to solve or as an opportunity to exploit)*
Planned Objectives:	*Identify what product or service is to be delivered at the end of the project, and at any interim delivery points. Describe the product sufficiently to enable the project team to create it, and for agreement to be reached at product delivery time that the product has been correctly produced*
High level project description:	*Briefly explain the requirements for the project and a description of the project to afford an understanding of known needs and tasks to accomplish project*
High level product description:	*Briefly identify major deliverables to be created by this project*
Planned schedule:	*Identify what milestones will be a key factor to reach to project objectives*
Initial budget:	*Use a Rough Order of Magnitude estimate to show budget requirements*
Program or Portfolio Links:	*Identify how the project links to the work of the organization and any programs being managed in the organization*
Assignment of Project Manager, responsibility and authority	*Often the Project Manager will have already been decided before hand or during the charter. Identify who the Project Manager is and what their responsibility is during the project and what authority level they have (decision making, budget, approving, etc.)*
Name and Title of Sponsor:	*Identify who the project sponsor is (persons or groups) and explain what their authority will be within the project*
Other:	*Identify and explain any other matters that are important for the initiation and conduct of the project. Focus on charter issues of importance between the project sponsor and the project manager. This section is not for describing the project plan*
Approval:	Sponsor: Date:

Application Aid

This form is available
individually or as
part of a set at:
www.TrueSolutions.com

Process Tasks

The Develop Project Charter process aligns with several of the defined tasks that a project manager performs when managing a project:

Initiating Task #1: "Perform project assessment based upon available information and meetings with the sponsor, customer and other subject matter experts, in order to evaluate the feasibility of the new products or services within the given assumptions and/or constraints".

Initiating Task #2: "Define the high-level scope of the project based on the business and compliance requirements, in order to meet the customer's project expectations".

Initiating Task #4: "Identify and document high-level risks, assumptions and constraints based on current environment, historical data and/or expert judgment, in order to identify project limitations and propose and implementation approach".

Initiating Task #5: "Develop the project charter by further gathering and analyzing stakeholder requirements, in order to document project scope, milestones and deliverables".

Initiating Task #6: "Obtain approval for the project charter from the sponsor and customer (if required), in order to formalize the authority assigned to the project manager and gain commitment and acceptance for the project".

Think About It

Instructions Use this exercise to compare how you practice project management to what is specified in the *PMBOK® Guide Fifth Edition.*

Best Practices suggest that the following items are used during the Develop Project Charter process.

Which of these items do you use when practicing project management?

- ☐ 1-5 page document
- ☐ High Level Overview of Project
- ☐ High Level list of deliverables
- ☐ Business Case
- ☐ Planned Schedule
- ☐ Initial Budget
- ☐ Project Manager assignment
- ☐ Authority level for PM specified
- ☐ Signature of sponsor

How would you change your use of this process in your organization to resolve any gaps in application?

_____

_____

Must Know Concepts
- -

These are the basic concepts you need to know about the process Develop Project Charter.

1. The Develop Project Charter process is intended to formally authorize a new project.

2. The primary deliverable (Output) of the Develop Project Charter process is the Project Charter.

3. The Project Charter is a high-level document that communicates preliminary project characteristics, authorizes the project, and identifies and authorizes the project manager.

4. The Project Charter is typically issued by a project initiator or sponsor, external to the immediate project organization, at a funds-providing management level.

5. The project's business need, and product or service description should be clearly defined and documented in the Project Charter.

6. Chartering a project links the project to the ongoing work of the performing organization.

7. The project manager should be assigned as early as possible, prior to project planning, preferably during Project Charter development.

8. The Project Charter should be relatively brief (broad, not deep), perhaps 1-5 pages in length.

9. Enterprise Environmental Factors are internal or external factors that influence the project.

10. Organizational Process Assets are assets that may be used to influence project success, such as templates, procedures, historical data and published guidelines.

Additional Reading
- -

- PMBOK® Guide Fifth Edition: Section 4.0   Introduction, Project Integration Management
- PMBOK® Guide Fifth Edition: Section 4.1   Develop Project Charter

Lesson Quiz

Instructions: The actual PMP exam is done via computer. These questions are representative of what you will encounter. Circle the correct answer. Answer Key in Appendix A.

1. Develop Project Charter inputs include all of the following *except* _____.

    A. organizational process assets
    B. enterprise environmental factors
    C. agreements
    D. expert judgment

2. Which of the following statements is *most* true?

    A. The Project Charter identifies the names of project management team members.
    B. The Project Charter tracks a project's history.
    C. The Project Charter names and authorizes the project manager.
    D. The Project Charter describes the details of what needs to be done to satisfy quality improvement objectives.

3. Your project is characterized by frequent changes to the Project Charter. Authorizing Project Charter changes should typically be the responsibility of _____.

    A. Senior management
    B. The project manager
    C. The project management team
    D. Project stakeholders

4. Which of the following is *most* true?

    A. The Project Charter is developed during closing.
    B. The Project Charter is developed during initiating.
    C. The Project Charter is developed during executing.
    D. The Project Charter is developed during planning.

5. You can generally say each of the following is true *except*:

    A. The Project Charter identifies major task interdependencies.
    B. The Project Charter includes the initial product description.
    C. The Project Charter defines the business need(s) that the project was undertaken to address.
    D. The Project Charter is issued by a senior manager external to the project.

6. Agreements may include:

    A. A contract with a third-party customer
    B. Service level agreements
    C. Verbal agreements
    D. All of the above

7 You have just been assigned to manage a new project, which will create the marketing campaign for a new line of women's clothing. You have formed your core project team and met with your sponsor, who is the Director of Marketing for Chic Woman, Inc. The director is very firm about budget and schedule for the marketing campaign rollout, because expectations have been set in the marketplace that the new line will roll out within 6 months, before the Spring buying season starts. You decide you will need to use conflict resolution and problem solving to get the Project Charter developed. These are:

A. Inputs to the Develop Project Charter process
B. Tools and techniques to the Develop Project Charter process
C. Facilitation Techniques
D. Part of Organizational Process Assets

End of Lesson 5

Lesson 6
Identify Stakeholders

Objectives

At the end of this lesson, you will be able to:

- Describe the purpose of the Identify Stakeholders process
- Describe the Inputs, Tools and Techniques, and Outputs of the Identify Stakeholders process
- Identify who Key Stakeholders would be for a typical project

Process Locator for the PMBOK Guide

	Initiating	Planning	Executing	M&C	Closing
Integration					
Scope					
Time					
Cost					
Quality					
Human Resource					
Communications					
Risk					
Procurement					
Stakeholder					

Very early in the life of a project, it is critical to identify all of the organizations and people who may have an impact on the project, and all those who may be impacted by the project.

A "Stakeholder" is any person or organization that is actively involved in a project, or whose interests may be affected positively or negatively by execution of a project. Stakeholders can be internal to the organization or external. In many projects the public at large will become a stakeholder to be considered on the project. The challenge for the project manager when the public is a stakeholder will be to act while considering public needs. Often there is no direct representative of the public to be consulted during project planning and execution.

A project manager must be sure to identify and list all potential stakeholders for a project. Potential stakeholders include but not limited to:

- Employees

- Shareholders

- Investors

- Government and regulatory agencies

- Suppliers

- Labor unions

- Prospective employees

- Prospective customers

- Local communities

- State or Regional communities

- National communities

- Public at large (Global Community)

- Competitors

The project manager must document relevant information for all identified stakeholders. This information may include the stakeholder's interests, involvement, expectations, importance, influence, and impact on the projects execution as well as any specific communications requirements that may be required. It is important to note that although some identified stakeholders may not actually require any communications, those stakeholders should be identified.

When identifying stakeholders and rating their level of interest and involvement in the project it will become important to use some sort of a tool, a rating scale an influence diagram or some chart form to identify the level of power, influence, interest or impact that the stakeholder may have on the project. There is a sample of a stakeholder needs and expectations form in the forms section of this lesson.

Process Elements

The Identify Stakeholders process has the following Inputs:

- Project Charter - High-level document that authorizes the project and assigns/authorizes the project manager

- Procurement Documents - Identifies procurement contract stakeholders

- Enterprise Environmental Factors - Consideration factors such as; culture, structure, standards, trends, practices

- Organizational Process Assets - Consideration factors such as templates, lessons learned, stakeholder registers from former projects

The Identify Stakeholders process uses the following Tools & Techniques:
Stakeholder Analysis - Gathering and assessing information to determine whose interests should be taken into account for a project (i.e. Power/Interest Grid)

- Expert Judgment - Expert technical and/or managerial judgment (from any qualified source)

- Meetings – Profile analysis meetings to identify and develop an understanding of stakeholders and their needs and expectations

The Identify Stakeholders process has the following Output:
- Stakeholder Register - A document identifying all project stakeholder information, requirements and classification

Identify Stakeholders		
This process identifies all persons/organizations impacted by a project and documents their interests, involvement, and impact on the project		
Inputs	**Tools and Techniques**	**Outputs**
• Project Charter	• Stakeholder Analysis	• Stakeholder Register
• Procurement Documents	• Expert Judgment	
• Enterprise Environmental Factors	• Meetings	TSI Study Aid
• Organizational Process Assets		This chart is part of the study aid poster series available at: www.TrueSolutions.com

Figure 6.1. Process Elements within the Identify Stakeholder

Process Documents

During the Identify Stakeholders process, the Stakeholder Register document is created. A stakeholder expectations questionnaire may be used to analyze specific stakeholder influences and needs. An example of a Stakeholder Register is shown below.

True Solutions, Inc.
Project Management Template
Version 2: Stakeholder Register Template

Stakeholder Register Template

Project Name:				
Prepared by:				
Date:				
Project Stakeholder Name	**Specific Information Needs** *Types & Frequency of Communication*	**Project Interests** *Specific Areas of Interest and Participation*	**Impact on Project** *Positive, Negative, Influencer, Supporter, Roadblock*	**Role** *Decision Maker, Collaborator, Participant, Consultant, Information Recipient*

Application Aid

This form is available individually or as part of a set at: *www.TrueSolutions.com*

A stakeholder register may be used to record the general overview of each stakeholder and their planned/forecast role on the project.

Process Tasks

The Identify Stakeholders process aligns with one of the defined tasks that a project manager performs when managing a project:

Initiating Task #3: "Perform key stakeholder analysis using brainstorming, interviewing, and other data gathering techniques, in order to ensure expectation alignment and gain support for the project".

Think About It

When applying the "Identify Stakeholders" process, it is important to note that overlooking this process often ends with sometimes disastrous results.

While working as project manager for a major automotive manufacturer during Y2K, I was leading a project to change the way automotive replacement parts were sold and distributed. We already had identified a rather large, overwhelming project team intended to work together to create and deploy the systems and new business processes. But we failed to clearly identify all of the stakeholders and their interests.

When we started the implementation planning it was quickly determined that the end users needs and the technical specifications of systems that the end users were using had not been properly identified. The goals and objectives of the end users were mostly different than the plan. Additionally, political factions within the project began to have internal wars over stated objectives and how to achieve the objectives from a technical standpoint. Major portions of the overall organization considered themselves to be stakeholders, yet were not identified on any list as a project stakeholder.

Using the "Identify Stakeholders" process effectively could have saved many hours of misdirection and resource misallocation (and lots of money). Ultimately, our project was only moderately successful with a small group of end-users that were deployed during that fiscal year. But we could have been highly successful if we had indentified all of our stakeholders and their needs before committing to action.

Contributed by Tim Bergmann, PMP

Must Know Concepts
----

1. A "stakeholder" is any person or organization that is actively involved in a project, or whose interests may be affected positively or negatively by execution of a project.

2. The Identify Stakeholders process is used to identify all people or organizations that maybe impacted or have an impact on a project.

3. A key output of the Identify Stakeholders process is the Stakeholder Register which lists the projects stakeholders and relevant information for each stakeholder or stakeholder group.

4. Stakeholder Analysis is a technique used to determine stakeholder interests, influence, participation and expectations for a project.

Additional Reading

- PMBOK Guide® Fifth Edition: Section 13.0   Introduction, Project Stakeholder Management
- PMBOK Guide® Fifth Edition: Section 13.1   Identify Stakeholders

Lesson Quiz

Instructions: The actual PMP exam is done via computer. These questions are representative of what you will encounter. Circle the correct answer. Answer Key in Appendix A.

1. Which of the following best describes the Identify Stakeholder process:

   A. The Identify Stakeholders process is used to identify all people or organizations that may be impacted or have an impact on a project.
   B. The Identify Stakeholders process is used to determine the communication needs of project stakeholders.
   C. The Identify Stakeholders process is used to make project information available to project stakeholders.
   D. The Identify Stakeholders process is used to ensure that communications with project stakeholders is productive and meets the needs and desires of those stakeholders.

2. You have just been appointed as the project manager to an organization that you are not familiar with. One of your first tasks is to identify stakeholders for your project. What are the three steps you would perform to analyze stakeholders:

   A. Identify internal stakeholders, identify external stakeholders, and develop a stakeholder communications plan.
   B. Identify all potential stakeholders, identify the potential impact or support of each stakeholder, and assess how they might respond to various situations.
   C. Identify all potential stakeholders, ask how they would like to be communicated with, and build alliances with those who are the most important stakeholders.
   D. Identify all potential stakeholders, identify the potential impact or support of each stakeholder, and build alliances with only the most important stakeholders.

3. The key output for identify stakeholders include:

   A. Communications Management Plan
   B. Stakeholder register
   C. Stakeholder issues report
   D. Stakeholder analysis

End of Lesson 6

This page intentionally blank.

Lesson 7
Planning Process Group

Objectives

At the end of this lesson, you will be able to:

- Understand what processes are used in the Planning Process Group
- Understand the purpose for using Planning processes for the project or project phase

Process Locator for the PMBOK® Guide

	Initiating	Planning	Executing	M&C	Closing
Integration					
Scope					
Time					
Cost					
Quality					
Human Resource					
Communications					
Risk					
Procurement					
Stakeholder					

The Planning Process Group consists of twenty-four processes that are intended to plan a project or project phase.

The primary purpose that these Planning processes are performed is to define the elements and work for a project (or phase). Planning processes cover all ten knowledge areas of the *PMBOK® Guide Fifth Edition.*

During the Planning processes, the project is fully defined. At the end of the Planning processes, the Project Management Plan and all related documentation is completed and accepted by the project stakeholders. Usually, after the Project Management Plan and all defining documents are accepted, then change control processes are employed to manage all subsequent changes to the project baseline.

Of particular importance are the project baselines for project scope, schedule and budget.

In general, when a change is made to the project baseline while the project is in the executing phases of the project, the project manager returns to the Planning processes in order to update the affected documentation.

Planning Tasks

On your PMP Exam, you will encounter many questions that will test your understanding of planning processes. These questions will generally focus on the following tasks, that are in turn, related to specific processes and process actions in planning. As a PMP or project manager planning a project (or project phase) you may be required to:

1. Assess detailed project requirements, constraints, and assumptions with stakeholders based on the project charter, lessons learned from previous projects, and the use of requirement-gathering techniques (e.g., planning sessions, brainstorming, focus groups), in order to establish the project deliverables.

2. Create the work breakdown structure with the team by deconstructing the scope, in order to manage the scope of the project.

3. Develop a budget plan based on the project scope using estimating techniques, in order to manage project cost.

4. Develop a project schedule based on the project timelines, scope, and resource plan, in order to manage timely completion of the project.

5. Develop a human resource management plan by defining the roles and responsibilities of the project team members in order to create an effective project organization structure and provide guidance regarding how resources will be utilized and managed.

6. Develop a communications plan based on the project organization structure and external stakeholder requirements, in order to manage the flow of project information.

7. Develop a procurement management plan based on the project scope and schedule, in order to ensure that the required project resources will be available.

8. Develop a quality management plan based on the project scope and requirements, in order to prevent the occurrence of defects and reduce the cost of quality.

9. Develop a Change Management Plan by defining how changes will be handled, in order to track and make changes.

10. Develop a risk management plan by identifying, analyzing, and prioritizing project risks and defining risk response strategies, in order to manage uncertainty throughout the project life cycle.

11. Present the project plan to the key stakeholders, in order to obtain approval to execute the project.

12. Conduct a kick-off meeting with all key stakeholders, in order to announce the start of the project, communicate the project milestones, and share other relevant information.

Knowledge Requirements

As a PMP applying Planning processes in real-world projects, you will be required to possess in-depth knowledge in several project specific areas, as well as a broad knowledge of project management in general. The PMP Exam will test your understanding of these knowledge specifics.

Remember, the PMP or project manager is always required to have a very broad base of knowledge to work from. The project manager has to work across the entire organization spectrum in many cases to effectively perform project management.

As a PMP or project manager applying Planning processes, you may be expected to have knowledge of:

- Requirements gathering techniques
- WBS tools and techniques
- Time, budget & cost estimation techniques
- Scope management techniques
- Resource planning process
- Workflow diagramming techniques
- Types and uses of organization charts

- Elements, purpose and techniques associated with:
  - Project planning
  - Communications planning
  - Procurement planning
  - Quality management planning
  - Change management planning
  - Risk management planning

Knowledge Check

Read the recommended chapters in the PMBOK Guide, associated with the Planning Process Group processes before attempting this exercise.

After you have read all of the lesson material and the readings in the PMBOK Guide, your goal is to match the planning processes to the Planning Process Group and correct PMBOK Guide Knowledge Area. Use the TSI Ultimate PMP Exam Prep Match Card Set to perform this exercise.

If you do not have a Match Card Set, create a 3x5 card for each Process Group, Knowledge Area and Process and match them by placing the correct planning process in a grid relative to the Process Group and Knowledge Area.

Use page 61 in the PMBOK Guide as your example and to check your matches after you have performed the matching exercise.

End of Lesson 7

Lesson 8
Plan Stakeholder Management

Objectives
At the end of this lesson, you will be able to:
- Describe the purpose of the Plan Stakeholder Management process
- Describe the Inputs, Tools and Techniques, and Outputs of the process
- Identify stakeholder engagement models to be considered when planning the project

Process Locator for the PMBOK Guide

	Initiating	Planning	Executing	Monitoring & Controlling	Closing
Integration					
Scope					
Time					
Cost					
Quality					
Human Resources					
Communications					
Risk					
Procurement					
Stakeholders		▓			

It is critical to identify all of the organizations, people and their expectations for the project. Stakeholder management focuses on managing interests and engagement.

A "Stakeholder" is any person or organization that is actively involved in a project, or whose interests may be affected positively or negatively by execution of a project. Once stakeholders have been identified, it is imperative to develop management strategies for ensuring that the stakeholders are engaged and participating throughout the life of the project. This can be done by creating an actionable plan showing the intent of the project manager and team for interaction levels based on individual stakeholder needs.

Plan Stakeholder Management identifies how the project will affect individual stakeholders. From this information, the project manager can tailor a plan to keep each stakeholder engaged and participating in the project by addressing specific interests and elements which affect that stakeholder.

The project manager may use analytical techniques to compare actual stakeholder involvement and engagement to planned involvement. This is usually done using a five-point scale ranging from an "Unaware" condition to a "Leading" condition.

Stakeholder Involvement & Engagement Compared to Planned Involvement

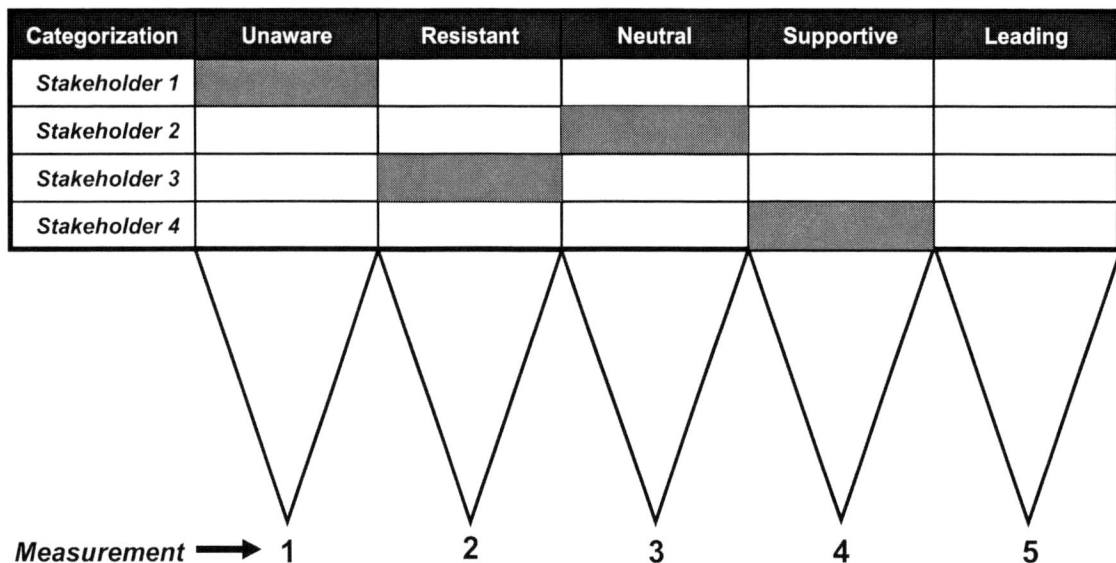

Categorization	Unaware	Resistant	Neutral	Supportive	Leading
Stakeholder 1	�© 🔲				
Stakeholder 2			▒		
Stakeholder 3		▒			
Stakeholder 4				▒	

| Measurement ➡ | 1 | 2 | 3 | 4 | 5 |

Figure 8.1 Stakeholder Involvement 5-Point Scale Illustration

Process Elements

The Plan Stakeholder Management process has the following Inputs:
- Project Management Plan – Document recording management approaches and techniques for communication among stakeholders

- Stakeholder Register – Identifies project stakeholders

- Enterprise Environmental Factors – Considers factors such as; culture, systems, procedures, industry standards

- Organizational Process Assets – Considers factors such as lessons learned and historical information

The Plan Stakeholder Management process uses the following Tools & Techniques:
- Expert Judgment – Expert technical and/or managerial judgment (from any qualified source)

- Meetings – Face to face meetings to determine stakeholder needs and participating levels

- Analytical Techniques – Comparing current levels of engagement to planned levels for project stakeholders

The Plan Stakeholder Engagement process has the following Output:
- Stakeholder Management Plan – Defines the approach to increase stakeholder support and reduce negative impacts represented in a stakeholder analysis matrix

- Project Documents Updates – Updates to schedule or stakeholder register

Plan Stakeholder Management		
This process develops management strategies to engage stakeholders throughout the project life cycle		
Inputs	**Tools and Techniques**	**Outputs**
• Project Management Plan • Stakeholder Register • Enterprise Environmental Factors • Organizational Process Assets	• Expert Judgment • Meetings • Analytical Techniques	• Stakeholder Management Plan • Project Documents Updates

Figure 8.1 Process Elements within the Plan Stakeholder Management Process

TSI Study Aid

This chart is part of the study aid poster series available at: *www.TrueSolutions.com*

Process Documents

The Stakeholder Management Plan document becomes part of the overall Project Management Plan. This document identifies chosen strategies for managing and engaging stakeholders throughout the project life cycle.

Some of the elements that might be included in the Stakeholder Management Plan are:

- Project Name

- Desired and current level of engagement level

- Impact of change to stakeholders by project

- Interrelationships and overlap between stakeholders

- Initial stakeholder communication requirements

- Method and reasons for updating the Stakeholder Management Plan

For specific PMP exam guidance on the Stakeholder Management Plan document and its contents, please refer directly to the PMBOK® Guide Fifth Edition, section 13.2.3.1.

The following form reflects a template that can be used to record all of the preliminary project information and define a Stakeholder Management Plan.

True Solutions, Inc.
Project Management Template
Volume 1: Stakeholder Management Plan

Project Name: _____
Document Prepared By: _____ Date: _____

Stakeholder Name	Engagement Levels		Change Impact	Overlaps with Other SH	Information Requirements		
	Current	Desired			Info Needed	Transmit Method	Frequency
Reasons to Update Plan							
Method to Update							
Approval Required:							

Plan Approved By: _____ Date: _____

Application Aid

This form is available individually or as part of a set at:
www.TrueSolutions.com

Process Tasks

The Plan Stakeholder Management process aligns with many of the defined planning tasks that a project manager performs when managing a project. No specific task deals with stakeholder management. Stakeholders are referred to in these tasks:

Planning Task #11: "Present the project plan to the key stakeholders (if required), in order to obtain approval to execute the project".

Planning Task #12: "Conduct a kick-off meeting with all stakeholders, in order to announce the start of the project, communicate the project milestones, and share other relevant information".

Think About It

How does your organization differ from the description of "Plan Stakeholder Management" as described in the PMBOK Guide? Do you spend more effort, or less effort in defining a management strategy for stakeholders on your projects?

Must Know Concepts

----

1. The Plan Stakeholder Management process is performed to develop appropriate management strategies to engage stakeholders throughout the project.

2. A key output of the Plan Stakeholder Management process is the Stakeholder Management Plan which lists the project's stakeholders and relevant information for each stakeholder or stakeholder group, their communications needs and expectations.

3. The project team should determine the desired level of engagement by each stakeholder for the current phase of the project. Using the five levels of stakeholder engagement (PMBOK 13.2.2.3) project teams must analyze current and desired state of stakeholder engagement.

Additional Reading

- PMBOK Guide® Fifth Edition: Section 13.2   Plan Stakeholder Management

Lesson Quiz

Instructions: The actual PMP exam is done via computer. These questions are representative of what you will encounter. Circle the correct answer. Answer Key in Appendix A.

1. Which of the following best describes the Plan Stakeholder Management process?

   A. The Plan Stakeholder Management process is used to identify all people or organizations that may be impacted or have an impact on a project.
   B. The Plan Stakeholder Management process is used to determine the communications needs of project stakeholders.
   C. The Plan Stakeholder Management process is used to make project information available to project stakeholders.
   D. The Plan Stakeholder Management process is used to identify stakeholder expectations, needs, interests and impacts in order to encourage participation and engagement of stakeholders throughout the project.

2. Stakeholder engagement levels can include all of these, except:

   A. Leading
   B. Resistant
   C. Supportive
   D. Roadblock

3. The key output from Plan Stakeholder Management is:

   A. Communications Management Plan
   B. Stakeholder Analytical Technique
   C. Stakeholder Management Plan
   D. Stakeholder Analysis Report

End of Lesson 8

Lesson 9
Plan Communications Management

Objectives
At the end of this lesson, you will be able to:
- Describe the purpose of the Plan Communications Management process
- Describe the Inputs, Tools and Techniques, and Outputs of the Plan Communications process
- Understand the importance of effective communications to the project
- Understand when to perform Plan Communications Management
- Understand what elements should be included in a Communications Management Plan

Process Locator for the PMBOK® Guide

	Initiating	Planning	Executing	M&C	Closing
Integration					
Scope					
Time					
Cost					
Quality					
Human Resource					
Communications		███			
Risk					
Procurement					
Stakeholder					

Effective communication in project management is considered a critical success factor.

When troubled projects are evaluated, it is typical to find poor communication as a major source of negative conflict and negative outcomes. It is a commonly accepted heuristic (rule of thumb) that good project managers spend up to 90% of their time communicating.

Communication provides the vital connections between people, concepts and information throughout the project environment. Good communication management ensures that important information is generated, collected, distributed and stored in an appropriate and effective manner. Effective communications can facilitate success and enable the project to succeed. The lack of effective communications almost always contributes to project confusion, deficiencies and failure.

The Plan Communications process is applied to determine the communication needs of project stakeholders. This includes determining:

- What information is needed

- When it is needed

- How it will be delivered

Communications needs for the project are typically determined by first engaging identified project stakeholders (communication requirements analysis), to determine their detailed information needs, then documenting the details in a Communications Management Plan. The initial identification of stakeholders occurs early in the project during project initiation. During the initial identification of stakeholders, communications requirements are identified at a high level. In the Plan Communication process, the initial requirements are further detailed and recorded. The Plan Communications process will be executed at the beginning of planning processes. The fact that this process is performed so early in the project attests to the overall importance of having an effective communications plan.

Communication Skills

Project Communications Management does not necessarily involve general communication skills. It is more concerned with information structure. However, understanding basic communication skills is essential to good project management. Communicating is one of the eleven key interpersonal skills that a project manager must use to facilitate project success.

Study Tip
Communication is a two-way activity. Communication is not complete until sender confirms the receiver has understood the intended message. Effective listening can be an important part of good communication. It can develop rapport, trust and respect.

It is important for the project manager to understand several elements associated with Communicating. The project manager should understand types of interpersonal communications, elements that may prevent or block communications and how to measure the number of communications channels.

There are five types of Interpersonal Communications:

- Informal Verbal Communication - "Hallway chat" and ad-hoc discussions
- Formal Verbal Communication - formal presentations, briefings
- Non-Verbal Communication - voice tones, body language (Non-verbal communication is much more powerful and expressive than words)
- Informal Written Communication - E-mail messages, memos, text messaging, notes
- Formal Written Communication - legal documents, plans, project reports, standards, procedures, letters, proposals

Communications Interference

Effective communication can become increasingly difficult if 'blockers' interfere. Communication blockers can include:

- Language differences between sender and receiver

- Physical distance between sender and receiver

- Physical background noise

- Negative comments from sender or receiver

- Hostility between sender and receiver

- Cultural differences between sender and receiver

- Bias

Care should be taken to minimize or eliminate blockers before engaging in meaningful communication.

Communication Channels

The number of communication channels increase in an exponential fashion as more stakeholders become engaged in a project.

Study Tip
The number of communication channels in a project is calculated using the equation: $N(N-1)/2$ (N= the number of people/stakeholders)

As an example, if a project team has eight members, the number of communication channels would be calculated like this:

8(8-1)/2 = 8(7)/2 = 56/2 = 28

Process Elements

The Plan Communications process has the following Inputs:

- Project Management Plan - A document identifying all project baseline information on how the project will be executed, monitored, controlled and closed

- Stakeholder Register - A document identifying all project stakeholder information, requirements and classification

- Enterprise Environmental Factors - Factors such as; culture and structure of an organization

- Organizational Process Assets - Factors such as lessons learned and historical information

The Plan Communications process uses the following Tools & Techniques:

- Communication Requirements Analysis - Determining the total of information needs among project stakeholders

- Communication Technology - The methodologies used to transfer information among project stakeholders

- Communication Models - A model of how communications occur between two parties

- Communication Methods - Individual/group meetings, video/audio conferences, other communication methods, Interactive, push and pull communication

- Meetings – Discussion and dialogue to determine the appropriate way to manage communications for the project

The Plan Communications process has the following Outputs:

- Communications Management Plan - Details the management of all project communications

- Project Documents Updates - Updates to other project documentation (i.e. project schedule, stakeholder register and stakeholder management strategy)

Plan Communications Management		
This process determines who needs what information, when, and how they get it		
Inputs	**Tools and Techniques**	**Outputs**
• Project Management Plan • Stakeholder Register • Enterprise Environmental Factors • Organizational Process Assets	• Communication Requirements Analysis • Communication Technology • Communication Models • Communication Methods • Meetings	• Communications Management Plan • Project Documents Updates TSI Study Aid This chart is part of the study aid poster series available at: *www.TrueSolutions.com*

Figure 9.1 Process Elements within the Plan Communications Management Process

Process Documents

The Communications Management Plan is the key output from the Plan Communications Management process. The Communications Management Plan documents the overall communications needs of project stakeholders at a detailed level. Many organizations have a pre-determined Communications Management Plan that will be executed for each project in the organization.

As with any other project management process, the size and complexity of the Communications Management Plan should be in accordance with the procedures of the organization and appropriate to the size and complexity of the project. As a simple example, a 2 week project to move a small department within the corporate headquarters building would have minimal communications requirements. An engineering project to create a new jet fighter using multiple corporations working in multiple global locations would require significant communications management activities.

A simple Communications Management Plan could consist of the following elements:

- Identifying information for the project and plan
  - Project name
  - Project manager
  - Revision number
  - Revision date
- Report (or Communications document) name

- Description of document
  - Elements to be included

- Level of detail
- Document recipients
- Document distribution schedule
- Document distribution method (or methods)

True Solutions, Inc.
Project Management Template
Version 2: Communications Plan Template

Communications Plan

Project Name:						
Prepared by:						
Date:						
Key Stakeholders (Distribution Schedule) ▼	**Stakeholder Issues**	**Key Messages to Communicate**	**Communication Methods to be Used** (written, one-on-one, electronic, meetings, etc.)	**Description of Specific Communications** (content, format, level of detail, etc.)	**Timing Issues** (see also *Bar Chart, Project Schedule*)	**Other**
Client						
Senior Management						
Sponsor						
Project Team Members						
Employees						
Subcontractors						
Suppliers						
Unions						
Government Agencies						
News Media						
Community						
Other						

Application Aid

This form is available individually or as part of a set at:
www.TrueSolutions.com

Process Tasks

The Plan Communications Management process aligns with one of the defined tasks that a project manager performs when managing a project:

Planning Task #6: "Develop a communications management plan based on the project organization structure and external stakeholder requirements, in order to manage the flow of project information".

Think About It

The Plan Communications Management process focuses on planning all communications that will be conducted for the project. Plan Communications does this by involving the stakeholders and meeting their requirements for document formats, frequencies and distribution. Plan Communications is done by:

- ☐ Involving stakeholders
- ☐ Documenting communications needs
- ☐ Determining what documents to use
- ☐ Determining formats
- ☐ Determining frequency for document to be distributed
- ☐ Determining who the documents will be distributed to
- ☐ Determining what media will be used for distribution

Which of these elements do you use in your organization for communications management? _____

Must Know Concepts
----

1. The Plan Communications Management process is applied to determine the communications needs of project stakeholders. This includes what information is needed, when it is needed and how it will be delivered.

2. The primary deliverable (Output) of the Plan Communications process is the Communications Management Plan.

3. Effective communications in project management is a critical success factor; it is an accepted heuristic that good project managers spend up to 90% of their time communicating.

4. Communication is a two-way activity. Communication is not complete until the sender confirms the receiver has understood the intended message.

5. The number of communication channels within a project increases exponentially as the number of stakeholders increases. The equation used to calculate communications channels is $N(N-1)/2$.

Additional Reading

- PMBOK® Guide Fifth Edition: Section 10.1   Plan Communications Management

Lesson Quiz

Instructions: The actual PMP exam is done via computer. These questions are representative of what you will encounter. Circle the correct answer. Answer Key in Appendix A.

1. Which of the following statements best describes the Plan Communications process?

   A. The Plan Communications Management process is applied to determine the number of communication channels within the project and use that data as justification for keeping the number of stakeholders to a minimum.

   B. The Plan Communications Management process is applied to determine informal verbal communication needs, formal verbal communication needs, informal written communication needs, formal written communication needs and non-verbal communication needs.

   C. The Plan Communications Management process is applied to determine the communications needs of project stakeholders, including what information is needed, when it is needed and how it will be delivered.

   D. The Plan Communications Management process is applied to satisfy stakeholder wishes.

2. Which statement is *most* true?

   A. Active listening (effective listening) is an outdated communications technique. It seldom enhances communication between sender and receiver.

   B. Formal written communication is the preferred method for all project communications. This ensures everything is formally documented for later review and use in lessons learned.

   C. Non-verbal communication is important.

   D. Stakeholders should be provided with information on a strict need-to-know basis. You and your project team are best served by keeping project information closely held.

3. A small project currently has 6 stakeholders in the communications loop. If two more stakeholders are added, how many more channels of communication will result?

   A. 2
   B. 13
   C. 15
   D. 28

End of Lesson 9

This page intentionally blank.

Lesson 10
Plan Scope Management

Objectives
At the end of this lesson, you will be able to:
- Describe the purpose of the Plan Scope Management process
- Describe the Inputs, Tools and Techniques, and Outputs of the Plan Scope Management process
- Understand the importance of scope management to the project
- Understand when to plan project scope
- Understand what elements should be included in a Scope Management Plan

Process Locator for the PMBOK® Guide

	Initiating	Planning	Executing	M&C	Closing
Integration					
Scope		▓▓▓			
Time					
Cost					
Quality					
Human Resource					
Communications					
Risk					
Procurement					
Stakeholder					

Scope is a critical success factor for every project.

This process helps us plan to manage project scope.

In versions one through four of the PMBOK Guide, there were three undefined "processes" that we have referred to over time, as the "hidden processes". PMI has taken action and corrected this ambiguity by including three new processes into the PMBOK Guide Fifth Edition. One of these formerly "hidden" processes is the process of Plan Scope Management.

Plan Scope Management is a very simple process. It is the process of creating a scope management plan that will document how project scope will be defined, documented, validated and controlled throughout the project life cycle. Using the very simplest definition, the Scope Management Plan might say something like: "Any changes to project scope must be approved by these key stakeholders".

The Scope Management Plan will document how scope is to be developed. This implies that the level of detail required and the format for the project scope statement will be defined here. This also includes development of the scope baseline which occurs in Create WBS. The Scope Management Plan should define what level of detail will go into the work breakdown structure/scope baseline.

The level of detail defined will then dictate how scope will be tracked and managed throughout the project. For example, if it is decided that the scope statement will only define deliverables at a milestone level, then, when tracking the project, the project manager and team will presumably only have to report at the milestone level.

If, on the other hand, the Scope Management Plan indicates that each deliverable will be defined to the task and hour level, then the team has a much more detailed tracking requirement for the project.

The Plan Scope Management process creates the Scope Management Plan and Requirements Management Plan, both which are considered part of the overall Project Management Plan.

Process Elements

The Plan Scope Management process has the following Inputs:
- Project Management Plan – A document that includes subsidiary plans used to create and influence the approach taken to managing scope

- Project Charter - The document authorizing the project to begin

- Enterprise Environmental Factors - Factors such as; culture, infrastructure, personnel administration and marketplace conditions

- Organizational Process Assets - Factors such as lessons learned, historical information, policies and procedures

The Plan Scope Management process uses the following Tools & Techniques:
- Expert Judgment – Expertise with specialized skill and knowledge in developing scope management plans

- Meetings – Discussion and dialogue to determine the appropriate way to manage scope for the project

The Plan Scope Management process has the following Outputs:

- Scope Management Plan - Details the management of scope definition, development, verification and monitoring

- Requirements Management Plan – Document which describes how requirements will be analyzed, documented and managed

Plan Scope Management		
This process documents how project scope is defined, validated and controlled		
Inputs	**Tools and Techniques**	**Outputs**
• Project Management Plan • Project Charter • Enterprise Environmental Factors • Organizational Process Assets	• Expert Judgment • Meetings	• Scope Management Plan • Requirements Management Plan

Figure 10.1 Process Elements within the Plan Scope Management Process

Process Documents

The Scope Management Plan is the key output from the Plan Scope Management process. The Scope Management Plan documents the overall plan to define, develop and manage scope at a detailed level. Many organizations have a pre-determined Scope Management Plan that will be executed for each project in the organization.

As with any other project management process, the size and complexity of the Scope Management Plan should be in accordance with the procedures of the organization and appropriate to the size and complexity of the project.

A simple Scope Management Plan could consist of the following elements:

1. Identifying information for the project and plan
   - Project name
   - Preparer name
   - Revision date

2. Person or persons who can request a scope change

3. Person or persons who can approve a scope change

4. Change reasons

5. Impacts to the project

6. Other information, such as:

- Process to develop the scope statement
- Process to define requirements

Project Management Template
Volume 1: Scope Management Plan Template

Scope Management Plan Template

Project Name:		
Prepared by:		
Date:		
Person(s) authorized to request scope changes (see Scope Change Request):		
Name:	Title:	Location:
Name:	Title:	Location:
Name:	Title:	Location:
Person(s) to whom Scope Change Request forms must be submitted for approval:		
Name:	Title:	Location:
Name:	Title:	Location:
Name:	Title:	Location:

Acceptable reasons for changes to Project Scope (e.g., changes to requirements, realization of a new process or procedure that improves outcomes, etc.):

Describe how you will calculate and report on the projected impact of any scope changes (time, cost, quality, etc.):

Describe any other aspects of how changes to the project scope will be managed:

Application Aid

This form is available individually or as part of a set at:
www.TrueSolutions.com

©Copyright 2013 True Solutions, Inc.
5001 LBJ Freeway, Suite 125-B Dallas, Texas 75244
Tel: 972.770.0900   Fax 972.770.0922   www.truesolutions.com

Process Tasks

The Plan Scope Management process aligns with one of the defined tasks that a project manager performs when managing a project:

Planning Task #9: "Develop a change management plan by defining how changes will be handled, in order to track and manage changes".

Think About It

The Plan Scope Management process focuses on planning all requirements and scope definitions that will be performed for the project. Plan Scope Management does this by involving the stakeholders and soliciting their requirements for change control. Plan Scope Management is done by:

- ☐ Involving stakeholders
- ☐ Documenting scope definition and management needs
- ☐ Determining what documents to use
- ☐ Determining formats
- ☐ Determining frequency for monitoring scope condition
- ☐ Determining who can request scope or requirements changes
- ☐ Determining who can approve changes

Which of these elements do you use in your organization for scope, requirements and change management? _____

_____

_____

Must Know Concepts

1. The Plan Scope Management process is applied to create a Scope Management Plan that documents how project scope will be defined, controlled and validated.

2. The primary deliverable (Output) of the Plan Scope Management process is the Scope Management Plan. A secondary, companion output from this process is the Requirements Management Plan.

3. Scope Management is part of the overall Project Management Plan.

Additional Reading

- PMBOK® Guide Fifth Edition: Section 5.1 Plan Scope Management

Lesson Quiz

Instructions: The actual PMP exam is done via computer. These questions are representative of what you will encounter. Circle the correct answer. Answer Key in Appendix A.

1. Which of the following statements best describes the Plan Scope Management process?

    A. The Plan Scope Management process is applied to determine the number of scope changes planned for the project and use that data as justification for keeping the number of stakeholders to a minimum.
    B. The Plan Scope Management process is applied to determine how to define, manage and control scope for the project.
    C. The Plan Scope Management process creates the Project Scope Statement.
    D. The Plan Scope Management process is applied to satisfy stakeholder expectations.

2. Which statement is *most* true?

    A. The Scope Management Plan is the only output from Plan Scope Management.
    B. Expert judgment is used in Plan Scope Management in order to determine how many scope changes we can anticipate for the project.
    C. Non-scope change requests are not important.
    D. There are two important outputs from Plan Scope Management, both of which are intended to manage scope for the project.

3. Which of these are not defined as an input to Plan Scope Management?

    A. Project Scope Statement
    B. Project Management Plan
    C. Enterprise Environmental Factors
    D. Lessons Learned Information

4. Your project team is working on creation of the Scope Management Plan, which they know will help to reduce the risk of project scope creep. They ask for your guidance as project manager. What is your best response?

   A. Think about what requirements may be developed and build the Scope Management Plan around those prospective requirements
   B. Include processes for developing and maintaining the Project Scope Statement and WBS
   C. Develop a process for how requirements will be tracked
   D. All of the above

5 What needs to be included in the Requirements Management Plan?

   A. How requirements will be planned, tracked, and reported
   B. Traceability structure
   C. Configuration management activities
   D. All of the above

End of Lesson 10

This page intentionally blank.

Lesson 11
Collect Requirements

Objectives
At the end of this lesson, you will be able to:
- Describe the purpose of the Collect Requirements process
- Describe the Inputs, Tools and Techniques, and Outputs of the Collect Requirements Process
- Describe methods for gathering requirements and making decisions
- Describe key documents which come from this process

Process Locator for the PMBOK® Guide

	Initiating	Planning	Executing	M&C	Closing
Integration					
Scope		■			
Time					
Cost					
Quality					
Human Resource					
Communications					
Risk					
Procurement					
Stakeholder					

The Collect Requirements process defines and documents the product and project features that are required to meet the expectations and requirements of the projects stakeholders.

Project "requirements" are the conditions and capabilities that must be achieved through the projects' execution. Requirements must be documented in sufficient detail to allow measurement in determining the status of project completion and in determining whether or not the documented requirements have been met.

The identified expectations and requirements will be used in other processes, such as cost, quality, and schedule planning, to ensure that the project is properly planned and will meet stakeholder expectations.

There are many tools and techniques than can used to help facilitate identifying requirements, such as; focus groups, workshops, brainstorming, mind mapping, surveys, observation, and others.

A key output of this process is the Requirements Documentation. Requirements Documentation describes how the identified requirements fulfill the business needs of the project. This documentation is normally progressively elaborated as a project progresses. In addition, a Requirements Traceability Matrix links each requirement to the business objectives to ensure that each requirement is adding value to the project and organization. Typical attributes used in the requirements traceability matrix may include:
- A unique identifier
- A textual description of the requirement
- The rationale for inclusion
- Owner
- Source
- Priority
- Version
- Current status (such as active, cancelled, deferred, added, approved, assigned, completed)
- Status date

Additional attributes to ensure that the requirement has met stakeholders' satisfaction may include stability, complexity and acceptance criteria.

A project's success is directly influenced by the accuracy and completeness in identifying all of the requirements and expectations through this process.

Process Elements

The Collect Requirements process has the following Inputs:
- Scope Management Plan – Document describing how scope will be developed and managed

- Requirements Management Plan - A document describing how requirements for the project will be analyzed, documented and managed

- Stakeholder Management Plan – Documents stakeholder areas of interest and strategies for engaging the stakeholders throughout the project

- Project Charter – Authorization to start the project along with high level scope and objectives

- Stakeholder Register – The list of project stakeholders

The Collect Requirements process uses the following Tools & Techniques:
- Interviews - Formal and informal approach to determine stakeholder information requirements and expectations

- Focus Groups - Bringing together prequalified stakeholders and subject matter experts to determine project and product expectations

- Facilitated Workshops - Focused sessions to define requirements and reconcile stakeholder differences

- Group Creativity Techniques - Activities organized to identify project and product requirements (i.e. brainstorming, idea/mind mapping, etc.)

- Group Decision Making Techniques - group assessment of alternatives which produce future actions (i.e. unanimity, majority, etc.)

- Questionnaires and Surveys - Form containing a set of questions distributed to gather information from a wide number of participants in a timely manner

- Observations - Directly viewing individuals or groups in their environment capturing actual job/task performance

- Prototypes – Developing a product model and soliciting feedback prior to actual build

- Benchmarking – Comparing planned processes or outcomes to industry standards or competitive products

- Context Diagrams – A scope model which visually depicts the business system

- Document Analysis – Analyzing documentation and identifying information relevant to the requirements

The Collect Requirements process has the following Outputs:
- Requirements Documentation - Documentation describing how individual requirements fulfill the business needs of the project

- Requirements Traceability Matrix - A grid which associates requirement origin history throughout the project life cycle

Collect Requirements		
This process defines and documents the project and product features and functions needed to fill stakeholder's needs and expectations		
Inputs	**Tools and Techniques**	**Outputs**
• Scope Management Plan • Requirements Management Plan • Stakeholder Management Plan • Project Charter • Stakeholder Register	• Interviews • Focus Groups • Facilitated Workshops • Group Creativity Techniques • Group Decision Making Techniques • Questionnaires and Surveys • Observations • Prototypes • Benchmarking • Context Diagrams • Document Analysis	• Requirements Documentation • Requirements Traceability Matrix

Figure 11.1 Process Elements within the Collect Requirements Process

Process Documents

During the Collect Requirements process the project manager creates Requirements Documentation and a Requirements Traceability Matrix. In the sample form shown following, a Project Requirements Documentation template and Requirements Traceability Matrix are combined in one form.

It should be also noted that the form shown has been condensed for presentation purposes. A template for this process may be much larger and wider, or may simply use linked information to refer to other, more lengthy documents.

Project Requirements

Project Name:	
Prepared by:	
Date:	
Ways to attain information	
Do Interview	Talk to them about their requirements in some detail
Facilitate workshops	Sort, prioritize, and set goals that meet the requirement needs
Questionnaires	Identify best questions to give you control of information
Focus Groups	Create a group specific to this need
Group Creativity and/or Group Decision	Use brainstorming, idea mapping, etc. to find the needs required then use a group decision methodology to count the 'vote'
Observations	Job shadow while they are working to see where the needs are
Stakeholder needs	Interview and Identify the need requirements of the sponsors for this project
Project	**Product**
Business requirements	Technical requirements
Project management requirements	Security requirements
Delivery requirements	Performance requirements
Acceptance requirements	Quality requirements
Requirement Assumptions	Impact area (internal) requirements
Requirement Restraints	Impact area (external) requirements
Traceability requirements	Support and Training requirements

TSi **Application Aid**

This form is available individually or as part of a set at:
www.TrueSolutions.com

Process Tasks

The Collect Requirements process aligns with one of the defined tasks that a project manager performs when managing a project:

Planning Task #1: "Assess detailed project requirements, constraints, and assumptions with stakeholders based on the project charter, lessons learned from previous projects, and the use of requirement-gathering techniques (e.g., planning sessions, brainstorming, focus groups), in order to establish the project deliverables".

Think About It

Instructions Use this exercise to compare how you practice project management to what is specified in the *PMBOK® Guide Fifth Edition.*

Think about how you collect requirements in your organization. Write a brief description of how you use this process:

_____

_____

_____

_____

Must Know Concepts

----

1. The Collect Requirements process defines and documents the product and project features that are required to meet the expectations and requirements of the projects stakeholders.

2. A key output of the Collect Requirements process is the Requirements Documentation.

3. A Requirements Traceability Matrix links requirements to business objectives to ensure each requirement is adding value to the project and organization. Typical attributes used in the requirements traceability matrix may include:
   - A unique identifier
   - A textual description of the requirement
   - The rationale for inclusion
   - Owner
   - Source

- Priority
- Version
- Current status (such as active, cancelled, deferred, added, approved, assigned, completed)
- Status date

4. A project's success is directly influenced by the accuracy and completeness in identifying all of the requirements and expectations through this process.

Additional Reading

- -

- PMBOK® Guide Fifth Edition: Section 5.2 Collect Requirements

Lesson Quiz

Instructions: The actual PMP exam is done via computer. These questions are representative of what you will encounter. Circle the correct answer. Answer Key in Appendix A.

1. Which of the following is most correct regarding the Collect Requirements process?

    A. The Collect Requirements process defines and documents stakeholder needs for managing customer expectations throughout the project.
    B. The only input for Collect Requirements is the Project Charter.
    C. Project requirements include technical, security and performance requirements
    D. Product requirements include project management, business and delivery requirements.

2. Collect Requirements tools and techniques include all of the following *except*:

    A. Prototypes
    B. Brainstorming
    C. Agile methods
    D. Focus Groups

3. Project Scope Management includes the following processes:

    A. Collect Requirements, Validate Scope, Perform Scope Control
    B. Verify Scope, Create WBS, Develop Project Management Plan
    C. Plan Scope Management, Collect Requirements, Control Scope, Validate Scope, Create WBS
    D. Define Scope, Control Scope, Report Scope Performance

4. You are project manager for a project that has a very aggressive schedule. You have a signed project charter and the project sponsor wants to begin actual work right away. Which of these choices is probably not appropriate in this situation?

    A. Refuse to start any work until all project and product requirements are fully defined.
    B. Do an initial project and product requirement definition, then document a plan to use rolling wave planning to define requirements and work as the project progresses.
    C. Identify small work elements that have little or no interdependencies and have less risk of requiring re-work that can be started immediately.
    D. Define requirements and scope for the project; when enough work elements are clearly identified that subject matter experts are able to start work, begin work while continuing to develop all requirements and scope in detail.

5. Which of these are management plans that are input to Collect Requirements?

    A. Human Resource Management Plan, Scope Strategy, Requirements Documentation
    B. Scope Management Plan, Requirements Management Plan, Stakeholder Management Plan
    C. Scope Management Plan, Communications Management Plan, Requirements Management Plan
    D. Risk Management Plan, Stakeholder Management Plan, Requirements Management Plan

6   You and your project team are planning the Blue Print project, which will result in creation of architectural design software. You are holding a facilitated workshop and a stakeholder has suggested that you add the ability to print design documents. What is the stakeholder describing?

    A. Business requirement
    B. Stakeholder requirement
    C. Solution requirement
    D. Transition requirement

7. In a facilitated workshop, you as the project manager are facilitating creation of a scope model for your project. The scope model shows the business system and how people and other systems interact with it. What are you developing?

    A. Benchmarking
    B. Requirements Documentation
    C. Prototype
    D. Context Diagram

8. You and your project team are working with stakeholders to collect requirements. You are conducting a focus group to analyze marketing literature, agreements, requests for proposal, logical data models, and business rules in order to elicit requirements. What Tool and Technique are you using?

    A. Benchmarking
    B. Observations
    C. Document Analysis
    D. Prototypes

End of Lesson 11

This page intentionally blank.

Lesson 12
Define Scope

Objectives
At the end of this lesson, you will be able to:
- Describe the purpose of the Define Scope process
- Describe the Inputs, Tools and Techniques, and Outputs of the Define Scope Process
- Understand that the Project Scope Statement is critical to project success by providing a common understanding of the project for stakeholders

Process Locator for the PMBOK® Guide

	Initiating	Planning	Executing	M&C	Closing
Integration					
Scope		████			
Time					
Cost					
Quality					
Human Resource					
Communications					
Risk					
Procurement					
Stakeholder					

The Define Scope process is applied to create the Project Scope Statement.

The Project Scope Statement defines the projects deliverables and the work required to create those deliverables. During scope definition, you and your team create the major deliverables, assumptions and constraints by progressively elaborating on data that was defined during project initiation. Stakeholders' needs and desires, as defined in the Requirements Document, are analyzed and developed into firm work requirements. Assumptions and constraints can be further analyzed and the opinions of domain experts can be solicited.

It is important to understand that your Project Scope Statement will serve to provide a common understanding of the project scope among stakeholders. The process of Define Scope creates a detailed Project Scope Statement. The Project Scope Statement is required to complete detailed project planning. The Work Breakdown Structure, Activity List and Project Schedule will derive from key information that is documented in this process.

During project execution the Project Scope Statement will be used to guide decisions. When changes to the project scope are approved, the Project Scope Statement will be updated.

A detailed and thorough Project Scope Statement is critical to the success of a project.

Process Elements

The Define Scope process has the following Inputs:
- Scope Management Plan – Document describing how scope will be developed and managed for the project

- Project Charter - High-level document that authorizes the project and assigns/authorizes the project manager

- Requirements Documentation - Documentation describing how individual requirements fulfill the business needs of the project

- Organizational Process Assets - Consideration factors such as processes, procedures and corporate knowledge base

The Define Scope process uses the following Tools & Techniques:
- Expert Judgment - Expert technical and/or managerial judgment (from any qualified source)

- Product Analysis - Generally accepted methods for translating high-level product descriptions into tangible deliverables

- Alternatives Generation - Technique used to generate different approaches to accomplish the work of the project

- Facilitated Workshops - Focused cross-functional sessions to gain a common understanding of the project objectives

The Define Scope process has the following Outputs:
- Project Scope Statement - Detailed description of a projects deliverables and work required to create them

- Project Documents Updates - Updates to other project documentation (i.e. stakeholder register, requirements documentation, etc.)

Define Scope		
This process defines and documents the project and product features and functions needed to fill stakeholder's needs and expectations		
Inputs	**Tools and Techniques**	**Outputs**
• Scope Management Plan	• Expert Judgment	• Project Scope Statement
• Project Charter	• Product Analysis	• Project Documents Updates
• Requirements Documentation	• Alternatives Generation	
• Organizational Process Assets	• Facilitated Workshops	

Figure 12.1 Process Elements within the Define Scope Process

Process Documents

During the Define Scope process one of the most important documents for the project is created. The Project Scope Statement is a narrative description of the scope (work to be performed) of the project. This document should describe the project scope in sufficient detail to provide a common understanding of the project scope for stakeholders.

While the Project Scope Statement can contain a wide variety of information, it is recommended that as a minimum the following be included in the Project Scope Statement:

- Project and Product Scope Description
- Acceptance Criteria
- Project Deliverables
- Project Limitations, such as exclusions, constraints and assumptions

Previously discussed in the Collect Requirements process, it is important to link project requirements and products requirements to the work of the project. Therefore, Functional Requirements documentation and Technical Requirements documentation is often linked to the Project Scope Statement. Other elements that are often included in the Project Scope Statement (to facilitate common understanding) are:

- Planned Schedule
- Planned Budget
- Resource Requirements
- Executive Summary (usually found at the beginning of the document)
- A summary of identified project risks
- Specific approaches planned towards executing the project

A simplified example of a Project Scope Statement template is shown below.

True Solutions, Inc.
Project Management Template
Version 2: Scope Statement Template

TSI

Scope Statement

Project Name:	
Prepared by:	
Date:	
Revision:	
Product Description:	*A brief summary of the product or service description*
Project Acceptance Criteria	*A statement that defines the criteria and the processes for completed result*
Project Deliverables:	*A list of the summary-level sub products whose full and satisfactory delivery marks completion of the project*
Deliverable A	
Deliverable B	
Deliverable C	
Deliverable D	
Deliverable E	
Known Exclusions	*This is where you define what is "not" in scope*
Project Constraints	*This is where you would list any constraint that limit your options (like budget)*
Project Assumptions	*This is where you would put anything you accept to be true (like you can work on a certain day in the future and it won't rain)*

TSI | Application Aid

This form is available
individually or as
part of a set at:
www.TrueSolutions.com

Process Tasks

The Define Scope process fits between two of the defined tasks that a project manager performs when managing a project (although neither task totally describes this process):

Planning Task #1: "Assess detailed project requirements, constraints, and assumptions with stakeholders based on the project charter, lessons learned from previous projects, and the use of requirement-gathering techniques (e.g., planning sessions, brainstorming, focus groups), in order to establish the project deliverables".

Planning Task #2: "Create the work breakdown structure with the team by deconstructing the scope, in order to manage the scope of the project".

Think About It

I was engaged to manage an application implementation project for a local company. Immediately upon arrival I reviewed the documentation to find that key areas of the project had a scope statement and list of deliverables for the vendor company to perform. What was missing, however, was a comprehensive contract document associated with the scope of work. As a result of this, the vendor proved to be a continual challenge to manage, since there were no associated contract terms which encouraged good work performance.

The project scope statement is an essential tool for defining what is, and what is not, part of the project. But without companion documentation, its value can diminish in many project scenarios.

Contributed by Tim Bergmann, PMP

Must Know Concepts

1. The Define Scope process is intended to create the Project Scope Statement.

2. The Project Scope Statement defines the projects deliverables and the work required to create those deliverables. It defines what is and what is not, part of the project.

3. The Project Scope Statement serves as a documented basis for common understanding of project scope among stakeholders.

4. Alternatives generation that is used during Define Scope is a key technique for generating different approaches for defining and performing project work.

Additional Reading

- PMBOK® Guide Fifth Edition: Section 5.3 Define Scope

Lesson Quiz

Instructions The actual PMP exam is done via computer. These questions are representative of what you will encounter. Circle the correct answer. Answer Key in Appendix A.

1. Define Scope inputs include all of the following except _____.

   A. Requirements Documentation
   B. Project Charter
   C. Project Scope Statement
   D. Organizational Process Assets

2. Which of the following statements is true?

   A. The Project Scope Statement may serve to provide a documented basis for making many future project decisions.
   B. The Project Scope Statement serves as a documented basis for common understanding of scope among stakeholders.
   C. The Project Scope Statement may be revised as the project progresses, to reflect approved changes to the project scope.
   D. All of the above.

3. The Define Scope process is intended to _____.

   A. Create the Scope Management Plan
   B. Create the Work Breakdown Structure (WBS), which provides a comprehensive definition of project scope
   C. Create the Project Scope Statement
   D. Create the Preliminary Project Scope Statement

4. Which of the following is most true?

   A. The Scope Statement should include a description of project deliverables, either at a summary-level or in detail.
   B. The Scope Management Plan should include the work breakdown structure.
   C. The Scope Management Plan should be as brief as possible.
   D. The Project Scope Statement should include the Work Breakdown Structure.

End of Lesson 12

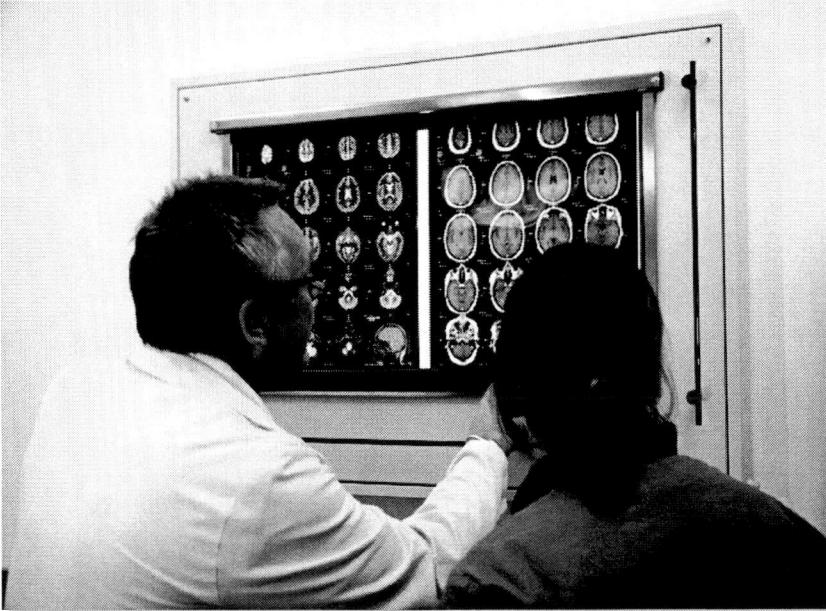

Lesson 13
Create WBS

Objectives
At the end of this lesson, you will be able to:
- Describe the purpose of the Create Work Breakdown Structure process
- Describe the Inputs, Tools and Techniques, and Outputs of the Create WBS process
- Be able to create or interpret a Work Breakdown Structure
- Understand that all of the work on the project should be contained and depicted in the WBS

Process Locator for the PMBOK® Guide

	Initiating	Planning	Executing	M&C	Closing
Integration					
Scope		▓▓▓			
Time					
Cost					
Quality					
Human Resource					
Communications					
Risk					
Procurement					
Stakeholder					

The WBS serves as an excellent communication tool, clearly illustrating the total scope of project work to stakeholders and, although there is no time associated with a WBS, the first level of decomposition often somewhat defines the project life cycle of the project.

Experienced project managers understand it is simply not possible to visualize and manage an entire project without some sort of tool. Instead of trying to manage the whole project at once, all the time, the project must be broken down into manageable sized pieces, and then the pieces can be easily managed. The Create Work Breakdown Structure process facilitates this goal by decomposing (subdividing) major project deliverables into smaller, more manageable components.

This process is typically the first process applied after the Project Scope Statement has been developed.

The primary deliverable from the Create Work Breakdown Structure process is the Scope Baseline. The WBS may be the most important tool for management of a project. When properly developed, the WBS illustrates all of the work elements that define the project and serves as the basis for most planning activities from this point forward.

The WBS documents all the work required to successfully complete the project. The WBS must identify **all of the work required, and only the work required**, to successfully complete the project. "Scope Creep" or continual changes in a project's work requirements can be eliminated by carefully defining scope and managing it using the WBS.

Effective application of the Create Work Breakdown Structure process is critical to project success. Work Packages are critical to developing the budget, the schedule and in tracking the project during monitoring and controlling. The completed Project Scope Statement, WBS, and WBS Dictionary form the Scope Baseline for the project.

Study Tip

The following concepts are important in creation of the WBS:

- WBS deliverables should be decomposed (subdivided) to a level where adequate cost and duration estimates are possible
- WBS deliverables should be decomposed to a level where acceptance criteria can be easily defined and the work can be effectively assigned, managed and measured
- There is no predefined limit to the number of sublevels in a WBS
- The WBS has no time frame, it defines work only
- The lowest level elements of the WBS are termed "Work Packages"
- Work Packages should require no more than 80 hours to complete (the '80 hour' thumb-rule/heuristic)
- Detailed work package descriptions and information are documented and collected to form a "WBS Dictionary"
- Work Packages are typically decomposed into smaller components called activities that represent the work effort required to complete the Work Package

---

Process Elements

The Create Work Breakdown Structure process has the following Inputs:

- Scope Management Plan – Document describing how scope will be developed and managed for the project

- Project Scope Statement - Detailed description of a projects deliverables and work required to create them

- Requirements Documentation - Documentation describing how individual requirements fulfillthe business needs of the project

- Enterprise Environmental Factors – Industry-specific WBS standards

- Organizational Process Assets - Consideration factors such as processes, procedures and corporate knowledge base

The Create Work Breakdown Structure process uses the following Tools & Techniques:

- Decomposition - The process of subdividing project scope into manageable-sized work packages

- Expert Judgment – Judgment provided by subject matter experts to decompose the deliverables into smaller, more manageable elements

The Create Work Breakdown Structure process has the following Output:

- Scope Baseline - The approved Project Scope Statement + the WBS + the WBS Dictionary

- Project Documents Updates - Updates to other project documentation (i.e. requirements documentation)

Create WBS		
This process subdivides major deliverables into manageable components		
Inputs	**Tools and Techniques**	**Outputs**
• Scope Management Plan	• Decomposition	• Scope Baseline
• Project Scope Statement	• Expert Judgment	• Project Documents Updates
• Requirements Documentation		
• Enterprise Environmental Factors		
• Organizational Process Assets		

TSI Study Aid

This chart is part of the study aid poster series available at: *www.TrueSolutions.com*

Figure 13.1 Process Elements within the Create WBS Process

Process Documents

During Create WBS we create a Work Breakdown Structure for the project. As previously discussed, the WBS is where ALL of the work to be performed on the project will be depicted. Typically a WBS is organized by:

* Phase
* Function to be performed
* Material use

Each WBS will be unique, but the WBS many times is derived from a previous similar WBS which is used as a template to create the new WBS. If your organization has a project management methodology in use, details of how to organize the WBS and what elements must be present will usually be defined as part of the project management methodology.

A sample WBS is depicted below:

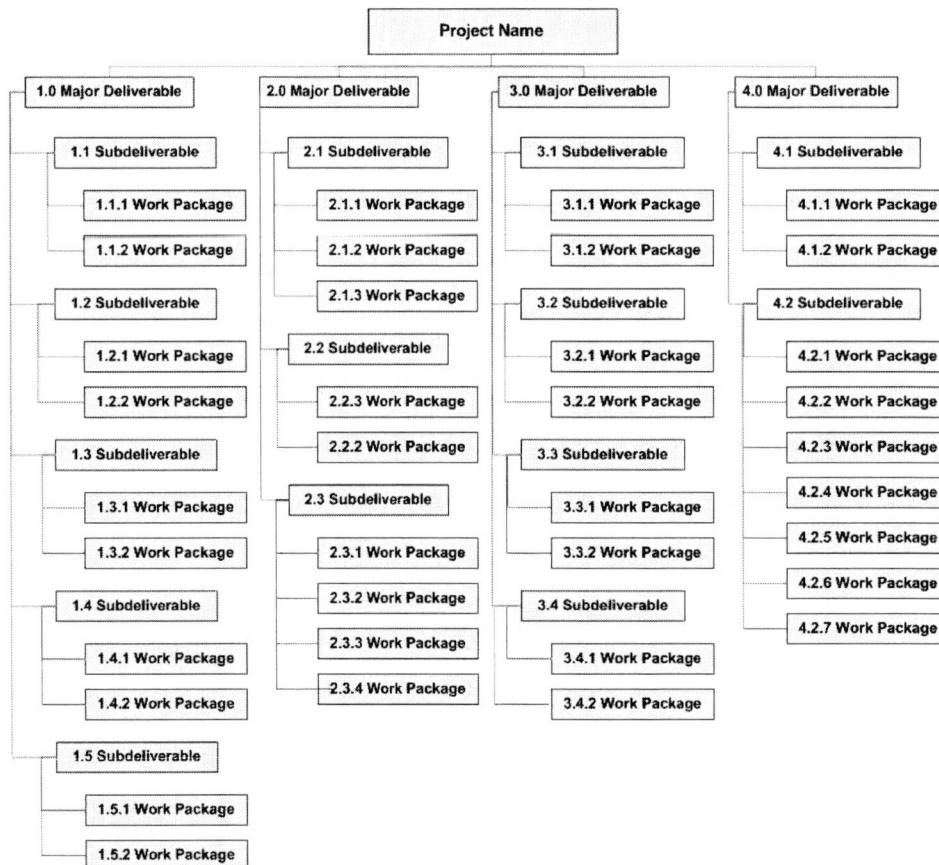

Figure 13.2 Work Breakdown Structure Example

Process Tasks

The Create WBS process is described as one of the defined tasks that a project manager performs when managing a project:

Planning Task #2: "Create the Work Breakdown Structure with the team by deconstructing the scope, in order to manage the scope of the project".

Think About It

Instructions Use this exercise to compare how you practice project management to what is specified in the *PMBOK® Guide Fifth Edition.*

Think about how this process is defined, used and documented in your organization. Write a brief description of how you use this process:

_____

_____

_____

Must Know Concepts

---

1. The Create Work Breakdown Structure process is intended to decompose (subdivide) major project deliverables into manageable sized components.

2. The primary deliverable from the Create Work Breakdown Structure process is the Scope Baseline, which is made up of the Scope Statement, WBS and WBS Dictionary.

3. The Scope Baseline describes all of the work to be performed on the project. This is described graphically in the WBS.

4. There is no predefined limit to the number of sublevels in a WBS. The lowest level in a WBS is a "Work Package". Activities represent the work effort of work packages.

5. Work Packages in the WBS should be decomposed to a level where adequate cost and duration estimates are possible and where acceptance criteria can be easily defined.

6. The WBS has no time frame. In its purest form, the WBS defines work only.

Additional Reading

- PMBOK® Guide Fifth Edition: Section 5.4   Create WBS

Lesson Quiz

Instructions: Circle the correct answer. Answer Key in Appendix A.

1. The decomposed illustration of all project scope (work) is called _____.

   A. A Project Breakdown Structure (PBS)
   B. An Organizational Breakdown Structure (OBS)
   C. A Work Breakdown Structure (WBS)
   D. A Contractual Work Breakdown Structure (CWBS)

2. The subdivision of major project deliverables, as identified in the Project Scope Statement, into smaller, more manageable components, is performed by applying _____.

   A. Configuration management
   B. Constrained optimization
   C. The Create WBS process
   D. The 80-hour rule

3. Which of the following statements is most true?

   A. Creating the WBS results in a compressed project schedule.
   B. Creating the WBS identifies activities on the project's critical path.
   C. Creating the WBS identifies key project risk events.
   D. Creating the WBS can enhance team buy-in.

4. All of the following are false, *except*:

   A. The Work Breakdown Structure communicates the total project scope (work) to stakeholders.
   B. The Work Breakdown Structure identifies the schedule objectives for defined deliverables.
   C. The Work Breakdown Structure describes the business need for each work package.
   D. The Work Breakdown Structure assigns the responsible organization for each major deliverable.

5. The primary Output of the Create WBS process includes the approved Project Scope Statement, the WBS, and the WBS Dictionary, and is a component of the Project Management Plan. What is this Output called?

   A. Project Documents Updates
   B. Scope Baseline
   C. Activities List
   D. Scope Management Plan

End of Lesson 13

This page intentionally blank.

Lesson 14
Plan Schedule Management

Objectives
At the end of this lesson, you will be able to:
- Describe the purpose of the Plan Schedule Management process
- Describe the Inputs, Tools and Techniques, and Outputs of the Plan Schedule Management process
- Understand when to perform Plan Schedule Management
- Understand what elements should be included in a Schedule Management Plan

Process Locator for the PMBOK® Guide

	Initiating	Planning	Executing	M&C	Closing
Integration					
Scope					
Time		▓▓▓			
Cost					
Quality					
Human Resource					
Communications					
Risk					
Procurement					
Stakeholder					

Time is a critical success factor for every project. This process helps us plan to manage the project schedule.

In versions one through four of the PMBOK Guide, there were three undefined "processes" that we have referred to over time, as the "hidden processes". PMI has taken action and corrected this ambiguity by including three new processes into the PMBOK Guide Fifth Edition. One of these formerly "hidden" processes is the process of Plan Schedule Management.

Plan Schedule Management is a very simple process. It is the process of creating a schedule management plan that will document how the project schedule will be defined, documented, validated and controlled throughout the project life cycle. Using the very simplest definition, the Schedule Management Plan might say something like: "Any changes to project schedule must be approved by these key stakeholders".

The Schedule Management Plan will document how the schedule is to be developed. This implies that the level of detail required and the format for the project schedule will be defined here. This also includes development of the schedule baseline which occurs in Develop Schedule. The Schedule Management Plan should define what level of detail will go into the schedule; whether you are tracking at the task or activity level, or tracking at a higher work package, deliverable or milestone level.

The Plan Schedule Management process creates the Schedule Management Plan which is considered part of the overall Project Management Plan.

Process Elements

The Plan Schedule Management process has the following Inputs:
- Project Management Plan - A document identifying all project information on how the project will be managed, including scope baseline

- Project Charter - The document authorizing the project to begin

- Enterprise Environmental Factors - Factors such as; culture, systems, software, etc.

- Organizational Process Assets - Factors such as templates and historical information

The Plan Schedule Management process uses the following Tools & Techniques:
- Expert Judgment – Expert technical and/or managerial judgment from any qualified source

- Analytical Techniques – Choosing strategies to manage the schedule, such as methods, estimating approaches, formats and project management software tools

- Meetings – Discussion and dialogue to determine the appropriate way to manage the schedule for the project

The Plan Schedule Management process has the following Outputs:
- Schedule Management Plan - Details the management of schedule, development, controlling and monitoring the schedule

Plan Schedule Management		
This process determines how the project schedule will be developed and managed		
Inputs	**Tools and Techniques**	**Outputs**
• Project Management Plan • Project Charter • Enterprise Environmental Factors • Organizational Process Assets	• Expert Judgment • Analytical Techniques • Meetings	• Schedule Management Plan TSI Study Aid This chart is part of the study aid poster series available at: *www.TrueSolutions.com*

Figure 14.1 Process Elements within Plan Schedule Management Process

Process Documents

The Schedule Management Plan is the key output from the Plan Schedule Management process. The Schedule Management Plan documents the overall plan to define, develop and manage the project schedule at a detailed level. Many organizations have a pre-determined Schedule Management Plan that will be executed for each project in the organization.

As with any other project management process, the size and complexity of the Schedule Management Plan should be in accordance with the procedures of the organization and appropriate to the size and complexity of the project.

A simple Schedule Management Plan could consist of the following elements:

- Identifying Information for the project and plan
  - Project Name
  - Preparer Name
  - Revision Date
- Person or Persons who can approve a schedule change
- Change reasons
- Impacts to the project
- Other Information, such as:
  - Process to develop the project schedule

A Schedule Management Plan template follows.

Schedule Management Plan

Project Name:		
Prepared by:		
Date:		

Person(s) authorized to request schedule changes (see Schedule Change Request):

Name:	Title:	Location:
Name:	Title:	Location:
Name:	Title:	Location:

Person(s) to whom Schedule Change Request forms must be submitted for approval:

Name:	Title:	Location:
Name:	Title:	Location:
Name:	Title:	Location:

Acceptable reasons for changes to Project Schedule *(e.g., delays due to material or personnel availability; weather; need to resolve related issue before proceeding; acceleration permitted due to early completion of a phase or process, etc.):*

Describe how you will calculate and report on the projected impact of any schedule changes *(time, cost, quality, etc.):*

Describe any other aspects of how changes to the project schedule will be managed:

Application Aid

This form is available
individually or as
part of a set at:
www.TrueSolutions.com

Process Tasks

The Plan Schedule Management process aligns with one of the defined tasks that a project manager performs when managing a project:

Planning Task #9: "Develop a change management plan by defining how changes will be handled, in order to track and manage changes".

Think About It

The Plan Schedule Management process focuses on planning all schedule requirements and definitions for the project. Plan Schedule Management does this by involving the stakeholders and considering the availability of resources. Plan Schedule Management is done by:

- ☐ Involving stakeholders
- ☐ Documenting the schedule and schedule management needs
- ☐ Determining what documents to use to present and track the schedule
- ☐ Determining frequency for monitoring schedule variances
- ☐ Determining who can request schedule changes
- ☐ Determining who can approve changes

Which of these elements do you use in your organization for schedule management?

_____

_____

_____

Must Know Concepts

1. The Plan Schedule Management process is applied to create a Schedule Management Plan that documents how the schedule will be defined, controlled and validated.

2. The primary deliverable (Output) of the Plan Schedule Management process is the Schedule Management Plan.

3. The Schedule Management Plan is part of the overall Project Management Plan.

Additional Reading

- PMBOK® Guide Fifth Edition: Section 6.1   Plan Schedule Management

Lesson Quiz

Instructions: The actual PMP exam is done via computer. These questions are representative of what you will encounter. Circle the correct answer. Answer Key in Appendix A.

1. Which of the following statements best describes the Plan Schedule Management process?

    A. The Plan Schedule Management process is applied to determine the number of schedule changes planned for the project and use that data as justification for keeping the project scope minimized.
    B. The Plan Schedule Management process is applied to determine how to define, manage and control the project schedule.
    C. The Plan Schedule Management process creates the Project Schedule
    D. The Plan Schedule Management process is applied to satisfy stakeholder reporting requirements.

2. Which statement is *most* true?

    A. The Schedule Management Plan is the only output from Plan Schedule Management.
    B. Expert Judgment is used in Plan Schedule Management in order to determine how many schedule changes we can anticipate for the project.
    C. Non-schedule change requests are not important.
    D. There are two important outputs from Plan Schedule Management, both of which are intended to manage the project schedule.

3. Which of these are not defined as an input to Plan Schedule Management?

    A. Expert Judgment
    B. Project Management Plan
    C. Enterprise Environmental Factors
    D. Lessons Learned information

4. You and your project team are in the process of planning how you are going to manage the project's schedule. You are considering scheduling methodology, scheduling tools that you may use, how to approach estimating, formats, and software. What are you doing specifically?

    A. Using Expert Judgment
    B. Using Analytical Techniques
    C. Using Decomposition
    D. All of the above

End of Lesson 14

Lesson 15
Define Activities

Objectives

At the end of this lesson, you will be able to:

- Describe the purpose of the Define Activities process
- Describe the Inputs, Tools and Techniques, and Outputs of the Define Activities process
- Understand how to use the Work Breakdown Structure to create the Activity List

Process Locator for the PMBOK® Guide

	Initiating	Planning	Executing	M&C	Closing
Integration					
Scope					
Time		▓▓▓			
Cost					
Quality					
Human Resource					
Communications					
Risk					
Procurement					
Stakeholder					

The Define Activities process identifies the specific activities necessary to complete the project deliverables.

The process of Define Activities logically follows closely after the Create WBS process. The WBS identifies the total of all project work in terms of deliverables. The WBS is deliverables-oriented. To adhere to this definition, our WBS should identify work using descriptive nouns, as opposed to action-oriented verbs. We apply the Define Activities process to convert our WBS work packages (lowest level elements) into action-oriented activities.

The primary deliverable from the Define Activities process is the project's Activity List; the Activity List becomes an extension of the WBS.

The primary Tool & Technique used to create the Activity List is "decomposition." This is basically the same decomposition method used to create the WBS. The difference is that, in Define Activities, decomposition is used to further subdivide work packages into manageable sized activities, and the final output is described in terms of activities, rather than deliverables.

Ideally, Define Activities is applied immediately following Create WBS. In real-world practice, however, the two processes are many times applied in parallel. In many projects, Rolling Wave Planning can be an effective tool to support activity definition. In Rolling Wave Planning, only near-term work is planned in detail, leaving future work summarized with less detail. As future work draws nearer, detailed planning is performed.

Process Elements

The Define Activities process has the following Inputs:
- Schedule Management Plan – Details the management of schedule development

- Scope Baseline - The project deliverables, constraints, and assumptions

- Enterprise Environmental Factors - Consideration factors such as; culture, systems, structure including the project management information system (PMIS)

- Organizational Process Assets - Consideration factors such as activity planning related policies, procedures, guidelines and lessons learned knowledge base

The Define Activities process uses the following Tools & Techniques:
- Decomposition - The process of subdividing WBS work packages into manageable-sized schedule activities

- Rolling Wave Planning - A form of progressive elaboration planning where only near term work is planned in detail

- Expert Judgment – Project team members and other experts experienced in defining activities

The Define Activities process has the following Outputs:
- Activity List - The comprehensive list and description of all schedule activities

- Activity Attributes - An extension of the activity list, intended to provide more detail (i.e. activity ID)

- Milestone List - The documented list of both mandatory and optional schedule milestones

Define Activities		
This process specifically identifies all schedule activities		
Inputs	**Tools and Techniques**	**Outputs**
• Scope Management Plan	• Decomposition	• Activity List
• Scope Baseline	• Rolling Wave Planning	• Activity Attributes
• Enterprise Environmental Factors	• Expert Judgment	• Milestone List
• Organizational Process Assets		

Figure 15.1 Process Elements within the Define Activities Process

Process Documents

The Activity List documents specific project activities – or tasks – that will be performed on the project. The project management methodology in the organization that you are working in will define the level of granularity or detail that is required in an Activity List. This document can be very high level or very detailed based upon project and organization need. Many Activity Lists are developed using Microsoft Project or a similar project management tool.

At a minimum, the Activity List should include:

- Project Name
- Project Manager
- Date for document
- Project Phases
- Project Deliverables or Milestones
- Project Work Packages
- Project Activities (associated with work packages)

Typically, additional information such as the duration of the activity, start date, end date and resource assigned is also shown on an Activity List.

A simple example of an Activity List follows.

True Solutions, Inc.
Project Management Template

Activity List

TSi

Project Name:							
Prepared by:							
Date:							
Project Phase				Duration	Start Date	End Date	Resource
	Deliverable						
		Work Package					
			Activity				
Development Phase							
	Develop Black Box						
		Materials					
			Determine specific components				
			Order components through Purchasing				
			Receive and Inventory components				
		Components Assembly					
			Attach CPU chip to motherboard				
			Attach heat sink and CPU fan				
			Attach CPU fan power cable				
			Insert RAM chips in motherboard slots				
			Install motherboard in CPU case				
		Test					
			Plug in power supply				
			Turn power switch to "on" position				
			Check BOIS settings				
			Place OS media in media slot				
			Boot				

TSi **Application Aid**

Process Tasks

The Define Activities process aligns with one of the defined tasks that a project manager performs when managing a project:

Planning Task #4: "Develop a project schedule based on the project timeline, scope, and resource plan, in order to manage timely completion of the project".

Think About It

Instructions: Use this exercise to compare how you practice project management to what is specified in the *PMBOK® Guide Fifth Edition.*

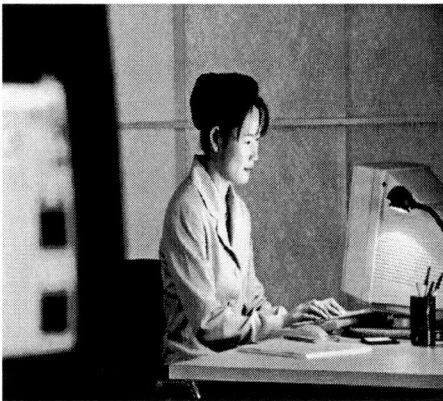

Best Practices suggest that each of the following items is used during the Define Activities process. Which of these items do you use when practicing project management?

☐ Decompose WBS to create Activity List

☐ List individual detailed activities

☐ Document activity attributes

☐ Document milestones for the project

☐ Use Rolling Wave Planning

How would you change your use of this process in your organization to resolve any gaps in application?

_____

_____

Must Know Concepts

1. The Define Activities process identifies the specific activities necessary to complete the project deliverables.

2. The Define Activities process is intended to decompose or subdivide WBS work packages into manageable sized activities.

3. The primary deliverable (Output) from the Define Activities process is the Activity List.

4. The Activity List may be viewed as an extension of the WBS.

5. Decomposition is the primary methodology (Tool/Technique) used to create the Activity List.

6. In some projects, Rolling Wave Planning can be an effective tool to support activity definition. In Rolling Wave Planning, only near-term work is planned in detail, leaving future work summarized with less detail. As future work draws nearer, detailed planning is performed.

Additional Reading

- PMBOK® Guide Fifth Edition: Section 6.2   Define Activities

Lesson Quiz

Instructions: Circle the correct answer. Answer Key in Appendix A.

1. The document that identifies all the activities that will be performed on a project is called _____.

   A. The Work Breakdown Structure (WBS)
   B. The Scope Statement
   C. The Activity List
   D. The Work Package List

2. Each of the following is false, *except*:

   A. The Activity List may be viewed as an extension of the Work Breakdown Structure.
   B. The lowest level elements of the WBS (work packages) automatically identify all the project activities necessary to produce identified project deliverables.
   C. The lowest level elements of the WBS (work packages) should be documented in terms of action-oriented activities, to help facilitate and expedite the Define Activities process.
   D. All of the above are false.

3. Define Activities inputs include all of the following, except _____.

   A. Enterprise environmental factors
   B. Organizational process assets
   C. Scope baseline
   D. Milestone list

4. Which of the following statements is true?

   A. Decomposition is the primary methodology (Tool/Technique) used to further subdivide WBS work packages into manageable sized activities.
   B. Decomposition is the primary methodology (Tool/Technique) used to further subdivide WBS major deliverables into manageable sized work packages.
   C. Decomposition is a primary methodology (Tool/Technique) used in both Create WBS and Define Activities.
   D. All of the above are true.

5. You are the project manager for the Dallas Co-Op project, which will consolidate information for local farm co-ops and locate the information in a centralized database. The data will then be used to build a website that customers and prospective customers can use to locate a farm co-op that meets their produce needs. Your business sponsor is interested in getting the website up and running prior to the summer growing season. You and the team are in the Define Activities process and are making a decision on the appropriate level of detail needed to appropriately manage the schedule. What input do you need to review?

   A. Scope Management Plan
   B. Requirements Management Plan
   C. Scope Baseline
   D. Schedule Management Plan

End of Lesson 15

This page intentionally blank.

Lesson 16
Sequence Activities

Objectives

At the end of this lesson, you will be able to:

- Describe the purpose of the Sequence Activities process
- Describe the Inputs, Tools and Techniques, and Outputs of the Sequence Activities process
- Be able to create and interpret a project network diagram

Process Locator for the PMBOK® Guide

	Initiating	Planning	Executing	M&C	Closing
Integration					
Scope					
Time		▓▓			
Cost					
Quality					
Human Resource					
Communications					
Risk					
Procurement					
Stakeholder					

Sequence Activities is the process of identifying the interrelationships between individual project activities, then documenting them using, what is generically termed, a Project Schedule .Network Diagram

Sequence Activities is an essential step that must be performed accurately prior to the development of a realistic and achievable schedule. The output from this process is a Project Network Logic Diagram, aka, Project Schedule Network Diagram. Project Diagrams are often, though not correctly, referred to as PERT Charts.

When sequencing activities, intuitive sense tells us that certain project activities must be completed before others may start. These activities are called "mandatory" dependency. In some cases, certain activities may be moved around or performed in parallel; these activities are known as "discretionary". Other types of dependency relationships include "external" and "internal" dependencies based upon enterprise environmental factors.

When planning sequences, certain activities must start before others can finish. There are four possible inter activity logical relationships:

- Finish-to-Start – One activity must finish before the next activity may start. F-S is the most common type of interdependency.

- Finish-to-Finish – The completion of the successor activity depends upon the completion of the predecessor activity.

- Start-to-Start – One activity must start before the next activity may start.

- Start-to-Finish – One activity must finish before the next activity may finish. S-F is the least common type of interdependency.

These relationships must be identified and documented in some form of Network Diagram. This is what activity sequencing is all about.

As you might imagine, in a project with hundreds or thousands of identified activities, activity sequencing can be a very complex process. In real-world project planning, most project managers rely on the use of project management software to automate and expedite the process. However, a project manager should have the ability to manually create and analyze simple network diagrams. To accomplish this, the project manager must learn the fundamentals of Network Logic Diagramming, then spend time with hands-on practice.

Because there is a lot of important information in the Sequence Activities process (compared to other processes), expect to devote a little more time learning this process.

Process Elements

The Sequence Activities process has the following Inputs:
- Schedule Management Plan – Identifies the scheduling method on how activities may be sequenced

- Activity List - The comprehensive list and description of all schedule activities

- Activity Attributes - An extension of the activity list that may describe the predecessor or successor relationships

- Milestone List - The documented list of both mandatory and optional schedule milestones

- Project Scope Statement - Detailed description of a projects deliverables including constraints and assumptions that may affect activity sequencing

- Enterprise Environmental Factors – Consideration factors such as systems, tools, industry standards

- Organizational Process Assets - Project files from corporate knowledge base used for scheduling methodology

The Sequence Activities process uses the following Tools & Techniques:
- Precedence Diagramming Method (PDM) - Activity-on-Node (AON) project network diagramming technique

- Dependency Determination - Mandatory dependencies, discretionary dependencies, internal dependencies, external dependencies

- Applying Leads and Lags - Further defined 'overlaps (leads)' and 'delays (lags)' in activity dependencies

The Sequence Activities process has the following Outputs:
- Project Schedule Network Diagrams - Schematic displays of the project's activities and their logical relationships

- Project Documents Updates - Updates to other project documentation (i.e. Activity lists, Activity attributes, Milestone list and Risk register)

Sequence Activities		
This process indentifies and documents dependencies among schedule activities		
Inputs	**Tools and Techniques**	**Outputs**
• Schedule Management Plan • Activity List • Activity Attributes • Milestone List • Project Scope Statement • Enterprise Environmental Factors • Organizational Process Assets	• Precedence Diagramming Method (PDM) • Dependency Determination • Leads and Lags	• Project Schedule Network Diagrams • Project Documents Updates TSI Study Aid This chart is part of the study aid poster series available at: www.TrueSolutions.com

Figure 16.1 Process Elements within the Sequence Activities Process

Process Documents

To master all there is to know about Network Logic Diagramming; we could spend a graduate-level semester dedicated just to this one subject. It can be quite complex with many specific techniques and technique-variations to consider. To prepare for the PMP Exam, however, we need to master only the fundamentals. Here they are.

Precedence Diagramming Method (PDM)

This is the method used by most modern project management software programs. It constructs the project network diagram using boxes (called *nodes*) to represent project activities, and connects them with arrows which illustrate their interdependencies. Here is a simple network diagram, drawn using PDM:

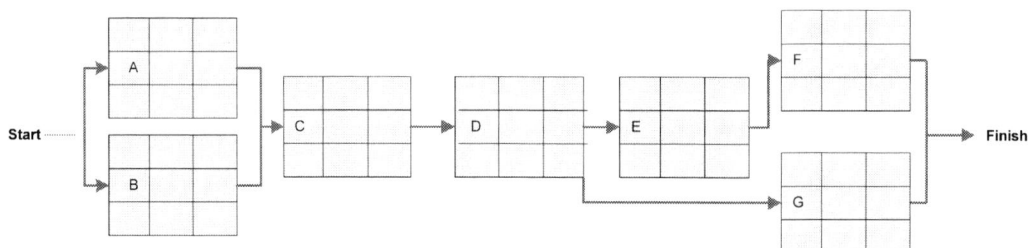

Figure 16.2 Precedence Diagramming Method example #1

In this simplified example, the project consists of seven activities, A - G. We see that activities A and B have no predecessor constraints and can start right away. We see that A and B must finish before activity C can start. We see that C must finish before D can start. D must finish before E or G can start. E must finish before F can start. Finally, F and G must finish before the project can finish.

Precedence Diagrams are also called Activity-On-Node (AON) Diagrams (Activity information is identified directly on the node). Precedence Diagrams can illustrate four types of interdependencies; a simplified depiction of each model is shown:

Finish-to-Start (F-S)
- Activity A must Finish before Activity B may Start.

F-S is the most common type of interdependency. This dependency type has no overlaps.

- Start-to-Finish (S-F)

Activity A must Start before Activity B may Finish.
S-F is the least common type of interdependency.

- Start-to-Start (S-S)

Activity A must Start before Activity B may Start.
S-S is a less common type of interdependency.

- Finish-to-Finish (F-F)

Activity A must Finish before Activity B may Finish.
F-F is a less common type of interdependency.

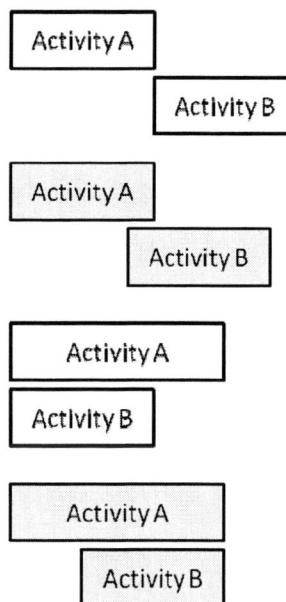

Figure 16.3 Precedence Diagramming Method example #2

PDM Conventions

When properly constructed and annotated, Network Diagrams can communicate an enormous amount of essential information. During planning, this helps the project team in creating the project schedule, obtaining resources and in identifying risks. Here is the way information is typically annotated on PDM Network Diagrams (Activity-on-Node AON). The numbers indicated in this example are work units. Typically, work units are hours, shifts, days, weeks, etc.

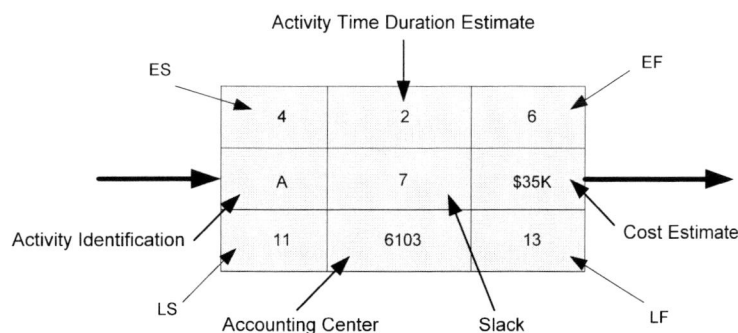

Figure 16.4 Precedence Diagramming Method Convention example

Once the Network is constructed and work units for each activity are estimated, we can then determine the following for each activity:

- **Earliest Start Time** (ES) and **Earliest Finish Time** (EF). We can determine ES and EF by making a *forward pass* (left-to-right) through the Network. The earliest start time (ES) of a successor activity is the latest of the early finish times of its predecessors. The earliest finish time (EF) is the total of the earliest start time and the activity duration

- **Latest Starting Time** (LS) and **Latest Finish Time** (LF). We can determine LS and LF by making a *backward pass* (right-to-left) through the Network. The latest finish time (LF) for an activity entering a node is the same as smallest value latest start time (LS) of the activities exiting the node. The latest start time (LS) of an activity is the latest finish time (LF) minus the activity duration

- **Slack** (also referred to as *float, reserve, total float, path float*). We can determine Slack in an activity by subtracting its ES from its LS. Many non-critical project activities may have Slack time, allowing greater flexibility in scheduling and resource allocation. Activities on the network's Critical Path typically have zero Slack

Applying Leads and Lags

To accurately define the logical relationship between many project schedule activities, the team will need to apply *leads* and/or *lags*. The best time to first determine and apply leads and lags is now, during Sequence Activities.

Leads - Lead time may be viewed as an *overlap* between tasks. For example, in a finish-to-start dependency with a 10-day lead, the successor activity can start 10-days before the predecessor has finished. Lead time allows project teams to add realism and flexibility to their schedule.

Lags - Lag time is *waiting time*. For example, if Activity A involves pouring concrete that requires 4 days to set, then Activity B may have a 4 day lag ... meaning Activity B cannot start until 4 days after Activity A is finished. Lead time is termed 'negative lag' in some software programs.

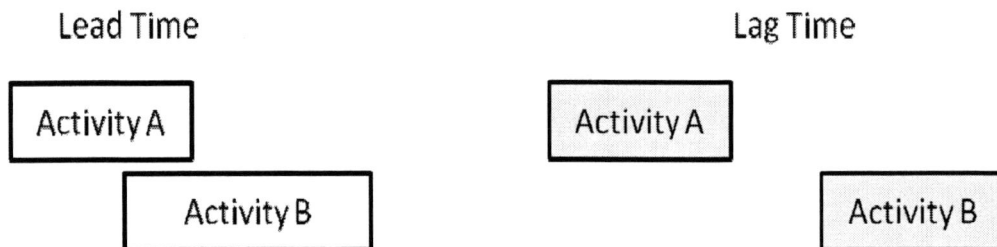

Lead Time   Lag Time

Activity A

Activity A

Activity B

Activity B

Figure 16.5 Applying Leads and Lags example

Critical Path

Network Diagrams illustrate all of the project's activities and their interrelationships/ dependencies, from project start to project finish. They also annotate, at minimum, identification of each activity and the estimated time duration of each activity. Typically a PMP Exam Question will use a simple diagram and may look something like this:

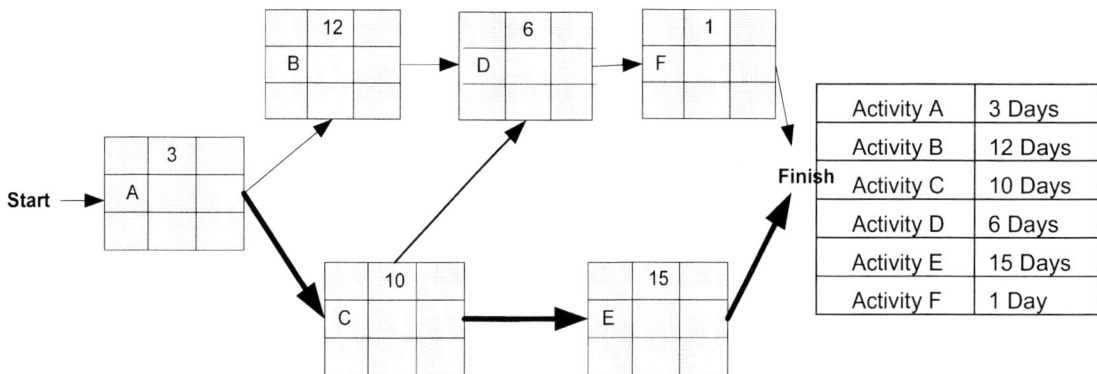

Figure 16.6 Critical Path example

Activity A	3 Days
Activity B	12 Days
Activity C	10 Days
Activity D	6 Days
Activity E	15 Days
Activity F	1 Day

- In this simple example, the project is comprised of six activities, A-F.

- All predecessor/successor relationships are Finish-to-Start (F-S).

- Activity A will require 3 days for completion, Activity B 12 days, Activity C 10 days, and so on.

- There are three possible paths through this Network from start-to-finish; Path 1) Start-A-B-D-F-Finish, Path 2) Start-A-C-E-Finish and Path 3) Start-A-C-D-F-Finish.

- Add the associated Activity time estimates to find that Path 1 is 22 days long, Path 2 is 28 days long and Path 3 is 20 days long.

- Path 2 is the longest path through the Network Diagram (28 days), and is therefore identified as the **Critical Path**. *The Critical Path is the longest path through a Network Diagram.* The Critical Path also defines the shortest period of time in which the project may be completed (here, 28 days).

- The Critical Path can be indicated with a heavier arrowed line and has "0" slack.

Process Tasks

The Define Activities process aligns with one of the defined tasks that a project manager performs when managing a project:

Planning Task #4: "Develop a project schedule based on the project timeline, scope, and resource plan, in order to manage timely completion of the project".

Think About It

Instructions: Use this exercise to compare how you practice project management to what is specified in the *PMBOK® Guide Fifth Edition.*

Think about how this process is defined, used and documented in your organization. Write a brief description of how you use this process:

_____

_____

_____

_____

_____

_____

Must Know Concepts

---

1. The Sequence Activities process is intended to identify and document interactivity logical relationships.

2. The primary deliverable (Output) of the Sequence Activities process is the project schedule network diagram.

3. The project schedule network diagram illustrates all project activities and their predecessor/successor relationships/interdependencies. It also identifies the project's Critical Path and all of the activities on the Critical Path.

4. The Critical Path is the longest path through a network diagram. It defines the shortest period of time in which the project may be completed. A project may have more than one critical path, or dual critical paths at certain times in the project.

5. Project schedule network diagrams are typically created and documented using the Precedence Diagramming Method (PDM) technique.

6. PDM is also referred to as Activity-on-Node (AON). In AON diagrams, activities are represented by nodes which are connected by arrowed lines to illustrate their interdependencies.

7. AON diagrams can show four types of interdependencies (F-S), (S-F), (F-F) and (S-S). Dummies are not needed to illustrate network logic in AON diagrams.

8. A Forward Pass (left-right through the network) may be performed to determine Earliest Start times (ES) and Earliest Finish times (EF) for each project activity.

9. A Backward Pass (right-left through the network) may be performed to determine Latest Start times (LS) and Latest Finish times (LF) for each project activity.

10. Slack (also referred to as float, reserve, path float or total float) for any given activity may be determined by subtracting ES from LS. Activities on the Critical Path typically have zero slack.

11. Subnet (or fragnet or subnetwork) is a subdivision of a network diagram.

12. Hammock is group of related activities illustrated as a single summary activity.

13. Lead time and Lag time allows project teams to add realism and flexibility to their schedule. Lead time may be viewed as an overlap between tasks. Lag time is waiting time.

Additional Reading

- PMBOK® Guide Fifth Edition: Section 6.3   Sequence Activities

Lesson Quiz

Instructions: The actual PMP exam is done via computer. These questions are representative of what you will encounter. Circle the correct answer. Answer Key in Appendix A.

1. The longest path through a project network diagram is termed, _____.

    A. Path float
    B. Latest finish time (LF)
    C. Latest start time (LS)
    D. Critical path

2. Which of the following statements is most true?

    A. A project network diagram may identify more than one critical path.
    B. A project network diagram can illustrate only one critical path. If more than one critical path is identified, a mistake has been made somewhere in construction of the network logic.
    C. A project network diagram should always use a template from a previous project.
    D. A project network diagram is essentially the same as a project WBS. They are interchangeable.

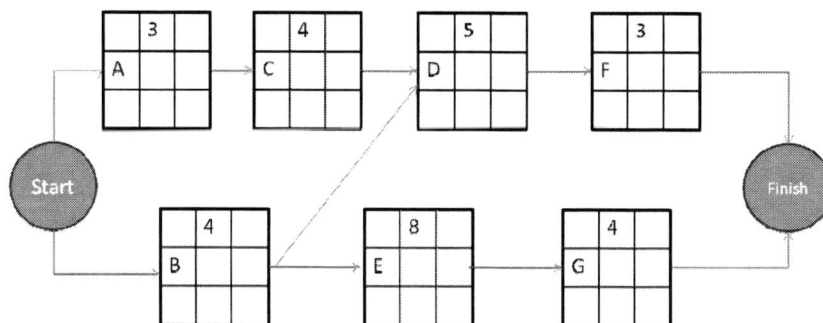

3. In the simplified network diagram shown above, how many paths exist, from start to finish?

    A. 6
    B. 1
    C. 5
    D. 3

4. Referring to the project network diagram in question 3, identify the critical path.

    A. Start-A-C-D-F-Finish
    B. Start-B-D-F-Finish
    C. Start-B-E-G-Finish
    D. Start-A-B-D-E-Finish

5. Referring to the diagram in question 4, how long will this project take to be completed?

   A. 14 days
   B. 20 days
   C. 31 days
   D. 16 days

6. From the given information, determine how many paths exist through this project's network diagram.

Activity	Activity Duration	Predecessors
A	1 week	none
B	7 weeks	none
C	5 weeks	A and B
D	12 weeks	B
E	10 weeks	C and D
F	6 weeks	E
G	3 weeks	F

   A. 1
   B. 2
   C. 3
   D. 4

7. Referring to the information given in question 6, identify the project's critical path.

   A. Start-A-C-E-F-G-Finish
   B. Start-B-D-E-F-G-Finish
   C. Start-B-C-E-F-G-Finish
   D. Start-A-C-E-F-Finish

8. Referring to the information given in question 6, identify the shortest period of time in which this project may be completed.

   A. 25 weeks
   B. 31 weeks
   C. 38 weeks
   D. Insufficient information

9. The Sequence Activities process is applied to _____.

   A. Identify all of the deliverables-oriented work within the scope of the project
   B. Further subdivide work packages into clearly defined activities
   C. Create the project schedule network diagram
   D. Schedule all of the project's defined activities

End of Lesson 16

This page intentionally blank.

Lesson 17
Estimate Activity Resources

Objectives
At the end of this lesson, you will be able to:
- Describe the purpose of the Estimate Activity Resources process
- Describe the Inputs, Tools and Techniques, and Outputs of the Estimate Activity Resources (people, materials, supplies and equipment) process
- Understand what resources must be estimated

Process Locator for the PMBOK® Guide

	Initiating	Planning	Executing	M&C	Closing
Integration					
Scope					
Time		▓▓▓			
Cost					
Quality					
Human Resource					
Communications					
Risk					
Procurement					
Stakeholder					

Estimate Activity Resources is the simple yet important process of determining the type and quantities of material, people, equipment or supplies (physical resources) needed.

Ideally, resource needs are determined at the lowest level components, then rolled-up to higher levels (major deliverables).

The primary deliverable of the Estimate Activity Resources process is a documented description of Activity Resource Requirements. Typically, the resource needs identified here will be obtained by later applying the Acquire Project Team process and/or Procurement processes.

The Activity Attributes provide the primary data input for Estimate Activity Resources. The Estimate Activity Resource process is closely coordinated with several processes, including Estimate Costs, Acquire Project Team, Estimate Activity Duration and Plan Procurements processes.

Process Elements

The Estimate Activity Resources process has the following Inputs:
- Schedule Management Plan – Identifies the level of accuracy and units of measure to be estimated

- Activity List - The comprehensive list and description of all schedule activities

- Activity Attributes - An extension of the activity list, intended to provide more attribute details

- Resource Calendars - Information on the availability of resources over the planned activity duration

- Risk Register – The comprehensive list of project uncertainties

- Activity Cost Estimates – Preliminary estimates for the cost of resources

- Enterprise Environmental Factors - Consideration factors such as resource availability and skills, resource location

- Organizational Process Assets - Consideration factors such as policies, procedures and historical data

The Estimate Activity Resources process uses the following Tools & Techniques:
- Expert Judgment – Experts in resource planning and estimating

- Alternatives Analysis - Used to identify alternatives to account for various resource capabilities, skills, and availability

- Published Estimating Data - Available published information on production rates and costs for an array of trades, materials, and equipment, and other resources

- Bottom-Up Estimating - Deriving project totals by estimating individual activities, then rolling-up to summary level

- Project Management Software - Any software that may help plan, organize, manage resource estimates and pools

The Estimate Activity Resources process has the following Outputs:
- Activity Resource Requirements - Types and quantities of resources needed for each activity

- Resource Breakdown Structure (RBS) - Hierarchal structure of identified resources (by category and type)

- Project Documents Updates - Updates to other project documentation (i.e. Activity List, Activity Attributes and Resource Calendars)

Estimate Activity Resources		
This process determines the physical resources needed for each activity		
Inputs	**Tools and Techniques**	**Outputs**
• Schedule Management Plan	• Expert Judgment	• Activity Resource Requirements
• Activity List	• Alternatives Analysis	• Resource Breakdown Structure (RBS)
• Activity Attributes	• Published Estimating Data	
• Resource Calendars		• Project Documents Updates
• Risk Register	• Bottom-up Estimating	
• Activity Cost Estimates	• Project Management Software	
• Enterprise Environmental Factors		
• Organizational Process Assets		

Figure 17.1 Process Elements within the Estimate Activity Resources Process

Process Documents

The primary document that comes from this process is the Activity Resource Requirements list. This document contains a list (at an appropriate level of detail) of all resources that are required for the project. This can be also arrayed as a Resource Breakdown Structure (RBS). The RBS can be depicted in list form or in a graphic "organization chart" like format.

An example of a Resource Requirements document is shown below.

Resource Requirements Worksheet

Project Name:				
Prepared by:				
Date:				

Work Breakdown Structure Element	Type of Resource Required:	Quantity	Involve Staff Acquisition? (Notes)	Involve Procurement? (Notes)
1.				
2.				
3.				
4.				
5.				
6.				
7.				
8.				

Additional Notes or Comments:

Submitted to:

Name:

Title:

Date:

Name:

Title:

Date:

©Copyright 2013 True Solutions, Inc.
5001 LBJ Freeway, Suite 125, Dallas, Texas 75244
Tel: 972.770.0900 Fax 972.770.0922 www.truesolutions.com

Process Tasks

The Estimate Activity Resources process aligns with one of the defined tasks that a project manager performs when managing a project; activity resources are part of the time/schedule project component:

Planning Task #4: "Develop a project schedule based on the project timeline, scope, and resource plan, in order to manage timely completion of the project".

Think About It

Instructions: Use this exercise to compare how you practice project management to what is specified in the *PMBOK® Guide Fifth Edition.*

Which of these items do you use when practicing project management?

☐ Define all resources: people, equipment, materials, supplies

☐ List all resources by individual detailed activities

☐ Use a specific resource list

☐ Document resources in a graphic Resource Breakdown Structure

☐ Update all documents when changes to resource plans occur

How would you change your use of this process in your organization to resolve any gaps in application?

_____

_____

_____

_____

_____

_____

Must Know Concepts

1. The Estimate Activity Resources process is intended to estimate the type and quantities of material, people, equipment or supplies required to perform each activity (physical resources).

2. The primary deliverable (Output) from the Estimate Activity Resources process is the documented description of Activity Resource Requirements.

3. Bottom-up estimating is often used in this process. It generally produces the most confident estimates, but is more costly and time consuming than it's opposite, analogous estimating. Typically, bottom-up estimating is performed by developing detailed estimates for each activity at the work package level of the WBS. They are then rolled-up to derive a project total.

4. Identified resource requirements will typically be obtained later by applying the Acquire Project Team process and the Procurement processes.

Additional Reading

- PMBOK® Guide Fifth Edition: Section 6.4 Estimate Activity Resources

Lesson Quiz

Instructions: the actual PMP exam is done via computer. These questions are representative of what you will encounter. Circle the correct answer. Answer Key in Appendix A.

1. The people, equipment, materials and supplies used to estimate activity resources are termed:

   A. Work breakdown structure (WBS) requirements
   B. Physical resources
   C. Work package requirements
   D. Estimate activity resources outputs

2. The Estimate Activity Resources process is applied to:

   A. Determine the type of physical resources required to perform each activity
   B. Determine the people required to perform each activity
   C. Determine the equipment required to perform each activity
   D. Determine the materials required to perform each activity

3. Estimate Activity Resources Tools & Techniques include:

   A. Alternatives analysis, expert judgment and project management software
   B. Resource pool description, expert judgment and project management software
   C. Organizational policies, expert judgment and project management software
   D. Resource calendars, expert judgment and project management software

4. Which of the following statements is most true:

   A. Activity Resource Requirements is the primary Output from Estimate Activity Resources, and describes the physical resources needed to perform/complete project activities.
   B. Activity Resource Requirements is the primary Output from Estimate Activity Resources, and describes the roles and responsibilities of assigned project personnel.
   C. Activity Resource Requirements is the primary Output from Estimate Activity Resources, and describes the resources potentially available to support identified project activities.
   D. Each of the above statements is equally true.

5. Which of these are inputs to the Estimate Activity Resources process?

   A. Schedule Management Plan, Risk Register, Activity Cost Estimates
   B. Scope Management Plan, Risk Register, Activity Cost Estimates
   C. Schedule Management Plan, Activity Resource Requirements, Activity Cost Estimates
   D. Project Documents Updates, Resource Breakdown Structure, Activity Cost Estimates

End of Lesson 17

This page intentionally blank.

170 Ultimate PMP® Exam Prep Study Guide

Lesson 18
Estimate Activity Durations

Objectives
At the end of this lesson, you will be able to:
- Describe the purpose of the Estimate Activity Durations process
- Describe the Inputs, Tools and Techniques, and Outputs of the Estimate Activity Durations process
- Understand the available methods for estimating activity durations

Process Locator for the PMBOK® Guide

	Initiating	Planning	Executing	M&C	Closing
Integration					
Scope					
Time		▓			
Cost					
Quality					
Human Resource					
Communications					
Risk					
Procurement					
Stakeholder					

Estimate Activity Durations is the process of estimating time durations for each defined activity resource, which will serve as an essential input for the Develop Schedule process.

In simpler projects, estimates are typically documented as deterministic, single-point values (one number). For example, a single-point estimate may be documented as; 7 days (with no plus/minus flexibility). Single point estimates are generally less confident. Using expert judgment or an analogous estimate (also known as top-down estimate) is simple and quick, and produces a producing a single point estimate.

In more complex projects, it is common to use sophisticated mathematics to determine probabilistic distributions for each activity, resulting in a time range estimate instead of a single time estimate. For example, a probabilistic estimate may be documented as a graphical curve indicating the probability of an activity finishing at any given time on the curve. Probabilistic estimates generally provide for more confident expectations. Probabilistic estimates usually use a method like three-point estimating to predict a range of outcomes. Duration estimates do not include any lags.

Three point estimates are sometimes called "PERT" estimates (Program Evaluation Review Technique). Three-point or PERT estimates can be determined using triangular or beta distributions. The formulas are:

Three point estimates using Triangular Distribution: $tE = (tO + tM + tP) / 3$

Three point estimates using Beta Distribution: $tE = (tO + 4tM + tP) / 6$

This Beta Distribution formula is equivalent to the most common PERT formula:
$E = (O + 4ML + P)/6$

O = Optimistic estimate
ML (or M) = Most Likely estimate
P = Pessimistic estimate

Estimates should from the person or group of people who have expert familiarity with the activity.

In most of today's project management software, it is common to estimate activity durations in terms of work periods (activity durations). The project team determines how best to define work periods for their particular project, typically days, shifts, hours or weeks.

Process Elements

The Estimate Activity Durations process has the following Inputs:
- Schedule Management Plan – Defines the method and level of accuracy to be used in estimating durations

- Activity List - The comprehensive list and description of all schedule activities

- Activity Attributes - An extension of the activity list, intended to provide more details

- Activity Resource Requirements - Types and quantities of resources needed for each activity

- Resource Calendars - Information on the availability of resources over the planned activity duration

- Project Scope Statement - Detailed description of a major deliverables (specifically assumptions and constraints)

- Risk Register – The comprehensive list of project uncertainties

- Resource Breakdown Structure – Hierarchical structure of identified resources

- Enterprise Environmental Factors - Consideration factors such as databases, productivity metrics and published commercial information

- Organizational Process Assets - Consideration factors such as historical information, project calendars, scheduling methodology and lessons learned

The Estimate Activity Durations process uses the following Tools & Techniques:
- Expert Judgment – Experts who can provide duration estimates from prior similar projects

- Analogous Estimating - Using actual values from a previous similar project to base current estimates

- Parametric Estimating - Uses a statistical relationship between historical data and other variables to calculate an estimate for activity parameters (i.e. Total labor hours = 6,000)

- Three-Point Estimating - Factoring most likely, optimistic and pessimistic estimates to derive a forecasted estimate

- Group Decision Making Techniques – Team approaches used to improve estimate accuracy and commitment

- Reserve Analysis - Determining appropriate amount of contingency reserve to compensate for schedule risk

The Estimate Activity Durations process has the following Outputs:
- Activity Duration Estimates - Quantitative assessments of the time likely needed to complete each activity

- Project Documents Updates - Updates to other project documentation (i.e. Activity Attributes and assumptions)

Estimate Activity Durations		
This process estimates the number of work periods for each schedule activity		
Inputs	**Tools and Techniques**	**Outputs**
• Schedule Management Plan • Activity List • Activity Attributes • Activity Resource Requirements • Resource Calendars • Project Scope Statement • Risk Register • Resource Breakdown Structure • Enterprise Environmental Factors • Organizational Process Assets	• Expert Judgment • Analogous Estimating • Parametric Estimating • Three-Point Estimating • Group Decision Making Techniques • Reserve Analysis	• Activity Duration Estimates • Project Documents Updates

TSI — Study Aid

This chart is part of the study aid poster series available at: **www.TrueSolutions.com**

Figure 18.1: Process Elements within the Estimate Activity Durations Process

Process Documents

The Activity Duration Estimate can come in many different formats. Activity Duration Estimates are a precursor to development of the project schedule. So, many times the project manager will incorporate the Activity Duration Estimate into an automated project management tool such as Microsoft Project or a similar scheduling tool and the output will simply be part of the project schedule.

Process Tasks

The Define Activities process aligns with one of the defined tasks that a project manager performs when managing a project:

Planning Task #4: "Develop a project schedule based on the project timeline, scope, and resource plan, in order to manage timely completion of the project".

Think About It

Instructions: Use this exercise to compare how you practice project management to what is specified in the *PMBOK® Guide Fifth Edition.*

Think about how this process is defined, used and documented in your organization. Write a brief description of how you use this process:

_____

_____

_____

Must Know Concepts

----

1. The Estimate Activity Durations process is estimating time durations for each defined activity resource. These estimates will ultimately be used to create the project schedule.

2. The primary deliverable (Output) from the Estimate Activity Durations process is the Activity Duration Estimates.

3. Deterministic (single-point) estimates are typically documented with only one value. Probabilistic (range) estimates typically report estimates in terms of probabilities, instead of hard numbers.

4. Estimating should originate from the person, or group of people, who are most knowledgeable about the activity, ideally by the person or people who will be doing the work.

5. Analogous estimating (also termed top-down estimating) typically involves basing an estimate on a known previous activity performed in the past. Analogous estimates are relatively quick to perform and inexpensive, because no detailed estimating protocols are necessary. Analogous estimates are also the least confident, typically proving to have a significant margin of error.

6. Three-Point Estimates uses the three estimates (Pessimistic, Most Probable and Optimistic) and may be used as a tool to help determine an approximate range for an activity's duration. PERT analysis calculates an expected activity duration using a weighted average of these estimates. A triangular [$tE = (tO + tM = tP) / 3$] or Beta Distribution formula [$tE = (tO + 4tM = tP) / 6$] may be used.

7. Estimators may choose to include reserve time (also termed time buffers) to proportionately compensate for the level of risk associated with the activity.

8. Duration estimates are typically documented in terms of work periods. Work periods are determined by the project team and are typically defined as shifts, hours, days or weeks.

9. Ideally, estimates should be reported with ranges of possible results such as; 8 days ±2 (indicating 6-10 days).

Additional Reading

- PMBOK® Guide Fifth Edition: Section 6.5   Estimate Activity Durations

Lesson Quiz

Instructions: The actual PMP exam is done via computer. These questions are representative of what you will encounter. Circle the correct answer. Answer Key in Appendix A.

1. The estimating technique that typically uses the past actual performance of a similar activity is termed?

    A. Bottom-up estimating
    B. Probabilistic estimating
    C. Analogous estimating (also termed top-down)
    D. Deterministic (sing-point) estimating

2. Which of the following is most true?

    A. Work periods should be reported with ranges of possible results such as 10 days +3; or 90% probability of finishing within 3 weeks
    B. Work periods should include time reserve (time contingency) to compensate for associated risk
    C. Work periods are typically defined by the project manager, then communicated to the project team
    D. Work periods are typically defined in terms of hours, days, shifts, weeks

3. Estimate Activity Durations outputs include which of the following:

    A. Activity duration estimates, project documents updates
    B. Activity duration estimates, three-point estimates
    C. Activity duration estimates, reserve analysis
    D. Activity duration estimates, resource calendars

4. Estimate activity durations are best prepared by:

    A. Functional managers, because they are on the front line and close to the work
    B. The project team, to ensure the project manager's expectations will be satisfied
    C. The project manager, to ensure the project schedule can be created to satisfy the sponsor's expectations
    D. The person or people who have the most knowledge about the work

5. The individuals on your project are developing duration estimates and you find that the estimates vary widely from person to person. You decide to use the Three-Point Estimate $tE = (tO + tM + tP) / 3$ to get the most realistic estimate possible. What is this form of the Three Point Estimate called?

    A. Triangular Distribution
    B. Beta Distribution
    C. PERT
    D. Parametric

6. The individuals on your project are developing duration estimates and you find that the estimates vary widely from person to person. You decide to use the Three-Point Estimate $tE = (tO + 4tM + tP) / 6$ to get the most realistic estimate possible. What is this form of the Three Point Estimate called?

    A. Triangular Distribution
    B. Beta Distribution
    C. PERT
    D. Parametric

7. Your team is determining activity duration estimates and need to perform reserve analysis to develop reserve amounts for "known-unknowns" and "unknown-unknowns". What are these reserves called?

    A. Management reserves and contingency reserves, respectively
    B. Contingency reserves
    C. Contingency reserves and management reserves, respectively
    D. Management reserves

8. Which of the following statements is most true?

    A. Management Reserves are included in the Schedule Baseline
    B. Management Reserves are not included in the Schedule Baseline
    C. Contingency Reserves and Management Reserves are included in the Schedule Baseline
    D. Contingency Reserves are not in the Schedule Baseline

End of Lesson 18

Lesson 19
Develop Schedule

Objectives

At the end of this lesson, you will be able to:
- Describe the purpose of the Develop Schedule process
- Describe the Inputs, Tools and Techniques, and Outputs of the Develop Schedule process
- Understand the typical methods that are used to Develop Schedule

Process Locator for the PMBOK® Guide

	Initiating	Planning	Executing	M&C	Closing
Integration					
Scope					
Time		▓▓▓			
Cost					
Quality					
Human Resource					
Communications					
Risk					
Procurement					
Stakeholder					

Develop Schedule is the process to create the project schedule based on activity sequences, durations, resource requirements and schedule constraints.

The project schedule is developed as the result of many detailed iterations and progressive elaboration across the entire planning phase.

Scheduling software has become an essential tool to help create the schedule. Most scheduling software today will allow project teams to input raw data, and then automate the process of maneuvering it to create the schedule baseline. Once the schedule has been baselined, then software can automate changes and tracking throughout the project's remaining phases.

Developing and maintaining a project schedule file can be quite time consuming and require expert support. In large projects, it is not unusual to assign one full-time scheduler for every thousand lines in the schedule.

The Develop Schedule process is applied to determine the start/finish dates for project activities.

Creating a Project Schedule

There are four primary methods used to calculate theoretical early/late start/finish dates for project activities:

- **Critical Path Method (CPM)** CPM determines start/finish dates using a one-time duration estimate for each activity by performing forward and backward passes. The Critical Path Method is the "most probable" time duration estimate.
- **Critical Chain Method** This method may be used to modify a project schedule to account for limited resources and project uncertainty. Critical chain methodology is characterized by a focus on the use and management of duration buffers.   Durations used do not include safety buffers for risk, logical relationships or resource availability; time buffers are added to compensate for project characteristics. The resource-constrained critical path is known as the critical chain.
- **Resource Optimization Techniques** Resource Leveling and Resource Smoothing are resource management tools sometimes used to adjust resource utilization across the project schedule, to minimize exaggerated peaks and valleys.
- **Modeling Techniques** What-if-Scenario Analysis and Simulation tools compute different scenarios to derive the schedule. Typically, this is done using Monte Carlo simulations to support this method.

Completed project schedules are typically illustrated using a Bar Chart (Gantt Chart), Milestone Chart or Dated Network Diagram.

Tools to Compress a Project Schedule

- **Crashing** This is the process of adding more resources to the activity. Crashing typically adds cost and potentially increases risk. The key to using this is to choose the most efficient and effective alternative. It is not always a feasible alternative.

- **Fast Tracking** The project schedule can sometimes be shortened by 'fast tracking' activities on the critical path. Fast tracking is the process of realigning normally sequential activities to be performed in parallel. Fast tracking typically increases risk and can cause rework. Like crashing, fast tracking is not always a feasible alternative.

Process Elements

The Develop Schedule process has the following Inputs:
- Schedule Management Plan – Identifies the scheduling method used to create the schedule

- Activity List - The comprehensive list and description of all schedule activities

- Activity Attributes - An extension of the activity list, intended to provide details used to build the schedule

- Project Schedule Network Diagrams - Schematic displays of the project's activities and their logical relationships

- Activity Resource Requirements - Types and quantities of resources needed for each activity

- Resource Calendars - Information on the availability of resources over the planned activity duration

- Activity Duration Estimates - Quantitative assessments of the time likely needed to complete each activity

- Project Scope Statement - Detailed description deliverables (specifically assumptions and constraints)

- Risk Register – The comprehensive list of project uncertainties

- Project Staff Assignments – What staff are assigned to specific activities

- Resource Breakdown Structure – Detailed description of planned resources

- Enterprise Environmental Factors - Consideration factors such as standards, scheduling tools, communication channels

- Organizational Process Assets - Consideration factors such as scheduling methodology and project calendar

The Develop Schedule process uses the following Tools & Techniques:
- Schedule Network Analysis - Technique that generates the project schedule, employs various analytical methods

- Critical Path Method - Calculates schedule dates without regard to resource limitations by performing forward and backward passes (i.e. buffers)

- Critical Chain Method - Modifies the project schedule to account for limited resources

- Resource Optimization Techniques – Techniques applied to create efficient resource-limited schedules (i.e. resource leveling, resource smoothing)

- Modeling Techniques - Explores various scenarios using simulation tools (i.e. Monte Carlo)

- Leads and Lags - Further defined 'overlaps (leads)' and 'delays (lags)' in activity dependencies

- Schedule Compression - Shortens the schedule without changing scope (fast-tracking, crashing)

- Scheduling Tool - Tool used to facilitate creation of the project schedule

The Develop Schedule process has the following Outputs:
- Schedule Baseline - Specific version of the project schedule, accepted and approved by authorized stakeholders to compare to actual results

- Project Schedule - Graphic presentation illustrating planned start and planned finish dates for each activity (i.e. milestone charts, bar charts, project schedule network diagrams)

- Schedule Data - The schedule milestones, schedule activities, activity attributes, and all documented assumptions and constraints

- Project Calendars – Identifies working days and shifts available for project activities

- Project Management Plan Updates – Updates to the schedule management plan and schedule baseline

- Project Documents Updates - Updates to other project documentation (i.e. activity resource requirements, activity attributes, calendar, risk register)

<table>
<tr><td colspan="3" align="center">Develop Schedule</td></tr>
<tr><td colspan="3" align="center">This process analyzes activities and constraints to create the project schedule</td></tr>
<tr><td align="center">Inputs</td><td align="center">Tools and Techniques</td><td align="center">Outputs</td></tr>
<tr>
<td>
<ul>
<li>Schedule Management Plan</li>
<li>Activity List</li>
<li>Activity Attributes</li>
<li>Project Schedule Network Diagrams</li>
<li>Activity Resource Requirements</li>
<li>Resource Calendars</li>
<li>Activity Duration Estimates</li>
<li>Project Scope Statement</li>
<li>Risk Register</li>
<li>Project Staff Assignments</li>
<li>Resource Breakdown Structure</li>
<li>Enterprise Environmental Factors</li>
<li>Organizational Process Assets</li>
</ul>
</td>
<td>
<ul>
<li>Schedule Network Analysis</li>
<li>Critical Path Method</li>
<li>Critical Chain Method</li>
<li>Resource Optimization Techniques</li>
<li>Modeling Techniques</li>
<li>Leads and Lags</li>
<li>Schedule Compression</li>
<li>Scheduling Tool</li>
</ul>
</td>
<td>
<ul>
<li>Schedule Baseline</li>
<li>Project Schedule</li>
<li>Schedule Data</li>
<li>Project Calendars</li>
<li>Project Management Plan Updates</li>
<li>Project Documents Updates</li>
</ul>

TSI   Study Aid
This chart is part of the study aid poster series available at:
www.TrueSolutions.com
</td>
</tr>
</table>

Figure 19.1 Process Elements within Develop Schedule

Process Documents

Two important documents are finalized in the Develop Schedule process. The baseline Project Schedule will be developed during this process. Completed project schedules are typically illustrated using a Bar Chart (Gantt Chart), Milestone Chart or Dated Network Diagram. An example of the most common form – the Bar Chart/Gantt Chart is shown below as well as a Milestone Form Template.

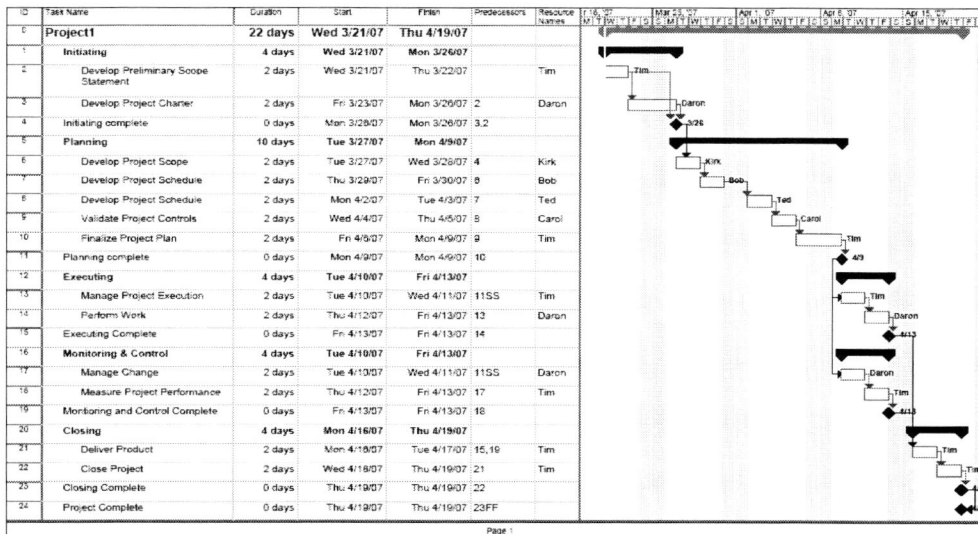

ID	Task Name	Duration	Start	Finish	Predecessors	Resource Names
0	Project1	22 days	Wed 3/21/07	Thu 4/19/07		
1	Initiating	4 days	Wed 3/21/07	Mon 3/26/07		
2	Develop Preliminary Scope Statement	2 days	Wed 3/21/07	Thu 3/22/07		Tim
3	Develop Project Charter	2 days	Fri 3/23/07	Mon 3/26/07	2	Daron
4	Initiating complete	0 days	Mon 3/26/07	Mon 3/26/07	3,2	
5	Planning	10 days	Tue 3/27/07	Mon 4/9/07		
6	Develop Project Scope	2 days	Tue 3/27/07	Wed 3/28/07	4	Kirk
7	Develop Project Schedule	2 days	Thu 3/29/07	Fri 3/30/07	6	Bob
8	Develop Project Schedule	2 days	Mon 4/2/07	Tue 4/3/07	7	Ted
9	Validate Project Controls	2 days	Wed 4/4/07	Thu 4/5/07	8	Carol
10	Finalize Project Plan	2 days	Fri 4/6/07	Mon 4/9/07	9	Tim
11	Planning complete	0 days	Mon 4/9/07	Mon 4/9/07	10	
12	Executing	4 days	Tue 4/10/07	Fri 4/13/07		
13	Manage Project Execution	2 days	Tue 4/10/07	Wed 4/11/07	11SS	Tim
14	Perform Work	2 days	Thu 4/12/07	Fri 4/13/07	13	Daron
15	Executing Complete	0 days	Fri 4/13/07	Fri 4/13/07	14	
16	Monitoring & Control	4 days	Tue 4/10/07	Fri 4/13/07		
17	Manage Change	2 days	Tue 4/10/07	Wed 4/11/07	11SS	Daron
18	Measure Project Performance	2 days	Thu 4/12/07	Fri 4/13/07	17	Tim
19	Monitoring and Control Complete	0 days	Fri 4/13/07	Fri 4/13/07	18	
20	Closing	4 days	Mon 4/16/07	Thu 4/19/07		
21	Deliver Product	2 days	Mon 4/16/07	Tue 4/17/07	15,19	Tim
22	Close Project	2 days	Wed 4/18/07	Thu 4/19/07	21	Tim
23	Closing Complete	0 days	Thu 4/19/07	Thu 4/19/07	22	
24	Project Complete	0 days	Thu 4/19/07	Thu 4/19/07	23FF	

Microsoft Project™

True Solutions, Inc.
Project Management Template
Version 2: Milestone Chart Template

TSI

Milestone Chart

| Project Name: |
| Prepared by: |
| Date: |

Current

Event	Jan	Feb	March	April	May	June	July	August
Subcontracts Signed	△▼							
Specifications Finalized		△						
Design Reviewed		△						
Subsystem Tested			△					
First Unit Delivered			△					
Production Plan Completed				△				

There are many other acceptable ways to display project information on a milestone chart

Planned = △
Actual = ▼

TSI   Application Aid

This form is available
individually or as
part of a set at:
www.TrueSolutions.com

Note: The arrows above are AutoShapes. Select an arrow from the Key, select Edit->Copy, then select Edit->Paste. Click and drag the new arrow to move to the desired table cell.

©Copyright 2013 True Solutions, Inc.
5001 LBJ Freeway, Suite 125, Dallas, Texas 75244
Tel: 972.770.0900 Fax 972.770.0922 www.truesolutions.com

Figure 19.2 Milestone Chart Example

Process Tasks

The Develop Schedule process aligns with one of the defined tasks that a project manager performs when managing a project:

Planning Task #4: "Develop a project schedule based on the project timeline, scope, and resource plan, in order to manage timely completion of the project".

Think About It

Instructions: Use this exercise to compare how you practice project management to what is specified in the *PMBOK® Guide Fifth Edition*.

Think about how this process is defined, used and documented in your organization. Write a brief description of how you use this process:

_____

_____

_____

What specific Inputs, Tools or Techniques do you use as part of this process in your organization?

_____

_____

Are the outcomes from this process different in your organization or experiences?

_____

_____

_____

_____

_____

Must Know Concepts

1. The Develop Schedule process is applied to create the project schedule based on activity sequences, durations, resource requirements and schedule constraints.

2. There are four primary methods used to calculate theoretical early/late start/finish dates for project activities; Critical Path Method (CPM), Critical Chain Method, Resource Optimization Techniques and Modeling Techniques.

3. Care must be taken to differentiate the actual effort-time (performance-time) required to perform the activity work and the calendar-time (elapsed-time) required to completed the activity. Some activities may have non-work waiting time involved.

4. The primary deliverables (Outputs) of the Develop Schedule process include the Schedule Baseline and the Project Schedule.

5. There are two primary methods used to shorten schedules; Crashing and Fast Tracking.

6. Completed project schedules are typically illustrated using Bar Charts (also called Gantt Charts), Milestone Charts or Project Schedule Network Diagrams.

7. Resource Optimization Techniques include Resource Leveling and Resource Smoothing which are tools to 'level' resources across the project schedule, to minimize exaggerated peaks and valleys.

8. Schedule Modeling Tools include "What-if-Scenario Analysis" and Monte Carlo simulations; both are used to factor in uncertainties into the project schedule.

Additional Reading

- PMBOK® Guide Fifth Edition: Section 6.6   Develop Schedule

Lesson Quiz

Instructions: The actual PMP exam is done via computer. These questions are representative of what you will encounter. Circle the correct answer. Answer Key in Appendix A.

1. The Develop Schedule process is applied to:

   A. Document all duration estimates, using the scheduling software
   B. Document how changes to the project schedule will be managed
   C. Add realism and flexibility to the project schedule
   D. Create the project schedule based on activity sequences, durations, resource requirements and schedule constraints

2. You have been requested to shorten the project schedule by two weeks. You and your project team can:

   A. Explore the feasibility of crashing and/or fast tracking activities on the critical path. But, this can result in higher costs and/or greater risk.
   B. Explore the feasibility of resource leveling. But, this can result in higher costs and/or greater risk.
   C. Explore the feasibility of employing effective conflict resolution skills to respectfully deny the request. But this can result in hard feelings.
   D. Explore the feasibility of extending lead times and/or shortening lag times. But this can result in unnecessary quality problems.

3. Develop schedule outputs include all the following except:

   A. The schedule baseline
   B. The project schedule
   C. Schedule data
   D. Activity duration estimates

4. Which of the following statements is least true:

   A. Completed project schedules are typically illustrated using Bar Charts, Milestone Charts or Network Diagrams.
   B. There are two primary methods used to shorten schedules: crashing and fast tracking
   C. Resource leveling heuristics can be used to reduce the number of estimated resources, resulting in lower project costs.
   D. Lead time and lag time allows project teams to add realism and flexibility to their schedule. Lead time may be viewed as an overlap between tasks. Lag time is waiting time.

5. All of the following statements are true about project scheduling methods except?

    A. The Critical Path Method is used without regard to resource limitations
    B. The Critical Chain Method is used when there are certain resource limitations
    C. Resource Optimization Techniques include Resource Leveling and Resource Smoothing
    D. Modeling Techniques include Leads and Lags

End of Lesson 19

Lesson 20
Plan Human Resource Management

Objectives

At the end of this lesson, you will be able to:

- Describe the purpose of the Plan Human Resource Management process
- Describe the Inputs, Tools and Techniques, and Outputs of the Plan Human Resource Management process
- Understand organization types and cultures and their potential effects on the project

Process Locator for the PMBOK® Guide

	Initiating	Planning	Executing	M&C	Closing
Integration					
Scope					
Time					
Cost					
Quality					
Human Resource		▓▓▓			
Communications					
Risk					
Procurement					
Stakeholder					

The Plan Human Resource Management process is applied to develop, document and assign project roles, responsibilities and reporting relationships and to develop a Staffing Plan.

Plan Human Resource Management typically involves creating a project organization chart, a Human Resource Management Plan, defining team policies/procedures and creating a Staffing Management Plan.

Logically, human resource planning is one of the earliest processes applied in project planning. Because the organization structure will greatly influence the project's communications requirements, human resource planning is closely linked with communications planning.

Projects can be staffed by people external to the organization, internal to the organization, or by a mix of both. As you may imagine, a project team comprised of staff members who are temporarily borrowed from various groups within an organization will be quite different from a project team comprised of members who are all hired from the outside. To better understand the dynamics of different project organizations, it is helpful to understand the way different organizations tend to staff their projects. Accordingly, this lesson begins with a presentation of some important fundamentals in organizational theory.

Organizational Theory

As a project manager, you may be expected to have a practical understanding of different types of organizational structures, especially with relation to project staffing. Generally, we recognize three primary types of organizations:

- Functional Organizations
- Matrix Organizations
- Projectized Organizations

Functional Organizations

In Functional organizations, little, if any, cross-functional work is organized/performed as projects. In these organizations, staff members typically work strictly within their functional specialty, such as Finance, Engineering, Marketing, Quality and Manufacturing.

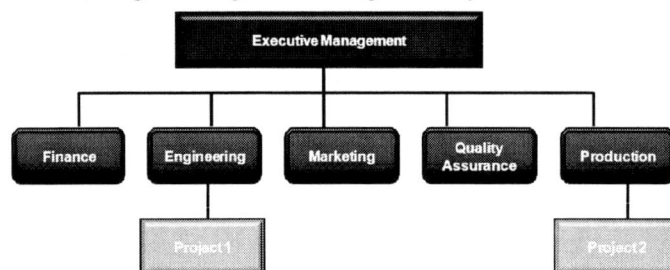

Figure 20.1 Functional Organization example

In Functional organizations, the functional managers usually assume all responsibility and authority. A project manager may be assigned, but only as a project coordinator or project expediter.

Matrix Organizations

In Matrix organizations, the structure is similar to a functional organization, except some work is organized and performed as projects. Typically, project teams are comprised of people temporarily borrowed from various functional areas within the organization. When their project work is done, they return to their functional area. There are several matrix organization variants.

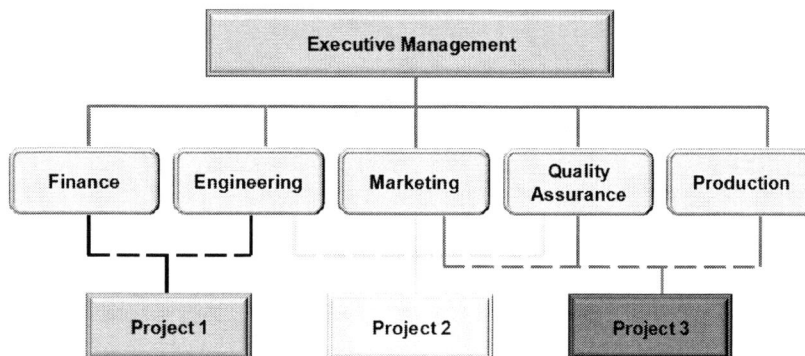

Figure 20.2 Matrix Organization example

In a balanced matrix organization, the project manager equally shares responsibility and authority with functional managers during the project.

In a strong matrix, the PM has more authority than the Functional Manager.

In a weak matrix, the PM has less authority than the Functional Manager.

Projectized Organizations

In Projectized organizations, all work is organized and performed as projects. A building contractor firm could exemplify a projectized organization. In these organizations, project teams are usually hired solely to support a project, then let go as soon as their work is done.

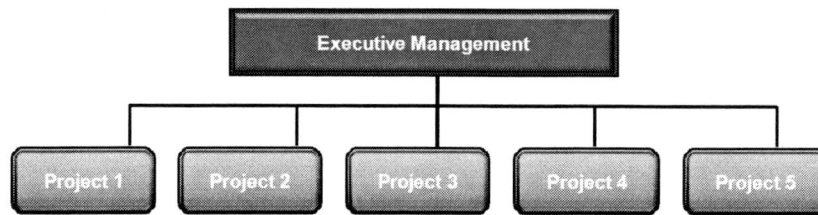

Figure 20.3 Projectized Organization example

In Projectized organizations, the project manager usually assumes full profit/loss responsibility and authority.

Process Elements

The Plan Human Resource Management process has the following Inputs:
- Project Management Plan – Documented plan to manage the project including how work will be executed

- Activity Resource Requirements - Types and quantities of resources needed for each schedule activity

- Enterprise Environmental Factors - Consideration factors such as; culture, policies, marketplace conditions

- Organizational Process Assets - Consideration factors such as processes, policies, lessons learned and escalation procedures

The Plan Human Resource Management process uses the following Tools & Techniques:
- Organization Charts and Position Descriptions - Displays illustrating project reporting relationships and positions (i.e. hierarchical, matrix and text-oriented)

- Networking – Formal and informal interaction to better understand political and interpersonal factors in an organization or industry

- Organizational Theory - The body of knowledge that describes how people, teams and organizations behave

- Expert Judgment – Experts used to list skills, roles, reporting relationships, etc.

- Meetings – Planning meeting to assess human resource needs

The Plan Human Resource Management process has the following Outputs:
- Human Resource Management Plan - Describes how resources should be defined, staffed, managed and released

Plan Human Resource Management		
This process documents project roles, responsibilities and reporting relationships		
Inputs	**Tools and Techniques**	**Outputs**
• Project Management Plan • Activity Resource Requirements • Enterprise Environmental Factors • Organizational Process Assets	• Organizational Charts and Position Descriptions • Networking • Organizational Theory • Expert Judgment • Meetings	• Human Resource Management Plan *TSI* Study Aid This chart is part of the study aid poster series available at: *www.TrueSolutions.com*

Figure 20.4 Process Elements within the Develop Human Resource Plan process

Process Documents

The Human Resource Management Plan that is the output from this process is really a collection of documents. The Human Resource Management Plan may combine the Roles and Responsibility Chart (RACI Chart), the Staffing Management Plan (when resources come and go), the Project Organization Chart and other human resource related information into one collection of documents. This is a volume of information that will take multiple pages to define and document.

A simple example of a template for human resource planning is shown below.

Human Resource and Staffing Management Plan

Project Name:	
Prepared by:	
Date:	
Project Manager:	
Staffing Management Plan Number: (original is #1)	
Project Team Roles and Responsibilities:	
List Each Team Member and Role: Responsibility, Accountability, Consult, Inform • •	
Insert Project Organization Chart Here:	

Staff Management Plan:

Resource Description	Estimated Number	Projected Timing to Join Project	Projected Completion Date for Release
1.			
2.			
3.			
4.			
5.			
6.			
7.			
8.			

Training Needs:

Type of Training	Dates of Training
•	
•	
•	

Projected Approach and Schedule for Updating Staffing Management Plan:

Triggering Event	Expected Timing
•	
•	
•	

Resource Calendar – note differences to standard calendar here:
1.
2.
Additional Notes:

TSI   Application Aid

Process Tasks

The Plan Human Resource Management process aligns with one of the defined tasks that a project manager performs when managing a project:

Planning Task #5: "Develop a Human Resource Management Plan by defining the roles and responsibilities of the project team members in order to create an effective project organization structure and provide guidance regarding how resources will be utilized and managed".

Think About It

Instructions Use this exercise to compare how you practice project management to what is specified in the *PMBOK® Guide Fifth Edition.*

Best Practices suggest that the following items are used during the Plan Human Resource Management process.

Which of these items do you use when practicing project management?

☐ Define all roles and responsibilities

☐ Create an organization chart

☐ Use tools like a RACI chart or Responsibility Matrix

☐ Document a Staffing Management Plan to show when resources come & go

☐ Document a complete Human Resource Management Plan to cover the entire project time period

☐ Update all documents when changes to resource plans occur

How would you change your use of this process in your organization to resolve any gaps in application?

_____

_____

_____

Must Know Concepts

1. The Plan Human Resource Management process is applied to develop, document and assign project roles, responsibilities and reporting relationships.

2. The primary output of the Plan Human Resource Management process is the project's Human Resource Management Plan.

3. The Human Resource Management Plan describes how/when human resources will be brought into the project and how/when human resources will leave the project. A Resource Histogram is often used to illustrate some of this information.

4. Roles (who does what) and responsibilities (who decides what) are often illustrated using a Responsibility Assignment Matrix (RAM).

5. A Responsibility Assignment Matrix (RAM) illustrates assignments and levels of authority/responsibility, as a function of WBS elements. There is no time associated with a RAM.

6. A RACI Chart (Responsible, Accountable, Consult, Inform) is a type of RAM. In the RACI chart, there can be only one person accountable.

7. Functional organizations typically do not perform much work as cross-functional projects. When they do, projects are usually the full responsibility of a functional manager. Project managers in functional organizations typically have very little authority and are often termed project coordinators or project expediters.

8. In matrix organizations, projects are performed using human resources borrowed from functional areas within the organization. In matrix organizations, project managers typically share responsibility and authority with functional managers.

9. In projectized organizations, most work is performed as projects. In projectized organizations, the project manager typically assumes full profit/loss responsibility and authority and staffs the project with dedicated (not borrowed) human resources.

Additional Reading

- PMBOK® Guide Fifth Edition: Section 9.0   Introduction, Project Human Resource Management
- PMBOK® Guide Fifth Edition: Section 9.1   Plan Human Resource Management

Lesson Quiz

Instructions: The actual PMP exam is done via computer. These questions are representative of what you will encounter. Circle the correct answer. Answer Key in Appendix A.

1. The Plan Human Resource Management process is applied to _____.

   A. Develop, document and assign the project resource histogram
   B. Develop, document and assign project roles, responsibilities and reporting relationships
   C. Develop the project's Responsibility Assignment Matrix
   D. Identify which organizational standards are applicable to the project, then determine how to satisfy them.

2. Which statement is least true?

   A. In matrix organizations, project managers typically share responsibility an authority with functional managers.
   B. In strong matrix organizations, project managers may have more authority than functional managers.
   C. Project managers in functional organizations may have little authority and are often termed project coordinators or project expeditors.
   D. In projectized organizations, the project manager typically assumes no profit/loss responsibility/authority and staffs the project with human resources borrowed from various functional areas within the organization.

3. Plan Human Resource Management tools and techniques include:

   A. Staffing management plan, networking, communicating
   B. Organization charts and position descriptions, networking, organizational theory
   C. Organization charts and position descriptions, negotiating, organizational theory
   D. Project management plan, activity resource requirements, networking

End of Lesson 20

This page intentionally blank.

Lesson 21
Plan Cost Management

Objectives

At the end of this lesson, you will be able to:

- Describe the purpose of the Plan Cost Management process
- Describe the Inputs, Tools and Techniques, and Outputs of the Plan Cost Management process
- Understand when to perform Plan Cost Management
- Understand what elements should be included in a Cost Management Plan

Process Locator for the PMBOK® Guide

	Initiating	Planning	Executing	M&C	Closing
Integration					
Scope					
Time					
Cost		▓▓▓			
Quality					
Human Resource					
Communications					
Risk					
Procurement					
Stakeholder					

Cost is a critical success factor for every project. This process helps us plan to manage the project budget.

In versions one through four of the PMBOK Guide, there were three undefined "processes" that we have referred to over time, as the "hidden processes". PMI has taken action and corrected this ambiguity by including three new processes into the PMBOK Guide Fifth Edition. One of these formerly "hidden" processes is the process of Plan Cost Management.

Plan Cost Management is a simple process in terms of change control, and can be compared to the similar processes of Plan Scope Management and Plan Schedule Management. In this process a Cost Management Plan that will document how the project budget will be defined, documented, validated and controlled throughout the project life cycle. Using the very simplest definition, the Cost Management Plan might say something like: "Any changes to the project budget must be approved by key stakeholders".

The Cost Management Plan will document how the budget is to be developed. This implies that the level of detail required and the format for the project budget will be defined here.

The Cost Management Plan will also define what level of detail will go into the tracking the budget as the project is executed. An important part of the Cost Management Plan is the definition of accuracy levels, thresholds for reporting and earned value rules for performance measurement.

The Plan Cost Management process creates the Cost Management Plan which is considered part of the overall Project Management Plan.

Process Elements

The Plan Cost Management process has the following Inputs:
- Project Management Plan - A document identifying all project baseline information on how the project will be managed

- Project Charter - The document authorizing the project to begin

- Enterprise Environmental Factors - Factors such as culture, systems, procedures, standards

- Organizational Process Assets - Factors such as lessons learned and historical information

The Plan Cost Management process uses the following Tools & Techniques:
- Expert Judgment – Expert technical or managerial judgment from any qualified source

- Analytical Techniques – Choosing strategies to manage the budget, such as self-funding, funding with equity or funding with debt

- Meetings – Discussion and dialogue to determine the appropriate way to manage the project budget

The Plan Cost Management process has the following Outputs:
- Cost Management Plan - Details budget definition, development, validation and monitoring levels of detail and accuracy as well as performance measurement rules

Plan Cost Management		
This process determines how the project Cost will be developed and managed		
Inputs	**Tools and Techniques**	**Outputs**
• Project Management Plan	• Expert Judgment	• Cost Management Plan
• Project Charter	• Analytical Techniques	
• Enterprise Environmental Factors	• Meetings	
• Organizational Process Assets		

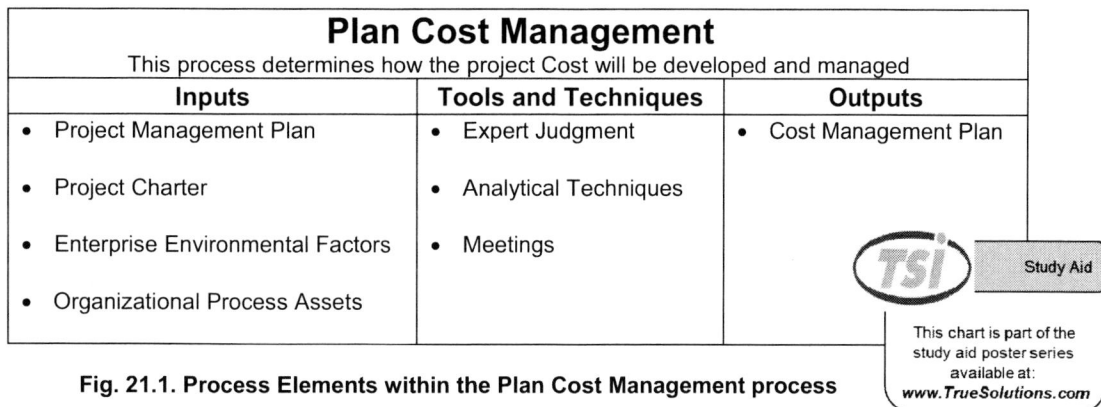

Fig. 21.1. Process Elements within the Plan Cost Management process

Process Documents

The Cost Management Plan is the key output from the Plan Cost Management process. The Cost Management Plan documents the overall plan to define, develop and manage the project cost at a detailed level. Many organizations have a pre-determined Cost Management Plan that will be executed for each project in the organization.

As with any other project management process, the size and complexity of the Cost Management Plan should be in accordance with the procedures of the organization and appropriate to the size and complexity of the project.

A simple Cost Management Plan could consist of the following elements:

- Identifying information for the project and plan
  - Project name
  - Preparer name
  - Revision date

- Person or persons who can request a cost change

- Person or persons who can approve a cost change

- Change reasons

- Impacts to the project

- Other information, such as:
  - Process to develop the project cost
  - Precision levels, units of measure, control thresholds to be used to measure cost performance

A Cost Management Plan template follows.

Cost Management Plan

Project Name:		
Prepared by:		
Date:		
Person(s) authorized to request cost changes (see Cost Change Request):		
Name:	Title:	Location:
Name:	Title:	Location:
Name:	Title:	Location:
Person(s) to whom Cost Change Request forms must be submitted for approval:		
Name:	Title:	Location:
Name:	Title:	Location:
Name:	Title:	Location:

Acceptable reasons for changes in Project Cost *(e.g., approved scope changes, increased raw material costs, etc.)*:

Describe how you will calculate and report on the projected impact of any cost changes *(time, quality, etc.)*:

Describe any other aspects of how changes to the Project Cost will be managed:

Application Aid

This form is available individually or as part of a set at:
www.TrueSolutions.com

Process Tasks

The Plan Cost Management process aligns with one of the defined tasks that a project manager performs when managing a project:

Planning Task #9: "Develop a change management plan by defining how changes will be handled, in order to track and manage changes".

Think About It

The Plan Cost Management process focuses on planning all cost requirements and definitions for the project. Plan Cost Management does this by involving the stakeholders and considering the availability of resources. Plan Cost Management is done by:

☐ Involving stakeholders

☐ Documenting the budget and cost management needs

☐ Determining what documents to use to present and track the budget

☐ Determining frequency for monitoring cost variances

☐ Determining who can request budget changes

☐ Determining who can approve changes

Which of these elements do you use in your organization for cost management?

_____

_____

_____

Must Know Concepts

1. The Plan Cost Management process is applied to create a Cost Management Plan that documents how the cost will be defined, controlled and validated.

2. The primary deliverable (Output) of the Plan Cost Management process is the Cost Management Plan.

3. The Cost Management Plan is part of the overall Project Management Plan.

Additional Reading

- PMBOK® Guide Fifth Edition: Section 7.0   Project Cost Management
- PMBOK® Guide Fifth Edition: Section 7.1   Plan Cost Management

Lesson Quiz

Instructions: The actual PMP exam is done via computer. These questions are representative of what you will encounter. Circle the correct answer. Answer Key in Appendix A.

1. Which of the following statements best describes the Plan Cost Management process?

    A. The Plan Cost Management process is applied to determine the number of cost changes planned for the project and use that data as justification for keeping the project scope minimized
    B. The Plan Cost Management process is applied to determine how to define, manage and control the project budget
    C. The Plan Cost Management process creates the project budget
    D. The Plan Cost Management process is applied to satisfy stakeholder accounting requirements

2. Which statement is *most* true?

    A. The Cost Management Plan is the only output from Plan Cost Management
    B. Expert judgment is used in Plan Cost Management in order to determine how many budget changes we can anticipate for the project
    C. Non-budgetary change requests are not important
    D. There are two important outputs from Plan Cost Management, both of which are intended to manage the project budget

3. Which of these are not defined as an input to Plan Cost Management?

    A. Project Schedule Baseline
    B. Project Management Plan
    C. Enterprise Environmental Factors
    D. Lessons Learned information

4. You and your team are in the Planning Process Group and are considering how to develop and track your budget. You are considering things such as self-funding, funding with equity, renting, leasing, buying, payback periods, return on investment, etc. What Tool and Technique are you using?

    A. Analytical Techniques
    B. Meetings
    C. Expert Judgment
    D. Control Thresholds

5. Which of these are components of the Cost Management Plan?

    A. Results of earned value analysis
    B. The budget
    C. Results of variance analysis – under or over budget, magnitude of variance, recommended corrective action, if any
    D. Units of measure, levels of precision and accuracy, control thresholds, rules for performance measurement, reporting formats, process descriptions

6. You have been asked to take over a project that is seriously over budget. Upon completing an initial review, you discover that the final budget was developed using analogous estimating and that budget tracking and monitoring procedures had never really been thought through. What do you do first?

    A. Call all stakeholders together and request bottom-up estimates for all activities.
    B. Work with your project team and key stakeholders to develop the Cost Management Plan.
    C. Request that your finance department provide additional funding to the project.
    D. Call a meeting with your business sponsor to request additional people resources for the project.

End of Lesson 21

This page intentionally blank.

Lesson 22
Estimate Costs

Objectives
At the end of this lesson, you will be able to:
- Describe the purpose of the Estimate Costs process
- Describe the Inputs, Tools and Techniques, and Outputs of the Estimate Costs process
- Understand the tools to be used to develop cost estimates
- Understand the different types of cost estimates to be used

Process Locator for the PMBOK® Guide

	Initiating	Planning	Executing	M&C	Closing
Integration					
Scope					
Time					
Cost		▓▓▓			
Quality					
Human Resource					
Communications					
Risk					
Procurement					
Stakeholder					

Estimate Costs is the process of determining the estimated costs of resources that will be applied to complete all project schedule activities.

Estimate Costs includes direct resources such as labor, materials and equipment plus other indirect costs such as contingency cost reserves, inflation allowances, cost of quality and overhead. Estimates may be documented and reported in detail or in summary form.

It is important to distinguish between cost and price. For example, in a competitive bid scenario, a construction company may estimate its total cost to build an office complex then submit a bid with its price to the client. Typically the price will be higher than the cost. The difference represents the construction company's potential profit. Generally, price is negotiable, whereas cost is not.

Like activity duration estimates, cost estimates should be prepared and documented with ranges of possible outcomes, instead of inflexible single-point values. For example, $9,300 +/- 10%.

One tool or technique that is mentioned in this process is the Three-Point Estimate. Three-Point estimates are estimates derived using three values: most likely estimate, optimistic estimate and pessimistic estimate. This method of estimating is also known as "PERT" – Program Evaluation Review Technique. The PMBOK® Guide uses a new formula with new designations for the values. Most Likely value = Cm, Optimistic = Co, Pessimistic = Cp.

The Three-Point Estimate can use a Triangular Distribution formula: $cE = (cO + cM = cP)/3$, or a Beta Distribution formula: $cE = (cO + 4cM + cP) / 6$.

This is more simply expressed by the old PERT formula of: $O+4ML+P/6$.

Many organizations use an established chart of accounts for financial tracking and reporting. It is good practice to code each cost estimate in alignment with the organization's chart of accounts (or with a project-specific chart of accounts, if an existing one is not available). This can facilitate financial tracking and reporting across the project life-cycle.

Study Tip
Financial Accounting Terms As a project manager, you may be expected to work closely at times with financial accounting professionals, primarily to support the cost budgeting, tracking, reporting and analysis aspects of your project. Therefore, it is very useful to have a general understanding of key accounting terms.

Here are the associated financial accounting terms you are most likely to encounter:

- Accelerated Depreciation = Costs amortized over a period of time at some faster rate than straight line depreciation

- Benefit Cost Ratio (BCR) = Benefit / Cost. BCR<1 = costs greater than benefits, BCR >1 = benefits greater than costs, BCR = 1 means costs equal benefits

- Direct Costs = Costs that are directly applied to work on the project

- Fixed Costs = Non-recurring costs that don't change in proportion to the amount of work. One-time set-up/ tear-down costs, special training costs, etc.

- Indirect Costs = Overhead items. These are costs typically incurred to cover general administration costs across an organization

- Internal Rate of Return (IRR) = In essence, IRR may be viewed as the interest rate an organization will realize on the money invested in a project

- Law of Diminishing Returns = increasingly the more you put in, the increasingly less benefit you get out. For example: Devoting 100 hours of guided study and preparation to pass a Certification Exam may ensure a passing score of 150. Spending 200 hours may ensure a score of 160. Spending 400 hours may ensure a score of 165. In this example, 100 hours is sufficient to achieve the goal. The first doubling of effort (100 hours - 200 hours) returns only a 5% improvement. The second doubling of effort (200 hours - 400 hours) returns even less, a 2.5% improvement

- Net Present Value (NPV) = the value today of all associated cash flows in the future. It is calculated by adding all of the Present Values (PVs), by accounting period (see Present Value below). For example, if a project is expected to finish two years from now, there may be eight quarterly accounting periods. The NPV equals the sum of the eight quarterly PVs

- Opportunity Cost = The loss of potential gain from other alternatives when one alternative is chosen

- Payback Period = The time to recover costs; this period begins when the project ends

- Present Value (PV) = The value today of cash flows in the future

- Present Value = $FV/(1+r)^n$; where r = interest rate n= number of time periods, FV = Future Value

- Straight Line Depreciation = Costs amortized by an equal amount each year

- Sunk Costs = Expended costs; Special Note: Accounting standards suggest that sunk costs should not be considered when deciding to continue with a troubled project

- Value Analysis = The systematic use of appropriate techniques to find a less costly way to accomplish the same scope of work

- Variable Costs = Costs that change in proportion to the amount of materials, supplies, equipment and labor applied to the project. More labor, more costs. More supplies, more costs, etc.

- Working Capital = The amount of money an organization has available to invest

Study Tip
Cost estimates used by the project manager are often defined by the organization for PMP study, you will focus on two defined estimates.

- Order of Magnitude Estimate (or Rough Order of Magnitude ROM) - This is one of the standard project cost estimates. It defines the confidence or range of an estimate to be: -25%, to +75%

- Definitive Estimate - This is the most accurate standard project estimating type. It defines the estimate to be: +/- 5%, to +10%. This would typically be the budget baseline accuracy range.

Other cost elements and tools to be considered, include:

- Life Cycle Costing - Life Cycle Costing is an important concept to factor in project planning. It suggests that post-project operating costs should be carefully considered when planning project strategies. The intent is to avoid strategies that will lower immediate project costs in such a way that they will increase post-project operating costs

- Analogous Estimating (top-down) - Analogous estimating (also termed top-down estimating) typically involves basing an estimate on a known previous activity performed in the past. Analogous estimates are relatively quick to perform and inexpensive, because no detailed estimating protocols are necessary. All that is involved is recalling history. Analogous estimates are also the least confident, typically proving to have a significant margin of error after-the-fact

- Bottom-up Estimating - Bottom-up estimating generally produces the most confident estimates, but is more costly and time consuming than analogous estimating. Typically, bottom up estimating is performed by developing detailed estimates for each activity at the work package level of the WBS. They are then rolled-up to derive a project total

- Parametric Estimating – This tool is used when you have repeatable elements in the project. For example if you have to run multiple cables for workstations and each cable takes 1.5 hours (the parameter), then you can produce an estimate based on the number of times you use the parameter.

- Chart of Accounts - Most performing organizations use an established chart of accounts for financial tracking and reporting. It is good practice to code each cost estimate in alignment with the organization's chart of accounts to facilitate financial tracking and reporting for the project.

Process Elements

The Estimate Costs process has the following Inputs:
- Cost Management Plan – Documented plan to manage the project budget

- Human Resource Management Plan – Documented plan for using human resources

- Scope Baseline - Scope baseline = the approved project scope statement + the WBS + the WBS dictionary

- Project Schedule - Graphic presentation illustrating planned start and planned finish dates for each t activity

- Risk Register - List of identified risks and their mitigating costs

- Enterprise Environmental Factors - Consideration factors such as; culture, systems, procedures, industry standards (i.e. market conditions and published commercial data)

- Organizational Process Assets - Consideration cost factors such as policies, templates, historical information and lessons learned

The Estimate Costs process uses the following Tools & Techniques:
- Expert Judgment - Expert technical and/or managerial judgment (from any qualified source)

- Analogous Estimating - Using actual results from a previous project to base current estimates

- Parametric Estimating - Use of project 'parameters' to calculate predicted costs

- Bottom-Up Estimating - Estimating individual activities, then rolling-up the summary

- Three-Point Estimating - Factoring most likely, optimistic and pessimistic estimates to get an estimate

- Reserve Analysis - Determining an estimate of contingency reserve and management reserves, to compensate for cost risk

- Cost of Quality - Total costs incurred to achieve project quality (conformance to requirements)

- Project Management Software - Cost estimating applications, spreadsheets, simulations, and statistical tools

- Vendor Bid Analysis - Analyzing vendor bids to determine project costs

- Group Decision Making Techniques – Team approaches used to improve estimate accuracy and commitment

The Estimate Costs process has the following Outputs:
- Activity Cost Estimates - a quantitative assessment of probable costs required to complete an activity

- Basis of Estimates - Documentation that supports the cost estimates

- Project Documents Updates - Updates to other project documentation (i.e. risk register)

Estimate Costs

This process approximates the costs of resources needed to complete project activities

Inputs	Tools and Techniques	Outputs
• Cost Management Plan • Human Resource Management Plan • Scope Baseline • Project Schedule • Risk Register • Enterprise Environmental Factors • Organizational Process Assets	• Expert Judgment • Analogous Estimating • Parametric Estimating • Bottom-up Estimating • Three-Point Estimating • Reserve Analysis • Cost of Quality • Project Management Software • Vendor Bid Analysis • Group Decision Making Techniques	• Activity Cost Estimate • Basis of Estimates • Project Documents Updates

TSI — Study Aid

This chart is part of the study aid poster series available at: www.TrueSolutions.com

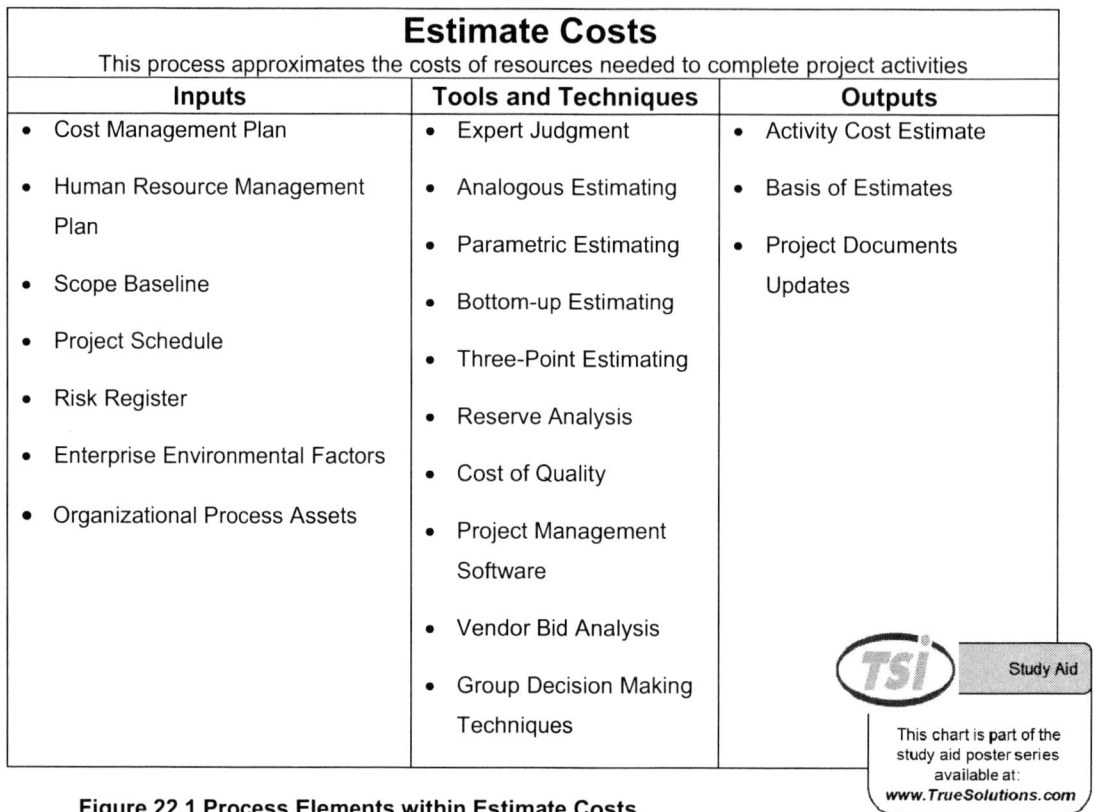

Figure 22.1 Process Elements within Estimate Costs

Process Documents

Two important documents come from the Estimate Costs process. First and foremost the project manager will create a Cost Estimate for the project. The Cost Estimate is usually provided in a spreadsheet format using one or more automated tools.

Task Description	Cost	Work Package #	Control Account	Project Cost	Contingency Reserve (Knowns)	Project Baseline	Accuracy Estimate
Develop Prelim Scope	$200						
Develop Project Charter	$200	A001			$200		
Develop Project Scope	$400						This Budget Estimate is considered the Order of Magnitude estimate with an accuracy of -25% to +75%. Date of Estimate: June 17, 2006
Develop Schedule	$300						
Validate Controls	$200						
Finalize Project Plan	$200	A002			$400		
Manage Project Execution	$1,000						
Perform Work	$2,000	B001	8840	$4,500	$500	$5,600	
Perform Change Control	$500						
Measure Performance	$400	B002	8875	$900	$100	$1,000	
Deliver Product	$1,000						
Obtain Formal Acceptance	$200						
Archive Information	$200	B003	8874	$1,400	$400	$1,800	
Totals				$6,800	$1,600	$8,400	

Process Tasks

The Estimate Costs process aligns with one of the defined tasks that a project manager performs when managing a project:

Planning Task #3: "Develop a budget plan based on the project scope using estimating techniques, in order to manage project cost".

Think About It

Instructions: Use this exercise to compare how you practice project management to what is specified in the *PMBOK® Guide Fifth Edition.* Think about how this process is defined, used and documented in your organization. Write a brief description of how you use this process:

_____

_____

_____

Must Know Concepts

1. The Estimate Costs process is applied to develop cost estimates for each identified project activity. Costs include direct costs for items such as labor, materials and equipment plus indirect costs for items such as administrative overhead and contingency reserves. These estimates will ultimately be used to create the cost baseline.

2. Estimating should be performed by the person, or group of people, who are most knowledgeable about the activity, ideally by the person or people who will be doing the work.

3. Cost estimates should be prepared and documented with ranges of possible outcomes, instead of inflexible single-point values. For example, $9,300 -5% to +10%.

4. An Order of Magnitude (or Rough Order of Magnitude ROM) estimate defines the confidence of an estimate to be: - 25%, to +75%.

5. A Definitive estimate defines the confidence of an estimate to be: - 5%, to +10%.

6. Some of the tools used for Estimate Costs include Analogous estimating (using a previous activity as the basis for the estimate), Bottom-up Estimating (developing detailed estimates

for each activity, then rolling up for a total), Three-Point Estimating (using Most Likely, Optimistic and Pessimistic values, then factoring).

7. It is helpful to document cost estimates using a coding structure aligned with some selected chart of accounts, typically the chart of accounts already in use by the performing organization.

Additional Reading

- PMBOK® Guide Fifth Edition: Section 7.2   Estimate Costs

Lesson Quiz

Instructions: The actual PMP exam is done via computer. These questions are representative of what you will encounter. Circle the correct answer. Answer Key in Appendix A.

1. When a project manager prepares cost estimates during the initiation phase, what is the range of a rough order of magnitude (ROM)?

    A. +/- 50%
    B. - 40%, to +80%
    C. - 25%, to +75%
    D. - 25%, to +100%

2. Estimating costs Tools & Techniques include which of the following:

    A. Analogous estimating, bottom-up estimates, chart of accounts
    B. Bottom-up estimating, parametric modeling, activity duration estimating
    C. Analogous estimating, bottom-up estimating, parametric estimating
    D. Bottom-up estimating, parametric estimating, estimating publications

3. Which of the following statements is least true?

    A. The estimating cost process is applied to create the cost baseline
    B. The estimating cost process is applied to develop cost estimates for each schedule activity
    C. Costs can include labor, materials, equipment, supplies, variable costs, indirect costs and direct costs
    D. The project cost management plan is developed as part of the Plan Cost Management process

4. Which of the following statements is most true?

    A. Price and cost are essentially interchangeable
    B. Price includes all direct project costs, whereas cost includes all indirect project costs
    C. Price and cost are not the same
    D. Price should be considered as life cycle costing factor, whereas costs should not

5. Cost estimates are best developed by:

    A. The project team
    B. The project manager
    C. The project cost engineer
    D. The person, or people who will be doing the actual work

End of Lesson 22

This page intentionally blank.

Lesson 23
Plan Procurement Management

Objectives
At the end of this lesson, you will be able to:
- Describe the purpose of the Plan Procurement Management process
- Describe the Inputs, Tools and Techniques, and Outputs of the Plan Procurement Management process
- Understand general criteria for the make or buy decision
- Understand contract types and applications

Process Locator for the PMBOK® Guide

	Initiating	Planning	Executing	M&C	Closing
Integration					
Scope					
Time					
Cost					
Quality					
Human Resource					
Communications					
Risk					
Procurement		▓			
Stakeholder					

The Plan Procurement Management process is the planning process used to document decisions regarding the purchase and acquisition of required project resources.

Plan Procurement Management process documents approaches, procurement decisions and identifies potential sellers for required project resources.

Required resources include more than just physical materials or components, and can include services and labor from outside the immediate project organization. For example, construction projects may require special permits. This process would be used to specify who and how those permits will be obtained.

There are several actions taken during the Plan Procurement Management Process:

- Make-or-buy decision making

- Identifying approaches and potential sellers

- Creating the Procurement Management Plan and the Procurement Statement of Work

Make or Buy decisions can often be difficult.

Some elements to consider when making the decision to "Make" the product are:
- Cost of using internal resources

- Ability to use readily available experienced subject matter experts

- Having more control of the work

- Maintaining control of the intellectual property

- You may consider the presences of proprietary data

When making the decision to "Buy" you may also consider:
- Cost; many times external resources can be more efficient or a shrink-wrapped product is available that can be customized

- In-house expertise may not be available

- If efficiency outweighs intellectual property considerations

- If the needed skills are readily available from vendors

The Plan Procurement Management process is closely coordinated with Project Time Management, Project Cost Management and Human Resource Management processes. It also must factor in consideration for project risks involved in purchasing decisions.

If it is determined during Plan Procurement Management that there are no products or services that need to be acquired outside of the project, then the remaining Project Procurement Management processes are not performed.

Types of Contracts

Considered to be part of the Organizational Process Assets used on the project, there are the three broad categories of contract types. From them, many variation possibilities (hybrids) may be crafted to suit specific project needs:

Fixed Price (also termed firm fixed price or lump sum) - Fixed price contracts require the seller to provide all contracted items for one firm price. When executed well, fixed price contracts provide confident, stable costs to the project, avoiding cost overruns. As a result, fixed price contracts can reduce cost risk to the buyer. Fixed price contracts are often used in projects, for the express purpose of reducing cost risk

Cost Reimbursable [sometimes structured as Cost-Plus-Fee (CPF), Cost-Plus-Fixed-Fee (CPFF), Cost-Plus- Incentive-Fee (CPIF), or Cost-Plus-Percentage of Cost (CPPC)]. - Cost reimbursable contracts require the buyer to reimburse the seller for his/her costs, plus some agreed-upon fee.

Total cost to the buyer will vary, depending on the amount and types of items supplied
Time and Materials (T&M) - T&M contracts reimburse the seller at an agreed-upon rate for each item to be provided. Total cost to the buyer will vary, depending on the amount and types of items supplied

At a very high level, there are some general reasons for choosing one contract form over another.

	Fixed Price	Cost Reimbursable	Time & Materials
Contract Forms	FP = Fixed price FPIF = Fixed price incentive fee FPEPA = Fixed Price economic price adjustment	CR = Cost Reimbursable CPFF = Cost plus fixed fee CPPC = Cost Plus percent of cost CPIF = Cost Plus Incentive Fee	T&M T&E = Time and Expense
Advantages	Less work for buyer to manage, less cost risk to buyer. Seller has incentive to control costs. Buyer knows total cost.	Simpler scope of work, sometimes provides lower cost since seller does not need to factor in as much risk.	Quick to create SOW, good choice for staff augmentation.
Best to use when	You know precisely what you need done.	You need help in determining what needs to be done.	Short term staff augmentation. Need someone right away.
Disadvantages	Seller may attempt to add-on with change orders. Needs a detailed SOW – changes have to be controlled closely.	Buyer has to closely control each seller invoice to avoid overpaying. Seller has a moderate incentive to control costs.	Seller has no incentive at all to control costs or to work efficiently. Requires daily management by the buyer.
Scope of work	Detailed – has to define all the work specifically.	Moderate detail – wants seller to help define the work.	Brief SOW – usually specified on a daily basis to resource.

Figure 23.1 Contract Form Description

Process Elements

The Plan Procurement Management process has the following Inputs:
- Project Management Plan – Documented plan to manage the project

- Requirements Documentation - Documentation describing how individual requirements fulfill the business needs of the project

- Risk Register - List of identified risks

- Activity Resource Requirements - Types and quantities of resources needed for each schedule activity

- Project Schedule - Graphic presentation illustrating planned start and planned finish dates for each project activity

- Activity Cost Estimates - a quantitative assessment of the probable costs required to complete an activity

- Stakeholder Register – Document identifying all project stakeholder information

- Enterprise Environmental Factors - Consideration factors such as; culture, systems, procedures, industry standards

- Organizational Process Assets - Consideration factors such as processes, procedures and corporate knowledge base

The Plan Procurement Management process uses the following Tools & Techniques:
- Make-or-Buy Analysis - General management technique used to determine which resources must be purchased outside of the organization

- Expert Judgment - Expert technical and/or managerial judgment (from any qualified source)

- Market Research – Examination of industry or specific vendor capabilities and information

- Meetings – Meetings to determine needed procurements

The Plan Procurements process has the following Outputs:
- Procurement Management Plan - Describes how the procurement process will be managed from documentation through contract closure

- Procurement Statement of Work - Detailed description of the "procurement item" for prospective suppliers (sellers)

- Procurement Documents – Documents used to inform sellers of the need, used to solicit responses

- Source Selection Criteria – Criteria used to help score or rate proposals submitted by prospective project suppliers

- Make-or-Buy Decisions - The documented decisions of what will be developed in-house and what will be purchased

- Change Requests - Request for changes to scope, schedule, costs, or processes or other project documentation

- Project Documents Updates - Documents Updates to other project documentation

Plan Procurement Management
This process documents purchasing decisions,
the procurement approach, and identifies potential sellers

Inputs	Tools and Techniques	Outputs
• Project Management Plan	• Make or Buy Analysis	• Procurement Management Plan
• Requirements Documentation	• Expert Judgment	• Procurement Statement of Work
• Risk Register	• Market Research	
• Activity Resource Requirements	• Meetings	• Procurement Documents
• Project Schedule		• Source Selection Criteria
• Activity Cost Estimates		• Make-or-Buy Decisions
• Stakeholder Register		• Change Requests
• Enterprise Environmental Factors		• Project Documents Updates
• Organizational Process Assets		

TSI Study Aid

This chart is part of the study aid poster series available at:
www.TrueSolutions.com

Chart 23.2. Process Elements within Plan Procurement Management

Process Documents

True Solutions, Inc.
Project Management Template
Version 2: Procurement Management Planning Checklist
Template

Procurement Management Planning Checklist

Project Name:		
Prepared by:		
Date:		
Identify types of contracts being used		
Independent estimates required?	Yes	No
If Yes, who will prepare?		
By when?		
Actions that Project Management Team can take independent of Procurement Department		
Source of standardized procurement documents, if needed		
How will multiple providers be managed?		
How will you coordinate Procurement with the following aspects of the project?		
Scheduling		
Performance Reporting		
Human Resources		
Other		

Application Aid

This form is available
individually or as
part of a set at:
www.TrueSolutions.com

Process Tasks

The Plan Procurement Management process aligns with one of the defined tasks that a project manager performs when managing a project:

Planning Task #7: "Develop a procurement plan based on the project scope and schedule, in order to ensure that the required project resources will be available".

Think About It

Instructions: Use this exercise to compare how you practice project management to what is specified in the *PMBOK® Guide Fifth Edition.* Think about how this process is defined, used and documented in your organization. Write a brief description of how you use this process:

Must Know Concepts

1. The Plan Procurement Management process is the planning process used to document decisions regarding the purchase and acquisition of required project resources.

2. Primary outputs of the Plan Procurement Management process are the Procurement Management Plan, Procurement Statements of Work, Procurement Documents and Source Selection Criteria.

3. If it is determined during Plan Procurement Management that there are no products or services that need to be acquired or developed outside of the project team, then the remaining Project Procurement Management processes do not need to be performed.

4. There are three primary activities during the Plan Procurement Management Process: Make-or-buy decision making, identifying approaches to procurement and potential sellers and creating the Procurement Management Plan and Statement of Work.

5. There are the three broad categories of contract types: Fixed Price, Cost Reimbursable and Time and Materials (T&M).

Additional Reading

- PMBOK® Guide Fifth Edition: Section 12.0 Introduction, Project Procurement Management
- PMBOK® Guide Fifth Edition: Section 12.1 Plan Procurement Management

Lesson Quiz

Instructions: The actual PMP exam is done via computer. These questions are representative of what you will encounter. Circle the correct answer. Answer Key in Appendix A.

1. After reviewing the detailed analysis associated with a particular project activity, you and your project team decide to contract with a specialist outside of your organization. You then prepare a document that details the complete scope of expected work, plus other important terms. This document is an example of _____.

   A. A work package
   B. A contractor's project charter
   C. A contract statement of work (SOW)
   D. Risk avoidance

2. Which of the following is *most* true?

   A. Creating the procurement management plan can also have an influence on the project schedule.
   B. Make-or-buy analysis only considers the direct costs associated with the procurement of an item.
   C. The amount of risk shared between the seller and the buyer is determined by teaming agreements.
   D. The procurement management plan includes seller selection for all procured items.

3. When preparing bid documents, the project team decides to include a section requiring each prospective seller to demonstrate their a) financial capacity, b) technical depth, c) management depth and d) understanding of scope. The team's intent is to provide important non-price information for them to consider when selecting the supplier. This could be an example of_____.

   A. Standard forms
   B. Expert judgment
   C. Source Selection criteria
   D. Benchmarking

End of Lesson 23

Lesson 24
Determine Budget

Objectives
At the end of this lesson, you will be able to:
- Describe the purpose of the Determine Budget process
- Describe the Inputs, Tools and Techniques, and Outputs of the Determine Budget process
- Understand the tools used to develop the Project Cost Baseline
- Understand how the Project Cost Baseline is documented

Process Locator for the PMBOK® Guide

	Initiating	Planning	Executing	M&C	Closing
Integration					
Scope					
Time					
Cost		▓			
Quality					
Human Resource					
Communications					
Risk					
Procurement					
Stakeholder					

The Determine Budget process is applied to formally aggregate all activity (and/or work package) cost estimates into a cohesive project budget and approved cost baseline.

Determine Budget is the process of aggregating cost estimates into a final project budget. The project budget is sometimes termed the "Project Cost Baseline" or "Performance Measurement Baseline (PMB). Formally, the cost performance baseline is the time-phased budget. It is used to monitor and measure project cost performance across remaining project phases. When measuring the project using Earned Value Techniques, the Cost Baseline is represented by the Budget at Completion (BAC) value. Cost baselines are typically illustrated using graphs. Plotted cost baselines usually form an S-Curve appearance.

Contingency reserves and management reserves are established in the Determine Budget Process or reevaluated if developed in Estimate Costs. However, management reserves are excluded from the cost baseline. Management reserves can become part of the cost baseline if approved as a result of change control during project execution.

Process Elements

The Determine Budget process has the following Inputs:
- Cost Management Plan – Documented plan to manage the project budget

- Scope Baseline - Scope baseline = the approved project scope statement + the WBS + the WBS dictionary

- Activity Cost Estimates - a quantitative assessment of the probable costs required to complete an activity

- Basis of Estimates - Documentation that supports the cost estimates by defining how the estimates were derived

- Project Schedule - Graphic presentation illustrating planned start and planned finish dates for each activity

- Resource Calendars - Information on the availability of resources over the planned activity duration

- Risk Register – List of identified risks

- Agreements - Applicable contract information for products and services to be purchased from external sources

- Organizational Process Assets - Consideration factors such as cost policies, procedures, guidelines and cost budgeting tools and reporting methods.

The Determine Budget process uses the following Tools & Techniques:
- Cost Aggregation - The process of aggregating schedule activity cost estimates by work packages

- Reserve Analysis - Determining appropriate amount of contingency and management reserves to compensate for project risk

- Expert Judgment - Expert technical and/or managerial judgment (from any qualified source)

- Historical Relationships - Analogous and Parametric Models used for cost estimation

- Funding Limit Reconciliation - the scheduling of work to avoid large variations in periodic expenditures

The Determine Budget process has the following Outputs:
- Cost Baseline - The time-phased budget used to measure, monitor and control project cost performance - aka Budget at Completion (BAC)

- Project Funding Requirements - Simply the funding needed and when it will be needed

- Project Documents Updates - Updates to other project documentation (i.e. risk register, cost estimates and project schedule)

Determine Budget This process aggregates individual activity costs to establish the project's Cost Baseline		
Inputs	**Tools and Techniques**	**Outputs**
• Cost Management Plan	• Cost Aggregation	• Cost Baseline
• Scope Baseline	• Reserve Analysis	• Project Funding Requirements
• Activity Cost Estimates	• Expert Judgment	
• Basis of Estimates	• Historical Relationships	• Project Documents Updates
• Project Schedule	• Funding Limit Reconciliation	
• Resource Calendars		
• Risk Register		
• Agreements		
• Organizational Process Assets		

TSI Study Aid

This chart is part of the study aid poster series available at: *www.TrueSolutions.com*

Figure 24.1 Process Elements within the Determine Budget process

Process Documents

The main document that is created as a result of the Determine Budget process is the Cost Baseline – a.k.a. Budget at Completion (BAC). This Cost Baseline is the best estimate of all costs of resources, reserves and other costs for the overall project. The Cost Baseline is a progressively elaborated document based on original Cost Estimates. The Cost Baseline could be depicted as a spreadsheet or as an "S-Curve" graphic.

Task Description	Cost	Work Package Cost	Control Account	Project Cost	Contingency Reserve (Knowns)	Project Baseline	Management Reserve (Unknowns)	Total Project Budget
Develop Prelim Scope	$200							
Develop Project Charter	$200	$400			$200		$100	
Develop Project Scope	$400							
Develop Schedule	$300							
Validate Controls	$200							
Finalize Project Plan	$200	$1,100			$400		$200	
Manage Project Execution	$1,000							
Perform Work	$2,000	$3,000	8840	$4,500	$500	$5,600	$500	$6,400
Perform Change Control	$500							
Measure Performance	$400	$900	8875	$900	$100	$1,000	$-0-	$1,000
Deliver Product	$1,000							
Obtain Formal Acceptance	$200							
Archive Information	$200	$1,400	8874	$1,400	$400	$1,800	$-0-	$1,800
Totals				$6,800	$1,600	$8,400	$800	$9,200

Figure 24.2 Project Cost Baseline example

Process Tasks

The Determine Budget process aligns with one of the defined tasks that a project manager performs when managing a project:

Planning Task #3: "Develop a budget plan based on the project scope using estimating techniques, in order to manage project cost".

Think About It

Instructions: Use this exercise to compare how you practice project management to what is specified in the *PMBOK® Guide Fifth Edition.* Think about how this process is defined, used and documented in your organization. Write a brief description of how you use this process:

_____

_____

What specific Inputs, Tools or Techniques do you use as part of this process in your organization?

_____

_____

Must Know Concepts

----

1. The Determine Budget process is applied to formally aggregate all activity cost estimates into a cohesive project budget, also known as the Cost Baseline.

2. The primary deliverable (Output) of the Determine Budget process is the cost baseline.

3. The Cost Baseline is the project's time-phased budget.

4. The Cost Baseline is used to monitor and measure project cost performance across project phases.

5. Cost Performance baselines are typically illustrated using graphs. Plotted cost performance baselines usually form an S-Curve appearance.

6. Management Reserves are excluded from the Cost Baseline, but are part of the overall Project Budget

Additional Reading

- PMBOK® Guide Fifth Edition: Section 7.3   Determine Budgets

Lesson Quiz

Instructions: The actual PMP exam is done via computer. These questions are representative of what you will encounter. Circle the correct answer. Answer Key in Appendix A.

1. The Determine Budget process is applied to:

   A. Formally estimate the cost of each identified work package
   B. Formally organize all activity cost estimates into a cohesive project budget
   C. Formally document the estimated cost of each WBS work package
   D. Formally document the estimated cost of each activity identified on the project's activity list

2. Your project team has just completed development of the cost baseline. The cost baseline is:

   A. A formal document that describes how earned value management (EVM) will be applied to measure and report project cost performance
   B. A formal document that describes how project cost variances will be managed
   C. A time-phased budget, used to monitor and measure cost performance
   D. A time-phased budget, used as supporting detail to justify activity cost estimates

3. Determine Budget inputs include all the following *except*:

   A. Cost baseline
   B. Activity cost estimates
   C. Resource calendars
   D. Project schedule

4. Which of the following statements is *most* true?

   A. Cost baselines are typically illustrated using graphs. Plotted cost baselines usually form an S-curve appearance
   B. Cost baselines are typically documented informally, as they are likely to change frequently
   C. Cost baselines are typically documented as a subsidiary plan to the overall project plan
   D. Cost baselines are typically illustrated using Gantt Charts (Bar Charts) or Milestones Charts

End of Lesson 24

Lesson 25
Plan Quality Management

Objectives
At the end of this lesson, you will be able to:
- Describe the purpose of the Plan Quality Management process
- Describe the Inputs, Tools and Techniques, and Outputs of the Plan Quality Management process
- Understand fundamental quality definitions

Process Locator for the PMBOK® Guide

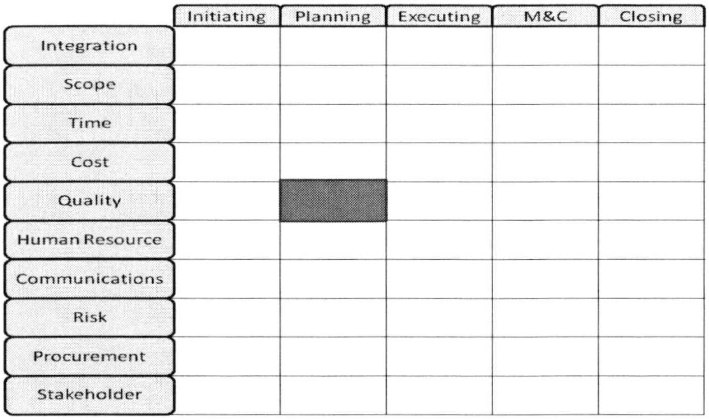
Initiating
Planning
Executing
M&C
Closing
Integration
Scope
Time
Cost
Quality
Human Resource
Communications
Risk
Procurement
Stakeholder

The Plan Quality Management process is applied to identify which quality standards are applicable to the project and then determine how to satisfy them.

Quality planning is often applied in parallel with other processes during project planning.

The term quality means different things to different people, depending on their specific orientation and application environment. For our purposes in project management, quality means delivering precisely what is promised. When a project team delivers on-time, within budget and has satisfied all scope requirements, then quality has been achieved.

It is important to understand, quality must be "planned-in" to the project, not "inspected-in".

It is also helpful to understand that the terms quality and grade are not identical. Quality is the totality of characteristics to satisfy requirements. Grade is a measurement of technical characteristics. For instance, a high-grade product would be characterized by having many complex features. A low-grade product would have few features. Both could be of high-quality. When speaking of quality and grade, low-quality is a problem, low-grade is not.

Study Tip

Quality Terms
The following are the key terms and concepts related to Project Quality:

Quality policy - An organization's quality commitment is generally referred to as the quality policy. The quality policy originates from the highest management levels in the organization. A corporate Quality Management Manual could serve to document the quality policy. In some projects, the organization's quality policy can be adopted directly, to serve the project's quality needs. In other projects, it may be necessary to create a project-specific quality policy. In all projects, the quality policy must be communicated to stakeholders and requirements must be met

Cost of quality (COQ) - The cost of quality is defined as a quality tool/technique. It includes all costs expended to achieve product/service quality objectives. Quality = conformance to requirements. These costs typically include prevention costs (planned-in quality), appraisal costs (quality control) and failure costs (warranty, rework)

Design of experiments (DOE) - Design of experiments is a quality tool/technique that employs statistical methods to analyze trade-offs. For instance, the project team may wish to evaluate the schedule/cost trade-offs associated with using senior engineers (higher costs, lower risks, possible shorter duration) opposed to using junior engineers (lower costs, higher risks, possible longer duration). Simulations (experiments) may be run to determine the optimum combination of junior engineers and senior engineers

Flowcharting - Flowcharts (also termed process maps or systems flow charts) are often used as a quality tool/technique. Flowcharts are graphical illustrations that show how elements of a system relate. A project network diagram is a flow chart.

Study Tip (continued)

Quality Terms (continued)

Cause-and-effect diagrams (also called fishbone diagrams or Ishikawa diagrams) - A cause-and-effect diagram is a specific type of flow chart. These type diagrams are often used to illustrate how different factors are linked to problems and are especially helpful in generating ideas and thinking when analyzing quality problems

Benchmarking - Benchmarking is defined as a quality tool/technique. Benchmarks are established standards and/or practices that may be used for comparison when the project team establishes its standards for measuring project performance. Benchmarks may be internal or external to the performing organization

ISO 9000|10000 - ISO 9000|10000 is an international quality standard used by organizations to ensure adherence to their own quality policies. ISO 9000|10000 is part of The International Organization for Standardization's series. ISO 9000|10000 is a brief document, not a detailed QA/QC policy. ISO 9000|10000 certified organizations are still responsible for developing their own specific quality policies. ISO 9000|10000 certification simply ensures adherence to those organization-specific quality policies

Just-in-Time (JIT) - JIT is the manufacturing management concept/practice of maintaining minimal inventory (ideally zero). JIT implementation typically requires higher quality standards to compensate for lower inventories (high failure rates cannot be tolerated in a JIT environment)

Quality Metrics (also called operational definitions) - Metrics are the specific parameters for measuring quality performance. These are the project elements selected for measurement and the quality control system that will be used to measure them

Process Improvement - Project teams should be ever-vigilant in looking for ways to improve project performance (cost reduction, schedule reduction) across the entire life-cycle, not just during planning. Such improvements increase overall benefits to project stakeholders. This is process improvement. Process improvement is any action taken to improve efficiency and effectiveness in project performance

Total Quality Management (TQM) - TQM is a concept/practice intended to help organizations achieve quality improvement objectives

Process Elements

The Plan Quality Management process has the following Inputs:
- Project Management Plan – Documented approaches and plans to manage the project

- Stakeholder Register - A document identifying all project stakeholder information

- Risk Register - List of identified risks

- Requirements Documentation – Documentation describing how individual requirements meet the business need of the project

- Enterprise Environmental Factors - Consideration factors such as; government regulations, rules, standards, guidelines, and conditions of the project/product which may affect quality

- Organizational Process Assets - Consideration factors such as quality policies, procedures, guidelines, historical databases, and lessons learned

The Plan Quality Management process uses the following Tools & Techniques:
- Cost-Benefit Analysis - The use of financial measures to assess the desirability of identified alternatives

- Cost of Quality - Total costs incurred to achieve project quality (cost of conformance and cost of nonconformance)

- Seven Basic Quality Tools – Tools such as Cause and Effect Diagrams, Flowcharts, Check-sheets, Pareto Diagrams, Histograms, Control Charts and Scatter Diagrams

- Benchmarking - Comparing performance to a selected 'standard,' primarily to generate ideas for improvement

- Design of Experiments (DOE) - A statistical method to help identify optimal solutions, factoring-in specific variables

- Statistical Sampling - Statistical analysis using a small group from an entire population

- Additional Quality Planning Tools – Brainstorming, force field analysis, nominal group technique, quality management and control tools, etc.

- Meetings – Meetings to develop the Quality Management Plan

The Plan Quality Management process has the following Outputs:
- Quality Management Plan - Describes how the team will implement the organization's quality policy

- Process Improvement Plan - Describes the steps for analyzing processes to eliminate wasteful activities (i.e. boundaries, configuration, metrics and targets for improved performance)

- Quality Metrics - Operational definitions. Project elements, and how they are to be measured by quality control

- Quality Checklists - Structured forms used to verify that a set of required steps has been performed in quality control

- Project Documents Updates - Updates to other project documentation

Plan Quality Management		
This process indentifies project quality standards and defines how they will be satisfied		
Inputs	**Tools and Techniques**	**Outputs**
• Project Management Plan	• Cost-Benefit Analysis	• Quality Management Plan
• Stakeholder Register	• Cost of Quality	• Process Improvement Plan
• Risk Register	• Seven Basic Quality Tools	
• Requirements Documentation	• Benchmarking	• Quality Metrics
	• Design of Experiments	• Quality Checklists
• Enterprise Environmental Factors	• Statistical Sampling	• Project Documents Updates
• Organizational Process Assets	• Additional Quality Planning Tools	
	• Meetings	

**Figure 25.1 Process Elements within the
Plan Quality Management process**

This chart is part of the study aid poster series available at:
www.TrueSolutions.com

Process Documents

Two documents are critical outputs from the Plan Quality Management process: the Quality Management Plan and the Process Improvement Plan.

The Quality Management Plan depicts (as a minimum):
- Quality Organization and Roles and Responsibilities (towards quality actions)
- Resources Required
- Quality Assurance actions planned
- Quality Control actions planned
- Quality Approaches

The Quality Management Plan services to describe how the project team will implement its organization's quality policy. The Quality Management Plan may be brief or comprehensive, whichever best suite the size and complexity of the project. A Quality Management Plan template example is shown following.

The Process Improvement Plan depicts (as a minimum)

- Process Boundaries (owner, purpose, process description)

- Process Configuration (flowcharts)

- Process Metrics (control parameters)

- Target for Process Improvement

The Process Improvement Plan details the steps for analyzing processes to identify and eliminate wasteful activities, thus increasing stakeholder value. The Process Improvement Plan may be brief or comprehensive to suit the size and complexity of the project.

True Solutions, Inc.
Project Management Template
Version 2: Quality Management Plan Template

Quality Management Plan

Project Name:	
Prepared by:	
Date:	
Description of Project Quality System:	

Describe in as much detail as needed specifically what will be required in each of the following areas to manage quality on this project:

ORGANIZATIONAL STRUCTURE

ROLES AND RESPONSIBILITIES

PROCEDURES

PROCESSES

RESOURCES

Describe how each of the following aspects of quality management will be addressed on this project:

QUALITY CONTROL

QUALITY ASSURANCE

QUALITY IMPROVEMENT

Application Aid

This form is available individually or as part of a set at:
www.TrueSolutions.com

Process Tasks

The Plan Quality Management process aligns with one of the defined tasks that a project manager performs when managing a project:

Planning Task #8: "Develop a quality management plan based on the project scope and requirements, in order to prevent the occurrence of defects and reduce the cost of quality".

Think About It

Instructions Use this exercise to compare how you practice project management to what is specified in the *PMBOK® Guide Fifth Edition.*

Think about how this process is defined, used and documented in your organization. Write a brief description of how you use this process:

_____

_____

_____

_____

Must Know Concepts

----

1. The Plan Quality Management process is applied to identify which quality standards are applicable to the project then determine how to satisfy them.

2. The primary outputs of the Plan Quality Management process are the project's Quality Management Plan and the Process Improvement Plan.

3. In project management, quality means delivering precisely what is promised. When a project team delivers on-time, within budget and has satisfied all scope requirements, then quality has been achieved.

4. Quality must be planned-in to a project, not inspected-in.

5. Quality and grade are not the same. Low-quality is a problem, low-grade is not.

6. Cost of quality includes all costs expended to achieve product/service quality objectives.

Additional Reading

- PMBOK® Guide Fifth Edition: Section 8.0 Introduction, Project Quality Management
- PMBOK® Guide Fifth Edition: Section 8.1 Plan Quality Management

Lesson Quiz

Instructions: The actual PMP exam is done via computer. These questions are representative of what you will encounter. Circle the correct answer. Answer Key in Appendix A.

1. The Plan Quality Management process is applied to:

    A. Help ensure high-grade, high quality project performance
    B. Create quality improvement
    C. Develop the project's cause-and-effect diagram
    D. Identify which quality standards are applicable to the project, then determine how to satisfy them

2. Plan Quality Management tools and techniques include:

    A. Cost-benefit analysis, benchmarking, cost of quality (COQ)
    B. Quality baseline, benchmarking, cost of quality (COQ)
    C. Cost-benefit analysis, quality checklists, cost of quality (COQ)
    D. Cost-benefit analysis, benchmarking, quality metrics

3. You and your project team have been studying the performance of a recently completely project in your organization that was a big success. That project was very similar in nature to yours. You decide to use several successful milestone achievements from the project to set measurement standards for your own project. This is an example of:

    A. Enterprise Environmental Factors
    B. Using templates
    C. Benchmarking
    D. Develop Schedule

4. You and your project management team completed the project on-time, within budget and you successfully delivered all that was defined in the scope of work, precisely to specification. Based on this scenario, which of the following statements is *most* true?

    A. You and your project team have achieved quality
    B. You and your project team may have missed some important project objective.
    C. You and your project team should immediately close the project
    D. You and your project team should re-check your requirements

End of Lesson 25

Lesson 26
Plan Risk Management

Objectives

At the end of this lesson, you will be able to:

- Describe the purpose of the Plan Risk Management process
- Describe the Inputs, Tools and Techniques, and Outputs of the Plan Risk Management process
- Know the definition of risk to be used for project management
- Understand the categories of risk to be considered on the project

Process Locator for the PMBOK® Guide

	Initiating	Planning	Executing	M&C	Closing
Integration					
Scope					
Time					
Cost					
Quality					
Human Resource					
Communications					
Risk		■			
Procurement					
Stakeholder					

Even though risk is found everywhere in the project environment, it can be identified, analyzed and managed to minimize potential negative impacts and maximize potential positive impacts.

Project risk management is a knowledge area that had been largely overlooked in past years, but is now recognized as one of the most important areas in all of modern project management.

Risk infiltrates into each and every aspect of a project. There are six closely associated processes in project risk management. In this lesson, we will discuss the first process, which is Plan Risk Management. In Plan Risk Management, we decide how to approach and plan our risk management activities for a particular project. Definitions of risk and how to quantify risk are developed in this process. The Plan Risk management process is intended and used to develop the project's Risk Management Plan.

There are several important things to understand concerning risk: **Project risk is any uncertain event or condition that, if it occurs, has a positive or negative effect on a project objective.** Therefore, project risks can be positive or negative! Negative risks are Threats and should be avoided. Positive risks are Opportunities and should be pursued.

When planning risk management for the project, the project manager must ascertain the stakeholder levels of risk tolerance. This can be expressed in terms of:
- Risk appetite: the degree of uncertainty the stakeholder group might be willing to undertake with the anticipation of a reward.
- Risk tolerance: the amount of risk the individual or group can withstand.
- Risk threshold: at what level of uncertainty will the stakeholder(s) have a specific interest in a project risk. Below a threshold, risk is commonly accepted, above the threshold, risk is often not tolerated.
- There are three types of Risk: Known – Known, Known – Unknowns, Unknowns – Unknowns.

Process Elements

The Plan Risk Management process has the following Inputs:
- Project Management Plan – Documented plans and approaches to managing the project

- Project Charter – High level document that authorizes the project and assigns the project manager

- Stakeholder Register – Document identifying all project stakeholder information

- Enterprise Environmental Factors – Consideration factors such as; risk attitudes and tolerances

- Organizational Process Assets – Consideration factors such as risk categories, risk definitions, formats, templates, roles & responsibilities, lessons learned and stakeholder register

The Plan Risk Management process uses the following Tools & Techniques:
- Analytical Techniques – Techniques used to define the risk management context for the project, including grouping methods, casual analysis, root cause analysis, failure mode and effect analysis (FMEA), fault tree analysis (FTA), reserve analysis, and trend analysis.

- Expert Judgment – Expert technical or managerial input from qualified sources

- Meetings – Meetings to develop the risk management plan

The Plan Risk Management process has the following Output:
- Risk Management Plan - Describes how project risk management will be structured and performed across the project

Plan Risk Management		
This process is intended and used to develop the project's Risk management Plan		
Inputs	**Tools and Techniques**	**Outputs**
• Project Management Plan	• Analytical Techniques	• Risk Management Plan
• Project Charter	• Expert Judgment	
• Stakeholder Register	• Meetings	
• Enterprise Environmental Factors		
• Organizational Process Assets		

TSI Study Aid

This chart is part of the study aid poster series available at: www.TrueSolutions.com

Figure 26.1 Process Elements within the Plan Risk Management process

Process Documents

The primary output from the Plan Risk Management process is the Risk Management Plan. The Risk Management Plan serves to document how project risk activities will be approached and planned. The Risk Management Plan can be brief or comprehensive, based on the needs of the project. The Risk Management Plan will become a subsidiary plan to the overall Project Management Plan. Following is a possible Risk Management Plan template.

In addition to the Risk Management Plan, the project manager and team may choose to document risk categories being considered for the project. A Project Risk Categorization Worksheet can also be termed as a Risk Breakdown Structure.

There are four generally accepted categories of risk in project environments. These four categories are sometimes expressed as a Risk Breakdown Structure (RBS):

- **Project management risks** - These type risks may be caused by poor use of project management disciplines
- **Organizational risks** - These type risks may be caused by resource conflicts, incompatible goals and/or inadequate funding
- **External risks** - These type risks are typically caused by regulatory issues and/or natural disasters

- **Technical, quality, performance risks** - These type risks may be caused by a reliance on unproven technology and/or unrealistic performance goals

True Solutions, Inc.
Project Management Template
Version 2: Project Risk Categorization Worksheet Template

(TSi)

Project Risk Categorization Worksheet

Project Name:
Prepared by:
Date:
NOTE: List all identified project risks within each category. Retain this information for reference throughout the risk management process:
Project-management risks—such as poor allocation of time and resources, inadequate quality of the project plan, poor use of project management disciplines.
Organizational risks—such as cost, time, and scope objectives that are internally inconsistent, lack of prioritization of projects, inadequacy or interruption of funding, and resource conflicts with other projects in the organization.
External risks—such as shifting legal or regulatory environment, labor issues, changing owner priorities, country risk, and weather. Force majeure risks such as earthquakes, floods, and civil unrest generally require disaster recovery actions rather than risk management.
Technical, quality, or performance risks—such as reliance on unproven or complex technology, unrealistic performance goals, changes to the technology used or to industry standards during the project.

(TSi) | Application Aid

This form is available
individually or as
part of a set at:
www.TrueSolutions.com

Risk Management Plan

Project Name:	
Prepared by:	
Date:	
Description of Risk Management Methodology to be Used:	
Approaches	
Tools	
Data Sources	
Roles and Responsibilities:	
Risk Management Action:	
Team Leader	
Team Members	
Support	
[Add sections as needed]	
Budget:	
Timing: (Describe how risk management will relate to the project life cycle, and at what points it will be reviewed during the execution of the project)	
Risk Categories: (you can generalize here or use the Project Risk Categorization Worksheet; similar to RBS[Risk Breakdown Structure])	
Risk Probability and Impact: (you can generalize here or use the Rating Impact for a Risk)	

TSI   Application Aid

This form is available
individually or as
part of a set at:
www.TrueSolutions.com

Process Tasks

The Plan Risk Management process aligns with one of the defined tasks that a project manager performs when managing a project:

Planning Task #10: "Develop a risk management plan by identifying, analyzing, and prioritizing project risks and defining risk response strategies, in order to manage uncertainty throughout the project life cycle".

Think About It

Instructions: Use this exercise to compare how you practice project management to what is specified in the *PMBOK® Guide Fifth Edition*.

Think about how this process is defined, used and documented in your organization. Write a brief description of how you use this process:

_____

_____

_____

_____

_____

What specific Inputs, Tools or Techniques do you use as part of this process in your organization?

_____

_____

_____

Are the outcomes from this process different in your organization or experiences?

_____

_____

Must Know Concepts

----

1. Project risk is any uncertain event or condition that, if it occurs, has a positive or negative effect on a project objective.

2. Project risks can be positive or negative.

3. Negative risks are Threats and should be avoided.

4. Positive risks are Opportunities and should be pursued.

5. Project risk management is comprised of six closely associated processes.

6. Plan Risk Management is the first of the risk processes and is applied to decide and document how project risk will be approached and planned.

7. There are four generally accepted categories of risk in project environments: project management risks, organizational risks, external risks. technical risks (technical, quality, performance),

8. The primary deliverable (Output) of the Plan Risk Management process is the Risk Management Plan.

9. Part of the Risk Management Plan may include the risk categories to be considered, documented as a Risk Breakdown Structure.

10. There are three types of risk attitudes: risk appetite, risk tolerance, and risk threshold.

Additional Reading

- PMBOK® Guide Fifth Edition: Section 11.0 Introduction, Project Risk Management
- PMBOK® Guide Fifth Edition: Section 11.1 Plan Risk Management

Lesson Quiz

Instructions The actual PMP exam is done via computer. These questions are representative of what you will encounter. Circle the correct answer. Answer Key in Appendix A.

1. Project risk is properly defined as:

    A. Any negative event or condition that, if it occurs, has an effect on a project objective.
    B. Any cause that has a negative consequence to a project objective.
    C. Any uncertain event or condition that, if it occurs, has a negative or positive effect on a project objective.
    D. Any opportunity that has a negative or positive effect on a project objective.

2. Which of the following statements is most incorrect?

    A. A risk has a cause and, if it occurs a consequence.
    B. There are negative risks and positive risks.
    C. Positive risks may be viewed as opportunities and should be pursued.
    D. Negative risks must be eliminated before project plan execution.

3. Plan Risk management inputs include all the following, except:

    A. Organizational process assets
    B. The risk management plan
    C. The project management plan
    D. Internal and external factors affecting the enterprise

4. The six project risk management processes are:

    A. Plan Risk Management, Identify Risks, Perform Qualitative Risk Analysis, Perform Quantitative Risk Analysis, Plan Risk Responses, Control Risks
    B. Plan Risk Management, Identify Risks, Perform Qualitative Risk Analysis, Perform Quantitative Risk Analysis, Perform Risk Response Planning, Monitor and Control Risks
    C. Plan Risk Management, Identify Risks, Perform Qualitative Risk Analysis, Perform Probabilistic Risk Analysis, Perform Risk Response Planning, Perform Risk Mitigation
    D. Plan Risk Management, Identify Risks, Perform Qualitative Risk Analysis, Perform Quantitative Risk Analysis, Perform Risk Mitigation, Perform Risk Control

End of Lesson 26

Lesson 27
Identify Risks

Objectives
At the end of this lesson, you will be able to:
- Describe the purpose of the Identify Risks process
- Describe the Inputs, Tools and Techniques, and Outputs of the Identify Risks process
- Understand methods for identifying project risk

Process Locator for the PMBOK® Guide

	Initiating	Planning	Executing	M&C	Closing
Integration					
Scope					
Time					
Cost					
Quality					
Human Resource					
Communications					
Risk		▓			
Procurement					
Stakeholder					

The Identify Risks process is applied to determine which risks may affect the project and to document their characteristics.

Identify Risks is the second of our five risk processes that occur in the Planning process group. The primary objective of Identify Risk is to create a list of identified risks, along with the indications that the risk has occurred or is about to occur. These indications are termed triggers or risk symptoms or warning signs. Each identified risk will be analyzed during the application of subsequent risk management processes. To help identify as many risks as possible, many knowledgeable people should participate in the process. Several iterations are likely before an exhaustive list of risks is developed.

While most risk identification is done during planning, identifying risks is a process that should be encouraged frequently throughout the project life cycle. In many projects, new risks can surface daily and others dissipate.

Identify Risks Fundamentals

First of all, remember the definition of risk: *Project risk is an uncertain event or condition that, if it occurs, has a positive or negative effect on a project objective. A risk has a cause, and if it occurs, a consequence.*

It is common in project management to encounter documented risks that are not risks at all.

Study Tip
Some project managers have difficulty identifying what a risk is. Here are a few tips: • Risk is an uncertain event or condition. Uncertainty is the key. If an event or condition is certain, then it is not a risk • A problem is not a risk. It is a certain negative condition • An issue is not a risk. It is a matter to be decided

Information gathering techniques are used to help identify project risks. They include:

- **Brainstorming sessions** - with knowledgeable people
- **Delphi Technique** - This technique solicits and shares information among experts on an anonymous basis, to build consensus without personal bias
- **Interviewing** - Simple one-on-one interviews with key people can be very productive
- **Root Cause Identification** - Investigation to determine essential causes of project risks

SWOT analysis is another technique for analyzing the organization's Strengths, Weaknesses, Opportunities and Threats that can bring risks to the surface.

Diagramming techniques can be applied to help identify project risks. They include:

- **Cause and Effect Diagrams** (also termed fishbone diagrams or Ishikawa diagrams) - These can help identify the causes of risk

- **Systems flowcharts** (or process maps) - Analyzing the project network diagram, for example, can bring risks to light
- **Influence diagrams** - help identify associated causes

Process Elements

The Identify Risks process has the following Inputs:
- Risk Management Plan - Describes how project risk management will be structured and performed across the project

- Cost Management Plan - Defines how risk budgets, contingencies, and management reserves will be managed

- Schedule Management Plan - Defines how changes to the project schedule will be managed

- Quality Management Plan - Describes how the team will implement the organization's quality policy

- Human Resource Management Plan - Describes how and when human resources will be applied to the project

- Scope Baseline - Scope baseline = the approved project scope statement + the WBS + the WBS dictionary

- Activity Cost Estimates - a quantitative assessment of the probable costs required to complete an activity

- Activity Duration Estimates - Quantitative assessments of the time likely needed to complete each activity

- Stakeholder Register - A document identifying all project stakeholder information, requirements and classification

- Project Documents - Additional project documentation that aids in identification of risks (i.e. assumptions log, work performance reports, earned value reports, network diagrams, and baselines)

- Procurement Documents – Documents used to inform sellers of need, used to solicit sellers responses

- Enterprise Environmental Factors - Consideration factors such as; published information, academic studies, published checklists, benchmarking, industry studies and risk attitudes

- Organizational Process Assets - Consideration factors such as project files, organizational and project process controls, risk statement templates and lessons learned

The Identify Risks process uses the following Tools & Techniques:
- Documentation Reviews - A structured review of all project documentation

- Information Gathering Techniques - Various techniques used to help in identification of risks (i.e. brainstorming, Delphi technique, interviewing, root cause analysis)

- Checklist Analysis - Checklists based on historical risks identified for previous similar projects

- Assumptions Analysis - Analysis of project assumptions to identify possible risks

- Diagramming Techniques - Risk diagramming techniques (Ex: Cause and Effect diagrams, system flow charts, influence diagrams)

- SWOT Analysis - Strengths, Weaknesses, Opportunities, and Threats (SWOT) Analysis

- Expert Judgment - Expert technical and/or managerial judgment (from any qualified source)

The Identify Risks process has the following Output:
- Risk Register - List of identified risks

Identify Risks		
This process is applied to determine which risks may affect the project and documents their characteristics.		
Inputs	**Tools and Techniques**	**Outputs**
• Risk Management Plan	• Documentation Reviews	• Risk Register
• Cost Management Plan	• Information Gathering Techniques	
• Schedule Management Plan		
• Quality Management Plan	• Checklist Analysis	
• Human Resource Management Plan	• Assumptions Analysis	
	• Diagramming Techniques	
• Scope Baseline	• SWOT Analysis	
• Activity Cost Estimates	• Expert Judgment	
• Activity Duration Estimates		
• Stakeholder Register		
• Project Documents		
• Procurement Documents		
• Enterprise Environmental Factors		
• Organizational Process Assets		

Figure 27.1 Process Elements within the Identify Risks process

Process Documents

As an output from the Identify Risks process, the project manager and stakeholders create the Risk Register. The document created at this stage of the project is not the final Risk Register document. The current document output from Identify Risks is the preliminary list of risks for the project. Subsequent processes will make updates to this Risk Register by providing more detail.

True Solutions, Inc.
Project Management Template

Risk Register/Evaluation Grid

Project Name:
Prepared by:
Date:

Risk ID#	Risk Description	Risk Owner	Rating or Priority of Risk	Symptoms & Warning Signs	Root Cause	Trigger	Impact (P/I Score)	Quantitative Score	Risk Response Action Type	Response Trigger	Response Owner	Response Description	Expected Impact

Application Aid

This form is available individually or as part of a set at: **www.TrueSolutions.com**

Process Tasks

The Identify Risks process aligns with one of the defined tasks that a project manager performs when managing a project:

Planning Task #10: "Develop a risk management plan by identifying, analyzing, and prioritizing project risks and defining risk response strategies, in order to manage uncertainty throughout the project life cycle".

Think About It

During the early days of E-Commerce over the Internet, I was assigned to replace the existing project manager on a project to create a website for a paint company. What I found when I took over the project was that there was very little documentation available. Most of the project had been managed very loosely by the previous project manager and from only a short list of project risks was developed.

This paint company website was planned to have all of the usual tools for the customer to find information about paint, how to choose paint, how to apply paint and search options to search out specific products that they could use to paint their home or business. But one particular feature was a very risky element for the entire project.

The person or persons who had collected the requirements and defined the scope for the project had included a feature to allow customers to go online and match *customized* paint colors over the Internet. Now when I began to ask the technical staff involved with the project about this, they told me this was not a problem, since the customer would be expected to have (or purchase?) a special monitor calibration tool – a special piece of hardware and software that would read the monitor colors and calibrate them so that the matching of paint would come out correctly.

I suspect that you already know the outcome of this particular project. We were not able to economically create this website feature. In the end, the customer felt like the project was a failure since they did not get the "special feature" (paint matching) that they wanted. The performing organization felt like the project was a failure since they did not get to build and maintain the special feature and since the project terminated early as a result (less money for the company). And the technical resources were all disappointed since they did not get to play with the technical feature to make it work.

Proper risk identification on the front of the project would have identified how difficult it would have been to build this special paint match feature. Proper risk identification would have determined how immature the technology was and how unlikely it would be that a customer who wanted to match paint would have a monitor color calibration tool or would be willing to purchase one. Again, proper use of project management processes, in their appropriate order, would have saved everyone involved from disappointment and misuse of resources.

Contributed by Tim Bergmann, PMP

Must Know Concepts

1. Project risk is an uncertain event or condition that, if it occurs, has a positive or negative effect on a project objective. A risk has a cause, and if it occurs, a consequence.

2. The Identify Risks process is applied to determine which risks may affect the project and to document their characteristics.

3. Identifying risks is a process that should be encouraged frequently throughout the project life cycle. In many projects, new risks can surface daily.

4. Information gathering techniques used to help identify project risks include: brainstorming, Delphi technique, interviewing, root cause identification,

5. Diagramming techniques can be applied to help identify project risks including: cause and effect diagrams (also termed fishbone or Ishikawa), systems flowcharts (also termed process maps), influence diagrams.

6. SWOT analysis is another technique for analyzing the organization's Strengths, Weaknesses, Opportunities and Threats that can bring risks to the surface.

7. Indications that a risk has occurred, or is about to occur, are termed triggers (or risk symptoms or warning signs).

8. The primary output of the Identify Risks process is the Risk Register. The Risk Register is created during risk identification and then used to capture the outputs of all subsequent risk processes.

Additional Reading

- PMBOK® Guide Fifth Edition: Section 11.2   Identify Risks

Lesson Quiz

Instructions The actual PMP exam is done via computer. These questions are representative of what you will encounter. Circle the correct answer. Answer Key in Appendix A.

1. The Identify Risks process is applied to:

   A. Determine which risks are serious enough to warrant further analysis
   B. Determine which risks may affect the project and to document their characteristics
   C. Determine which risks are low enough to accept
   D. Determine which risks should be mitigated

2. Identify Risks Tools & Techniques include the following:

   A. Information gathering techniques, diagramming techniques, documentation reviews
   B. Assumptions analysis, checklist analysis, diagramming techniques
   C. Diagramming techniques, documentation reviews, assumptions analysis
   D. All the above

3. Which of the following statements is most true?

   A. Identifying risks is a process that must be applied properly during project planning, because once execution begins, there are no more opportunities to incorporate new risks in the plan
   B. Identifying risks is a process that is normally contained to members of the project core team
   C. Identifying risks is a process that should be encouraged frequently throughout the project life cycle. In many projects, new risks can surface daily
   D. Identifying risks is a process that should be performed by functional managers, because they are closest to the work

4. Diagramming techniques can be applied to help identify project risks. These techniques may include:

   A. Cause and effect diagrams (also termed fishbone or Ishikawa)
   B. Systems flowcharts (also termed process maps)
   C. Influence diagrams
   D. All of the above

5. Indications that a risk has occurred, or is about to occur, are termed:

   A. Uncertainties
   B. Triggers (or risk symptoms or warning signs)
   C. Consequences
   D. Threats

End of Lesson 27

Lesson 28
Perform Qualitative Risk Analysis

Objectives

At the end of this lesson, you will be able to:

- Describe the purpose of the Perform Qualitative Risk Analysis process
- Describe the Inputs, Tools and Techniques, and Outputs of the Perform Qualitative Risk Analysis process
- Understand how to apply a Risk Matrix in order to score and prioritize risks for the project

Process Locator for the PMBOK® Guide

	Initiating	Planning	Executing	M&C	Closing
Integration					
Scope					
Time					
Cost					
Quality					
Human Resource					
Communications					
Risk		▓▓▓			
Procurement					
Stakeholder					

Perform Qualitative Risk Analysis is the process of assessing the impact and likelihood of identified risks.

Perform Qualitative Risk Analysis is the third of five risk planning processes, and is logically applied as the next step after the Identify Risks process.

Perform Qualitative Risk Analysis is intended to help prioritize identified risks and identify those risks serious enough to warrant further analysis. As you may imagine, some identified risks have very little probability of occurring, and if they occur, would have only a slight impact. As a result of the Perform Qualitative Risk Analysis process, these risks would be appropriately listed low in priority. Other identified risks may have high probabilities of occurring and/or significant impact if they occur. These risks may be listed high in priority.

A probability/impact (P-I) risk rating matrix is used as the primary tool in Qualitative Risk Analysis to determine the impact and likelihood of identified risks.

Risk Probability/Impact (P-I) Matrix

A probability/impact (P-I) matrix is a tool that combines both risk probability and risk impact into a single score. It is used to help determine qualitative risk rankings.

Probability/Impact Matrix						
		Multiply P x I = Risk Score				
Risk Probability Low → High	.9					
	.7					
	.5					
	.3					
	.1					
	Risk Impact→	.1	.3	.5	.7	.9
		Very Low	Low	Moderate	High	Very High

Figure 28.1 Probability/Impact Matrix example

Using this P-I matrix type of qualitative assessment, each identified risk may be assigned a score by plotting it appropriately in the matrix. In this simple P-I matrix example, risks that are assessed with scores in the lower left portion of the matrix indicate low-probability with low-impact. Risks scored in the upper right indicate high-probability with high impact.

Typically, these high-high risks would receive higher priority for either further analysis or for immediate action. Notice that the probability y-axis goes no higher than 0.9 in this example. By definition, the probability of a risk occurring must be less than 100%. If the probability is 100%, then the event or condition is certain to occur and therefore not a risk at all. Risks are uncertain events or conditions.

Process Elements

The Perform Qualitative Risk Analysis process has the following Inputs:

- Risk Management Plan - Describes how project risk management will be structured and performed across the project

- Scope Baseline – The approved Scope Statement, WBS and WBS Dictionary

- Risk Register - List of identified risks

- Enterprise Environmental Factors - Consideration factors such as; published information, academic studies, published checklists, benchmarking, industry studies and risk attitudes

- Organizational Process Assets - Consideration factors such as similar completed projects, studies, risk databases

The Perform Qualitative Risk Analysis process uses the following Tools & Techniques:
- Risk Probability and Impact Assessment - Qualitative assessment of individual risk probability/impact

- Probability and Impact Matrix - A matrix that rates/prioritizes risks by combining probabilities and impacts

- Risk Data Quality Assessment - Technique to determine the level (confidence) to which a risk is useful

- Risk Categorization - Technical risks, external risks, project management risks, organizational risks

- Risk Urgency Assessment - Identification of risks which may require near-term responses

- Expert Judgment - Expert technical and/or managerial judgment (from any qualified source)

The Perform Qualitative Risk Analysis process has the following Output:
- Project Documents Updates- Updates to the risk register and assumptions list

Perform Qualitative Risk Analysis		
This process prioritizes risks by analyzing their combined probability and impact		
Inputs	**Tools and Techniques**	**Outputs**
• Risk Management Plan • Scope Baseline • Risk Register • Enterprise Environmental Factors • Organizational Process Assets	• Risk Probability and Impact Assessment • Probability and Impact Matrix • Risk Data Quality Assessment • Risk Categorization • Risk Urgency Assessment • Expert Judgment	• Project Documents Updates

TSI Study Aid

This chart is part of the study aid poster series available at: *www.TrueSolutions.com*

Figure 28.2 Process Elements within the Perform Qualitative Risk Analysis process

Process Documents

The Perform Qualitative Risk Analysis process documents results by populating the Probability-Impact Matrix shown previously in this chapter. Risk scores which result from the P-I Matrix will be entered into the Risk Register as an update.

Process Tasks

The Perform Qualitative Risk Analysis process aligns with one of the defined tasks that a project manager performs when managing a project:

Planning Task #10: "Develop a risk management plan by identifying, analyzing, and prioritizing project risks and defining risk response strategies, in order to manage uncertainty throughout the project life cycle".

Think About It
- -

Instructions Use this exercise to compare how you practice project management to what is specified in the *PMBOK® Guide Fifth Edition*.

Best Practices suggest that the following items are used during the Perform Qualitative Risk Analysis process.

Which of these items do you use when practicing project management?

☐ Identify risks in a separate process before you rank risks
☐ Rank risks using a Probability-Impact Matrix
☐ Use a cardinal scale (numbers) to score risks
☐ Use an ordinal scale (descriptive words; low-med-high)
☐ Identify a single risk score for each risk
☐ Normally have more risks than you can address due to constraints

How would you change your use of this process in your organization to resolve any gaps in application?

_____

_____

_____

Must Know Concepts

1. The Perform Qualitative Risk Analysis process is applied to assess the impact and likelihood of identified risks. It is intended to help prioritize identified risks and identify those risks serious enough to warrant further analysis.

2. A risk probability/impact (P-I) matrix is a tool that combines both risk probability and risk impact into a single score. It is used to help determine qualitative risk rankings.

3. The primary output of the Perform Qualitative Risk Analysis process is updates to project documents, which are new inputs to the Risk Register, including a list of risks for additional analysis, a list of prioritized risks, a list of risks requiring near-term response, risks grouped by category, and more.

Additional Reading

- PMBOK® Guide Fifth Edition: Section 11.3   Perform Qualitative Risk Analysis

Lesson Quiz

Instructions The actual PMP exam is done via computer. These questions are representative of what you will encounter. Circle the correct answer. Answer Key in Appendix A.

1. The perform qualitative risk analysis process is applied to:

   A. Assess the probability/impact of high priority risks in order to mitigate immediate threats
   B. Determine which risks may affect the project and to document their characteristics
   C. Further assess those risks that scored high-high on the probability/impact (P-I) matrix
   D. Assess the impact and likelihood of identified risks. It is intended to help prioritize identified risks and identify those risks serious enough to warrant further analysis

2. A probability/impact (P-I) risks rating matrix is:

   A. A defined tool/technique of the Perform Qualitative Risk Analysis process
   B. A defined input to the Perform Qualitative Risk Analysis process
   C. A tool that combines both risk probability and risk impact into a single score
   D. A and C

Probability/Impact Matrix						
		Multiply P x I = Risk Score				
Risk Probability Low → High	.9					
	.7					
	.5					
	.3					
	.1					
	Risk Impact →	.1	.3	.5	.7	.9
		Very Low	Low	Moderate	High	Very High

3. Using this P-I matrix shown, you and your team determine that an identified risk has a 0.3 probability of occurring and, if it occurs, an impact potential of .7. What is the overall score for this risk?

   A. 0.21
   B. 2.10
   C. 21.0
   D. None of the above

4. Using this P-I matrix, what is the highest possible risk score and the lowest possible risk score?

   A. 0.81, 0.01
   B. 0.9, 0.1
   C. 90.0, 1.0
   D. 0.9, .001

End of Lesson 28

.

This page intentionally blank.

Lesson 29
Perform Quantitative Risk Analysis

Objectives

At the end of this lesson, you will be able to:

- Describe the purpose of the Perform Quantitative Risk Analysis process
- Describe the Inputs, Tools and Techniques, and Outputs of the Perform Quantitative Risk Analysis process
- Understand that this process is applied when it is necessary for project success

Process Locator for the PMBOK® Guide

	Initiating	Planning	Executing	M&C	Closing
Integration					
Scope					
Time					
Cost					
Quality					
Human Resource					
Communications					
Risk		▆			
Procurement					
Stakeholder					

Perform Quantitative Risk Analysis is applied to determine a numerical value for overall project risk.

The Perform Quantitative Risk Analysis process is applied to guide the additional analysis of individual risks, to determine the numerical value of its probability of occurrence and the numerical value of its consequence on project objectives, should it occur. Perform Quantitative Risk Analysis is the fourth of five risk planning processes and is normally applied as the logical next step following perform qualitative risk analysis.

Today's powerful desktop computers and application software allows project teams to perform sophisticated quantitative risk analyses, which contributes to higher confidence in schedule estimates, cost estimates and overall quality. Monte Carlo simulation and Expected Monetary Value (EMV) analysis are commonly used tools to apply perform quantitative risk analysis. (Reference PMBOK® 5th Edition p. 339.)

Quantitative Risk Analysis Tools

There are numerous Tools & Techniques available to support quantitative risk analysis. Five tools & techniques stand-out as generally recognized and practiced in a widespread fashion throughout the project management community.

Modeling Techniques

Expected Monetary Value Analysis (EMV) - EMV is calculated by multiplying the value of each possible outcome by its probability of occurrence, then adding them all together. A common way to show EMV is by using *__decision tree analysis__*. – Decision Tree Diagrams illustrate the decision being considered, along with all of the implications of choosing various alternatives, including costs, risks and rewards. Solving a decision tree yields the path with greatest expected value.

Sensitivity Analysis - Sensitivity analysis is a simple risk analysis technique that looks at the overall project risk in a somewhat cursory fashion. Here is an example: Assume that Project X has a cost $100K, with a projected Return on Investment (ROI) of 400% and a 60% probability of complete failure. Project XX has the same cost of $100K, but with a potential ROI of 35% and a 10% probability of complete failure. Using sensitivity analysis, the project selection decision is based on the level of risk our organization is willing to take. An organization that is willing to accept high risk may find Project X appealing, while Project XX may be better suited for a more risk adverse organization.

Simulation - Today's powerful desktop computers allow project teams of any size to perform sophisticated computer simulations. These simulations can provide confident numerical analyses for cost risk, schedule risk and other project risks. Monte Carlo algorithms provide the underlying 'engines' of many simulation software packages. Using Monte Carlo, project managers can input specific parameter values into a program, then automatically run hundreds or thousands of simulations. The results are typically reported in graphical form to predict project performance. One such application could be to predict activity time durations. In this application, activity time duration estimates would be input to a simulation program, along with other key information. When the simulation is run and reported, the result is a graph that illustrates the probability of completion on any calendar date on the curve. Some project risk specialists believe that Monte Carlo simulation programs serve as today's best available quantitative analysis tool ... and they predict actual project performance with a high degree of accuracy.

Data Gathering and Representation Techniques

Interviewing - Interviews with stakeholders and subject matter experts (SME's) can be an effective approach in quantifying risks. For instance; you, as interviewer, could ask an expert stakeholder to estimate the cost for a particular activity; a high estimate, a low estimate and a most-probable estimate. With these estimate ranges, you and your project risk team can perform a sophisticated quantitative analysis that should provide a complete and confident range of numerical cost probabilities for that activity.

Probability Distributions – In order to represent uncertainty in values such as schedule duration and cost of project components, a probability distribution might be used. Widely used examples of this tool include beta distribution and triangular distribution models. These models depict shapes that are common with data normally developed during quantitative risk analysis.

Process Elements

The Perform Quantitative Risk Analysis process has the following Inputs:
- Risk Management Plan - Describes how project risk management will be structured and performed across the project

- Cost Management Plan - Defines how risk budgets, contingencies, and management reserves will be managed

- Schedule Management Plan - Defines how changes to the project schedule will be managed

- Risk Register - List of identified risks

- Enterprise Environmental Factors - Consideration factors such as culture, systems, procedures or industry standards

- Organizational Process Assets - Consideration factors such as similar completed projects, studies, risk databases

The Perform Quantitative Risk Analysis process uses the following Tools & Techniques:
- Data Gathering and Representation Techniques - Interviewing, probability distributions

- Quantitative Risk Analysis and Modeling Techniques - Sensitivity analysis, EMV, decision tree, simulation

- Expert Judgment - Expert technical and/or managerial judgment (from any qualified source)

The Perform Quantitative Risk Analysis process has the following Output:
- Project Documents Updates- Updates to other project documentation, assumptions, technical documentation or change requests that might occur

Perform Quantitative Risk Analysis

This process numerically analyzes the effect of risks on overall project objectives

Inputs	Tools and Techniques	Outputs
• Risk management plan • Cost management plan • Schedule management plan • Risk register • Enterprise environmental factors • Organizational process assets	• Data gathering and representation techniques • Quantitative risk analysis and modeling techniques • Expert judgment	• Project documents udpates

This chart is part of the study aid poster series available at: www.TrueSolutions.com

Figure 29.1 Process Elements within Perform Quantitative Risk Analysis

Process Documents

Process documents used in this process will vary depending on the tools employed. Interview records, simulation outcomes, probability distributions all may be employed and documented as part of this process. The results from using these tools will be documented in updating the Risk Register.

Process Tasks

The Perform Quantitative Risk Analysis process aligns with one of the defined tasks that a project manager performs when managing a project:

Planning Task #10: "Develop a risk management plan by identifying, analyzing, and prioritizing project risks and defining risk response strategies, in order to manage uncertainty throughout the project life cycle".

Think About It

Instructions Use this exercise to compare how you practice project management to what is specified in the *PMBOK® Guide Fifth Edition.* Which of these items do you use when practicing project management?

☐ Interviewing subject matter experts to determine ranges of probabilities in order to use probability distributions

☐ Using sensitivity analysis

☐ Using EMV forecasts and decision trees

☐ Modeling or simulation of outcomes

Which of these do you use in your organization?

_____

_____

_____

Must Know Concepts

----

1. The Perform Quantitative Risk Analysis process is applied to guide the additional analysis of individual risks, to determine the numerical value of its probability of occurrence and the numerical value of its consequence on project objectives, should it occur. This process is also applied to determine a numerical value for overall project risk.

2. Data gathering and representation techniques used include interviewing and probability distributions.

3. Quantitative risk analysis and modeling techniques used include sensitivity analysis, expected monetary value analysis and modeling and simulation tools.

4. Expected Monetary Value Analysis (EMV) is calculated by multiplying the value of each possible outcome by its probability of occurrence, then adding them all together. EMV= V (value $) x P (probability). Decision tree analysis uses EMV to illustrate the decision being considered, along with all the implications of choosing various alternatives. Solving a decision tree yields the path with the greatest expected monetary value.

5. The primary output of the Perform Quantitative Risk Analysis process is Project Documents Updates represented by new input information to the Risk Register including, probabilistic analysis of the project, probability of achieving cost and time objectives, a prioritized list of quantified risks, and more.

Additional Reading

- PMBOK® Guide Fifth Edition: Section 11.4   Perform Quantitative Risk Analysis

Lesson Quiz

1. The Perform Quantitative Risk Analysis process is applied to:
   A. Develop the project's risk management plan
   B. Determine which risks may affect the project and to document their characteristics
   C. Assess the impact and likelihood of identified risks
   D. Guide the additional analysis of individual risks, to determine the numerical value of its probability of occurrence and the numerical value of its consequence on project objectives, should it occur

2. After careful comparison, the decision is made by your project sponsor to choose one particular project strategy over another, because the chosen strategy has less associated risk. This decision is consistent with her risk adverse policies. This could be an example of using _____ to base a decision.
   A. Subjective analysis
   B. Expert power
   C. Title power
   D. Sensitivity analysis

3. Perform Quantitative Risk Analysis Tools & Techniques include:

   A. Probability and Impact Matrix, quantitative risk analysis and modeling techniques
   B. Data gathering and representation techniques, probability and impact matrix
   C. Data gathering and representation techniques, quantitative risk analysis and modeling techniques
   D. Checklist analysis, quantitative risk analysis and modeling techniques

4. To help determine and justify a cost contingency for your project, you decide to further evaluate four identified risks using EMV analysis. Risk 1 has a 10% probability of occurring, and if it occurs, will result in $10,000 added cost to the project. Risk 2 has a 70% probability of occurring, and if it occurs, will result in $8,000 added cost to the project. Risk 3 has a 60% probability of occurring, and if it occurs, will result in $10,000 less cost to the project. Risk 4 has a 20% probability of occurring, and if it occurs, will result in $800 added cost to the project. What is the combined EMV of these four risks?

   A. -$12,760
   B. $760
   C. -$760
   D. Not enough information

End of Lesson 29

This page intentionally blank.

270 Ultimate PMP® Exam Prep Study Guide

Lesson 30

Plan Risk Responses

Objectives

At the end of this lesson, you will be able to:

- Describe the purpose of the Plan Risk Responses process
- Describe the Inputs, Tools and Techniques, and Outputs of the Plan Risk Responses process
- Understand the risk responses for negative risks
- Understand the risk responses for positive risks
- Understand different options for response plans

Process Locator for the PMBOK® Guide

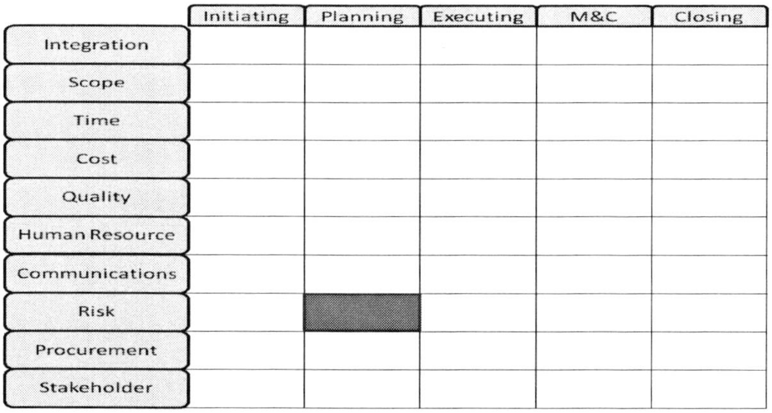
Initiating
Planning
Executing
M&C
Closing
Integration
Scope
Time
Cost
Quality
Human Resource
Communications
Risk
Procurement
Stakeholder

A primary objective of the Plan Risk Responses process is to create the project's Risk Response Plan as part of the Risk Register.

The Plan Risk Responses process is applied to develop options and determine actions to enhance opportunities (positive risks), and to develop options and determine actions to reduce threats (negative risks).

Once a risk has been identified and analyzed (qualitatively/quantitatively), a decision must be made on what to do about the risk. It is the intent of Plan Risk Responses to guide that decision, by planning an appropriate response to the risk.

For instance: Inclement weather is a risk that threatens many outdoor events. A project team managing such an event may choose to respond to this negative risk by planning in advance. That planning may be:

- To change the plan, making it an indoor event (this action avoids the risk)
- To arrange in parallel an alternate indoor venue that may be substituted at the last minute, should the risk occur (this action accepts the risk, with a contingency plan in place)
- To purchase insurance to cover losses, should the risk occur and the event is cancelled (this action transfers the risk, shifting the consequence to another party)
- To plan one or more rain dates (this action mitigates the risk by lowering the probability of complete cancellation, should the risk occur)

An example of a positive risk in relation to the above outdoor event might be if the weather is much better than usual for that time of the year and the crowd is much larger than planned. Positive risk response options:

- If the project team determines 30 days or so prior to the event that the long-term weather outlook is positive, they may choose to advertise the event further in advance or advertise the forecast weather outlook (attempting to enhance the risk).
- If the project team determines immediately prior to event that a highly positive condition exists they may attempt to notify the public or advertise a special event fee or expanded events (exploiting the risk).
- Accepting this risk might involve a contingency plan (as above – only geared to the positive outcomes). An example of a contingency plan might be to plan for more food consumption at the event or arrange for more contingent parking.
- Sharing the risk might involve bringing other organizations into the event if positive conditions are present.

Risk Response Options

Strategies for Negative Risks or Threats

- Avoidance - Avoidance is any action that changes the project plan, or condition within the plan, to eliminate the risk. If feasible, risk avoidance is the best option available to reduce overall negative project risk. If an avoidance strategy can be reasonably implemented for a particular negative risk, then the risk is completely eliminated
- Transference - Risk transfer is the action of shifting the consequence and ownership of a risk to a third party. It is important to understand this does not eliminate the risk (avoidance

eliminates a risk). It transfers the consequence and ownership. For instance: Risk may be transferred by a) purchasing insurance, b) obtaining guarantees, warranties and/or performance bonds, c) using fixed-price contracts, transferring cost risk to the seller, d) transferring liability through a contract

- Mitigation - Mitigation is any action that reduces the probability and/or impact of an adverse risk to an acceptable threshold. Many creative possibilities may exist to develop reasonable mitigation plans
- Accept - This strategy is used when the team decides that no changes to the Project Management Plan will occur for a risk, or when no response strategy can be defined for a risk

Strategies for Positive Risks or Opportunities

- Exploit - Seeking ways to make the opportunity happen
- Share - Sharing the opportunity with a third party, who may be better able to make it happen
- Enhance - Seeking to increase the size and/or probability of the opportunity
- Accept - Used when no action is planned for taking advantage of a positive risk.

Accepting a risk (with no other actions) is a reasonable response strategy in many instances, especially when the risk probability and impact is low. Risks may be accepted actively or passively.

Active acceptance requires the advance development of an appropriate contingency action to respond to the risk, should it occur. An active acceptance strategy for any particular risk could include a) developing a contingency action plan, b) developing a fallback action in advance, or c) adding a contingency reserve (contingency allowance) to the project schedule and/or budget as appropriate.

Passive acceptance is a reasonable option with very low probability/impact risks. Passive acceptance requires no response action planned in advance. Instead a planned action is developed only if and when the risk occurs (a workaround).

Process Elements

The Plan Risk Responses process has the following Inputs:
- Risk Management Plan - Describes how project risk management will be structured and performed across the project

- Risk Register - List of identified risks

The Plan Risk Responses process uses the following Tools & Techniques:
- Strategies for Negative Risks or Threats - Avoid, transfer, mitigate, accept

- Strategies for Positive Risks or Opportunities - Exploit, share, enhance, accept

- Contingent Response Strategies - Responses planned for implementation if/when certain conditions occur

- Expert Judgment - Expert technical and/or managerial judgment (from any qualified source)

The Plan Risk Responses process has the following Outputs:
- Project Management Plan Updates - Updates to the Project Management Plan as a result of this process (i.e. schedule/cost/quality/procurement/human resource management plans, scope baseline, schedule baseline, cost baseline)

- Project Documents Updates - Updates to other project documentation (i.e. assumptions log updates, technical documentation updates, change requests.

Plan Risk Responses		
This process develops options & actions to reduce threats and enhance opportunities		
Inputs	**Tools and Techniques**	**Outputs**
• Risk Management Plan • Risk Register	• Strategies for Negative Risks or Threats • Strategies for Positive Risks or Opportunities • Contingent Response Strategies • Expert Judgment	• Project Management Plan Updates • Project Documents Updates TSI Study Aid This chart is part of the study aid poster series available at: *www.TrueSolutions.com*

Figure 30.1 Process Elements within Plan Risk Responses

Process Documents

The main output to this process is an update to the Risk Register, in the project documents updates output. As an output from Plan Risk Responses, the Risk Register is now the complete document with all risk information documented.

There are potentially updates to many of the ancillary plans that make up the Project Management Plan. Common management plans that are part of the Project Management Plan like scope, time and cost may be updated. Also, quality, procurement and human resources plans may also see updates.

Process Tasks

The Plan Risk Responses process aligns with one of the defined tasks that a project manager performs when managing a project:

Planning Task #10: "Develop a risk management plan by identifying, analyzing, and prioritizing project risks and defining risk response strategies, in order to manage uncertainty throughout the project life cycle".

Think About It

Instructions: Use this exercise to compare how you practice project management to what is specified in the *PMBOK® Guide Fifth Edition.*

Think about how this process is defined, used and documented in your organization. Write a brief description of how you use this process:

_____

_____

_____

Must Know Concepts

----

1. The Plan Risk Responses process is applied to develop options and determine actions to enhance opportunities (positive risks), and to develop options and determine actions to reduce threats (negative risks).

2. The primary output of the Plan Risk Responses process is the project's completed Risk Register, characterized as Project Documents Updates.

3. Avoidance is one of the strategies for negative risks or threats. Avoidance involves changing the project plan, or condition within the plan, to eliminate the risk.

4. Transference is one of the strategies for negative risks or threats. Risk transfer involves shifting the consequence and ownership of a risk to a third party.

5. Mitigation is one of the strategies for negative risks or threats. Mitigation involves reducing the probability and/or impact of a negative risk to an acceptable threshold.

6. Acceptance is a strategy for both threats and opportunities. With active acceptance, a contingency plan is developed in advance to respond to the risk, should it occur. With passive acceptance, a response action is developed only if and when the risk event occurs.

7. Exploit, Share and Enhance are strategies for positive risks or opportunities.

8. Contingency action is any planned response action to a risk, should it occur.

9. Contingency allowance (or contingency reserve) is a cost buffer or time buffer included in the project plan to compensate for risk and to help reduce the probability of overruns.

Additional Reading

- PMBOK® Guide Fifth Edition: Section 11.5 Plan Risk Responses

Lesson Quiz

Instructions: Circle the correct answer. Answer Key in Appendix A.

1. The Plan Risk Responses process is applied to:

    A. Develop options and determine actions to create positive risks and develop options and determine actions to mitigate negative risks
    B. Develop options and determine actions to enhance opportunities (positive risks) and develop options and determine actions to reduce threats (negative risks)
    C. Develop options and determine actions to eliminate (avoid) negative risks and develop options and determine actions to accept positive risks
    D. Develop options and determine actions to create opportunities for positive risks and develop options and determine contingency actions to negative risks

2. After reviewing the detailed analysis of a risk associated with a particular project activity, you and your project team decide to respond to the risk by contracting with a specialist outside of your organization. This could be an example of:

    A. Active acceptance
    B. Passive acceptance
    C. Mitigation
    D. Transference

3. Plan Risk Responses outputs include:

    A. Project documents updates, project management plan updates
    B. Risk response plan updates, list of residual risks, list of mitigated risks
    C. Risk response plan updates, alleviated risks, contractual agreements
    D. Risk response plan, secondary risks, list of unused potential responses

End of Lesson 30

This page intentionally blank.

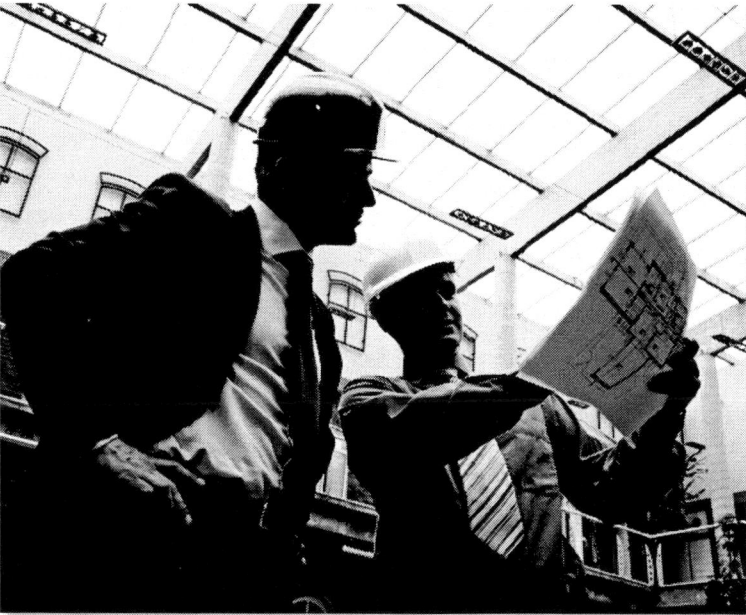

Lesson 31
Develop Project Management Plan

Objectives
At the end of this lesson, you will be able to:
- Describe the purpose of the Develop Project Management Plan process
- Describe the Inputs, Tools and Techniques, and Outputs of the Develop Project Management Plan Process
- Understand what ancillary management plans make up the Project Management Plans
- Understand that the project schedule is part of, but is not the Project Management Plan

Process Locator for the PMBOK® Guide

	Initiating	Planning	Executing	M&C	Closing
Integration					
Scope					
Time					
Cost					
Quality					
Human Resource					
Communications					
Risk					
Procurement					
Stakeholder					

The Develop Project Management Plan simply defines, integrates and coordinates all subsidiary plans and the outputs from other planning processes into a single, cohesive document; the Project Management Plan.

The Develop Project Management Plan process represents both the first step and the final step in project planning.

As the Planning Process Group starts, the Project Charter is a key output from Initiating. The Project Charter becomes a key input to the Develop Project Management Plan process. This signifies that the Develop Project Management Plan process actually starts as soon as the Planning processes are begun and continues concurrently with the other planning processes throughout planning.

Once approved and authorized, the Project Management Plan is used to:

- serve as the baseline for monitoring and measuring project performance during execution
- facilitate stakeholder communications during execution and control
- guide all aspects of the project through execution, monitoring & control, and closing
- document project planning decisions, strategies, alternatives and assumptions

The Project Management Plan is progressively elaborated through updates throughout a project's life cycle. The Project Management Plan consists of two categories of documents: baselines and subsidiary plans. All of these are part of the inputs to this process and are developed during project planning.

The Project Management Plan and Project Schedule are not one and the same. In common application, many persons, including project managers, tend to use "project plan" to mean a Microsoft Project Schedule; however these documents are two distinct things.

Process Elements

The Develop Project Management Plan process has the following Inputs:
- Project Charter - High-level document that authorizes the project and assigns the project manager

- Outputs From Other Processes - Planning documents from the other project planning processes

- Enterprise Environmental Factors - Consideration factors such as; culture, systems, procedures, industry standards

- Organizational Process Assets - Consideration factors such as processes, procedures and corporate knowledge base

The Develop Project Management Plan process uses the following Tools & Techniques:
- Expert Judgment - Expert technical and/or managerial judgment from any qualified source

- Facilitation Techniques - Used to guide development of the project management plan

The Develop Project Management Plan process has the following Output:
- Project Management Plan - The consolidated package of the subsidiary management plans and baselines

Develop Project Management Plan		
This process documents all actions required to define, prepare, integrate, and coordinate all subsidiary plans		
Inputs	**Tools and Techniques**	**Outputs**
• Project Charter • Outputs from Other Processes • Enterprise Environmental Factors • Organizational Process Assets	• Expert Judgment • Facilitation Techniques	• Project Management Plan

Figure 31.1 Process Elements within Develop Project Management Plan

Process Documents

The Project Management Plan is a collection of documents that define the baseline and the approach for the project. Since it is a collection of documents, each document has its own format based on the needs of that particular portion of the project. The Project Management Plan could consist of:

- Project Charter
- Communications Management Plan
- Cost Management Plan
- Human Resource Management Plan
- Procurement Management Plan
- Process Improvement Plan
- Quality Management Plan
- Requirements Management Plan
- Risk Management Plan
- Schedule Management Plan
- Scope Management Plan
- Stakeholder Management Plan
- Cost Baseline
- Schedule Baseline
- Scope Baseline
- Change Management Plan
- Life Cycle and description of project approaches
- Documentation describing key management reviews to be performed during the project

The Project Management Plan should be as detailed as required by project conditions. Some project management plans may summarize the overall project or include less document content if a highly detailed plan is not required.

Process Tasks

The Develop Project Management Plan process aligns with all 12 of the defined tasks that a project manager performs when planning a project. These tasks, in general, cover developing requirements, scope, budget, schedule, human resources, communications, procurement, quality, change management and risk management plans. Specifically, these 2 tasks are highly relevant:

Planning Task #11: "Present the project plan to the key stakeholders (if required), in order to obtain approval to execute the project". This is a formal written document that should have signed approval.

Planning Task #12: "Conduct a kick-off meeting with all key stakeholders, in order to announce the start of the project, communicate the project milestones, and share other relevant information".

Think About It

Instructions: Use this exercise to compare how you practice project management to what is specified in the *PMBOK® Guide Fifth Edition*.

Think about how this process is defined, used and documented in your organization. Write a brief description of what a typical project management plan consists of in your company:

_____

_____

_____

_____

_____

Must Know Concepts

----

1. The Develop Project Management Plan process represents the first process started during planning and the final step in project planning.

2. The Develop Project Management Plan process is applied to gather the outputs from all other planning processes, all subsidiary plans, then assemble them into a single, cohesive document; the Project Management Plan.

3. The primary deliverable (Output) of the Develop Project Management Plan process is the Project Management Plan.

4. The Project Management Plan documents project planning decisions, strategies, alternatives and assumptions.

5. The Project Management Plan serves as the baseline for monitoring and measuring project performance during executing, monitoring & controlling and closing.

6. The Project Management Plan facilitates stakeholder communications during executing, monitoring & controlling and closing.

7. The Project Management Plan guides all aspects of the project through executing, monitoring & controlling and closing.

Additional Reading

- PMBOK® Guide Fifth Edition: Section 4.2   Develop Project Management Plan

Lesson Quiz

Instructions: The actual PMP exam is done via computer. These questions are representative of what you will encounter. Circle the correct answer. Answer Key in Appendix A.

1. Which of the following best describes the Develop Project Management Plan process?

    A. The Develop Project Management Plan process may use a PMIS to help assemble the integrated project plan.
    B. The Develop Project Management Plan process represents the last step in project planning.
    C. The Develop Project Management Plan process is applied to gather the outputs from all other planning processes, along with all subsidiary plans, and assemble them into a single, cohesive document; the Project Management Plan.
    D. The Develop Project Management Plan process is ongoing throughout the project planning phase.

2. You and your project team may use your Project Management Plan to _____.

    A. Document project planning decisions, strategies, alternatives and assumptions
    B. Serve as the baseline for monitoring and measuring project performance during execution and control
    C. Guide all aspects of your project through executing, monitoring & controlling and closing
    D. All of the above

3. Develop Project Management Plan inputs include all of the following except:

    A. Project charter
    B. Past project files
    C. Expert judgment
    D. Project management information system

4. Most project planning work is now complete and your project team is preparing to assemble the integrated Project Management Plan. They look to you for guidance. Your best recommendation may be what?

    A. The size and complexity of the Project Management Plan should be in sensible proportion to the size and complexity of the project.
    B. The Project Management Plan must include all planning outputs, in as much detail as is available.
    C. The Project Management Plan must be as condensed as possible, so as not to overwhelm risk adverse stakeholders.
    D. All of the above.

5   The Project Management Plan includes all of these except:

   A. Baselines
   B. Management plans
   C. Project Documents
   D. All of the above

End of Lesson 31

This page intentionally blank.

Lesson 32
Executing Process Group

Objectives

At the end of this lesson, you will be able to:

- Understand what processes are used in the Executing Process Group
- Understand the purpose for using Executing processes for the project or project phase

Process Locator for the PMBOK® Guide

	Initiating	Planning	Executing	M&C	Closing
Integration					
Scope					
Time					
Cost					
Quality					
Human Resource					
Communications					
Risk					
Procurement					
Stakeholder					

The Executing Process Group consists of eight processes that are intended to manage the work during a project or project phase.

The primary purpose that these Executing processes are performed is to manage the work so that the intended deliverables of the project or phase are created as planned. Executing processes occur in Project Integration Management, Project Quality Management, Project Human Resource Management, Project Communications Management, Project Procurement Management and Project Stakeholder Management knowledge areas in the *PMBOK® Guide Fifth Edition*.

If there was a "keyword" to characterize the Executing Process Group, it might be "deliverables". The most important output of the entire process group is the deliverables created for the project.

The Executing processes work very closely and have a high degree of interaction with each other. In addition, these Executing processes also work very closely with the processes in the Monitoring and Controlling process group. Executing processes focus on producing deliverables, the Monitoring and Controlling processes concentrate on confirming that the planned deliverables are created and that these outputs meet the planned specifications and requirements.

Executing Tasks

On your PMP Exam, you will encounter many questions that will test your understanding of Executing processes. These questions will generally focus on the following Executing tasks.

As a PMP or project manager executing a project (or project phase), you may be required to:

1. Obtain and manage project resources including out-sourced deliverables by following the procurement plan, in order to ensure successful project execution.

2. Execute the tasks as defined in the project management plan, in order to achieve the project deliverables within budget, schedule and defined quality.

3. Implement the quality management plan using the appropriate tools and techniques, in order to ensure that work is being performed according to required quality standards.

4. Implement approved changes according to the change management plan, in order to meet project requirements.

5. Implement approved actions (e.g. workarounds) by following the risk management plan, in order to minimize the impact of the risks on the project.

6. Maximize team performance through leading, mentoring, training, and motivating team members.

Knowledge Requirements

As a PMP applying Executing processes in real-world projects, you will be required to possess in-depth knowledge in several project specific areas, as well as a broad knowledge of project management in general. The PMP Exam will test your understanding of these knowledge specifics.

By developing a familiarity with these knowledge specifics, you will better understand the context of many PMP Exam questions. As you progress through the Ultimate PMP Exam Prep Guide, you will see each of these areas mentioned. Please give some thought to each item as it relates to your own project management experiences with past and current projects.

Remember, the PMP or project manager is always required to have a very broad base of knowledge to work across the entire organization, and effectively perform project management.

As a PMP or project manager applying Executing processes, you may be expected to have knowledge of:

1. Project monitoring tools and techniques

2. Elements of a statement of work

3. Interaction of WBS elements within the project schedule

4. Project budgeting tools and techniques

5. Quality standard tools

6. Continuous improvement processes

Process Group Interactions

Study Tip
Be sure to understand the Process Group Interactions We have previously exposed and discussed information about process group interactions. During the Executing phases or portions of the project a high degree of interaction occurs between the Executing *process group* and the Monitoring and Controlling *process group*. The intent of the Executing process group is to create project deliverables. The intent of the Monitoring and Controlling process group is to make sure they are the right deliverables. When completing the work of the project, processes from both process groups have to work together very closely and interact frequently in order to manage the project and its outcomes. **As you read the Ultimate PMP Exam Prep Guide,** *remember to look for process flows (defined by one output becoming the input to another process) that define the flows and interactions that occur on a typical project.*

Knowledge Check

Read the recommended chapters in the PMBOK® Guide, associated with the Executing Process Group processes before attempting this exercise.

After you have read all of the lesson material and the readings in the PMBOK® Guide, your goal is to match the executing processes to the Executing Process Group and correct PMBOK® Guide Knowledge Area. Use the TSI Ultimate PMP Exam Prep Match Card Set to perform this exercise.

If you do not have a Match Card Set, create a 3x5 card for each Process Group, Knowledge Area and Process and match them to the correct Executing process in a grid relative to the Process Group and Knowledge Area.

Use page 61 in the PMBOK® Guide as your example and to check your matches after you have performed the matching exercise.

End of Lesson 32

Lesson 33
Direct and Manage Project Work

Objectives

At the end of this lesson, you will be able to:

- Describe the purpose of the Direct and Manage Project Work process
- Describe the Inputs, Tools and Techniques, and Outputs of the Direct and Manage Project Work process
- Describe the key interpersonal skills which are required for effective project management in project environments

Process Locator for the PMBOK® Guide

	Initiating	Planning	Executing	M&C	Closing
Integration			▓▓▓		
Scope					
Time					
Cost					
Quality					
Human Resource					
Communications					
Risk					
Procurement					
Stakeholder					

Direct and Manage Project Work is the process of coordinating and directing all the resources that exist across the project, in carrying out the Project Management Plan.

Direct and Manage Project Work is performed in order to successfully execute the Project Management Plan. The project manager and team must constantly monitor and measure performance against baselines, so that timely corrective action can be taken, as appropriate. Changes must be incorporated into the project as approved and, cost and schedule forecasts must be updated periodically, as appropriate.

During project execution, it is typical that most project costs are expended during this period.

The understanding and appropriate use of general management skills is most important during project execution. Accordingly, this chapter begins with primers in three essential people-skills in project environments: conflict management, negotiation, and leadership.

Conflict Management

Three truths about conflict in project environments

1. Conflict manifests when there are incompatible goals, thoughts or emotions within or between individuals or groups.
2. Conflict is inevitable in project environments, but it does not have to be destructive.
3. Project staff should be sensitive to both the positive and negative values of conflict and its effect on performance

The 'Seven Sources of Conflict' in Project Environments

From studies conducted by Thamhain & Wilemon (1975) and Posner (1986):

1. Schedules
2. Cost/Budget
3. Priorities
4. Human Resources
5. Technical Trade-offs
6. Personality
7. Administrative Procedures

Resolving Conflict in Project Environments

Here are six common approaches for resolving conflicts. Project managers should select the approach most appropriate for any particular situation.

Confronting (also termed Problem Solving or Negotiating) - Confronting tackles the disagreement head-on. Successful confronting usually requires mature, competent parties who are genuinely interested in finding an acceptable solution. Confronting takes longer, but can provide an ultimate resolution

Collaborating - This may be a good approach when the situation can't be compromised. It incorporates viewpoints from both parties to help build a consensus resolution. Collaborating can provide a long-term resolution

Compromising (also termed Bargaining) - Compromising incorporates the use of trade-off exchanges, to bring some satisfaction to both parties. A permanent resolution can be achieved, but some aspects of the issue may be compromised. With compromising, both sides lose something and hard feelings can return

Smoothing (also termed Accommodating) - This can be a good interim approach to temporarily keep-the-peace. With smoothing, agreements are emphasized, disagreements are avoided. Smoothing typically provides short-term relief, but fails to provide a permanent resolution

Withdrawing (also termed Avoidance) - Better termed throwing-in-the-towel, retreat, refusal to deal with the conflict, ignoring it or denial. This may not be an ideal approach, as withdrawing never resolves a conflict. It can, however, be a sensible temporary approach when 'cooling off' will help

Forcing - This involves the use of dominance. Forcing is typically a technique of last resort reserved for times when there is no common ground, when time is of the essence, or when the parties are uncooperative. Forcing can be fast and decisive, but generally leaves hard feelings. Forcing can provide a definitive resolution.

Negotiating In Project Environments

Negotiating in project environments typically involves bargaining for resources, bargaining for information and/or bargaining for actual work.

Negotiation is the process through which parties with differing interests reach agreement.

Negotiable items in the project environment may include items and elements such as: issues, changes, services and supplies, resources and performance measurement criteria.

When you are negotiating your project parameters, your negotiating partners generally include all or some of your stakeholders. For example: executives, functional managers, other project managers, subject matters experts, clients or customer and procurement specialists.

There are 3 primary steps to successful negotiating:

1. Separate the problem from the people
   - Put yourself in the other persons position
   - Separate the substance of negotiation from relationships and personalities
   - Find ways to give credit for the advice and ideas of others
   - Develop options that are fair to all parties
   - Attack the problem, not each other
   - Define the problem – not the symptom

2. Focus on common interests
   - Explore your shared interests instead of opposing views
   - Acknowledge the interests of the other party
   - Be firm in dealing with the problem, but flexible in exploring solutions and ideas

3. Create options that include shared interests

- Before starting negotiation, create possible solutions that reflect shared interests
- Focus on adjusting the most mutually attractive solution to reach a final agreement

Project Leadership

Leadership in project environments is the process of
- Creating a vision
- Communicating that vision to others
- Communicating a realistic plan to achieve the vision
- Translating the vision into reality through people, rather than over people

Effective leadership skills are essential to ensure long term success as a project manager. Successfully managing a project team, motivating stakeholders and creating a high-performance, innovative project environment requires good leadership, influence skills, and political awareness in order to navigate a project to completion.

There are several types of power found in the leadership role. These types of power include:

Reward Power - This type power is derived from the leader's authority to reward desired behavior ... with salary increases, promotions, vacations, perks and/or other positive incentives

Punishment Power - This type of power is derived from the leader's authority to punish undesirable behavior ... with termination, pay docking, reprimands and/or other negative incentives

Referent Power - Referent power is earned power. Leaders who are admired by others as a role model, usually get desired behavior from their people through this referent (or earned) power

Expert Power - This is closely related to referent power. It is earned when the leader is viewed as an expert and gains desired behavior because people believe their leader 'knows best'

Title Power - This is the type of power derived by the actual title or position of the leader, as authorized by senior/executive management. It is also known as Legitimate Power.

Information Power - This type power is derived by controlling the distribution of key information to people. 'Information is power'

Charismatic Power - This type of power is derived through the use of extraordinary communication skills. This type of 'influence' power can be very useful for project managers who function in environments where they have limited formal authority

Contacts Power - This type of power is derived through alliances and networks with influential people in the organization

Total power is often derived from a combination of several individual sources.

Process Elements

The Direct and Manage Project Work process has the following Inputs:
- Project Management Plan - The consolidated package of the subsidiary plans and baselines

- Approved Change Requests - Documented, authorized changes that expand or reduce scope

- Enterprise Environmental Factors - Consideration factors such as; culture, systems, procedures, industry standards

- Organizational Process Assets - Consideration factors such as processes, procedures and corporate knowledge base

The Direct and Manage Project Work process uses the following Tools & Techniques:
- Expert Judgment - Expert technical and/or managerial judgment (from any qualified source)

- Project Management Information System - (PMIS) Automated system to help the team execute planned activities

- Meetings - Meetings required to direct and manage project work

The Direct and Manage Project Work process has the following Outputs:
- Deliverables - Results, products and/or capabilities (unique, verifiable outcomes) of activities performed

- Work Performance Data - Raw data related to deliverable status, schedule progress, and costs incurred

- Change Requests - Requests for changes to scope, cost, budget, schedule, or policies and procedures

- Project Management Plan Updates - Updates to the Project Management Plan as a result of this process

- Project Documents Updates - Updates to other project documentation

Direct and Manage Project Work		
This process executes the work defined in the project management plan		
Inputs	**Tools and Techniques**	**Outputs**
• Project Management Plan	• Expert Judgment	• Deliverables
• Approved Change Requests	• Project Management Information System	• Work Performance Data
• Enterprise Environmental Factors	• Meetings	• Change Requests
• Organizational Process Assets		• Project Management Plan Updates
		• Project Documents Updates

Figure 33.1 Process Elements within Direct and Manage Project Work

Process Documents

The key result from the process and Direct and Manage Project Work is work results or deliverables. The project manager may manage work through use of a work authorization system. Most work authorization systems employ specific documentation to track work results.

An example of a simple work results document is shown below.

Work Results Guidelines

Project Name:		
Prepared by:		
Date:		
Deliverable #1		
Completed as of Scheduled Date:		
Not completed as of Scheduled Date:		
Reason, if not completed		
Quality Standards:	**Met**	**Not Met**
Quality Issues		
Costs Incurred		
On Budget	**Under Budget by**	**Over Budget by**
Additional Remarks:		
Deliverable #2		
Completed as of Scheduled Date:		
Not completed as of Scheduled Date:		
Reason, if not completed		
Quality Standards:	**Met**	**Not Met**
Quality Issues		
Costs Incurred		
On Budget	**Under Budget by**	**Over Budget by**
Additional Remarks:		
Reported by	**Date**	

Application Aid

This form is available individually or as part of a set at:
www.TrueSolutions.com

Process Tasks

The Direct and Manage Project Work process aligns with all 6 of the defined tasks that a project manager performs when executing a project. These tasks, in general, cover managing resources, task execution, quality, changes and team performance. Specifically, one task is highly relevant:

Executing Task #2: "Execute the tasks as defined in the project plan, in order to achieve the project deliverables within budget and schedule".

Think About It

Instructions: Use this exercise to compare how you practice project management to what is specified in the *PMBOK® Guide Fifth Edition.* Think about how this process is defined, used and documented in your organization. Write a brief description of how you use manage project work:

_____

_____

_____

_____

_____

Must Know Concepts

----

1. The Direct and Manage Project Work process is applied by the project manager and project team to coordinate and direct all the resources to carry out the Project Management Plan.

2. When using the Direct and Manage Project Work process, the project manager and team must monitor and measure performance against baselines, so corrective action can be taken.

3. The primary deliverable (Outputs) of the Direct and Manage Project Work process are work results (deliverables).

4. Approved change requests become a key input to Direct and Manage Project Work in order to incorporate changes into the project.

5. The effective use of people skills is essential to achieve success during project execution.

6. Formal work authorization systems are helpful to control project work, especially with respect to minimizing unnecessary scope expansion (scope creep).

Additional Reading

- PMBOK® Guide Fifth Edition: Section 4.3   Direct and Manage Project Work

Lesson Quiz

Instructions: The actual PMP exam is done via computer. These questions are representative of what you will encounter. Circle the correct answer. Answer Key in Appendix A.

1. The conflict resolution technique in which both sides lose something is called?

   A. Bargaining
   B. Negotiating
   C. Problem Solving
   D. Accommodating

2. Which of the following is *least* true?

   A. To successfully execute the project management plan, the project manager and team must constantly monitor and measure performance against baselines, so correction action can be taken.
   B. The effective use of people skills is essential to achieve success during project execution.
   C. In most projects, most of the project budget is spent during the project execution phase.
   D. Formal work authorization systems are used to account for project spending, by category, in accordance with the cost budget chart of accounts.

3. Direct and Manage Project Work outputs include _____.

   A. Deliverables, project documents
   B. Deliverables, project management plan updates
   C. Deliverables, project schedule
   D. Deliverables, stakeholder register

4. You, as project manager, are in the fortunate position of having a loyal, motivated and respectful project core team. This is largely due to the fact that you have thirty years of hands-on experience, successfully bringing-in projects on-time, on-budget and within scope. This position of personal leadership power you possess could be an example of

   _____.

   A. Expert power
   B. Title power
   C. Contacts power
   D. Charismatic power

5 You are in the executing phase of your project and are holding meetings with your project team and other stakeholders to discuss the progress of the project deliverables. Your meetings are not progressing well; people are not focused on the meeting topics and seem to be distracted. As project manager, what may be your best recommendation for getting stakeholders engaged?

A. Try to accomplish multiple purposes to get more done in one meeting
B. Hold face-to-face meetings
C. Hold virtual meetings using conferencing tools
D. Document meeting minutes

6 Project Management Plan Updates, an Output of Direct and Manage Project Work, may include updates to all of the following except:

A. Scope Management Plan
B. Project Documents
C. Cost Management Plan
D. Process Improvement Plan

7 Project Documents Updates, an Output of Direct and Manage Project Work, may include updates to all of the following except:

A. Requirements Documentation
B. Project Management Plan
C. Project Logs
D. Stakeholder Register

End of Lesson 33

This page intentionally blank.

Lesson 34
Acquire Project Team

Objectives
At the end of this lesson, you will be able to:
- Describe the purpose of the Acquire Project Team process
- Describe the Inputs, Tools and Techniques, and Outputs of the Acquire Project Team process
- Describe common methods to acquire the project team
- Describe when the project manager will acquire the project team

Process Locator for the PMBOK® Guide

	Initiating	Planning	Executing	M&C	Closing
Integration					
Scope					
Time					
Cost					
Quality					
Human Resource			▓		
Communications					
Risk					
Procurement					
Stakeholder					

The Acquire Project Team process is applied to get needed human resources assigned and working on the project.

When considering people to support the project, the project team should factor things such as experience, availability, competencies, personal characteristics and whether or not the potential resource has an interest in working on the project. Many times, especially in matrix organizations, you as project manager may need to use your best negotiating skills to get the people you want from their functional manager(s).

The Acquire Project Team process is defined as an executing process in the *PMBOK® Guide Fifth Edition*. This does not mean that the project manager has to wait until late in the project to acquire the project team. Best practice guidelines would suggest that a core project team will be acquired early in the project – immediately after the project charter is issued. Other human resources will be brought on throughout the project as needed. It will be important that the project manager plan carefully and not acquire resources without first considering the Develop Human Resource Plan process and its outcomes: the Staffing Management Plan and Roles and Responsibilities for the project.

An important consideration for the project manager will be to negotiate for and acquire resources which have the needed levels of competency that are required to execute the project. If the available resources do not have the required competencies and experience, if there are not sufficient resources available to perform project activities or if resources cannot be acquired in a timely manner, the project manager will return to the planning processes and re-plan portions of the project that are affected by differences in planned human resources.

The Acquire Project Team process is complete when the project is reliably staffed with appropriate people. Many project teams publish a formal team directory when staffing is complete.

Process Elements

The Acquire Project Team process has the following Inputs:
- Human Resource Management Plan – Documented human resource requirements for the project

- Enterprise Environmental Factors - Consideration factors such as; culture, systems, procedures, industry standards

- Organizational Process Assets - Consideration factors such as processes, procedures and corporate knowledge base

The Acquire Project Team process uses the following Tools & Techniques:
- Pre-Assignment - Predefined project staff assignments. Example: Staff was identified in the project charter

- Negotiation - Influential discussions (typically with functional managers) to fill project staff assignments

- Acquisition - Obtaining project staff from outside sources (if necessary), using project procurement management

- Virtual Teams - Teams with shared goals working with little or no face-to-face communications

- Multi-Criteria Decision Analysis – Basing selection criteria on multiple elements such as availability, cost, experience, ability, knowledge, skills, attitude and international factors

The Acquire Project Team process has the following Output:
- Project Staff Assignments -The appropriate people, reliably assigned to staff the project

- Resource Calendars - Documents the time periods each team member can work on the project

- Project Management Plan Updates - Updates to the Project Management Plan as a result of this process

Acquire Project Team		
This process obtains needed project human resources		
Inputs	**Tools and Techniques**	**Outputs**
• Human Resource Management Plan • Enterprise Environmental Factors • Organizational Process Assets	• Pre-Assignment • Negotiation • Acquisition • Virtual Teams • Multi-Criteria Decision Analysis	• Project Staff Assignments • Resource Calendars • Project Management Plan Updates *TSI* Study Aid This chart is part of the study aid poster series available at: *www.TrueSolutions.com*

Figure 34.1 Process Elements within Acquire Project Team

Process Documents

Process documents used in this process will vary depending on the tools employed. Interview records, selection outcomes, resource calendars showing availability all may be employed and documented as part of this process. The results from using these tools will be documented in hiring or acquisition decisions.

Process Tasks

The Acquire Project Team process aligns with one of the defined tasks that a project manager performs when managing a project:

Executing Task #1: "Obtain and manage project resources including out-sourced deliverables by following the procurement plan, in order to ensure successful project execution".

Think About it

Instructions: Use this exercise to compare how you practice project management to what is specified in the *PMBOK® Guide Fifth Edition.*

Think about how this process is defined, used and documented in your organization. Write a brief description of how you use this process:

_____

_____

_____

_____

_____

What specific Inputs, Tools or Techniques do you use as part of this process in your organization?

_____

_____

_____

_____

Are the outcomes from this process different in your organization or experiences?

_____

_____

_____

Must Know Concepts

1. The Acquire Project Team process is applied to obtain and assign needed human resources (people) to the project.

2. The project manager will negotiate with functional managers and other sources of possible project team members as necessary to obtain the people a project manager desires.

3. The project manager will use procurement processes to acquire staff if external staff are used for the project

4. The primary deliverable (Output) of the Acquire Project Team process is project staff assignments.

Additional Reading

- PMBOK® Guide Fifth Edition: Section 9.2   Acquire Project Team

Lesson Quiz

Instructions: The actual PMP exam is done via computer. These questions are representative of what you will encounter. Circle the correct answer. Answer Key in Appendix A.

1. Which of the following best describes the Acquire Project Team process?

   A. The Acquire Project Team process is applied to obtain needed human resources (people) from functional managers.
   B. The Acquire Project Team process is applied to assign needed human resources (people) to the project directory.
   C. The Acquire Project Team process is applied to assign project team roles and responsibilities.
   D. The Acquire Project Team process is applied to obtain and assign needed human resources (people) to the project.

2. Which statement is *least* true?

   A. In matrix organizations, project managers may have to negotiate with functional managers to obtain needed people.
   B. In strong matrix organization, project managers may have more authority than functional managers.
   C. In functional organizations, it is the project sponsor's responsibility to assign project staff.
   D. A Responsibility Assignment Matrix (RAM) illustrates assignments and levels of authority/responsibility, as a function of WBS elements. There is no time associated with a RAM.

3. Acquire project team tools and techniques include:

   A. Pre-assignment, resource calendars
   B. Negotiation, acquisitions
   C. Virtual teams, resource calendars
   D. Project staff assignments, acquisitions

4. You are assigned to manage an important project for your organization. This project is the direct result of your company winning a competitive bid. You are told that your project team is already selected and assigned. What is the likely reason for staff being assigned before the project even begins?

   A. Your project sponsor does not fully trust you to make staff assignment decisions.
   B. Specific staff members were part of your company's winning proposal.
   C. Staff assignment is the responsibility of your company's Human Resources department.
   D. Your company assigns the same personnel to every project.

End of Lesson 34

Lesson 35
Develop Project Team

Objectives

At the end of this lesson, you will be able to:

- Describe the purpose of the Develop Project Team process
- Describe the Inputs, Tools and Techniques, and Outputs of the Develop Project Team process
- Understand ways that the project manager can facilitate team building within the project team

Process Locator for the PMBOK® Guide

	Initiating	Planning	Executing	M&C	Closing
Integration					
Scope					
Time					
Cost					
Quality					
Human Resource			▓		
Communications					
Risk					
Procurement					
Stakeholder					

Develop Project Team is the process of enhancing the ability of individual team members (skills and team cohesiveness) to enhance overall project performance.

In practice, team development is a continuous process applied from the time the project team comes together until the team disbands. In concept, stronger individuals will naturally create a stronger team.

Generally, Develop Project Team tools include:

- Training
- Team-building activities
- Recognition and rewards
- Co-location

Some project managers like to establish a project war room where core team members can be co-located to work in close proximity during the project.

In some matrix organizations, team development can be extra challenging when team members report to both the project manager and to their functional manager. In most organizations, the resource will be more closely aligned with their functional manager and will minimize input from the project manager on any organizational issues other than those directly relating to the project.

Successful team development requires a practical understanding of the dynamics of human behavior to create a project environment in which team members feel motivated to excel.

- Team members should desire to stay and grow with the project
- Team members should desire to fulfill their responsibilities and perform assigned tasks
- Team members should desire to go beyond average performance, to demonstrate creativity and innovation

Because motivation is a key management skill in team development, we begin this lesson with a motivation primer.

Motivation Theories

Motivation is internal, triggered by the needs and desires that create drive in people. Motivational theories are broken into two categories.

Content Theories focus on motivating desired behavior by satisfying specific motivation factors, such as money, shelter, security, growth and achievement.

Maslow's Hierarchy of Needs - This is probably the best known content theory. Maslow identifies five levels of needs, in ascending order of priority: Physiological, Safety, Social, Esteem, Self Actualization. According to this theory, a person must satisfy lower level needs before ascending the pyramid. Maslow believes it is 'unfulfilled needs' that serve as motivators. The diagram is shown below.

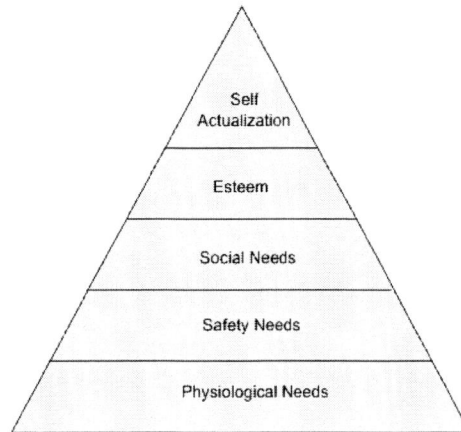

Figure 35.1 Maslow's Hierarchy of Needs

Alderfer's ERG Needs - Alderfer maintains that people have three sets of equally important fundamental motivators; Existence Needs (food, shelter), Relatedness Needs (relationships) and Growth Needs (development)

Herzberg's Motivator/Hygiene Theory - Herzberg maintains that hygiene factors (money, environment, relationships) are essential to maintain harmony, but do not motivate. Herzberg's motivators include advancement, recognition and responsibility

Process Theories focus on producing desired behavior by employing specific motivational processes.

- McGregor's Theory X - Theory Y - probably the best known process theory, McGregor maintains that Theory X managers assume all people dislike work and try to avoid it. They motivate accordingly, usually with a strict hand. Theory Y managers assume all people can be high achievers when motivated, then motivate accordingly

- Morse & Lorsch's Contingency Theory - motivation is driven by the desire to achieve competence

- Latham & Locke's Goal-setting Theory - motivation is driven by the desire to achieve goals

- Vroom's Expectancy Theory - motivation is driven by the expectation of a reward

- Skinner's Reinforcement Theory - motivation is driven by the influence of a previous experience

- Adams' Equity Theory - motivation is driven by a core desire to be treated equitably

Process Elements

The Develop Project Team process has the following Inputs:
- Human Resource Management Plan – Documented human resource requirements for the project

- Project Staff Assignments - The appropriate people, reliably assigned to staff the project

- Resource Calendars - Documents the time periods each team member can work on the project

The Develop Project Team process uses the following Tools & Techniques:
- Interpersonal Skills - The broad set of 'soft skills' important to team development

- Training - Activities designed to enhance the competencies of project team members

- Team-Building Activities - Actions designed to enhance interpersonal relationships among team members

- Ground Rules - Documented team rules to establish clear expectations with respect to acceptable behavior

- Co-Location -The placing of team members in the same physical location, to enhance team performance

- Recognition and Rewards - Formal management actions that recognize and reward desirable behavior

- Personnel Assessment Tools - Surveys, assessments, interviews, skill tests and focus groups

The Develop Project Team process has the following Outputs:
- Team Performance Assessments - Formal and/or informal assessments of the team's effectiveness

- Enterprise Environmental Factors Updates - Updates to employee training records and skill assessments

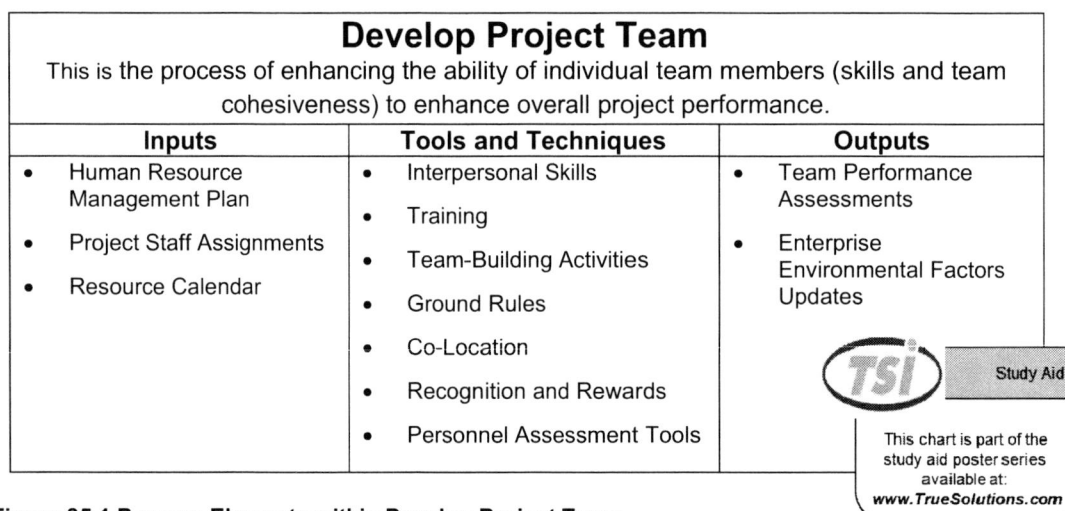

Develop Project Team
This is the process of enhancing the ability of individual team members (skills and team cohesiveness) to enhance overall project performance.

Inputs	Tools and Techniques	Outputs
• Human Resource Management Plan • Project Staff Assignments • Resource Calendar	• Interpersonal Skills • Training • Team-Building Activities • Ground Rules • Co-Location • Recognition and Rewards • Personnel Assessment Tools	• Team Performance Assessments • Enterprise Environmental Factors Updates

TSI Study Aid

This chart is part of the study aid poster series available at: www.TrueSolutions.com

Figure 35.1 Process Elements within Develop Project Team

Process Tasks

The Develop Project Team process aligns with one of the defined tasks that a project manager performs when managing a project:

Executing Task #6: "Maximize team performance through leading, mentoring, training and motivating team members".

Think About It

Instructions: Use this exercise to compare how you practice project management to what is specified in the *PMBOK® Guide Fifth Edition.* Best Practices suggest that the following items are used during the Develop Project Team process.

Which of these items do you use when practicing project management?

☐ Training

☐ Co-location of the team

☐ Ground rules for behavior

☐ Team-building activities

☐ Recognition and rewards

Which of these tools do you use for team building?

_____

_____

Must Know Concepts
----

1. Develop Project Team is the process of enhancing the ability of individual team members (skills and team cohesiveness) to enhance overall project performance.

2. In some matrix organizations, team development can be extra challenging when team members report to both the project manager and to their functional manager.

3. The primary deliverable (Output) of the Develop Project Team process is team performance assessments.

4. Important content theories of motivation include Maslow's Hierarchy of Needs and Herzberg's Motivator/Hygiene Theory.

5. Important process theories of motivation include McGregor's Theory X - Theory Y.

Additional Reading

- PMBOK® Guide Fifth Edition: Section 9.3   Develop Project Team

Lesson Quiz

Instructions: The actual PMP exam is done via computer. These questions are representative of what you will encounter. Circle the correct answer. Answer Key in Appendix A.

1. Develop Project Team inputs include all of the following *except:*

    A. Project staff assignments
    B. Resource calendars
    C. Team-building activities
    D. Human Resources Management Plan

2. Which of these statements best describes the Develop Project Team process?

    A. Develop Project Team is the process of creating the project's rewards and recognition procedures.
    B. Develop Project Team is the process of enhancing the ability of individual team members to enhance overall project performance.
    C. Develop Project Team is the process of creating the project team's motivation procedures.
    D. Develop Project Team is the process of co-locating team members to a single project war room; which will serve as the team's headquarters during the project.

3. The highest level in Maslow's Hierarchy of Needs is:

    A. Safety
    B. Esteem
    C. Self Actualization
    D. Self Preservation

4. Which of the following statements is most true?

    A. Co-location can include moving team members into a more central area when team members already work at the same physical location, but should not include relocating team members from other geographic locations.
    B. Team development is generally easier in functional organizations
    C. In some organizations, team development can be extra challenging when team members report to both the project manager and to their functional manager
    D. Team development procedures should be developed during Develop Project Charter

End of Lesson 35

This page intentionally blank.

Lesson 36
Manage Project Team

Objectives
At the end of this lesson, you will be able to:
- Describe the purpose of the Manage Project Team process
- Describe the Inputs, Tools and Techniques, and Outputs of the Manage Project Team process
- Understand the use of an Issues Log in managing resources

Process Locator for the PMBOK® Guide

	Initiating	Planning	Executing	M&C	Closing
Integration					
Scope					
Time					
Cost					
Quality					
Human Resource			▓		
Communications					
Risk					
Procurement					
Stakeholder					

We apply the Manage Project Team process to address performance, behavior, issues and conflicts associated specifically with project team members.

Manage Project Team process involves tracking and appraising team member performance, resolving issues, observing team behavior, managing conflicts and providing feedback. In matrix organizations, dual reporting roles of team members typically create complications that must be managed properly by the project manager. Effectively managing these dual reporting situations is often a critical success factor in project environments.

Of course, the intended outcome of the Manage Project Team process is enhanced overall project performance.

Process Elements

The Manage Project Team process has the following Inputs:
- Human Resource Management Plan - Documented human resource requirements for the project

- Project Staff Assignments -The appropriate people, reliably assigned to staff the project

- Team Performance Assessments - Formal and/or informal assessments of the team's effectiveness

- Issues Log - A log of who is responsible for issues resolution

- Work Performance Reports - S-curves, bar charts, tables, histograms, etc. that summarize team member performance

- Organizational Process Assets - Consideration factors such as processes, procedures and corporate knowledge base

The Manage Project Team process uses the following Tools & Techniques:
- Observation and Conversation - Used to stay in-touch with project work and team member attitudes

- Project Performance Appraisals - Formal and/or informal appraisals to provide feedback to team members

- Conflict Management - Used to enhance productivity and create positive working relationships

- Interpersonal Skills - The broad set of 'soft skills' important to team development

The Manage Project Team process has the following Outputs:
- Change Requests - Request for changes to scope, schedule, costs, or processes or other project documentation

- Project Management Plan Updates – updates to the Project Management Plan as a result of this process

- Project Documents Updates - Updates to other project documentation

- Enterprise Environmental Factor Updates - Updates to employee training records and skill assessments

- Organizational Process Asset Updates - Updates to corporate docs, guidelines, procedures, historical information, etc.

Manage Project Team		
This process is applied to address performance, behavior, issues and conflicts associated specifically with project team members.		
Inputs	**Tools and Techniques**	**Outputs**
• Human Resource Management Plan	• Observation and Conversation	• Change Requests
• Project Staff Assignments	• Project Performance Appraisals	• Project Management Plan Updates
• Team Performance Assessments	• Conflict Management	• Project Documents Updates
• Issue Log	• Interpersonal Skills	• Enterprise Environmental Factor Updates
• Work Performance Reports		• Organizational Process Assets Updates
• Organizational Process Assets		

Figure 36.1 Process Elements within Manage Project Team

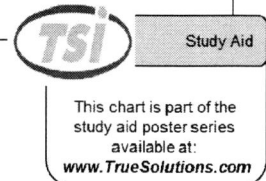

Process Documents

One of the most important documents that will be used in this process is the Issues Log. The Issues Log as applied to project management can be a public document concerned directly with all issues that are being addressed on the project. In this process, many times the project manager is addressing and documenting sensitive human resource issues. The issues log as applied here may be a semi-public document that is held by the project manager and discussed only with human resource personnel and project senior managers.

Sometimes this human resources Issues Log is simply a journal kept by the project manager – unless personnel action is required. The project manager should determine what is appropriate for the project and organizational culture that they are working in.

Process Tasks

The Manage Project Team process aligns with one of the defined tasks that a project manager performs when managing a project:

Executing Task #6: "Maximize team performance through leading, mentoring, training and motivating team members".

Think About It

We all know there will be conflicts on projects. In many cases, these situations can be resolved quickly. However, there are times when conflicts with team members cannot always be resolved. In this situation, I was brought in as the program manager from outside of an organization. Upon my arrival, one of the project managers appeared distant and uncooperative. We met and discussed her concerns. She explained she was previously promised my position and was extremely unhappy regarding my arrival to the PMO. After reviewing her concerns with my sponsor, I discovered her performance was not meeting the sponsor's expectations and he felt she was not ready to take on the additional responsibility. However, the sponsor and her supervisor had not documented their concerns nor communicated them to her during the past year.

The project manager and I sat down and put a plan together to position her to ultimately assume my role since I had only planned to remain in this position for six months. The first month was great, however, the second month I noticed her behavior reverting back to the original dissatisfactions. We continued to meet and I began to document the negative behavior on an issues report, reviewed only by the sponsor and myself. Despite the attempts to correct the problems, the project manager could not get past her resentment and anger of not having the program manager position. Finally, she was released from the company. The issues report became a key document used to make the case and show the attempts to resolve the problems.

Fortunately, within two weeks of her departure, the team improved their overall performance that impacted the entire organization. Unfortunately, her behavior was left unaddressed for a year and that negatively affected the organization. If an issues report had been used and her negative behavior addressed in a timely manner, she may have been the appropriate choice when the program manager position became available.

Contributed by Sharron Frohner, PMP

Must Know Concepts
----

1. The Manage Project Team process is applied to address performance, behavior, issues and conflicts associated specifically with project team members.

2. Observation and conversation are key methods to stay in touch with the work and attitudes of project team members.

3. Successful conflict management results in greater productivity and positive working relationships.

Additional Reading

- PMBOK® Guide Fifth Edition: Section 9.4   Manage Project Team

Lesson Quiz

Instructions: The actual PMP exam is done via computer. These questions are representative of what you will encounter. Circle the correct answer. Answer Key in Appendix A.

1. Manage Project Team inputs include:

    A. Team performance assessments, work performance reports, organizational process assets, issue log
    B. Team performance assessments, conflict management, organizational process assets, project staff assignments
    C. Observation and conversation, project staff assignments, issue log, change requests
    D. Project performance appraisals, interpersonal skills, project staff assignments, performance reports

2. Which of the following is *most* true?

    A. Staffing changes do not have to be processed through the Perform Integrated Change Control process
    B. An issue log is a written document which provides visibility and tracking of responsible party and resolution due dates for a particular issue
    C. Issues are also known as risks
    D. Conflict should be avoided at all costs during a project

3. The Manage Project Team process is applied to:

    A. Enhance the performance of project team members, to enhance the overall project performance
    B. Coordinate training for project team members and to create the project's reward and recognition system
    C. Address performance, behavior, issues and conflicts associated specifically with project team members
    D. Develop options and determine actions to create opportunities for project team member advancement

End of Lesson 36

This page intentionally blank.

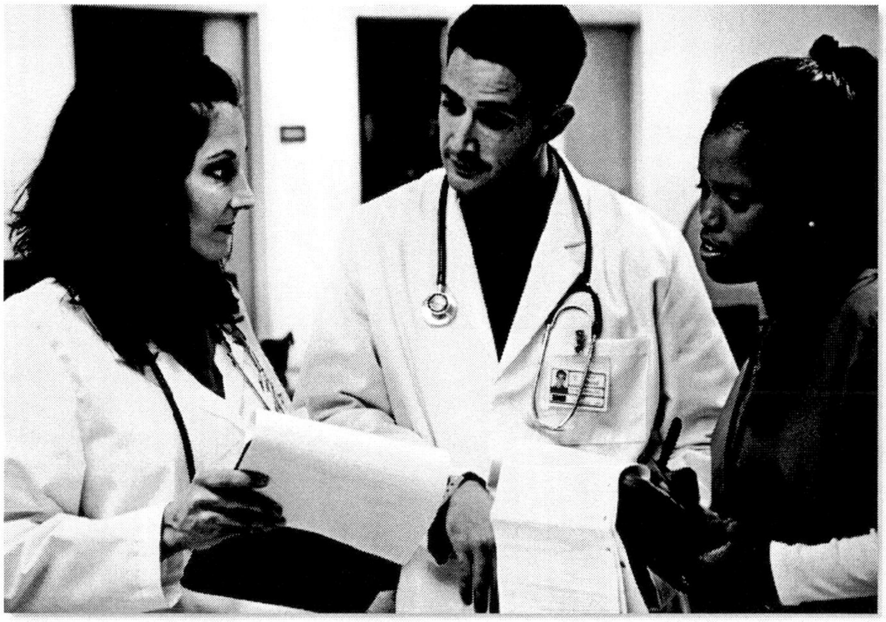

37

Lesson 37
Manage Communications

Objectives

At the end of this lesson, you will be able to:

- Describe the purpose of the Manage Communications process
- Describe the Inputs, Tools and Techniques, and Outputs of the Manage Communications process
- Understand that all project documents become part of "organizational process assets"

Process Locator for the PMBOK® Guide

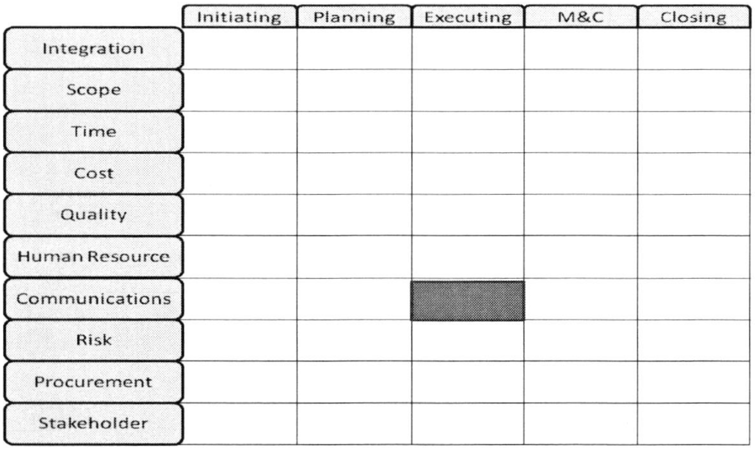
Initiating
Planning
Executing
M&C
Closing
Integration
Scope
Time
Cost
Quality
Human Resource
Communications
Risk
Procurement
Stakeholder

Manage Communications is the communications process of making project information available to project stakeholders, as determined and documented in the Communications Management Plan.

Manage Communications process involves the activities that are necessary to create, distribute, receive, acknowledge and understand project information. Communications methods should be appropriate to the project, the timeliness required and the culture of the organization that you are working in.

Communications can be done most effectively if there are effective retrieval systems available and put into use. And, in order to effectively communicate information, we have to remember that the project manager must possess good general communications skills. Information is often communicated to stakeholders that is clouded with technical terms or acronyms which are not readily understandable by managers or customers.

Effective communications techniques include:

- Sender-receiver models – understanding feedback and barriers to communication
- Choice of media - written, verbal or electronic based; based on needs of project
- Writing styles – using active vs. passive
- Meeting management - agendas and effective means for addressing conflict
- Presentation - body language and presentation aids
- Facilitation - obtaining consensus and overcoming obstacles

It is important to be mindful that communication is not complete until the sender is confident that the receiver understands the information, as intended. In a later process, Manage Stakeholder Engagement, the project manager will address any issues that arise from the distribution of information. Project success is most likely when all stakeholders have a shared understanding of the current condition of the project.

Process Elements

The Manage Communications process has the following Inputs:
- Communications Management Plan - The agreed upon plan for managing project communications

- Work Performance Reports - S-curves, bar charts, tables, histograms, etc. that summarize work performance measurements

- Enterprise Environmental Factors - Consideration factors such as culture, systems, procedures, industry standards

- Organizational Process Assets - Consideration factors such as policies, procedures, guidelines, templates, and historical information

The Manage Communications process uses the following Tools & Techniques:
- Communications Technology - Available systems or technology for communications

- Communications Models - Sender/Receiver models defining roles and responsibilities for communications

- Communication Methods - Individual/group meetings, video/audio conferences, other communication methods

- Information Management Systems - System tools for tracking, storing and/or communicating information

- Performance Reporting - Methods for reporting status, performance or forecasting

The Manage Communications process has the following Outputs:
- Project Communications - Updates to corporate documents, guidelines, procedures, historical information

- Project Management Plan Updates - Updates to the Project Management Plan as a result of this process

- Project Documents Updates - Updates to other project documentation

- Organizational Process Asset Updates - Updates to corporate documents, guidelines, procedures, historical information, etc.

Manage Communications		
This process provides needed information to stakeholders in a timely fashion		
Inputs	**Tools and Techniques**	**Outputs**
• Communications Management Plan	• Communication Technology	• Project Communications
• Work Performance Reports	• Communications Models	• Project Management Plan Updates
• Enterprise Environmental Factors	• Communication Methods	• Project Documents Updates
• Organizational Process Assets	• Information Management Systems	• Organizational Process Assets Updates
	• Performance Reporting	

Figure 37.1 Process Elements within Manage Communications

Process Documents

This process is intended to deliver a wide variety of project documents to project stakeholders. The process gets its basis from the planning process: Plan Communications Management. The Communications Management Plan document might be used in this process as a checklist to ensure that the appropriate documents are distributed to project stakeholders.

Process Tasks

The Manage Communications process aligns loosely with one of the defined tasks that a project manager performs when managing a project:

Executing Task #2: "Execute the tasks as defined in the project plan, in order to achieve the project deliverables within budget and schedule".

Think About It

While working on a project to implement a new system at a company in another city, I learned the value and the dangers associated with using a document management system for document storage and review.

It has always been my assertion that one of the primary responsibilities of the project manager is to communicate effectively with stakeholders. I have always purported that timely communication is important. As well as being timely, the feedback component is also important. The perception held by the stakeholder is their reality. In order to determine what that perception or understanding of information is you have to communicate directly with stakeholders to ascertain their view.

On our project we decided to use Microsoft SharePoint as our status and performance reporting tool for the project. While SharePoint is a lovely tool for storage and dissemination of information, it does lack a bit as far a feedback or interaction between the project manager and stakeholders. I was assured that it was part of that corporate culture that everyone always used SharePoint for information storage and that everyone was used to retrieving information from the system.

Since I was a contractor and since I was travelling part of the time, I first learned the value of timely status reporting. The status report was due on Friday before 5pm. If I did not have the status report in the SharePoint file at the appropriate time, I got five or six e-mails asking where the status report was. That meant that the process worked, right? Well, as I said, I would get five or six e-mails; but there were over forty (40) stakeholders officially identified for the project. So what about those folks?

Well, I am sure you can guess the answer...the remainder of the project stakeholders were not concerned about the status report since they never retrieved it and read it. Several of these very same folks would arrive for the bi-weekly status meeting totally devoid of any knowledge about what was happening on the project.

Communications Management cannot be complete without some sort of mechanism to ensure that the information is read, acknowledged or acted upon in some manner.

Contributed by Tim Bergmann, PMP

Must Know Concepts

----

1. Manage Communications is the process of making project information available to project stakeholders, as determined and documented in the communications management plan.

2. Communication is not complete until the sender is confident that the receiver understands the information, as intended.

3. Orderly record keeping, effective distribution methods (meetings, project intranet, presentations, email), effective retrieval systems, and good general communication skills facilitate information distribution.

Additional Reading

- PMBOK® Guide Fifth Edition: Section 10.2   Manage Communications

Lesson Quiz

Instructions: The actual PMP exam is done via computer. These questions are representative of what you will encounter. Circle the correct answer. Answer Key in Appendix A.

1. Manage Communications _____.
   A. Is the communications process of creating & distributing just project performance reports to project stakeholders, as determined & documented in the communications management plan
   B. Is the communications process of creating and making project information available to project stakeholders, as determined and documented in the communications management plan
   C. Is the communications process of distributing earned value reports to project stakeholders, as determined & documented in the communications management plan
   D. Is the communications process of preparing and delivering progress presentations to project stakeholders, as determined & documented in the communications management plan

2. You and your project team have just commenced the execution/controlling phases of the project. Today, at the end of week one, your first weekly project performance report was prepared, reviewed/approved by the project core team and sent to the appropriate distribution list via electronic mail. Based on this information, select the best statement.
   A. Your communication obligation is satisfied. Your weekly performance report, as agreed to in the communications management plan, has been prepared and distributed, on-time, to the appropriate stakeholders. Stakeholders must accept ownership of their obligation to acknowledge receipt, then read and understand the information.
   B. Your communication obligation is not yet satisfied. Although your weekly performance report, as agreed to in the communications management plan, has been prepared and distributed, on-time, to the appropriate stakeholders, you must verify that the reports were received for communication to be complete. It may be a good idea to use electronic receipt verification to automate this process.
   C. Your communication obligation may not yet be satisfied. Although your weekly performance report, as agreed to in the communications management plan, has been prepared and distributed, on-time, to the appropriate stakeholders, you should verify that the reports were received and that the recipients understood the information, as it was intended. It may be a good idea to interview a few recipients to ensure the reports satisfy their intended purpose, especially after distribution of the very first report.
   D. Your communication obligation is satisfied. Your weekly performance report, as agreed to in the communications management plan, has been prepared and distributed, on-time, to the appropriate stakeholders. You may confidently move to the next activity.

3. Manage Communications inputs include all the following *except*:
   A. Communications management plan
   B. Work performance reports
   C. Organizational process assets
   D. Communication methods

End of Lesson 37

Lesson 38
Manage Stakeholder Engagement

Objectives

At the end of this lesson, you will be able to:
- Describe the purpose of the Manage Stakeholder Engagement process
- Describe the Inputs, Tools and Techniques, and Outputs of the Manage Stakeholder Engagement process
- Understand what management skills are necessary to resolve issues with project stakeholders

Process Locator for the PMBOK® Guide

	Initiating	Planning	Executing	Monitoring & Controlling	Closing
Integration					
Scope					
Time					
Cost					
Quality					
Human Resources					
Communications					
Risk					
Procurement					
Stakeholders			▓▓▓		

The Manage Stakeholder Engagement Process is used to ensure that communications with project stakeholders is productive and meets the needs and desires of those stakeholders.

Manage Stakeholder Engagement process deals with communicating and working closely with stakeholders, resolving issues and keeping stakeholders interested and active throughout the project.

There is often a great deal of communications between the project management team and the project stakeholders. For the project to be managed effectively and efficiently the project manager should ensure that the stakeholder communications needs/desires are being met and that stakeholders are not being flooded with excessive and unnecessary communications.

Stakeholder engagement includes involving stakeholders at appropriate points in the project, negotiating and communicating with stakeholders, addressing stakeholder concerns before they become issues, then resolving issues that have been identified.

Process Elements

The Manage Stakeholder Engagement process has the following Inputs:
- Stakeholder Management Plan - Defines the approach to increase stakeholder support and reduce negative impacts

- Communications Management Plan - The agreed upon plan for managing project information

- Change Log - A log used to track changes that occur during a project

- Organizational Process Assets - Consideration factors such as communication requirements, issue management procedures, change control procedures and historical information

The Manage Stakeholder Expectations process uses the following Tools & Techniques:
- Communication Methods - Individual/group meetings, video/audio conferences, other communication methods

- Interpersonal Skills - The broad set of 'soft skills' important to stakeholder engagement: building trust, resolving conflict, active listening, overcoming resistance to change

- Management Skills - Presentation, writing, and public speaking skills as well as other general management skills

The Manage Stakeholder Expectations process has the following Output:
- Issues Log - Documented issues that require resolutions

- Change Requests - Requests for changes to scope, schedule, costs, or processes or other project documentation

- Project Management Plan Updates - Updates to the Communications Management Plan

- Project Documents Updates - Updates to other project documentation (i.e. stakeholder management strategy, stakeholder register, issue log)

- Organizational Process Asset Updates - Updates to causes of issues, supportive documentation for corrective actions and lessons learned

Manage Stakeholder Engagement		
This process manages communications to satisfy stakeholders requirement		
Inputs	**Tools and Techniques**	**Outputs**
• Stakeholder Management Plan • Communications Management Plan • Change Log • Organizational Process Assets	• Communication Methods • Interpersonal Skills • Management Skills	• Issues Log • Change Requests • Project Management Plan Updates • Project Documents Updates • Organizational Process Assets Updates

Figure 38.1 Process Elements within Manage Stakeholder Engagement

Process Documents

In this process the project manager communicates directly with the project stakeholders to resolve any project issues as they arise. While some issues may be of a sensitive nature and might not appear in a public Issues Log, the majority of project issues will be listed on an Issues Log.

A sample of an Issues Log is shown below.

PROJECT ISSUES AND QUESTIONS TRACKING LOG
Project Management Strategy

Project ID: Project Name:

Project Sponsor: Project Manager:

No.	From	Sent To	Assigned To	Item	Result	Sent	Closed	Dates Due	Status
1									
2									
3									
4									
5									
6									
7									
8									
9									
10									
11									
12									
13									
14									
15									
16									
17									
18									
19									
20									
21									
22									
23									
24									
24									
26									
27									
28									
29									
30									
31									
32									
33									
34									
35									

Application Aid

This form is available
individually or as
part of a set at:
www.TrueSolutions.com

Process Tasks

The Manage Stakeholder Engagement process aligns loosely with one of the defined tasks that a project manager performs when managing a project:

Executing Task #2: "Execute the tasks as defined in the project plan, in order to achieve the project deliverables within budget and schedule".

Think About It

Instructions: Use this exercise to compare how you practice project management to what is specified in the *PMBOK® Guide Fifth Edition*.

Think about how this process is defined, used and documented in your organization. Write a brief description of how you use this process:

_____

_____

_____

_____

Must Know Concepts

1. The Manage Stakeholder Engagement process is applied to ensure that communications with project stakeholders is productive and meets the needs and desires of those stakeholders.

2. Actively managing project stakeholders increases the likelihood that the project will not be negatively impacted by unresolved stakeholder issues.

3. An issue log (or action-item log) is used to document and monitor the resolution of issues.

Additional Reading

- PMBOK® Guide Fifth Edition: Section 13.3   Manage Stakeholder Engagement

Lesson Quiz

Instructions: The actual PMP exam is done via computer. These questions are representative of what you will encounter. Circle the correct answer. Answer Key in Appendix A.

1. The Manage Stakeholder Engagement process is applied to:

   A. Ensure each stakeholder is familiar with the project management plan, to the extent appropriate for the particular stakeholder
   B. Quantitatively determine the number of communication channels in a project environment
   C. Satisfy the needs of, and resolve issues with, project stakeholders
   D. Enhance the abilities of individual stakeholders to improve all project performance

2. During project execution, a key stakeholder becomes very upset. She claims that she was not aware of a project management plan element that impacts her division. Your best response would be:

   A. As soon as possible, arrange a face-to-face meeting with your sponsor to plan a resolution.
   B. As soon as possible, arrange a face-to-face meeting with the stakeholder.
   C. As soon as possible, with your project management team, create a workaround plan.
   D. As soon as possible, document the stakeholder's concern and communicate it to your sponsor/customer.

3. Manage Stakeholder Engagement tools & techniques include:

   A. Communication methods, communications management plan
   B. Communication methods, issue logs
   C. Communication methods, interpersonal skills
   D. Management skills, issue logs

End of Lesson 38

Lesson 39
Perform Quality Assurance

Objectives

At the end of this lesson, you will be able to:

- Describe the purpose of the Perform Quality Assurance process
- Describe the Inputs, Tools and Techniques, and Outputs of the Perform Quality Assurance process
- Understand the use of the Quality Audit

Process Locator for the PMBOK® Guide

	Initiating	Planning	Executing	M&C	Closing
Integration					
Scope					
Time					
Cost					
Quality			▓		
Human Resource					
Communications					
Risk					
Procurement					
Stakeholder					

Perform Quality Assurance (QA) is the application of all quality activities intended to ensure the project will employ all processes necessary to satisfy recognized requirements.

Quality activities should be applied across the entire project life cycle. An intended outcome of applying the Perform Quality Assurance process is continuous process improvement. This is accomplished through the audit of quality requirements and quality control measurements to ensure that quality standards and metrics or operational definitions have been met for the project. Continuous process improvement includes all actions to reduce waste and non-value-added activities, to increase project efficiency and effectiveness. Continuous process improvement is sometimes termed KAIZEN, representing the quality philosophy of achieving improvement via small incremental steps. ("Kaizen" is Japanese for improvement.) Note that process improvement is focused on improved project performance, not improved functionality of the product of the project.

While many organizations support quality assurance with dedicated departments, it is important to understand that project quality management is the responsibility of the project manager.

Process Elements

The Perform Quality Assurance process has the following Inputs:
- Quality Management Plan - The plan that describes how quality will be managed for the project

- Process Improvement Plan - The documented plan for encouraging constant process improvements

- Quality Metrics - Operational definitions. Project elements, and how they are to be measured by quality control

- Quality Control Measurements - Results of all quality control activities

- Project Documents - Any project documents which define project conditions

The Perform Quality Assurance process uses the following Tools & Techniques:
- Quality Management and Control Tools - The same T&Ts used to for the Control Quality process

- Quality Audits - Structured reviews to identify ineffective/inefficient processes/procedures as well as best practices and lessons learned

- Process Analysis - Implements the process improvement plan, to identify needed improvements

The Perform Quality Assurance process has the following Output:
- Change Requests - Requests for changes to take corrective action, preventive actions and/or perform defect repair

- Project Management Plan Updates - Updates to the Project Management Plan as a result of this process

- Project Documents Updates - Updates to other project documentation (i.e. quality audit reports, training plans and process documentation)

- Organizational Process Assets Updates – Updates to quality standards

Perform Quality Assurance		
This process ensures the project employs all processes needed to meet requirements		
Inputs	**Tools and Techniques**	**Outputs**
• Quality Management Plan • Process Improvement Plan • Quality Metrics • Quality Control Measurements • Project Documents	• Quality Management and Control Tools • Quality Audits • Process Analysis	• Change Requests • Project Management Plan Updates • Project Documents Updates • Organizational Process Assets Updates

Figure 39.1 Process Elements within Perform Quality Assurance

TSI Study Aid

Process Documents

The main purpose of the Perform Quality Assurance process is to determine if the project is progressing in the manner in which it was planned. Best practices for project management and creation of the project product (Metrics) are measured during the Perform Quality Assurance process.

A template for measuring quality metrics is shown below.

TSI

Quality Metrics

Project Name:		
Prepared by:		
Date:		
Project Manager:		
Project Phase:	**Overall Project Status:**	
Metrics Date:	**Metrics Number:**	**Metrics Leader:**
Metrics Team:		
Goal(s) of This Specific Metrics:		
Metrics of Management of Project:		
1. On time performance	Assessment:	Comment:
2. Budge Control	Assessment:	Comment:
3. (required project objective #3)	Assessment:	Comment:
4. (required project objective #4)	Assessment:	Comment:
Overall Assessment of Management of Project:		
Recommended Action(s)/Lessons Learned Regarding Management of the Project: 1. 2. 3.		
Metrics of the Product of the Project:		
1. Defect frequency	Assessment:	Comment:
2. Failure rate	Assessment:	Comment:
3. Reliability	Assessment:	Comment:
4. Test Coverage	Assessment:	Comment:
5. (required product characteristic #5)	Assessment:	Comment:
6. (required product characteristic #6)	Assessment:	Comment:
Overall Assessment about the Product of the Project:		
Recommended Action(s)/Lessons Learned Regarding the Product of the Project: 1. 2. 3.		
Additional Metrics Comments: 1. 2. 3.		
Have you attached additional material(s)?	yes	no
Name(s) of attachment(s): 1. 2.		
Metrics Report Submitted To:	Date:	

TSI   Application Aid

This form is available
individually or as
part of a set at:
www.TrueSolutions.com

Process Tasks

The Perform Quality Assurance process aligns with one of the defined tasks that a project manager performs when managing a project:

Executing Task #3: "Implement the quality management plan using the appropriate tools and techniques, in order to ensure that work is being performed according to required quality standards".

Think About It

Instructions: Use this exercise to compare how you practice project management to what is specified in the *PMBOK® Guide Fifth Edition.*

Think about how this process is defined, used and documented in your organization. Write a brief description of how you use this process:

_____

_____

_____

_____

_____

Must Know Concepts

1. Perform Quality Assurance is the application of the Quality Management Plan to ensure the project will employ all processes necessary to satisfy recognized quality requirements.

2. The primary deliverable (output) from this process is change requests.

3. Quality activities should be applied across the entire project life cycle.

4. An intended outcome of applying the Perform Quality Assurance process is continuous process improvement.

5. Continuous process improvement (quality improvement) is sometimes termed KAIZEN, representing the quality philosophy of achieving improvement via small incremental steps.

6. Continuous process improvement is focused on improved project performance, not improved functionality of the product of the project.

7. Remember that project quality management is the responsibility of the project manager.

Additional Reading

- PMBOK® Guide Fifth Edition: Section 8.2   Perform Quality Assurance

Lesson Quiz

Instructions: The actual PMP exam is done via computer. These questions are representative of what you will encounter. Circle the correct answer. Answer Key in Appendix A.

1. Which of the following best describes the perform quality assurance process?

    A. The perform quality assurance process provides confidence that the project will satisfy relevant quality standards
    B. The perform quality assurance process is applied to measure project performance, using quality assurance control charts
    C. The perform quality assurance process is applied to measure project performance, using earned value management (EVM)
    D. The perform quality assurance process is applied to improve the functionality of the product of the project

2. The responsibility for project quality management lies with:

    A. The project manager
    B. The project core team member assigned to manage project quality
    C. The highest ranking QA/QC manager in the performing organization
    D. The organization QA/QC manager assigned to oversee quality activities for this particular project

3. Perform quality assurance outputs include:

    A. Process analysis
    B. Recommended corrective actions
    C. Quality audits
    D. Results of quality control measurements

4. Which of the following statements is *least* true?

    A. Quality Assurance (QA) is the collective total of all activities intended to ensure the project satisfies recognized quality requirements
    B. Quality activities should be applied across the entire project life cycle
    C. Process improvement is sometimes termed KAIZEN, representing the quality philosophy of achieving improvement via small incremental steps
    D. Process improvement is focused on improving functionality of the product of the project

End of Lesson 39

Lesson 40
Conduct Procurements

Objectives
At the end of this lesson, you will be able to:
- Describe the purpose of the Conduct Procurements process
- Describe the Inputs, Tools and Techniques, and Outputs of the Conduct Procurements process
- Understand the notification, proposal and seller selection elements within this process

Process Locator for the PMBOK® Guide

	Initiating	Planning	Executing	M&C	Closing
Integration					
Scope					
Time					
Cost					
Quality					
Human Resource					
Communications					
Risk					
Procurement			▓▓▓		
Stakeholder					

The Conduct Procurements process is used to solicit and obtain the project's external resources. This process includes obtaining seller responses and bids, selection of a seller or sellers, and awarding contracts.

During the process of Conduct Procurements, the project manager (or purchasing department) will notify sellers of the potential need by providing appropriate procurement documents to the sellers. In response, the project manager (or purchasing department) will receive proposals from the seller on how the need can be satisfied by the vendor. The project manager or purchasing department will select a seller, negotiate and award a contract and ensure availability of the procured resources. Statements of work and evaluation criteria developed during Plan Procurements may be used in conjunction with notifying the vendor and evaluating their response or proposal.

This process is often repeated many times within the life-cycle of the project. In its simplest form, this may include searching for parts via the internet (for example) and placing an order from the cheapest source, or it can be a more complicated process of submitting procurement packages, reviewing seller bids, seller evaluations, negotiations, and contract award.

Successful procurement is often very critical to project success and can greatly impact the project's expenses.

Process Elements

The Conduct Procurements process has the following Inputs:
- Procurement Management Plan - The documented plan to acquire external resources for the project

- Procurement Documents - Documents used to solicit proposals from prospective sellers

- Source Selection Criteria - Criteria used to help score or rate proposals submitted by prospective project suppliers (sellers)

- Seller Proposals - Supplier (seller) responses that describe ability and willingness to provide requested services

- Project Documents - Risk Register and Risk Related Contract Decisions

- Make-or-Buy Decisions - The documented decisions of what will be developed in-house and what will be purchased

- Procurement Statement of Work – Description of products, services or resources needed for the project

- Organizational Process Assets - Consideration factors such as processes, procedures and corporate knowledge base

The Conduct Procurements process uses the following Tools & Techniques:
- Bidder Conference - Q&A type meetings with prospective project suppliers (sellers) prior to proposal preparation

- Proposal Evaluation Techniques - formal evaluation process defined by procurement policies

- Independent Estimates - prepared estimates used for benchmark on proposed seller responses

- Expert Judgment - Expert technical and/or managerial judgment (from any qualified source)

- Advertising - Public advertisements used to solicit potential sellers for contracted project goods and/or services

- Analytical Techniques – Analysis of the vendor to determine readiness and capability to provide services

- Procurement Negotiations - used to clarify structure and requirements for purchases between seller and purchaser

The Conduct Procurements process has the following Outputs:
- Selected Sellers - List of sellers selected using the process tools and techniques

- Agreements - The contract package for selected sellers

- Resource Calendars - Information on the availability of resources over the planned activity duration

- Change Requests - Request for changes to scope, schedule, costs, or processes or other project documentation

- Project Management Plan Updates - Updates to the Project Management Plan as a result of this process

- Project Documents Updates - Updates to other project documentation

Conduct Procurements

This process obtains seller responses, selecting sellers, and awarding contract

Inputs	Tools and Techniques	Outputs
• Procurement Management Plan	• Bidder Conference	• Selected Sellers
• Procurement Documents	• Proposal Evaluation Techniques	• Agreements
• Source Selection Criteria		• Resource Calendars
• Seller Proposals	• Independent Estimates	• Change Requests
• Project Documents	• Expert Judgment	• Project Management Plan Updates
• Make-or-Buy Decisions	• Advertising	
• Procurement Statement of Work	• Analytical Techniques	• Project Documents Updates
• Organizational Process Assets	• Procurement Negotiations	

TSI Study Aid

Figure 30. Process Elements within Conduct Procurements

Process Documents

As previously stated in the introduction to this process, there are multiple documents that can be used during the process of Conduct Procurements. The project manager or purchasing department will use the inputs from Plan Procurement Management as a guide for this process. During this process the project manager or purchasing department receive proposals. The format for each proposal could be set by the buyer or seller. Ultimately, the project manager or purchasing department will award a contract to the seller.

An example of the Contract Award Template is shown below.

True Solutions, Inc.
Project Management Template
Version 2: Procurement Contract Award Template

Procurement Contract Award

Project Name:	
Prepared by:	
Date:	
Statement of Work or Project Deliverables:	A statement of work that defines the need or deliverable from buyer that will meet sellers standard
Schedule Baseline	A statement that defines approximately when the buyer will be needed
Performance Reporting	The standard of work that is expected from buyer to meet the seller requirements
Pricing	The fixed price that is agreed upon by buyer and seller
Payment Terms	The method in which the obligation between buyer and seller will be satisfied
Fees and Retainage	The method of how the seller will be paid and what monies will be retained for warranty purposes
Inspection & Acceptance Criteria	The standard of work that is expected is agreed upon and acceptance criteria set
Penalties	If the standard of work is not met, what conditions will be placed upon buyer
Incentives	If the standard of work is met, what conditions will be placed upon seller
Insurance & Performance Bonds	This is protection for the buyer where a seller is required to pay for an insurance on work performed
Change Request Handling	This is the documentation that states how changes of work will be handled
Termination & ADR	This is where it is stated how termination of a seller is handled and how disputes about that are resolved

Application Aid

This form is available individually or as part of a set at:
www.TrueSolutions.com

Process Tasks

The Conduct Procurement process aligns with one of the defined tasks that a project manager performs when managing a project:

Executing Task #1: "Obtain and manage project resources including outsourced deliverables by following the procurement management plan, in order to ensure successful project execution".

Think About It

Instructions: Use this exercise to compare how you practice project management to what is specified in the *PMBOK® Guide Fifth Edition.* Which of these items do you use when practicing project management?

☐ Statements of work previously defined and documented

☐ Make-or-buy analysis results

☐ List of pre-qualified vendors

☐ Vendor evaluation criteria

☐ Standard contract forms

☐ Procurement award checklist

How would you address any gaps that are apparent between the best practice definition and the way you perform this process today?

_____

_____

Must Know Concepts

1. Conduct Procurements is the process of obtaining bids and proposals from sellers and selecting a seller to provide resources for the project.

2. The primary deliverable from this process is selected sellers and agreements.

3. Source selection criteria should be performed to determine the successful bidders.

4. The project manager should play an integral role throughout the contracting process.

5. Contracts are legally binding agreements between buyer and seller and may be simple or complex, proportional to the size and complexity of the procurement.

6. A purchase order is a contract.

Additional Reading

- PMBOK® Guide Fifth Edition: Section 12.2   Conduct Procurements

Lesson Quiz

Instructions: The actual PMP exam is done via computer. These questions are representative of what you will encounter. Circle the correct answer. Answer Key in Appendix A.

1. Conduct Procurements tools and techniques include _____.

   A. Bidder conferences
   B. Project documents
   C. Teaming agreements
   D. Source selection criteria

2. Which of the following statements is *most* true?

   A. The internet is a useful tool for conducting a bid based procurement effort.
   B. Independent estimates are required in complex procurement efforts.
   C. Bidder conferences are conducted to ensure that all prospective sellers clearly understand the procurement process and that all prospective sellers are treated equally and fair.
   D. Advertising for prospective bidders is best managed by advertising professionals.

3. The Conduct Procurements process is performed to _____.

   A. Develop and document the project's procurement management plan.
   B. Obtain responses, select a seller and award a contract.
   C. Determine the qualified sellers list.
   D. Advertise to prospective sellers to add to the company's vendor list.

End of Lesson 40

Lesson 41
Monitoring & Controlling Process Group

Objectives
At the end of this lesson, you will be able to:
- Understand what processes are used in the Monitoring and Controlling Process Group
- Understand the purpose for using Monitoring and Controlling processes for the project or project phase

Process Locator for the PMBOK® Guide

	Initiating	Planning	Executing	M&C	Closing
Integration					
Scope					
Time					
Cost					
Quality					
Human Resource					
Communications					
Risk					
Procurement					
Stakeholder					

The Monitoring and Controlling Process Group consists of eleven processes that are intended to control the work during a project or project phase.

The primary purpose that these Monitoring and Controlling processes are performed is to ensure that the work that is performed is the planned work or is changed to meet the requirements of the project in a controlled manner. Monitoring and Controlling processes occur in all knowledge areas except the Human Resource Management area in the *PMBOK Guide® Fifth Edition*.

A "key-word" that might characterize the Monitoring and Controlling Process Group could be "check". The most important element of Monitoring and Controlling is to check against the plan and the execution to ensure that the project is on track.

The Monitoring and Controlling processes work very closely and have a high degree of interaction with each other. In addition, these processes also work very closely with the processes in the Executing process group. Executing processes focus on producing deliverables, the Monitoring and Controlling processes concentrate on confirming that the planned deliverables are created and that these outputs meet the planned specifications and requirements.

When a change occurs on the project, the project manager will return to the Planning processes to update affected project documents to ensure that the entire project is constantly and properly documented.

Monitoring and Controlling Tasks

On your PMP Exam, you will encounter many questions that will test your understanding of Monitoring and Controlling processes. When studying, remember to focus on Earned Value topics, since many Monitoring and Controlling processes depend on Earned Value formulas for data measurement and forecasting. Other questions will generally focus on the following Monitoring and Controlling tasks. As a PMP or project manager monitoring and controlling a project or project phase, you may be required to:

1. Measure project performance using appropriate tools and techniques in order to identify and quantify any variances, perform approved corrective actions, and communicate with relevant stakeholders.

2. Manage changes to the project scope, schedule and costs by updating the project plan and communicating approved changes to the team, in order to ensure that revised project goals are met.

3. Ensure that project deliverables conform to quality standards established in the quality management plan by using appropriate tools and techniques (e.g., testing, inspection, control charts) in order to satisfy customer requirements.

4. Update the risk register and risk response plan by identifying any new risks, assessing old risks, and determining and implementing appropriate risk response strategies, in order to manage the impact of risks on the project.

5. Assess corrective actions on the issue register and determine next steps for unresolved issues by using appropriate tools and techniques in order to minimize the impact on project schedule, cost and resources.

6. Communicate project status to stakeholders for their feedback, in order to ensure the project aligns with business needs.

Knowledge Requirements

As a PMP applying Monitoring and Controlling processes in real-world projects, you will be required to possess in-depth knowledge in several project specific areas, as well as a broad knowledge of project management in general. The PMP Exam will test your understanding of these knowledge specifics.

By developing a familiarity with these knowledge specifics, you will better understand the context of many PMP Exam questions. As you progress through the Ultimate PMP Exam Prep Guide, you will see each of these areas mentioned. Please give some thought to each item as it relates to your own project management experiences with past and current projects.

Remember, the PMP or project manager is always required to have a very broad base of knowledge to work from. The project manager has to work across the entire organization spectrum in many cases to effectively perform project management.

As a PMP or project manager applying Monitoring and Controlling processes, you may be expected to have knowledge of:

- Performance measuring and tracking techniques

- Project control limits (thresholds, tolerances)

- Project performance metrics (efforts, costs, milestones)

- Cost analysis techniques

- Variance and trend analysis techniques

- Project plan management techniques

- Change management techniques

- Integrated change control processes

- Risk identification and analysis techniques

- Risk response techniques

- Problem solving

- Reporting procedures

Process Group Interactions

Study Tip
Be sure to understand the Process Group Interactions We have previously exposed and discussed information about process group interactions. During the Executing phases or portions of the project a high degree of interaction occurs between the Executing *process group* and the Monitoring and Controlling *process group*. The intent of the Executing process group is to create project deliverables. The intent of the Monitoring and Controlling process group is to make sure they are the right deliverables. When completing the work of the project, processes from both process groups have to work together very closely and interact frequently in order to manage the project and its outcomes. **As you read the Ultimate PMP Exam Prep Guide,** *remember to look for process flows (defined by one output becoming the input to another process) that define the flows and interactions that occur on a typical project.*

Knowledge Check

Read the recommended chapters in the PMBOK Guide, associated with the Monitoring and Controlling Process Group processes before attempting this exercise.

After you have read all of the lesson material and the reading in the PMBOK Guide, your goal is to match the monitoring and controlling processes to the Monitoring and Controlling Process Group and correct PMBOK Guide Knowledge Area. Use the TSI Ultimate PMP Exam Prep Match Card Set to perform this exercise.

If you do not have a Match Card Set, create a 3x5 card for each Process Group, Knowledge Area and Process and match them to the correct monitoring & controlling process in a grid relative to the Process Group and Knowledge Area.

Use page 61 in the PMBOK Guide as your example and to check your matches after you have performed the matching exercise.

End of Lesson 41

Lesson 42
Control Scope

Objectives

At the end of this lesson, you will be able to:

- Describe the purpose of the Control Scope process
- Describe the Inputs, Tools and Techniques, and Outputs of the Control Scope process
- Understand how the process of Control Scope interacts with the process of Perform Integrated Change Control

Process Locator for the PMBOK® Guide

	Initiating	Planning	Executing	M&C	Closing
Integration					
Scope				▓▓▓	
Time					
Cost					
Quality					
Human Resource					
Communications					
Risk					
Procurement					
Stakeholder					

Control Scope is the process of effectively managing changes in project scope, then integrating those changes across the entire project through the Perform Integrated Change Control process.

In Control Scope, scope changes are identified by utilizing the variance analysis tool. After a scope change has been identified it becomes an output from this process (as a change request), which becomes an input to Perform Integrated Change Control.

It is important to understand that it is the project manager's responsibility to discourage unnecessary scope changes. It is also important to understand that when changes are warranted, that they be made in strict accordance with the project's scope change control process, and that the established scope baseline remains intact. Scope changes are inevitable, but controlling scope minimizes uncontrolled "scope creep".

Some organizations utilize a change control board (CCB) to evaluate and approve/disapprove scope change requests.

Process Elements

The Control Scope process has the following Inputs:
- Project Management Plan - The consolidated package of the subsidiary management plans and baselines

- Requirements Documentation - Documentation describing how individual requirements fulfill the business needs of the project

- Requirements Traceability Matrix - a table which associates requirement origin and the relationship between requirements origin and history throughout the project life cycle

- Work Performance Data - Raw data related to deliverable status, schedule progress, and costs incurred

- Organizational Process Assets - Consideration factors such as processes, procedures and corporate knowledge base

The Control Scope process uses the following Tools & Techniques:
- Variance Analysis - Comparing scope performance objectives to actual outcomes, in order to assess the magnitude of variation

The Control Scope process has the following Outputs:
- Work Performance Information - Collection of project status information; technical performance measures, etc

- Change Requests - Request for changes to scope, schedule, costs, or processes or other project documentation

- Project Management Plan Updates - Updates to the Project Management Plan as a result of this process

- Project Documents Updates - Updates to other project documentation

- Organizational Process Assets Updates - Updates to corporate documents, guidelines, procedures, historical information, etc.

Control Scope		
This process controls changes to project scope		
Inputs	**Tools and Techniques**	**Outputs**
• Project Management Plan • Requirements Documentation • Requirements Traceability Matrix • Work Performance Data • Organizational Process Assets	• Variance Analysis	• Work Performance Information • Change Requests • Project Management Plan Updates • Project Documents Updates • Organizational Process Assets Updates

TSI Study Aid

This chart is part of the study aid poster series available at:
www.TrueSolutions.com

Figure 42.1 Process Elements within Control Scope

Process Documents

The main document that may be used in this process would be a Scope Change Request. Sometimes a generic change request will be used instead of the more specific Scope Change Request. A sample template is shown on the next page.

Scope Change Request

Project Name:		
Prepared by:		
Date:		
Person(s) Requesting Change:		
Change Number:		
Detailed Description of Scope Change Requested:		
Reason for Scope Change Requested:		
Effect on Project Cost:		
☐ Projected Cost *Overrun* of approximately	%	
☐ Estimated Cost *Reduction* of approximately	%	
Effect on Schedule:		
☐ Planned Project Completion Date:		
☐ New Project Completion Date:		
Additional Remarks:		
Approval	Project Manager	Date
Approval	(Other)	Date

Application Aid

This form is available
individually or as
part of a set at:
www.TrueSolutions.com

Process Tasks

The Control Scope process aligns with one of the defined tasks that a project manager performs when managing a project:

Monitoring and Controlling Task #1: "Measure project performance using appropriate tools and techniques, in order to identify and quantify any variances, perform approved corrective actions, and communicate with relevant stakeholders".

Monitoring and Controlling Task #2: "Manage changes to project scope, schedule and costs by updating the project plan and communicating approved changes to the team, in order to ensure that revised project goals are met."

Think About It

Instructions: Use this exercise to compare how you practice project management to what is specified in the *PMBOK® Guide Fifth Edition.* Think about how this process is defined, used and documented in your organization. Write a brief description of how you use this process:

_____

_____

_____

_____

_____

Must Know Concepts

----

1. Control Scope is the process of effectively managing changes in project scope, then integrating those changes across the entire project through the Perform Integrated Change Control process.

2. The primary deliverables (Outputs) of the Control Scope process include work performance information and change requests which, if approved, result in updates to all associated project plans and documents.

3. It is the project manager's responsibility to discourage unnecessary scope changes.

4. When legitimate scope changes are warranted, they should be made in accordance with the project's scope change control system.

Additional Reading

- -

- PMBOK® Guide Fifth Edition: Section 5.6   Control Scope

Lesson Quiz

- -

Instructions: The actual PMP exam is done via computer. These questions are representative of what you will encounter. Circle the correct answer. Answer Key in Appendix A.

1. Legitimate scope changes may be necessitated/justified by many conditions. Of the following, which does *not* typify a condition that would justify a scope change?

    A. A sponsor's decision to re-estimate activity costs
    B. A client's decision to add a feature to the product of the project
    C. A newly available technology that was not an option when project scope was initially documented
    D. A newly enacted government regulation

2. Control Scope inputs include all of the following *except*:

    A. Requirements documentation
    B. Project management plan
    C. Change requests
    D. Work performance data

3. Control Scope _____

    A. Is applied to guide the project change control board in approving or rejecting WBS change requests
    B. Is applied to determine and document how changes in project scope will be managed
    C. Is the process of re-baselineing scope
    D. Is the process of effectively managing changes in project scope, then integrating those changes across the entire project.

4. As a project manager, your first priority in relation to scope changes is to_____

    A. Manage each scope change immediately upon becoming aware of the request, in accordance with scope change control procedures
    B. Discourage and prevent unnecessary changes
    C. Ensure all scope changes are properly documented
    D. Discuss each scope change request with your project sponsor to ensure you have their approval before requesting the change

End of Lesson 42

Lesson 43
Control Schedule

Objectives

At the end of this lesson, you will be able to:

- Describe the purpose of the Control Schedule process
- Describe the Inputs, Tools and Techniques, and Outputs of the Control Schedule process
- Understand how Control Schedule interacts with the process of Perform Integrated Change Control

Process Locator for the PMBOK® Guide

	Initiating	Planning	Executing	M&C	Closing
Integration					
Scope					
Time				▓▓▓	
Cost					
Quality					
Human Resource					
Communications					
Risk					
Procurement					
Stakeholder					

Control Schedule is the process of monitoring the status of the project to update project progress and manage changes to the schedule baseline, then integrating those changes across the entire project through the Perform Integrated Change Control process.

In the process of Control Schedule, schedule changes are identified using various tools, including variance analysis. When a schedule change has been identified it becomes an output from this process in the form of a change request, which then becomes an input to Perform Integrated Change Control.

It is important to understand that it is the project manager's responsibility to discourage unnecessary schedule changes. It is also important to understand that when changes are warranted, that they be made in strict accordance with the project's schedule change control process that is defined in the Schedule Management Plan. In most methodologies, performance measurement is usually performed using the original baseline schedule as the measurement point.

Performance measurement formulas used in Control Schedule include Schedule Variance (SV) and Schedule Performance Index (SPI). We will discuss these in detail in Lesson 44 – Control Costs.

Process Elements

The Control Schedule process has the following Inputs:
- Project Management Plan - The consolidated package of the subsidiary management plans and baselines which contains the schedule management plan and the schedule baseline

- Project Schedule - The most recently version of the project schedule with updates

- Work Performance Data - Project progress such as which activities have started, their progress and which activities have finished

- Project Calendars - The documents describing work days and periods for project resources

- Schedule Data - Collection of information describing and controlling the schedule

- Organizational Process Assets - Consideration factors such as existing formal and informal schedule control-related policies, procedure, and guidelines, schedule control tools and monitoring and reporting methods to be used

The Control Schedule process uses the following Tools & Techniques:
- Performance Reviews – Reviews to measure, compare and analyze schedule performance

- Project Management Software - Any software that provides the track planned dates versus actual dates and forecast the effects of changes to the project schedule

- Resource Optimization Techniques - Techniques applied to create efficient resource limited schedules

- Modeling Techniques- Explores various scenarios to bring the schedule into alignment with the plan (i.e. Monte Carlo)

- Leads and Lags - Used to find ways to bring project activities that are behind into alignment with the plan

- Schedule Compression – Used to find ways to bring project activities that are behind into alignment with the plan - (i.e. fast tracking and crashing)

- Scheduling Tool - Tool used to perform schedule network analysis to generate an updated project schedule

The Control Schedule process has the following Output:
- Work Performance Information - Collection of project status information and calculated SV and SPI values

- Schedule Forecasts - Estimates or predictions of conditions or events in the future based on available information

- Change Requests - Request for changes to schedule baseline and/or other components of the project management plan

- Organizational Process Asset Updates - Updates to causes of variances, corrective action chosen and the reasons, and other types of lessons learned from project schedule control

- Project Management Plan Updates - Updates to the project management plan as a result of this process, specifically the schedule baseline, schedule management plan and cost baseline

- Project Documents Updates - Updates to other project documentation (i.e. Schedule Data and Project Schedule)

- Organizational Process Assets Updates - Updates to corporate docs, guidelines, procedures historical information, etc.

Control Schedule		
This process controls changes to the project schedule		
Inputs	**Tools and Techniques**	**Outputs**
• Project Management Plan • Project Schedule • Work Performance data • Project calendars • Schedule data • Organizational Process Assets	• Performance Reviews • Project Management Software • Resource Optimization Techniques • Modeling Techniques • Leads and Lags • Schedule Compression • Scheduling Tool	• Work Performance Information • Schedule Forecasts • Change Requests • Project Management Plan Updates • Project Documents Updates • Organizational Process Assets Updates

Figure 43.1 Process Elements within Control Schedule

Process Documents

In the Control Schedule process the primary document that might be used would be the Schedule Change Request. Again, the performing organization may choose to use a generic change request that covers all change areas instead of this more specific document. A sample template is show below.

Schedule Change Request

Project Name:	
Prepared by:	
Date:	
Person(s) Requesting Change:	
Change Number:	
Detailed Description of Schedule Change:	
Reason for Schedule Change Requested:	

Effect on Project Cost:
- ☐ Projected Cost *Overrun* of approximately _____ %
- ☐ Estimated Cost *Reduction* of approximately _____ %

Overall Effect on Schedule:
- ☐ Planned Project Completion Date: _____
- ☐ New Project Completion Date: _____

Additional Remarks:

Approval	Project Manager	Date
Approval	(Other)	Date

Application Aid

This form is available individually or as part of a set at:
www.TrueSolutions.com

Process Tasks

The Control Schedule process aligns with one of the defined tasks that a project manager performs when managing a project:

Monitoring and Controlling Task #1: "Measure project performance using appropriate tools and techniques, in order to identify and quantify any variances, perform approved corrective actions, and communicate with relevant stakeholders".

Monitoring and Controlling Task #2: "Manage changes to project scope, schedule and costs by updating the project plan and communicating approved changes to the team, in order to ensure that revised project goals are met."

Think About It

Instructions: Use this exercise to compare how you practice project management to what is specified in the *PMBOK® Guide Fifth Edition.*

Think about how this process is defined, used and documented in your organization. Write a brief description of how you use this process:

_____

_____

_____

_____

Must Know Concepts

----

1. Control Schedule is the process of effectively monitoring the project progress and managing project schedule baseline changes, then integrating those changes across the entire project through the Perform Integrated Change Control process.

2. The primary deliverables (Outputs) of the Control Schedule process include work performance information and change requests that, if they are approved, result in updates to all associated project plans and documents.

3. Control Schedule uses earned value to calculate SV and SPI values for the project schedule.

4. It is the project manager's responsibility to discourage unnecessary schedule changes.

5. When legitimate schedule changes are warranted, they should be made in accordance with the project's schedule change control system.

Additional Reading

- PMBOK® Guide Fifth Edition: Section 6.7 Control Schedule

Lesson Quiz

Instructions: The actual PMP exam is done via computer. These questions are representative of what you will encounter. Circle the correct answer. Answer Key in Appendix A.

1. Which of the following best describes the intended application of the control schedule process:

   A. Control schedule is the process of effectively monitoring the project progress and managing project schedule baseline changes, then integrating those changes across the entire project
   B. Control schedule is the process applied to prevent changes to the schedule baseline
   C. Control schedule is the process applied to guide the project manager when making approval/denial decisions with respect to schedule baseline change requests
   D. Control schedule is the process applied to determine the potential benefit value of schedule change requests

2. The project schedule change control system is intended to do what?

   A. Provide the procedural guidance by which schedule change requests are to be managed
   B. Provide the procedural guidance to integrate schedule change requests with the Project Management Information System (PMIS)
   C. Provide the procedural guidance to initiate corrective action with respect to the project schedule
   D. Provide the procedural guidance for the project manager and project team to ensure they authorize schedule changes in accordance with the performing organization's QA/QC standards

3. Control Schedule tools and techniques include all the following *except*:

   A. Performance reviews
   B. Schedule compression
   C. Project schedule
   D. Project management software

4. Work Performance Data is an Input to Control Schedule, which may include:

   A. Project reports
   B. Which activities have started
   C. Status reports
   D. Relative speed that data can be processed

5. You are in the process of Control Schedule and are considering various Project Calendars. Why?

   A. To see if you can compress the schedule
   B. A schedule model may require more than one project calendar to allow for different work periods for some activities to calculate schedule forecasts.
   C. To perform trend analysis
   D. All of the above

6. You are the business sponsor for the Wine Deep Distribution project. The project appears to be slightly behind, but the team is arguing over the magnitude of the schedule variance and if any corrective action is necessary. They finally agree to calculate SV and SPI to help them make some decisions. The results of the calculations are communicated to stakeholders. What is this output called?

   A. Performance Reviews
   B. Project Management Plan Updates
   C. Schedule Forecasts
   D. Work Performance Information

End of Lesson 43

Lesson 44
Control Costs

Objectives
At the end of this lesson, you will be able to:
- Describe the purpose of the Control Costs process
- Describe the Inputs, Tools and Techniques, and Outputs of the Control Costs process
- Understand how to use Earned Value Measurement to measure the project and report performance

Process Locator for the PMBOK® Guide

	Initiating	Planning	Executing	M&C	Closing
Integration					
Scope					
Time					
Cost				▓▓▓	
Quality					
Human Resource					
Communications					
Risk					
Procurement					
Stakeholder					

Control Costs is the process of effectively managing changes to the project budget, then integrating those changes across the entire project through the Perform Integrated Change Control process.

Control Costs is first of all a change control process. In this process, the project manager will monitor for changes that are occurring or need to occur, and if a change is warranted, a change request will be generated and sent as an input to Perform Integrated Change Control. In addition, in Control Costs, the application of earned value measurement (EVM) is a key tool used to measure project performance. Earned value analysis integrates cost, scope and schedule to derive measurement values that accurately assess project progress to date, as well as forecast future performance.

Scope, schedule or cost values alone can create false impressions. For example, a project can be well under budget at any given time. This may appear favorable. However, if the under-budget performance is the result of being well behind schedule, then the project may not be in a favorable status. Earned value analysis measures the overall project performance, focusing on scope, schedule and cost elements.

Earned value measurement allows project teams to determine a number of critical project factors:

- Schedule performance: Is the project ahead or behind schedule?
- Time efficiency: How efficiently is the project using time?
- Forecast completion: When is the project likely to be completed?
- Cost performance: Is the project over or under budget?
- Resource efficiency: How efficiently is the project utilizing resources?
- Forecast costs: What will the remaining project work cost? What will be the final project total cost?

Earned value measurement relies on four key data points:

Planned Value (PV) - (also termed Budgeted Cost of Work Scheduled BCWS) Planned value is the established baseline that indicates the amount of money planned for spending to date, at any particular point in time (regardless of what actual work has been performed). *Simplified: "what you intend to do, the value of the work planned".*

Earned Value (EV) - (also termed Budgeted Cost of Work Performed BCWP) Earned value is the established baseline that indicates the amount of money planned for spending on the actual work performed to date, at any particular point in time (regardless of other planned objectives). *Simplified: "what was accomplished and the value of the work accomplished – compared to Planned Value".*

Actual Cost (AC) - (also termed Actual Cost of Work Performed ACWP) Actual cost is the amount of money spent on the actual work performed to date, at any particular point in time (regardless of other planned objectives). *Simplified: "what was spent to achieve the earned value?"*

Budget at Completion (BAC) - Budget at completion is simply the amount of money planned for spending on the entire project.

Based on these data points, EVM Performance Analysis and Forecasting can be accomplished. Measurements occur at a specific point in the project. This measurement can be done on a periodic basis, like once per month or once per quarter. Measurements can be done at the end of a phase or when a milestone is scheduled for completion. Measurements can be done by WBS or by deliverable.

Once values for PV, EV, AC and BAC are identified, the project team can factor them into specific equations to determine variances, indices and forecasts.

Variance Formulas	Index Formulas	Forecast Formulas
• SV – Schedule Variance • CV – Cost Variance • VAC – Variance at Completion	• SPI – Schedule Performance Index • CPI – Cost Performance Index	• EAC – Estimate at Completion • ETC – Estimate to Complete • TCPI – To Complete Performance Index

Figure 44.1 Earned Value Measurement

Variance Formulas

Schedule Variance (SV)

SV = EV - PV

SV reveals schedule status ... at this time, is the project ahead of schedule or behind schedule? SV >0 = ahead of schedule. SV <0 = behind schedule.

Cost Variance (CV)

CV = EV - AC

CV reveals cost status ... at this time, is the project under budget or over budget? CV >0 = under budget. CV <0 = over budget.

Variance at Completion (VAC)

VAC = BAC - EAC

VAC forecasts final cost status ... when the project is complete, will it be under budget or over budget? VAC >0 = under budget. VAC <0 = over budget.

Index Formulas

Schedule Performance Index (SPI)

SPI = EV / PV

SPI indicates time efficiency ... at present, how efficiently is the project utilizing time? SPI>1 = ahead of schedule. SPI<1 = behind schedule.

Cost Performance Index (CPI)

CPI = EV / AC

CPI indicates cost efficiency ... at present, how efficiently is the project utilizing resources? CPI>1 = under budget. CPI<1 = over budget.

Forecast Formulas

The following describes the calculations to determine forecast values:

Estimate at Completion (EAC) (Choose one formula based on circumstances)

EAC = BAC/CPI   **(variances continue)**

EAC = AC + BAC - EV   **(variances ended)**

EAC = AC + Bottom up ETC   **(new view of project required)**

EAC = AC + [(BAC - EV) / CPI x SPI)]   **(worst case scenario)**

EAC forecasts final project costs ... at present, what is the updated estimate for final/total project costs?

Estimate to Complete (ETC)

ETC = EAC – AC

ETC = Re-estimate using bottom up estimate

ETC forecasts remaining project costs ... from this point forward, what will be the cost of remaining project work? ETC is listed in the PMBOK® Guide as a new bottom-up estimate.

To-Complete Performance Index (Choose formula based on circumstances)

TCPI = (BAC-EV)/(BAC-AC)   **(finish at BAC value)**

TCPI = (BAC-EV)/EAC-AC)   **(finish at EAC value)**

TCPI forecasts how efficient the remainder of the project must be in order to achieve project cost performance goals.

Formula #1 is used when the Budget at Completion is used as the cost performance goal.

Formula #2 is used when the Estimate at Completion is used as the cost performance goal. The EAC based formula is often used when management determines that the original BAC is not achievable and wants to use a more realistic measurement when calculating performance for the remainder of the project.

Process Elements

The Control Costs process has the following Inputs:
- Project Management Plan - The consolidated package of the subsidiary management plans and baselines which contains the cost performance baseline and cost management plan

- Project Funding Requirements – Simply the funding needed and when it will be needed

- Work Performance Data - Project progress such as which activities have started, their progress and which activities have finished

- Organizational Process Assets - Consideration factors such as processes, procedures, and corporate knowledge base

The Control Costs process uses the following Tools & Techniques:
- Earned Value Management (EVM) – Integrates scope, cost and schedule measurements to measure project performance and progress

- Forecasting – Estimates the project completion (ETC and EAC)

- To-Complete Performance Index (TCPI) – Calculated projection of cost performance that must be achieved on the remaining work

- Performance Reviews – Reviews to compare cost performance over time, schedule variances, and future expenditures forecasts

- Project Management Software - Any software that provides information on the three EVM dimensions (PV, EV, and AC)

- Reserve Analysis - Comparing project performance objectives to actual values, determining reserves available to address risk

The Control Costs process has the following Output:
- Work Performance Information - Collection of project status information and calculated CV, SV, CPI and SPI values

- Cost Forecasts - Calculated EAC value or bottom up EAC

- Change Requests - Request for changes to cost baseline and/or other components of the project management plan

- Project Management Plan Updates - Updates to the Project Management Plan as a result of this process, specifically the cost baseline, and cost management plan

- Project Documents Updates - Updates to other project documentation (i.e. cost estimates and basis of estimates)

- Organizational Process Assets Updates - Updates causes of variances, corrective action chosen and the reasons, and other types of lessons learned from project cost control

Control Costs		
This process controls changes to project costs		
Inputs	**Tools and Techniques**	**Outputs**
• Project Management Plan • Project Funding Requirements • Work Performance Data • Organizational Process Assets	• Earned Value Management • Forecasting • To-Complete Performance Index • Performance Reviews • Project Management Software • Reserve Analysis	• Work Performance Information • Cost Forecasts • Change Requests • Project Management Plan Updates • Project Documents Updates • Organizational Process Assets Updates

Figure 44.1 Process Elements within Control Costs

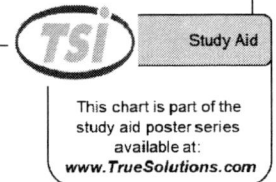

Process Tasks

The Control Costs process aligns with one of the defined tasks that a project manager performs when managing a project:

Monitoring and Controlling Task #1: "Measure project performance using appropriate tools and techniques, in order to identify and quantify any variances, perform approved corrective actions, and communicate with relevant stakeholders".

Monitoring and Controlling Task #2: "Manage changes to project scope, schedule and costs by updating the project plan and communicating approved changes to the team, in order to ensure that revised project goals are met."

Earned Value Application

This application exercise uses earned value to demonstrate tasks that a project manager performs when managing a project. Several important measurements are performed in this exercise.

• It shows you how large your gaps are from your cost and schedule baselines based on where you are on your project and where you are suppose to be on your project.

• It shows you how efficient you are on your budget and schedule.

- It helps you to determine how much more money you plan to spend based on your over/under runs.

- It helps you to determine how much money you will spend on your entire project based on over/under runs.

Your project has 4 tasks. Task A's value is $1,000. Task B's value is $5,000. Task C's value is $500. Task D's value is $2,000. Based on today's date, you are supposed to be completely done with task A and 50% done with task B. However, your Work Performance Information indicates you are completely done with task A and 75% done with task B. And, you have spent $5,000 so far on this project. Based on this information, how do you determine the components of your earned value?

Step 1: Draw out the project and document your assumptions:

Project ABC

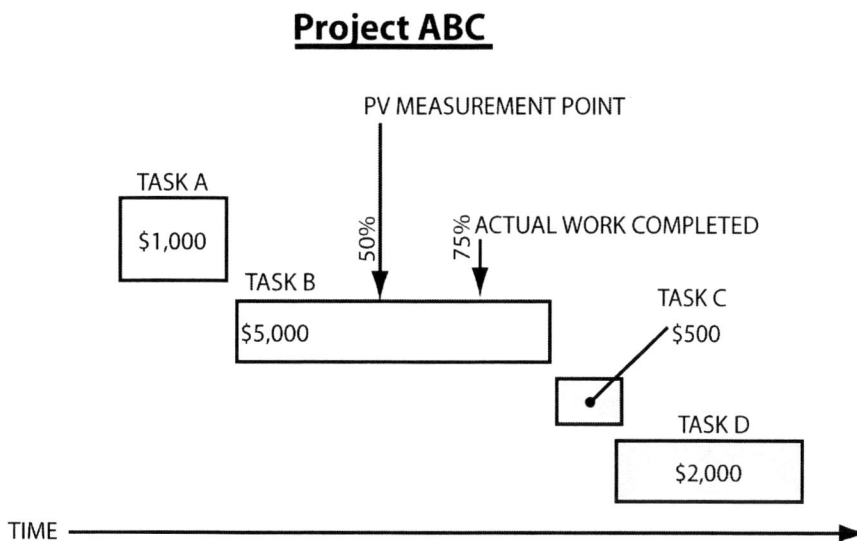

There are 4 tasks in this project
Task A is 100% completed, Task B is 75% completed.
$5,000 has been spent to date on this project
Based on today's date, you should have completed 100% of task A and 50% of Task B.

Step 2: Define the key data points:

PV (Planned Value)	What is the money value based on where you are supposed to be on this date (based on the authorized budget)? Also known as the performance measurement baseline (PMB) $1000 (Task A) + $2500 (50% of Task B) = $3,500 PV
EV (Earned Value)	What is the money value based on where you actually are (based on assigned work of the project schedule)? $1000 (Task A) + $3750 (75% of Task B) = $4,750 EV
AC (Actual Cost)	What is the actual amount of money spent (incurred) to

date?
$5,000 = AC

BAC (Budget at Completion)   What is the amount of money planned for spending
On the entire project (total planned value)?
$1000 (Task A) + $5000 (Task B) + $500 (Task C) +
$2000 (Task D) = $8,500

Step 3: Determine variances:
CV = EV – AC Cost variance   How far is the project from the cost baseline
(planned cost value)?
$4,750 (EV) - $5,000 (AC) = -$250 (CV)

Project is OVER budget by $250 (<0)
OR value of work completed compared to progress
made?

SV = EV – PV   Schedule variance – What is the monetary value of the
schedule baseline (behind or ahead of schedule)
$4,750 (EV) - $3,500 (PV) = $1,250 (SV)
Project is AHEAD of schedule by $1,250 (>0)
OR project achieved compared to project planned?

Step 4: Determine indices: (note, same data points but dividing instead of subtracting)
CPI = EV / AC   Project's cost performance to date – How efficient is the
project budget?
$4,750 (EV) / $5,000 (AC) = .95 (CPI)
Project is OVER budget (<1)
OR cost efficiency for the work completed

SPI = EV / PV   Project's schedule performance to date – How efficient
is the Project schedule?
$4,750 (EV) / $3,500 (PV) = 1.36 (SPI)
Project is AHEAD of schedule (>1)

TCPI (based on BAC)   (BAC – EV) / (BAC – AC)
($8,500 - $4,750) / ($8,500 - $5,000) = 1.07

TCPI (based on EAC)   (BAC – EV) / (EAC – AC)
($8,500 - $4,750) / $8,947 - $5,000) = .95

Step 5: Determine forecasts:
ETC = (BAC – EV) / CPI   Estimate to Complete
What is the amount of money you expect to spent to
Complete the project from this point?
($8,500 - $4,750) / .95 = $3,947 (ETC)
Based on past performance we plan to spend
$3,947

EAC = ETC + AC   Estimate at Completion
What is the expected cost for the entire project?

$3,947 (ETC) + $5,000 (AC) = $8,947 (EAC)
You expect to spend $8,947 that includes any
Current over or under runs

VAC = BAC − EAC   Variance at Completion
Will the project be under or over budget at completion?
$8,500 (BAC) - $8,947 (EAC) = -$447 (VAC)
You will be OVER budget by $447 at the end
Of your project

Must Know Concepts

1. Control Cost is the process of effectively managing changes to the project budget, then integrating those changes across the entire project through the Perform Integrated Change Control process.

2. The primary deliverables (outputs) from Control Costs are work performance information, forecasts and change requests. Approved change requests will result in project management plan updates.

3. Earned value measurement (EVM) is a key tool used to measure project performance. Earned value analysis integrates cost, scope and schedule to derive measurement values that accurately assess project progress to date, as well as forecasted future performance.

4. Planned Value PV (also termed Budgeted Cost of Work Scheduled BCWS) is the established baseline that indicates the amount of money planned for spending to date, at any particular point in time (regardless of what actual work has been performed).

5. Earned Value EV (also termed Budgeted Cost of Work Performed BCWP) is the established baseline that indicates the amount of money planned for spending on the actual work performed to date, at any particular point in time (regardless of other planned objectives).

6. Actual Cost AC (also termed Actual Cost of Work Performed ACWP) is the amount of money spent on the actual work performed to date, at any particular point in time (regardless of other planned objectives).

7. Budget at Completion BAC is simply the amount of money planned for spending on the entire project.

8. Schedule Variance (SV) SV = EV - PV SV>0 = ahead of schedule. SV<0 = behind schedule.

9. Cost Variance (CV) CV = EV - AC CV>0 = under budget. CV <0 = over budget.

10. Variance at Completion (VAC) VAC = BAC - EAC VAC>0 = under budget. VAC<0 = over budget.

11. Schedule Performance Index (SPI) SPI = EV/PV SPI>1 = ahead of schedule. SPI<1 = behind schedule.

12. Cost Performance Index (CPI) CPI = EV/AC CPI>1 = under budget. CPI<1 = over budget.

13. Estimate to Complete (ETC) forecasts remaining project costs. Two formulas are available: ETC = EAC – AC, or ETC = new bottom up estimate.

14. Estimate at Completion (EAC) forecasts final project cost total. Four formulas can be used: EAC = BAC/CPI, EAC = AC + BAC - EV, EAC = AC + Bottom up ETC or EAC = AC + [(BAC – EV) / (CPI x SPI)]. Formula use is based on project circumstances.

15. To Complete Performance Index (TCPI) forecasts how efficient the performance for the remainder of the project must be in order to achieve BAC or EAC. Two formulas are available: TCPI = (BAC – EV) / (BAC – AC) or TCPI = (BAC – EV) / (EAC – AC)

Additional Reading

- PMBOK® Guide Fifth Edition: Section 7.4   Control Costs

Lesson Quiz

Instructions: The actual PMP exam is done via computer. These questions are representative of what you will encounter. Circle the correct answer. Answer Key in Appendix A.

1. Of the following statements, which best describes the intended application of the Control Costs process?

    A. Control Costs is the process of effectively managing changes to the project cost baseline, then integrating those changes across the entire project
    B. Control Costs is the process applied to prevent changes to the cost baseline
    C. Control Costs is the process applied to guide the project manager when making approval/denial decisions with respect to cost baseline change requests
    D. Control Costs is the process applied to determine the potential benefit value of cost change requests

2. As budget changes are requested and approved during the execution/control phases of your project, it is most appropriate to:

    A. Integrate the changes as approved, then document/communicate a new project budget each time a change is made
    B. Document and communicate new project budgets, but only after all changes have been made and integrated
    C. Ensure your sponsor and key stakeholders are made aware of the changes as soon as possible after each change is made and integrated
    D. Integrate budget changes as you are authorized, but maintain the original cost baseline

3. The project cost change control system is intended to do what?

    A. Provide the procedural guidance by which cost change requests are to be managed
    B. Provide the procedural guidance to integrate cost changes with the Project Management Information System (PMIS)
    C. Provide procedural guidance to initiate corrective action with respect to the project budget
    D. Provide procedural guidance for the project manager and project team to ensure they authorize cost changes in accordance with the performing organization's QA/QC standards

4. Control Costs tools & techniques include all the following *except*:

    A. Project management software
    B. Performance measurements
    C. Forecasting
    D. Cost change control system

5. At the end of month three into a four month project, you find yourself 50% complete and have spent $600,000. You originally planned to spend $212,500 each month, with your work activities evenly scheduled at 25% each month. The total project budget is $850,000. What is the VAC?

    A. -$425,000
    B. $350,000
    C. $1,200,000
    D. -$350,000

6. While reviewing a progress report you see that the schedule variance is zero, the estimate to complete is $14,500 and the budgeted cost of work performed is $6,000. The earned value is:

    A. $8,500
    B. $20,500
    C. $6,000
    D. Not enough information

7. One way to determine the SPI is to:

    A. Subtract estimate at completion (EAC) from budget at completion (BAC)
    B. Divide budget at completion (BAC) by the cost performance index (CPI)
    C. Subtract actual cost of work performed (ACWP) from budgeted cost of work performed (BCWP)
    D. Divide budget cost of work performed (BCWP) by budgeted cost of work scheduled (BCWS)

8. A project was estimated to cost $1.5M and scheduled to last six months. After three months, the earned value analysis shows: BCWP = $650,000 BCWS = $750,000 ACWP = $800,000. What are the schedule and cost variances?

    A. SV = +$100,000 / CV = +$150,000
    B. SV = +$150,000 / CV = -$100,000
    C. SV = -$50,000 / CV = +$150,000
    D. SV = -$100,000 / CV = -$150,000

9. At the end of month three into a four month project, you find yourself 50% complete and have spent $600,000. You originally planned to spend $212,500 each month, with your work activities evenly scheduled at 25% each month. The total project budget is $850,000. What is your ETC?

    A. $212,500
    B. $600,000
    C. $1,062,500
    D. $425,000

End of Lesson 44

Lesson 45
Control Communications

Objectives

At the end of this lesson, you will be able to:

- Describe the purpose of the Control Communications process
- Describe the Inputs, Tools and Techniques, and Outputs of the Control Communications process
- Understand options for meeting information needs of stakeholders

Process Locator for the PMBOK® Guide

	Initiating	Planning	Executing	M&C	Closing
Integration					
Scope					
Time					
Cost					
Quality					
Human Resource					
Communications				■	
Risk					
Procurement					
Stakeholder					

Control Communications is the communications process of monitoring and controlling project information, throughout the project life cycle.

Control Communications is the process of monitoring and controlling project communications throughout the entire project life cycle. This implies that this process begins early in the project, immediately after the project is initiated and a Communications Management Plan is determined and documented.

An important part of Control Communications is to ensure that the level and detail of information reporting should be appropriate to the intended audience. Providing an excessive amount of performance data where it is unneeded or desired should be avoided.

Throughout the project life cycle, work performance information such as performance reports, status reports and forecasts will be communicated and controlled.

Process Elements

The Control Communications process has the following Inputs:
- Project Management Plan - The consolidated package of the subsidiary management plans and baselines

- Project Communications - The information communicated, such as deliverable status, progress, costs incurred

- Issues Log - Documented project issues requiring resolution

- Work Performance Data - Collection of project status information (planned vs. actuals); technical performance measures, etc.

- Organizational Process Assets - Consideration factors such as report templates, policies, procedures and organizationally defined variance limits

The Control Communications process uses the following Tools & Techniques:
- Information Management Systems - Standardized tools for storing and distributing information

- Expert Judgment - Expert technical and/or managerial judgment from any qualified source

- Meetings – Discussion and dialogue to determine the best ways to communication project information

The Control Communications process has the following Outputs:
- Work Performance Information - S-curves, bar charts, tables, histograms, etc. that summarize project performance

- Change Requests - Request for changes to scope, schedule costs, processes or other project documentation

- Project Management Plan Updates - Updates to the Project Management Plan as a result of this process

- Project Documents Updates - Updates to other project documentation

- Organizational Process Assets Updates - Updates to report formats and lessons learned

Control Communications		
This process monitors and controls communications throughout the project life cycle		
Inputs	**Tools and Techniques**	**Outputs**
• Project Management Plan • Project Communications • Issue Log • Work Performance Data • Organizational Process Assets	• Information Management Systems • Expert Judgment • Meetings	• Work Performance Information • Change Requests • Project Management Plan Updates • Project Documents Updates • Organizational Process Assets Updates

Figure 45.1 Process Elements within Control Communications

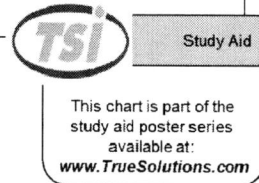

Process Documents

Control Communications monitors and controls a wide variety of communicated information. One of the most communicated items on the project is the project status report. Sample status report templates are shown below.

TSI

Department/Client Name
Status Report

Date of Status:	
Project Name:	
Project Manager:	
Project Sponsor:	
Delivery Manager	
Technical Lead:	
Start Date:	
Estimated End Date:	

Project Description	High level description
	
	Phase 1: Description
	
	   1. Deliverable 1
	
	   2. Deliverable 2
	
	   3. Deliverable 3
	
	   4. Deliverable 4
	
	Phase 2: Description
	
	   1. Deliverable 1
	
	   2. Deliverable 2
	
	   3. Deliverable 3
	
	   4. Deliverable 4

TSI — Application Aid

This form is available
individually or as
part of a set at:
www.TrueSolutions.com

Overall	Schedule	Resources	Technical	Cost
Red	Yellow	Green	N/A	

(You will need to quantify what each color means for the project during planning.)

Current Period's Accomplishments	• Phase 1 high level status with % complete
	• Key Status Point 1
	• Key Status Point 2
	• Key Status Point 3
	• Etc.

Next Period's Action Items	• Detailed deliverable/action with date/cost estimate where applicable.
	• Detailed deliverable/action with date/cost estimate where applicable.
	• Detailed deliverable/action with date/cost estimate where applicable.
	• Etc.

Milestones Status	Due Date	Revised Date	Status	Comments
Phase # - Milestone Name			R/Y/G	
Phase # - Milestone Name			R/Y/G	
Phase # - Milestone Name			R/Y/G	
Phase # - Milestone Name			R/Y/G	

#	Risks and Issues	Date Added	Assigned To	Status
01	Risk Description			Open/Closed
02	Risk Description			Open/Closed
03	Risk Description			Open/Closed
04	Risk Description			Open/Closed

Application Aid

This form is available individually or as part of a set at:
www.TrueSolutions.com

Process Tasks

The Control Communications process aligns with three of the defined tasks that a project manager performs when managing a project:

Monitoring and Controlling Task #1: "Measure project performance using appropriate tools and techniques, in order to identify and quantify any variances, perform approved corrective actions, and communicate with relevant stakeholders".

Monitoring and Controlling Task #5: "Assess corrective actions on the risk register and determine next steps for unresolved issues by using appropriate tools and technique in order to minimize the impact on project schedule, cost and resource."

Monitoring and Controlling Task #6: "Communicate project status to stakeholders for their feedback, in order to ensure the project aligns with business needs".

Think About It

When creating a status report for your project (or for your organization) you need to keep the corporate culture in mind when creating the report. I have previously reported lessons learned in terms of distributing information to project stakeholders. The lessons learned listed there carries over into the type of performance or status reporting that you choose to use. The tendency on the part of many stakeholders is to not read the information thoroughly. Most stakeholders are working on or participating in multiple projects most of the time – and usually they still have a "day-job" to work as well. Stakeholders are busy. Therefore it is often best to consider their work-load when crafting your project status report format.

I suggest that there are five major areas that need to be covered in a weekly status report:
- Red Flag items (issues that may stop the project execution)
- Risks and Issues
- Progress towards Objectives
- Forecast for work to be performed in the next reporting period
- Other (everything else that is happening on the project)

Some of my peers have accused me of being highly negative by putting "Red Flags" and "Risks and Issues" first in this format. I think this is just being realistic. If you think that your stakeholders are pressed for time and not going to have time to read your status report thoroughly, what portions of the report do you want them to read? Do you want them to understand that there are some risks and issues on the project? Or do you want them simply to see the "Progress" section and assume that all is well and the project is going great?

Contributed by Tim Bergmann, PMP

Must Know Concepts

1. Control Communications is the communications process of monitoring and controlling the communications for the project throughout the project life cycle.

2. Communicated information should meet the needs and desire of stakeholders by providing them with performance information, through the use of status reporting, progress reporting and forecasting.

3. The primary deliverable (output) from this process is work performance information.

Additional Reading

- PMBOK® Guide Fifth Edition: Section 10.3   Control Communications

Lesson Quiz

Instructions The actual PMP exam is done via computer. These questions are representative of what you will encounter. Circle the correct answer. Answer Key in Appendix A.

1. Control Communications is intended to monitor and control project information:

    A. During Planning and Executing
    B. During the entire project life cycle
    C. During Monitoring and Controlling
    D. During the project life cycle except for Initiating

2. All of these are outputs from Control Communications, except:

    A. Change Requests
    B. Project Management Plan Updates
    C. Project Forecasts
    D. Communications Management Plan updates

3. While reviewing a progress report you see that the project is falling seriously behind in one critical area. You decide that you need to discuss this issue with the functional manager. The best way to resolve this project issue would be to:

    A. List this as an issue on the issue log, then discuss at the team meeting
    B. Arrange for a face to face meeting with the functional manager to discuss the issue
    C. List the problem on the status report as a critical issue
    D. Talk to the sponsor and ask him to intercede with the functional manager

End of Lesson 45

Lesson 46
Control Stakeholder Engagement

Objectives

At the end of this lesson, you will be able to:

- Describe the purpose of the Control Stakeholder Engagement process
- Describe the Inputs, Tools and Techniques, and Outputs of the Control Stakeholder Engagement process
- Understand options for meeting information needs of stakeholders

Process Locator for the PMBOK® Guide

	Initiating	Planning	Executing	M&C	Closing
Integration					
Scope					
Time					
Cost					
Quality					
Human Resource					
Communications					
Risk					
Procurement					
Stakeholder				▓▓▓	

Control Stakeholder Engagement is the process of monitoring overall stakeholder relationships and adjusting strategies as needed, throughout the project life cycle.

Control Stakeholder Engagement is the process of monitoring and controlling overall project stakeholder relationships throughout the entire project life cycle. This implies that this process begins early in the project, immediately after the project is initiated and a Stakeholder Management Plan is determined and documented.

An important part of Control Stakeholder Engagement is to ensure that stakeholder interest and effectiveness is maintained during the project. As the project evolves and the project environment changes, the project manager may be required to adjust stakeholder management strategies in order to facilitate continued performance.

Process Elements

The Control Stakeholder Engagement process has the following Inputs:
- Project Management Plan - The consolidated package of the subsidiary management plans and baselines

- Issue Log - Documented project issues requiring resolution

- Work Performance Data - Collection of project status information (planned vs. actual); technical performance measures, etc.

- Project Documents – Documents that describe stakeholder interests, i.e., the schedule, stakeholder register, issue log, change log and project communications

The Control Stakeholder Engagement process uses the following Tools & Techniques:
- Information Management Systems – Standardized tools for storing and distributing information

- Expert Judgment – Expert technical and/or managerial judgment from any qualified source

- Meetings – Discussion and dialogue to determine the best ways to communication project information

The Control Stakeholder Engagement process has the following Outputs:
- Work Performance Information - S-curves, bar charts, tables, histograms, etc. that summarize project performance

- Change Requests - Request for changes to scope, schedule costs, processes or other project documentation

- Project Management Plan Updates - Updates to the Project Management Plan as a result of this process

- Project Documents Updates - Updates to other project documentation

- Organizational Process Asset Updates - Updates to report formats and lessons learned

Control Stakeholder Engagement		
This process monitors and controls stakeholder relationships throughout the project life cycle		
Inputs	**Tools and Techniques**	**Outputs**
• Project Management Plan • Issue Log • Work Performance Data • Project Documents	• Information Management Systems • Expert Judgment • Meetings	• Work Performance Information • Change Requests • Project Management Plan Updates • Project Documents Updates • Organizational Process Assets Updates

Figure 46.1 Process Elements within Control Communications

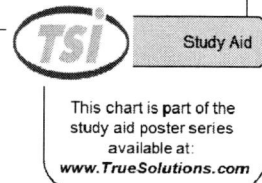

Process Documents

Control Stakeholder Engagement monitors and controls the stakeholder relationships on the project. Controlling stakeholder relationships will depend heavily on the interpersonal skills of the project manager. Face to face communications is often the best tool for engagement and for issues resolution, therefore, there is no specific document template provided for this process.

Process Tasks

The Control Stakeholder Engagement process aligns with one of the defined tasks that a project manager performs when managing a project:

Monitoring and Controlling Task #6: "Communicate project status to stakeholders for their feedback, in order to ensure the project aligns with business needs".

Think About It

Instructions: Use this exercise to compare how you practice project management to what is specified in the *PMBOK® Guide Fifth Edition.* Think about how this process is defined, used and documented in your organization. Write a brief description of how you use this process:

_____

_____

_____

_____

_____

Must Know Concepts

1. Control Stakeholder Engagement is the process of monitoring and controlling stakeholder relationships throughout the project life cycle.

2. As project conditions change during the project life cycle, it may be necessary to adjust stakeholder management strategies.

3. The primary deliverable (output) from this process is work performance information.

Additional Reading

*   PMBOK® Guide Fifth Edition: Section 13.4   Control Stakeholder Engagement

Lesson Quiz

- -

Instructions The actual PMP exam is done via computer. These questions are representative of what you will encounter. Circle the correct answer. Answer Key in Appendix A.

1. Control Stakeholder Engagement is intended to monitor and control stakeholders:

   A. During Planning and Executing
   B. During the entire project life cycle
   C. During Monitoring and Controlling
   D. During the project life cycle except for Initiating

2. All of these are named outputs from Control Stakeholder Engagement, except:

   A. Change Requests
   B. Project Management Plan Updates
   C. Stakeholder Management Plan updates
   D. Project documents updates

3. Work performance information shows that planned resources are not available from one functional area for the project. Your original stakeholder management plan indicated that the functional manager for this area was highly motivated to get the project completed. Now, it appears that he has reassigned his staff to other tasks. The best way to resolve this project issue would be to:

   A. Call a meeting and publicly demand an explanation from the functional manager.
   B. Arrange for a face to face meeting with the functional manager to discuss the issue; then use the results to modify the stakeholder management strategy to meet project and operations needs.
   C. List the problem on the status report as a critical issue.
   D. Talk to the sponsor and ask him to intercede with the functional manager.

End of Lesson 46

This page intentionally blank.

Lesson 47
Control Risks

Objectives
At the end of this lesson, you will be able to:
- Describe the purpose of the Control Risks process
- Describe the Inputs, Tools and Techniques, and Outputs of the Control Risks process
- Understand the use of workaround plans for responding to unanticipated project risk

Process Locator for the PMBOK® Guide

	Initiating	Planning	Executing	M&C	Closing
Integration					
Scope					
Time					
Cost					
Quality					
Human Resource					
Communications					
Risk				▩	
Procurement					
Stakeholder					

For the most part, Control Risks is the process of putting into action all of the risk planning done earlier in the project life-cycle.

The Control Risks process is applied to perform several functions for the project:
- Monitor identified risks

- Identify new risks

- Ensure the proper execution of planned risk responses

- Evaluate the overall effectiveness of the risk management plan in reducing risk

If a risk event occurs during project execution, there is a likelihood it was identified sometime earlier, it was analyzed and an appropriate response action was planned to deal with it (captured in the Risk Register). For the most part, Control Risks is the process of putting into action all of the risk planning done earlier in the project life-cycle.

It is important to understand that risk monitoring is intended to be a daily, on-going process across the entire project life-cycle. Project team members and stakeholders should be encouraged to be vigilant in looking for risk symptoms, as well as for new project risks. It is suggested that project risk always be an agenda item for all team meetings. Newly identified risks and symptoms of previously identified risks should be communicated immediately for evaluation and/or action.

Process Elements

The Control Risks process has the following Inputs:
- Project Management Plan - The consolidated package of the subsidiary management plans and baselines

- Risk Register – List of identified risks

- Work Performance Data - Raw data related to deliverable status, schedule progress and costs incurred

- Work Performance Reports - Project performance reports to track variance, earned value and forecasts

The Control Risks process uses the following Tools & Techniques:
- Risk Reassessment – New risk identification and frequent reassessment of existing risks

- Risk Audits – Examination and documentation of the effectiveness of risk responses and risk management processes

- Variance and Trend Analysis – Examination of project trends to help determine the impact of threats/opportunities

- Technical Performance Measurement

- Reserve Analysis – Determining appropriate amount of contingency reserve to compensate for project risk

- Meetings – Typically, risk management is an agenda item at each project status meeting

The Control Risks process has the following Outputs:
- Work Performance Information – Updates to project information used to support project decision making

- Change Requests - Request for changes to scope, schedule, costs, or processes or other project documentation

- Project Management Plan Updates – Updates to the Project Management Plan as a result of this process

- Project Documents Updates - Updates to other project documentation

- Organizational Process Assets Updates – Updates to corporate docs, guidelines, procedures, historical information, etc.

Control Risks		
Executes risk response plans and evaluates their effectiveness		
Inputs	**Tools and Techniques**	**Outputs**
• Project Management Plan • Risk Register • Work Performance Data • Work Performance Reports	• Risk Reassessment • Risk Audits • Variance and Trend Analysis • Technical Performance Measurement • Reserve Analysis • Meetings	• Work Performance Information • Change Requests • Project Management Plan Updates • Project Documents Updates • Organizational Process Assets Updates

Figure 47.1 Process Elements within Control Risks

Process Documents

During Control Risks, two functions occur: existing risks are monitored to determine if the risk is occurring and new risks are identified. If existing risks occur, the project manager often has a documented risk response prepared that can be put into action. When an existing risk occurs two documents will be addressed: the project manager will fill out a Change Request Form to request that the risk response be implemented and the Risk Register will be updated.

If a new risk occurs, it is likely that this risk was not previously identified, so it would not currently appear on the Risk Register. Responding to this previously unidentified risk would be done in the form of a Workaround Plan. The project manager would update the Risk Register to reflect the newly identified risk, use a Change Request Form to request a risk response be implemented and use a Workaround Planning Worksheet (shown below) to develop and document the workaround plan.

Risk Workaround Planning Worksheet

Project Name:	
Prepared by:	
Date:	
Description of Emerging Risk Identified:	
Person(s) Responsible:	
Results from Risk Analysis (if applicable):	
Description of Plan to Respond (avoidance, transference, mitigation, acceptance):	
Description of Residual Risk Level:	
Action Steps:	
Budget & Time for Response:	
Contingency/Fallback Plans:	
Additional Notes:	

Process Tasks

The Control Risks process aligns with one of the defined tasks that a project manager performs when managing a project:

Monitoring and Controlling Task #4: "Update the risk register and risk response plan by identifying any new risks, assessing old risks, and determining and implementing appropriate response strategies, in order to manage the impact of risks on the project".

Think About It

Instructions: Use this exercise to compare how you practice project management to what is specified in the *PMBOK® Guide Fifth Edition.*

Think about how this process is defined, used and documented in your organization. Write a brief description of how you use this process:

_____

_____

_____

_____

Must Know Concepts

1. The Control Risks process is applied to monitor identified risks, identify new risks, ensure proper execution of planned risk responses and evaluate overall effectiveness of the Risk Management Plan in reducing risk.

2. The primary outputs from Control Risks are work performance information and change requests.

3. Workarounds (or workaround plans) are responses to unanticipated (surprise) risk events after they occur. Workarounds are for risk events that were not previously identified, and have no advance planned response action. Workaround plans should be documented and incorporated into the Risk Register as soon as they are developed.

4. Risk monitoring is intended to be a daily, on-going process across the entire project life-cycle, from project start to project finish.

5. Project team members and stakeholders should be vigilant in looking for risk symptoms, as well as for new project risks.

Additional Reading

- PMBOK® Guide Fifth Edition: Section 11.6   Control Risks

Lesson Quiz

Instructions: The actual PMP exam is done via computer. These questions are representative of what you will encounter. Circle the correct answer. Answer Key in Appendix A.

1. The Control Risks process is applied to:

   A. Implement risk avoidance, risk transference, risk mitigation and risk acceptance (passive and active)

   B. Develop options and determine actions to enhance opportunities (positive risks) and develop options and determine actions to reduce threats (negative risks)

   C. Monitor identified risks, identify new risks, ensure proper execution of planned risk responses, and evaluate overall effectiveness of the Risk Management Plan in reducing risk

   D. Develop options and determine actions to create opportunities for positive risks and develop options and determine contingency actions for negative risks

2. During project execution, an odd risk event occurs, a risk that no one imagined in advance. But now that it has occurred, the project team must act. An appropriate response would be to:

   A. Request guidance from the project sponsor
   B. Create new risk response plan
   C. Create a workaround
   D. Transfer the risk as soon as possible

3. Control Risks tools & techniques include:

   A. Risk audits, reserve analysis, status meetings
   B. Work-around plans, reserve analysis, status meetings
   C. Risk audits, risk register updating, status meetings
   D. Risk audits, reserve analysis, recommended preventive actions

4. Which of the following statements is least true?

   A. Unanticipated risks (those not identified in advance) that occur during project execution must be ignored, because no advance plans exist to deal with them. The project must simply accept the consequences (either negative or positive).
   B. Project team members and stakeholders should be vigilant in looking for risk symptoms, as well as for new project risks.
   C. Risk monitoring is intended to be a daily, on-going process across the entire project life-cycle, from project start to project finish.
   D. Workarounds (or workaround plans) are responses to unanticipated (surprise) risk events after they occur.

End of Lesson 47

This page intentionally blank.

Lesson 48
Control Procurements

Objectives

At the end of this lesson, you will be able to:

- Describe the purpose of the Control Procurements process
- Describe the Inputs, Tools and Techniques, and Outputs of the Control Procurements process
- Understand the need to integrate the vendor team as part of the overall project team

Process Locator for the PMBOK® Guide

	Initiating	Planning	Executing	M&C	Closing
Integration					
Scope					
Time					
Cost					
Quality					
Human Resource					
Communications					
Risk					
Procurement				▓▓▓	
Stakeholder					

Monitoring the relationships created by a project's procurement needs, monitoring contract performance, and making procurement changes and corrections are accomplished through the Control Procurements process.

Part of this process includes validating that the seller's performance is meeting requirements and contract obligations.

In many organizations, the role of contract monitoring and control is performed by a specialized contracts department. This is often done because of the legalities associated with contracts. Regardless of who is performing contract administration, project team members should be aware of the legal obligations and impact of their actions in regard to contracts.

During the application of this process, each seller's performance should be recorded and documented. A performance review of sellers can lead to identification of issues to be resolved, and provides additional data for similar future projects in regards to contracts and purchases with sellers.

When applying this process the project manager will have a high degree of interaction with several other processes. It is important to integrate the vendor project team into the overall project team and stakeholder organization. Project management elements for managing work, for verifying work and deliverable conformance, for managing change and for developing the team are important during this process.

Some processes that may be closely coordinated with Control Procurements are:
- Direct and Manage Project Work

- Monitor and Control Project Work

- Validate Scope

- Control Quality

- Develop Project Team

- Manage Project Team

- Control Scope

- Control Schedule

- Control Cost

- Perform Integrated Change Control

- Close Procurements

- Close Project or Phase

Process Elements

The Control Procurements process has the following Inputs:

- Project Management Plan - The consolidated package of the subsidiary management plans and baselines which contains the procurement management plan

- Procurement Documents - Documents used to solicit proposals from prospective sellers

- Agreements - Procurement Contract and Information

- Approved Change Requests - documented, authorized changes that expand or reduce scope

- Work Performance Reports - Reports that summarize project performance

- Work Performance Data - Project performance related to quality standards being satisfied, paid invoices, and costs incurred

The Control Procurements process uses the following Tools & Techniques:
- Contract Change Control System - A system that defines the process by which a contract may be modified

- Procurement Performance Reviews - A procurement performance review of seller's conformance to contract terms

- Inspections and Audits - Required by the buyer, supported by the seller, conducted to verify seller's compliance

- Performance Reporting - Management information to assess the contractual performance of project suppliers

- Payment Systems - Reviews, approvals, payments made in accordance with contract terms

- Claims Administration - Procedures for resolving disputed/contested changes between buyer and seller

- Records Management System - Used by the project manager to manage contract documentation and records

The Control Procurements process has the following Outputs:
- Work Performance Information - Performance data associated with work completion

- Change Requests - Request for changes to scope, schedule, costs, or procurement management plan or other project documentation

- Project Management Plan Updates - Updates to the Project Management Plan as a result of this process specifically the procurement management plan and schedule baseline

- Project Documents Updates - Updates to other project documentation

- Organizational Process Asset Updates - Updates to correspondence, payment schedules and requests, and seller performance evaluation documentation

Control Procurements		
This process manages procurement relationships and contract performance		
Inputs	**Tools and Techniques**	**Outputs**
• Project Management Plan • Procurement Documents • Agreements • Approved Change Requests • Work Performance Reports • Work Performance Data	• Contract Change Control • Procurement Performance Reviews • Inspections and Audits • Performance Reporting • Payment Systems • Claims Administration • Records Management System	• Work Performance Information • Change Requests • Project Management Plan Updates • Project Documents Updates • Organizational Process Assets Updates

Figure 48.1 Process Elements within Control Procurements

Process Documents

As previously stated in this lesson, Control Procurements is closely linked to other project management processes in real-world application. The documents associated with these other processes will be used as part of this process.

Unique to this process is the need to communicate with the vendor company to notify them of status, change, conflict, etc. Formal communications (usually a letter) to the vendor company will become part of organizational process assets updates and ultimately part of the overall project archive.

Process Tasks

The Control Procurements process aligns with one of the defined tasks that a project manager performs when managing a project:

Monitoring and Controlling Task #1: "Measure project performance using appropriate tools and techniques, in order to identify and quantify any variances, perform approved corrective actions, and communicate with relevant stakeholders".

Think About It

Instructions: Use this exercise to compare how you practice project management to what is specified in the *PMBOK® Guide Fifth Edition.*

Best Practices suggest that the following items are used during the Control Procurements process.

Which of these items do you use when practicing project management?

☐ Communicate directly with the vendor to check on work

☐ Use Control Quality process to check work accuracy

☐ Create payment requests or make payments to the vendor

☐ Integrate vendor activities with other project processes

☐ Communicate formally to vendor about changes

☐ Formally accept work throughout the project

How would you change your use of this process in your organization to resolve any gaps in application?

Must Know Concepts

1. The Control Procurements process is used to manage procurement relationships, monitor contract performance, and make changes and corrections to procurements.

2. The primary outputs from Control Procurements are work performance information and change requests.

3. Many organizations utilize a contract administration department or office to administer procurement contracting due to the amount of legality involved in formal contracting.

4. Seller performance should be formally documented for use in future decisions and in evaluation of sellers.

5. Contract changes can be kept to a minimum by proper and thorough procurement planning but can be used to reduce risk, or when such amendments are beneficial for the buyer, the seller, or both.

Additional Reading

- PMBOK® Guide Fifth Edition: Section 12.3   Control Procurements

Lesson Quiz

Instructions: The actual PMP exam is done via computer. These questions are representative of what you will encounter. Circle the correct answer. Answer Key in Appendix A.

1. Control Procurements is:

   A. The procurement process of interfacing with the organization's central contract group
   B. The procurement process of approving and paying sellers' involves in a timely fashion
   C. The procurement process of ensuring that the seller's performance satisfies contractual obligations
   D. The procurement process of minimizing the number of contractors' change requests

2. You and your project team have completed evaluations of several proposals and have decided that one in particular appears to be present the most overall attractive offer. However, while checking references, you find this seller has a history of bidding low to get the work, then demanding many change requests to increase their revenue. You also found their quality of work is consistently excellent. Which of the following represents the best approach to this situation?

   A. Disqualify this seller's proposal. Their history demonstrates low integrity.
   B. Disqualify this seller's proposal. Your project may suffer schedule delays and cost overruns due to the many contract change requests you will certainly face from the seller.
   C. Do not disqualify this seller's proposal. They present the best offer. But, if you do ultimately select them, assign a core team member to watch them closely. They should not be trusted.
   D. Do not disqualify this seller's proposal. As long as you are confident that scope of work and terms are well-defined, contract changes should be minimal. Select this seller with confidence.

3. Control Procurements inputs include all the following except:
   A. Agreements
   B. Project management plan
   C. Change requests
   D. Work performance data

4. Which of the following statements is least true?
   A. Once negotiated and executed, a buy/seller contract becomes a legally binding agreement and cannot be changed.
   B. If a contract is well-planned, then the need for contract changes should be minimized.
   C. Contract changes that will need to improved project performance should be facilitated, but in accordance with the project's change control system.
   D. Unnecessary contract changes should be discouraged.

End of Lesson 48

This page intentionally blank.

Lesson 49
Control Quality

Objectives

At the end of this lesson, you will be able to:

- Describe the purpose of the Control Quality process
- Describe the Inputs, Tools and Techniques, and Outputs of the Control Quality process
- Understand that Control Quality is focused mostly on the product of the project
- Understand how various tools can be applied to measure the product of the project

Process Locator for the PMBOK® Guide

	Initiating	Planning	Executing	M&C	Closing
Integration					
Scope					
Time					
Cost					
Quality				■	
Human Resource					
Communications					
Risk					
Procurement					
Stakeholder					

Control Quality is the process of monitoring specific project results to ensure they comply with the project's quality standards.

Control Quality (QC) is the process of monitoring specific project results to ensure they comply with the project quality standards. Like quality assurance (QA), Control Quality should be applied across the entire project life cycle. The quality control process is also intended to identify ways to eliminate quality problems such as causes of weak processes or poor product quality. Process improvement is a natural adjunct of the Control Quality process.

Quality control monitors both product-related deliverables (work packages) and project management deliverables (cost/schedule/scope performance). This process focuses on outputs and uses tools that measure these outputs.

To effectively manage the QC aspects of a project, the project manager and project team should have a practical understanding of basic statistical quality control and probability. Accordingly, this lesson begins with a control quality primer.

Statistical Quality Control

Standard deviation (sigma) - For QC purposes, standard deviation is a measure indicating the distance from the mean (average). In the control chart illustration (next page), the upper control limit (UCL) and lower control limit (LCL) could be established at 3 sigma from the mean, or perhaps 6 sigma from the mean

Normal Distribution		
1 Sigma	+/- 68.26%	1 Standard Deviation
2 Sigma	+/- 95.46%	2 Standard Deviations
3 Sigma	+/- 99.73%	3Standard Deviations
6 Sigma	+/- 99.99%	6 Standard Deviations

Statistical Sampling - Statistical sampling is used as a QC technique to test a sample number of items from a larger population of items (opposed to testing every item). Statistical sampling can be effective and it can reduce overall QC costs. Statistical sampling has a body of knowledge all of its own

Other Statistical Quality Control Terms

Prevention = keeping errors out of the process
Inspection = keeping errors out of the hands of the customer
Attribute Sampling = results are determined as compliant or not compliant; go/no-go
Variables Sampling = results are measured on a continuous scale indicating degree of conformity
Special Causes = unusual events
Random Causes = normal process variation
Tolerances = results are acceptable if within tolerance ranges
Control Limits = result is in-control if it is within specified control limits

---

Figure 49.1 Statistical Quality Control

Common Quality Tools

- **Pareto Diagrams** - A Pareto diagram is a *histogram*, applied as a QC analysis tool to help illustrate the frequency of occurrences by category of causes. Pareto's Principle (the 80/20 principle) suggests that 80% of problems are caused by 20% of all possible causes. Pareto diagrams typically identify the root causes of quality problems, allowing the project team to focus their corrective actions on the small number of areas causing the largest number of problems

- **Checksheets** – Documented checklists used to determine compliance with documented quality standards or requirements

- **Scatter Diagrams** - Illustrate the pattern of relationship between two variables

- **Cause and Effect Diagrams** - (Ishikawa diagrams, fishbone diagrams). Illustrate how various factors may be linked to potential problems

- **Flowcharts (Process maps)** - Illustrate how various elements of a system interrelate

Process Control Charts

Control Charts are graphic displays of process results over time. They are used to monitor a process, to verify its continued stability. Control charts are used to monitor the results of any process, including project management processes. A typical control chart may look like this.

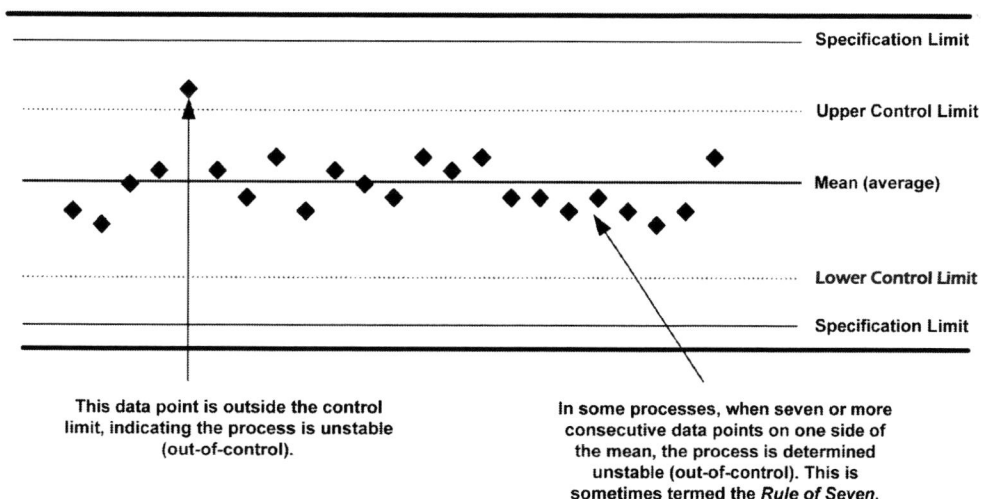

This data point is outside the control limit, indicating the process is unstable (out-of-control).

In some processes, when seven or more consecutive data points on one side of the mean, the process is determined unstable (out-of-control). This is sometimes termed the *Rule of Seven*.

Figure 49.2 Process Control Chart

Process Elements

The Control Quality process has the following Inputs:
- Project Management Plan - The consolidated package of the subsidiary management plans and baselines

- Quality Metrics - Operational definitions. Project elements, and how they are to be measured by quality control

- Quality Checklists - Structured forms used to verify that a set of required steps has been performed in quality control

- Work Performance Data - Collection of project status information (planned vs. actuals); technical performance measures, etc.

- Approved Change Requests - documented, authorized changes (i.e. defect repairs, revised work methods and revised schedule)

- Deliverables - Results, products and/or capabilities (unique, verifiable outcomes) of activities performed

- Project Documents – Agreements, quality audit reports, training plans and process documentation

- Organizational Process Assets - Consideration factors such as quality standards and policies, work guidelines, issue and defect reporting procedures and communication policies

The Control Quality process uses the following Tools & Techniques:
- Seven Basic Quality Tools - Quality tools such as Cause & Effect diagrams, Flowcharts, Check-sheets, Pareto Diagrams, Histograms, Control Charts, Scatter Diagrams

- Statistical Sampling - Statistical analysis using a small group from an entire population

- Inspection - Measuring, examining, testing (reviews, audits, walkthroughs) to ensure results conform to requirements and to validate defect repairs

- Approved Change Requests Review - A review of all approved change requests to verify implementation

The Control Quality process has the following Outputs:
- Quality Control Measurements - Results of all quality control activities

- Validated Changes - Notification of acceptance or rejection of changed or repaired items

- Verified Deliverables - Completed deliverables checked using the Perform Quality Control process

- Work Performance Information - Performance data associated with work completion

- Change Requests - Request for changes to take corrective action, preventive actions and/or perform defect repair

- Project Management Plan Updates - Updates to completed checklists and lessons learned documentation

- Project Documents Updates - Updates to other project documentation (i.e. quality management plan and process improvement plan)

- Organizational Process Asset Updates - Updates to corporate docs, guidelines, procedures, historical information, etc.

Control Quality		
Monitors project results against relevant quality standards to assess results and recommend changes		
Inputs	**Tools and Techniques**	**Outputs**
• Project Management Plan • Quality Metrics • Quality Checklists • Work Performance Data • Approved Change Requests • Deliverables • Project Documents • Organizational Process Assets	• Seven Basic Quality Tools • Statistical Sampling • Inspection • Approved Change Requests Review	• Quality Control Measurements • Validated Changes • Verified Deliverables • Work Performance Information • Change Requests • Project Management Plan Updates • Project Documents Updates • Organizational Process Assets Updates

Figure 49.3 Process Elements within Control Quality

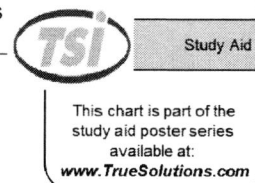

Process Documents

Documents that come from the process of Control Quality can be created in conjunction with other project management processes. In this process you may have the results of one or more tools being applied to project or product measurement and inspection.

Quality Control actions – specifically "inspection" is often tied to the Validate Scope process to verify that the work was completed correctly, meeting requirements and functional specifications. In this case, a formal acceptance form might be used in this process.

Process Tasks

The Control Quality process aligns with one of the defined tasks that a project manager performs when managing a project:

Monitoring and Controlling Task #3: "Ensure that project deliverables conform to the quality standards established in the quality management plan by using appropriate tools and techniques (e.g. testing, inspections, control charts), in order to satisfy customer requirements".

Think About It

Instructions: Use this exercise to compare how you practice project management to what is specified in the *PMBOK® Guide Fifth Edition.* Best Practices suggest that the following items are used during the Control Quality process.

Which of these items do you use when practicing project management?

☐ Cause and effect diagrams
☐ Control charts
☐ Flowcharts
☐ Histograms
☐ Pareto charts
☐ Scatter diagrams
☐ Statistical sampling
☐ Inspection procedures

If you do not use these tools – are there any of these tools that you see a need for?

_____

_____

_____

How can you close the gap between your current practices and best practices defined in the PMBOK?

_____

_____

Must Know Concepts

1. Control Quality is the process of monitoring specific project results to ensure they comply with the project's quality standards.

2. The primary deliverable (Output) of the Control Quality process is verified deliverables.

Test Tip

In the PMBOK® Guide Fifth Edition, the term "verified deliverables" appears to be used interchangeably with "validated deliverables." Therefore, a test question might use either term.

---

3. Control Quality monitors both product-related deliverables (work packages) and project management deliverables (cost/schedule/scope performance).

4. Statistical sampling is used as a QC technique to test a sample number of items from a larger population of items (opposed to testing every item). Statistical sampling can be effective and it can reduce overall QC costs.

5. A Pareto diagram is a histogram, applied as a QC analysis tool to help illustrate the frequency of occurrences by category of causes. Pareto's Principle (the 80/20 principle) suggests that 80% of problems are caused by 20% of all possible causes. Pareto diagrams typically identify the root causes of quality problems, allowing the project team to focus their corrective actions on the small number of areas causing the largest number of problems.

6. Standard deviation (sigma) is a measure indicating the distance from the mean (average). 1 sigma = 1 standard deviation = ± 68.26%. 2 sigma = 2 standard deviations = ± 95.46%. 3 sigma = 3 standard deviations = ± 99.73%. 6 sigma = 6 standard deviations = ± 99.99%.

7. Control Charts are graphic displays of process results over time. They are used to monitor a process, to verify its continued stability. Control charts are used to monitor the results of any process, including project management processes.

8. Scatter Diagrams, Flowcharts, Cause and Effect Diagrams, Check-sheets and Histograms are commonly used quality control tools.

Additional Reading

- PMBOK® Guide Fifth Edition: Section 8.3   Control Quality

Lesson Quiz

Instructions: The actual PMP exam is done via computer. These questions are representative of what you will encounter. Circle the correct answer. Answer Key in Appendix A.

1. Control Quality is the process of:

   A. Applying statistical testing to detect and analyze quality trends
   B. Monitoring the product of the project to ensure it satisfies product performance specifications
   C. Developing performance tolerance criteria, then documenting actual performance using a control chart
   D. Monitoring specific project results to ensure they comply with the project's quality standards

2. The upper control limit (UCL) and lower control limit (LCL) on a typical control chart indicates what?

   A. Process specification limits
   B. Product (of the project) performance specification limits
   C. Statistical validation that the product of the project satisfies performance specifications
   D. The acceptable range (upper and lower) of variation in a process

3. Control Quality tools and techniques include all the following *except*:

   A. Statistical sampling
   B. Pareto charts
   C. Control charts
   D. Quality metrics

4. Standard deviation (sigma):

   A. Is a performance measurement of how close you are to the schedule baseline for the project
   B. Is a performance measure of how far you are from a determined mean (average)
   C. Is a performance measurement of the precision of any statistical sample
   D. Is a performance measurement of how far out-of-control a process is at any given time

5. In project quality control, out-of-control could be indicated by:

   A. A charted process sample data point that falls outside (above or below) 1-sigma
   B. Any project core team member who has been authorized to declare an-out-of-control condition
   C. A charted process sample data point that falls outside an upper or lower control limit
   D. A charted process sample data point that violates the rule-of-seven

End of Lesson 49

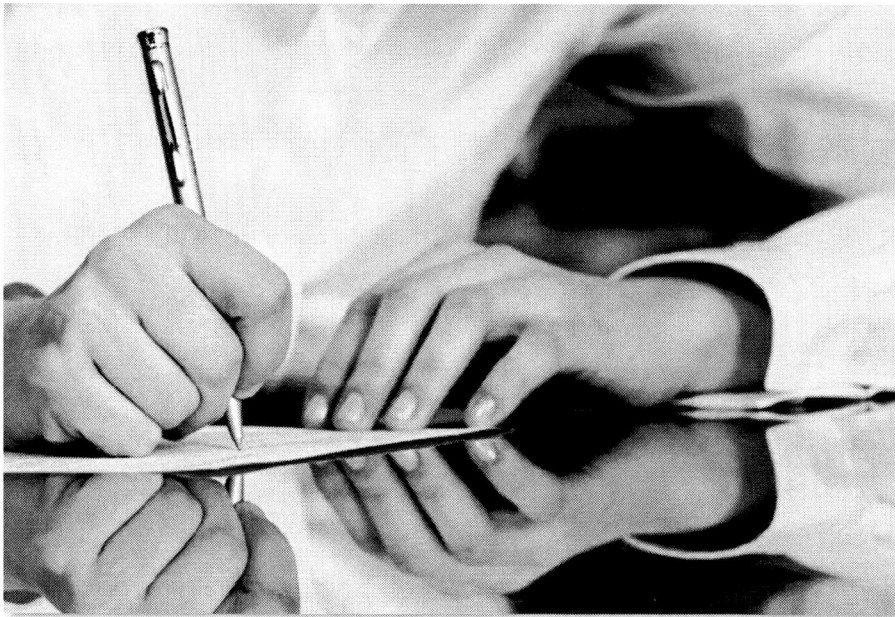

Lesson 50
Validate Scope

Objectives
At the end of this lesson, you will be able to:

6. Describe the purpose of the Validate Scope process
7. Describe the Inputs, Tools and Techniques, and Outputs of the Validate Scope process
8. Understand the relationship between Validate Scope, Control Quality and Close Project or Phase

Process Locator for the PMBOK® Guide

	Initiating	Planning	Executing	M&C	Closing
Integration					
Scope				▓▓▓	
Time					
Cost					
Quality					
Human Resource					
Communications					
Risk					
Procurement					
Stakeholder					

Validate Scope is the process of obtaining formal acceptance of project deliverables.

Validate Scope is the process of accepting completed project deliverables. It must be understood that a project deliverable is not complete until it has been formally accepted, by the individual or group authorized to accept it.

Scope validation differs from control quality. The Control Quality process focuses on the correctness of work. Scope validation focuses on formal acceptance of the work. In practice, control quality is performed first.

Formal acceptance must be documented. Scope validation can occur at any level of the project; it can be done for work, for a specific deliverable, for a milestone, for a phase or for the project overall. Validate Scope is often a predecessor to the closure of a project phase or when closing the overall project.

Process Elements

The Validate Scope process has the following Inputs:
- Project Management Plan - The consolidated package of the subsidiary management plans and baselines

- Requirements Documentation - Documentation describing how individual requirements fulfill the business needs of the project

- Requirements Traceability Matrix - A table which associates requirement origin and the relationship between requirement origin and history throughout the project life cycle

- Verified Deliverables - Completed deliverables checked using the Control Quality process

- Work Performance Data - Raw data related to deliverable status, schedule progress and costs incurred

The Validate Scope process uses the following Tools & Techniques:
- Inspection - Measuring, examining, testing (reviews, audits, walkthroughs) to ensure results conform to requirements

- Group Decision-Making Techniques - A process having multiple alternatives to reach a decision, such as Unanimity, Majority, Plurality or Dictatorship

The Validate Scope process has the following Outputs:
- Accepted Deliverables - Documentation of accepted deliverables from the Validate Scope process

- Change Requests - Request for changes to scope, schedule, costs, or processes or other project documentation

- Work Performance Information - Performance data associated with work completion

- Project Documents Updates - Updates to other project documentation

Validate Scope		
Formalizes acceptance of complete project deliverables		
Inputs	**Tools and Techniques**	**Outputs**
• Project Management Plan • Requirements Documentation • Requirements Traceability Matrix • Verified Deliverables • Work Performance Data	• Inspection • Group Decision Making Techniques	• Accepted Deliverables • Change Requests • Work Performance Information • Project Documents Updates

Figure 50.1 Process Elements within Validate Scope

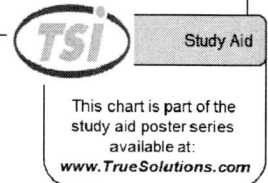

Process Documents

Validate Scope focuses on formal acceptance of project work. Validate Scope is often tied directly to the Control Quality process so that the accuracy of the work is inspected during the formal acceptance process. A formal acceptance form of some sort is the usual document associated with this process.

A sample template is shown below.

TSI

Formal Acceptance of Product or Phase

Project Name:	
Prepared by:	
Date:	
Name of Product:	
Name of Phase, if applicable:	
Name of Specific Deliverable, if applicable:	
Name of Client or Sponsor:	
Statement of Formal Acceptance:	

The undersigned formally accepts as complete the above identified product, project phase, or major deliverable and do hereby state that this project, project phase, or major deliverable meets or exceeds agreed upon performance standards for quality, schedule, and cost, and we state that we have seen documentation that all relevant legal and regulatory requirements have been met or exceeded.

[*In the case of a Phase:*] Acceptance of this Phase of the Project is conditional on the following: (e.g., satisfactory completion of all subsequent phases and meeting overall objectives of entire project)

Accepted by (name of client, sponsor, or other official)	*Date*
Accepted by (name of client, sponsor, or other official)	*Date*
Accepted by (name of client, sponsor, or other official)	*Date*
Signed form distributed to:	
Stakeholder name	*Date*
Stakeholder name	*Date*
Stakeholder name	*Date*

TSI Application Aid

This form is available
individually or as
part of a set at:
www.TrueSolutions.com

Process Tasks

The Validate Scope process aligns with one of the defined tasks that a project manager performs when managing a project:

Monitoring and Controlling Task #3: "Ensure that project deliverables conform to the quality standards established in the quality management plan by using appropriate tools and techniques (e.g. testing, inspections, control charts), in order to satisfy customer requirements".

Think About It

Instructions Use this exercise to compare how you practice project management to what is specified in the *PMBOK® Guide Fifth Edition*.

Think about how this process is defined, used and documented in your organization. Write a brief description of how you use this process

_____

_____

_____

Must Know Concepts

1. Validate Scope is the process of obtaining formal acceptance of project deliverables.

2. The primary deliverable (Output) of the Validate Scope process is accepted deliverables.

3. A project deliverable is not complete until it has been formally accepted, in writing by the individual or group authorized to accept it.

4. Validate Scope differs from quality control because Validate Scope focuses on formal acceptance of the work; whereas Control Quality focuses on correctness of work.

Additional Reading

* PMBOK® Guide Fifth Edition: Section 5.5   Validate Scope

Lesson Quiz

Instructions: The actual PMP exam is done via computer. These questions are representative of what you will encounter. Circle the correct answer. Answer Key in Appendix A.

1. Which of the following statements best depicts the difference between Validate Scope and Control Quality?

    A. Scope validation is primarily focused on the acceptance of project deliverables; Quality control is primarily focused on the correctness of deliverables
    B. Quality control is primarily focused on the acceptance of project deliverables; Scope validation is primarily focused on the correctness of deliverables
    C. Quality control is always performed before scope validation
    D. Scope validation is primarily focused on if deliverables meet the requirements; Quality control is primarily focused on the correctness of deliverables

2. Validate Scope inputs include all of the following except:

    A. Requirements documentation
    B. Requirements traceability matrix
    C. Verified deliverables
    D. Work performance information

3. Which of the following statements best describes the Validate Scope process?

    A. Validate Scope is applied to guide the parallel performance of quality control and formal acceptance of a project deliverable.
    B. Validate Scope is applied to verify the correctness of projcct deliverables.
    C. Validate Scope is the process of obtaining formal acceptance of project deliverables.
    D. Validate Scope is the process of verifying the correctness of identified project scope items.

4. Which of these is not an Output of Validate Scope?

    A. Work Performance Data
    B. Work Performance Information
    C. Project Documents Updates
    D. Change Requests

End of Lesson 50

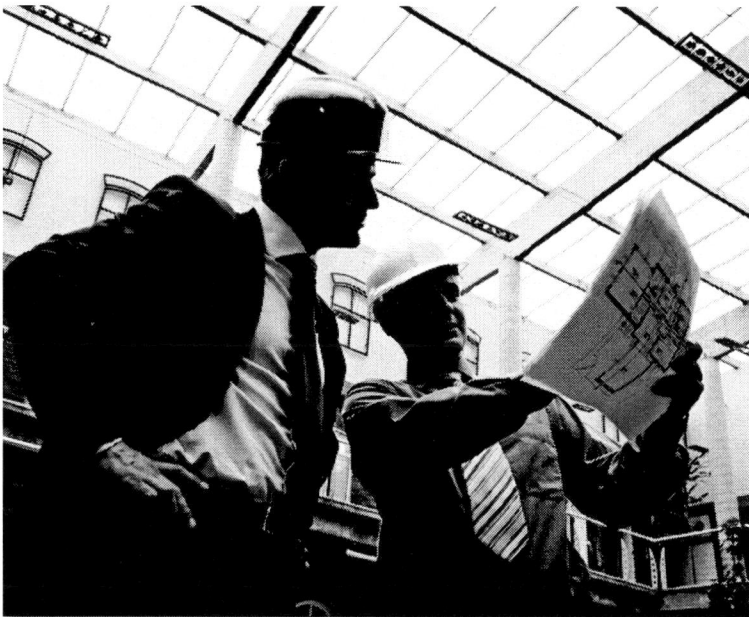

Lesson 51
Monitor & Control Project Work

Objectives
At the end of this lesson, you will be able to:
- Describe the purpose of the Monitor and Control Project Work process
- Describe the Inputs, Tools and Techniques, and Outputs of the Monitor and Control Project Work process

Process Locator for the PMBOK® Guide

	Initiating	Planning	Executing	M&C	Closing
Integration				███	
Scope					
Time					
Cost					
Quality					
Human Resource					
Communications					
Risk					
Procurement					
Stakeholder					

We apply the Monitor and Control Project Work process to monitor progress throughout the project in order to improve understanding of the project condition and take corrective or preventive actions when needed.

Monitor and Control Project Work is performed to track project work performance and take action when performance is different than planned. A good example of this might be the US Apollo space missions to the Moon during the 1960s and 1970s. Like many projects, at any given moment during a space capsule's flight to the Moon, the trajectory was considerably off-course. If the spacecraft were allowed to continue on its divergent path, the capsule would miss its target by a significant margin. Technology at that time was not capable of automating the capsule's flight path.

To compensate, ground controllers would continuously monitor the flight path and, using tiny on-board firing jets, making frequent corrective adjustments to bring the capsule back on-course. Ultimately, the capsule reached its objective.

This is a good comparison to the process of Monitor and Control Project Work.

As project managers, it is our responsibility to continuously monitor project work, and when we detect some aspect is heading off-course, we make controlling adjustments, as necessary, to bring the project back in alignment, to ultimately achieve our defined objectives.

Process Elements

The Monitor and Control Project Work process has the following Inputs:
- Project Management Plan - The consolidated package of the subsidiary management plans and baselines

- Schedule Forecasts - Estimates or predications of conditions or events in the future based on available information

- Cost Forecasts - Either a calculated EAC value or a bottom-up EAC value is documented and communicated to stakeholders

- Validated Changes - Notification of acceptance or rejection of changed or repaired items

- Work Performance Information - Collection of project status information, technical performance measures, etc.

- Enterprise Environmental Factors - Consideration factors such as; culture, systems, procedures, industry standards

- Organizational Process Assets - Consideration factors such as processes, procedures and corporate knowledge base

The Monitor and Control Project Work process uses the following Tools & Techniques:
- Expert Judgment - Expert technical and/or managerial judgment (from the project team)

- Analytical Techniques - Techniques used to monitor and control project work

- Project Management Information System - (PMIS) Automated system to help the team execute planned activities

- Meetings - Meetings required to monitor and control the project work

The Monitor and Control Project Work process has the following Output:
- Change Requests - Request for changes to scope, schedule, costs, or processes or other project documentation

- Work Performance Reports - S-Curves, bar charts, tables, histograms, etc., that summarize team performance

- Project Management Plan Updates - Updates to the Project Management Plan as a result of this process

- Project Documents Updates - Updates to other project documentation

Monitor and Control Project Work		
This process monitors and controls the processes used by the team		
Inputs	**Tools and Techniques**	**Outputs**
• Project Management Plan	• Expert Judgment	• Change Requests
• Schedule Forecasts	• Analytical Techniques	• Work Performance Reports
• Cost Forecasts		
• Validated Changes	• Project Management Information System	• Project Management Plan Updates
• Work Performance Information		
• Enterprise Environmental Factors	• Meetings	• Project Documents Updates
• Organizational Process Assets		

Figure 51.1 Process Elements within Monitor & Control Project Work

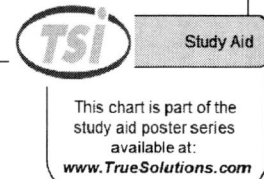

TSI Study Aid

This chart is part of the study aid poster series available at: www.TrueSolutions.com

Process Documents

Information gathered during the Monitor and Control Project Work process will be used in several other processes. A key document to use is the Change Request. This template is shown in the next lesson "Perform Integrated Change Control".

Process Tasks

The Monitor and Control Project Work process aligns with and uses elements of several of the defined tasks that a project manager performs when managing a project:

Monitoring and Controlling Task #1: "Measure project performance using appropriate tools and techniques, in order to identify and quantify any variances, perform approved corrective actions, and communicate with relevant stakeholders".

Monitoring and Controlling Task #2: "Manage change to the project scope, schedule, and costs by updating the project plan and communicating approved changes to the team, in order to ensure that revised project goals are met".

Monitoring and Controlling Task #5: "Assess corrective actions on the issue register and determine next steps for unresolved issues by using appropriate tools and techniques in order to minimize the impact on project schedule, cost and resources".

Think About It

Instructions: Use this exercise to compare how you practice project management to what is specified in the *PMBOK® Guide Fifth Edition.*

Think about how this process is defined, used and documented in your organization. Write a brief description of how you use this process:

_____

_____

_____

_____

_____

What specific Inputs, Tools or Techniques do you use as part of this process in your organization?

_____

_____

_____

Are the outcomes from this process different in your organization or experiences? Do you have a dedicated process like Monitor and Control Project Work formally defined?

_____

_____

_____

Must Know Concepts

1. The Monitor and Control Project Work process is applied to monitor all project work through initiating, planning, executing and closing in order to identify exceptions and take corrective or preventive actions, as needed.

2. The primary deliverable (output) from Monitor & Control Project Work is change requests.

3. Corrective actions are actions required to bring expected future project performance into conformance with the project management plan.

4. Preventive actions are actions required to reduce the probability of negative consequences associated with project risks.

Additional Reading

- PMBOK® Guide® Fifth Edition: Section 4.4 Monitor and Control Project Work

Lesson Quiz

Instructions: The actual PMP exam is done via computer. These questions are representative of what you will encounter. Circle the correct answer. Answer Key in Appendix A.

1. The monitor and control project work process is applied to _____

   A. Monitor all executing processes and take corrective or preventive actions, as needed
   B. Monitor all other processes through initiation, planning, executing and closing and implement risk response actions, if/when risk events occur
   C. Monitor all project work through initiation, planning, executing and closing and take corrective or preventive actions, as needed
   D. Provide guidance for all other monitoring & controlling processes and take corrective or preventive actions, as needed

2. During project execution, an opportunity arises to make a change that will significantly reduce the probability of an identified negative risk from occurring. You suggest making the change. This is an example of what?

   A. Expert judgment
   B. A preventive action
   C. A workaround plan
   D. A corrective action

3. Monitor and Control Project Work outputs include:

   A. Rejected change requests, recommended corrective actions, requested changes
   B. Forecasts, work performance reports, requested changes
   C. Project management plan updates, project documents updates, change requests
   D. Forecasts, recommended corrective actions, requested changes

4. The following are Inputs to Monitor and Control Project Work:

   A. Schedule Forecasts, Validated Changes, Cost Forecasts, Work Performance Information
   B. Schedule Forecasts, Validated Changes, Cost Forecasts, Work Performance Reports
   C. Schedule Forecasts, Validated Changes, Analytical Techniques, Work Performance Information
   D. Schedule Forecasts, Validated Changes, Meetings, Work Performance Reports

5. In Monitor and Control Project Work, Analytical Techniques is a Tool and Technique. Analytical Techniques include:

   A. Regression Analysis, Earned Value Management, Trend Analysis, Work Performance Information
   B. Regression Analysis, Meetings, Trend Analysis, FMEA
   C. Regression Analysis, Earned Value Management, Trend Analysis, FMEA
   D. Regression Analysis, Work Performance Reports, Trend Analysis, FMEA

End of Lesson 51

Lesson 52
Perform Integrated Change Control

Objectives

At the end of this lesson, you will be able to:

- Describe the purpose of the Perform Integrated Change Control process
- Describe the Inputs, Tools and Techniques, and Outputs of the Perform Integrated Change Control process
- Understand how Perform Integrated Change Control interacts with other control processes
- Understand how Configuration Management and Change Control work together

Process Locator for the PMBOK® Guide

	Initiating	Planning	Executing	M&C	Closing
Integration				▓▓▓	
Scope					
Time					
Cost					
Quality					
Human Resource					
Communications					
Risk					
Procurement					
Stakeholder					

Perform Integrated Change Control is the process of effectively managing changes and integrating them appropriately across the entire project.

Perform Integrated Change Control is the process of controlling changes for the project. The general goal of the project manager is to discourage unnecessary changes and focus on the project scope that is tied directly to requirements and strategic business needs. When changes are warranted, they must be made in strict accordance with the project's change control system, and established project baselines normally remain intact. Re-baselining the project and measuring performance against a new baseline is appropriate only in rare project situations when major changes in scope have occurred.

Configuration management, kept in the Enterprise Environmental Factors, is applied in conjunction with change control processes to control changes to the project baselines and product specifications. Configuration management is focused on specifications surrounding the deliverables and the specifications for processes that are used on the project. Change control works with configuration control. Change control documents and controls changes to the project baseline, scope, schedule, cost and product deliverables baseline. To oversimplify the description, configuration management applies mostly to the framework or specifications for the product and project processes. Change control deals with the deliverables planned for the project.

Configuration management activities included in this process include configuration identification (identifying the basis for the product definition), configuration status accounting (identifying and documenting when and how to check on the product configuration) and configuration verification and audit (auditing done to make sure the product configuration meets functional requirements).

Project changes, although often initiated verbally, should always be documented to allow tracking and control. Additionally, all project changes should be formally approved or rejected.

Change Requests that are used as inputs to the Perform Integrated Change Control process come from many sources. This process works closely with Control Scope and Control Schedule to manage change requests for formal approval or rejection. Other processes like Direct and Manage Project Work, Monitor and Control Project Work, Perform Quality Assurance, Control Quality and other also provide change requests to this process.

Some organizations utilize a change control board (CCB) to evaluate and approve/disapprove project change requests.

Process Elements

The Perform Integrated Change Control process has the following Inputs:
- Project Management Plan - The consolidated plan of the subsidiary management plans and baselines

- Work Performance Reports - Project performance reports to track variance, earned value and forecasts

- Change Requests - Request for changes to scope, schedule, costs, or processes or other project documentation

- Enterprise Environmental Factors - Consideration factors such as; culture, systems, procedures, industry standards

- Organizational Process Assets - Consideration factors such as processes, procedures and corporate knowledge base

The Perform Integrated Change Control process uses the following Tools & Techniques:
- Expert Judgment - Expert technical and/or managerial judgment (from any qualified source)

- Meetings - Change Control Board meetings to review change requests and approve/reject changes

- Change Control Tools - Manual and automated tools used to manage change requests and resulting decisions

The Perform Integrated Change Control process has the following Outputs:
- Approved Change Requests - Processed change requests

- Change Log - Documentation of changes that occur during a project

- Project Management Plan Updates - Updates to the Project Management Plan as a result of this process

- Project Documents Updates - Updates to other project documentation

Perform Integrated Change Control		
This process reviews, approves and controls changes to project deliverables		
Inputs	**Tools and Techniques**	**Outputs**
• Project Management Plan	• Expert Judgment	• Approved Change Requests
• Work Performance Reports	• Meetings	• Change Log
• Change Requests	• Change Control Tools	• Project Management Plan Updates
• Enterprise Environmental Factors		• Project Documents Updates
• Organizational Process Assets		

Figure 52.1 Process Elements within Perform Integrated Change Control

Process Documents

Two primary documents are associated with Perform Integrated Change Control: the Change Request Form and Change Log. Examples of each are shown below.

Generic Change Request

Project Name:		
Prepared by:		
Date:		
Person(s) Requesting Change:		
Change Number:		

Type of Change Requested:

Project Scope Change	Project Budget Change	Project Schedule Change
Project Procurement/Contract Change	Other (specify)	

Detailed Description of Change:

Reason for Change Requested:

Effect on Project Cost:

☐ Projected Cost *Overrun* of approximately   %

☐ Estimated Cost *Reduction* of approximately   %

Effect on Schedule:

☐ Planned Project Completion Date:

☐ New Project Completion Date:

Additional Remarks:

Approval	Project Manager	Date
Approval	(Other)	Date

Application Aid

This form is available individually or as part of a set at:
www.TrueSolutions.com

®Copyright 2013 True Solutions, Inc.
5001 LBJ Freeway, Suite 125, Dallas, Texas 75244
Tel: 972.770.0900 Fax 972.770.0922 www.truesolutions.com

Project Change Request Tracking Report

Project Name:				
Prepared by:				
Date:				
Project Manager:				
Project Change Request Administrator:				
Change Number	Change Name	Change Requestor	Status of Change	Comments

Application Aid

This form is available
individually or as
part of a set at:
www.TrueSolutions.com

Process Tasks

The Perform Integrated Change Control process aligns with and uses elements of two of the defined tasks that a project manager performs when managing a project:

Monitoring and Controlling Task #2: "Manage change to the project scope, schedule, and costs by updating the project plan and communicating approved changes to the team, in order to ensure that revised project goals are met".

Monitoring and Controlling Task #5: "Assess corrective actions on the issue register and determine next steps for unresolved issues by using appropriate tools and techniques in order to minimize the impact on project schedule, cost and resources".

Think About It

My company was engaged to provide project management of an implementation project for a software company. The actual project was to create a custom website portal for a financial organization so that they could access their financial system and upgrade to the newest version of the financial software package.

The project team consisted of a project manager and developers from the software company and a project manager and developers from a website company (most of the resources were off-shored) who were responsible for design and coding of the website portal. In addition, the customer team had a project manager and multiple functional experts.

The project had been delayed multiple times and was over budget by about $5,000,000. The customer was threatening to sue the software company for not delivering the implementation of the software. The software company had lost all credibility and did not how to fix the problem so they brought in my company as a third party Program Manager to be the neutral party and see if the project and the relationship could be recovered.

Our PM came in and within a week, assessed scope, requirements and project plan. The problem was identified as a lack of cohesive planning across all project teams and entities. Each of the above teams had a different scope document and working from different versions of the requirements. There were no plans or processes in place to synchronize their scope, requirements and changes.

The solution was getting all 3 parties to an agreed to a single scope and requirement document and then implementing stringent integrated change control for all parties. This solution was facilitated by holding requirement review sessions and producing one set of controlled requirements (owned by the functional users), and integrating all of the schedules into one master project schedule. Then we could see the gaps, issues and take action to put the project back on track. While the project ultimately ended with a severe cost overrun, the end result of the project was an upgraded financial system that was usable and internet accessible.

Contributed by Lorie Gibbons, PMP

Must Know Concepts

1. Perform Integrated Change Control is the process of effectively managing changes and integrating them appropriately across the entire project.

2. The primary deliverables (Outputs) of the Perform Integrated Change Control process include Approved Change Requests, Project Management Plan Updates and Project Document Updates.

3. Configuration management applies mostly to the framework or specifications for the product and project processes. Configuration management is an especially useful tool when the product of the project is very complex.

4. It is the project manager's responsibility to discourage unnecessary changes. When legitimate changes are warranted, they should be made in accordance with the project's change control system.

Additional Reading

- PMBOK® Guide Fifth Edition: Section 4.5 Perform Integrated Change Control

Lesson Quiz

Instructions: The actual PMP exam is done via computer. These questions are representative of what you will encounter. Circle the correct answer. Answer Key in Appendix A.

1. The Perform Integrated Change Control process occurs _____

   A. During Execution only
   B. During Initiating and Executing
   C. Throughout the project life cycle
   D. During Executing and Monitoring and Controlling

2. All of the following are Perform Integrated Change Control process outputs except:

   A. Updates to project documents
   B. Change request approvals
   C. Project management plan updates
   D. Change control meetings

3. Perform Integrated Change Control is _____.

   A. The process applied to guide the project change control board (CCB) in their decisions to approve or deny project change requests
   B. The process of effectively managing changes and integrating them appropriately across the entire project
   C. The process applied to encourage the project manager to use effective influencing skills to discourage unnecessary changes
   D. The process applied to guide the use of configuration management procedures across the project life cycle

4. Meetings is a Tool and Technique of Perform Integrated Change Control. What kind of meeting does this refer to specifically?

   A. Meeting to write Change Requests
   B. Discussion set up to preview potential changes that may be written
   C. Change Control Board meeting whose purpose is to decision Change Requests
   D. Status meeting set up to review issues

5. You are the project manager for the Lubbock Dirt Truck project, which will result in a new truck capable of working even during severe dust storms. The lead designer has discovered that modification of several key truck windshield features will really reduce the cost of the overall design. A Change Request is written and added to an automated system. What Tool and Technique is being used by the project team?

   A. Change Requests
   B. Enterprise Environmental Factors
   C. Change Log
   D. Change Control Tools

End of Lesson 52

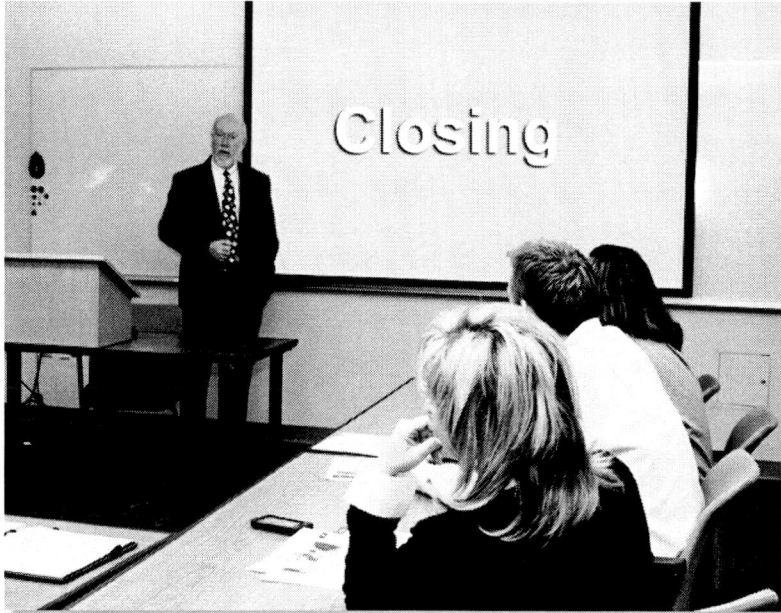

Lesson 53
Closing Process Group

Objectives

At the end of this lesson, you will be able to:

6. Understand what processes are used in the Closing Process Group
7. Understand the purpose for using Closing processes for the project or project phase

Process Locator for the PMBOK® Guide

	Initiating	Planning	Executing	M&C	Closing
Integration					
Scope					
Time					
Cost					
Quality					
Human Resource					
Communications					
Risk					
Procurement					
Stakeholder					

The Closing Process Group consists of two processes that are intended to end or close a project or project phase.

The primary purpose that these Closing processes are performed is to authorize the project (or phase) to end. End of phase reviews will be held as part of Closing processes. Closing processes occur in the Integration Management knowledge area and the Procurement Management knowledge area of the *PMBOK® Guide Fifth Edition.*

An important part of the Closing process group is the authorization for the vendor to terminate activities and for the overall project (or phase) to terminate.

When a project is closed, the sponsor, project manager and stakeholders have the final view of the project. Approvals for work, the product that was created and the project overall are obtained prior to closing the project or phase.

Once the project team and/or vendor team is released from the project, unless there is some form of warranty verbiage in contracts, then the team is done and the project is officially closed.

The PMBOK® Guide is very certain that the project ends when final approval for work, for the product and the project are obtained.

Closing Tasks

On your PMP Exam, you will encounter approximately several questions that will test your understanding of Initiating processes. These questions will generally focus on the following Closing tasks.

As a PMP or project manager closing a project (or project phase), you may be required to:

1. Obtain final acceptance of the project deliverables by working with the sponsor and/or customer, in order to confirm that project scope and deliverables were met.

2. Transfer the ownership or deliverables to the assigned stakeholders in accordance with the project plan, in order to facilitate project closure.

3. Obtain financial, legal and administrative closure using generally accepted practices, in order to communicate formal project closure and ensure no further liability.

4. Distribute the final project report including all project closure related information, project variances, and any issues, in order to provide the final project status to all stakeholders

5. Collate lessons learned through comprehensive project review, in order to create and/or update the organization's knowledge base.

6. Archive project documents and materials in order to retain organizational knowledge, comply with statutory requirements and ensure availability of data for potential use in future projects and internal or external audits.

7. Measure customer satisfaction at the end of the project by capturing customer feedback, in order to assist in project evaluations and enhance customer relationships.

Knowledge Requirements

As a PMP applying Closing processes in real-world projects, you will be required to possess in-depth knowledge in several project specific areas, as well as a broad knowledge of project management in general. The PMP Exam will test your understanding of these knowledge specifics.

By developing a familiarity with these knowledge specifics, you will better understand the context of many PMP Exam questions. Please give some thought to each item as it relates to your own project management experiences with past and current projects.

Remember, the PMP or project manager is always required to have a very broad base of knowledge to work from. The project manager has to work across the entire organization spectrum in many cases to effectively perform project management.

As a PMP or project manager applying Closing processes, you may be expected to have knowledge of:

- Contract closure requirements
- Basic project accounting principles
- Close-out procedures
- Feedback techniques
- Project review techniques
- Archiving techniques and statutory requirements
- Compliance (Statutory or organization requirements)
- Transition planning techniques

Read the *PMBOK® Guide Fifth Edition*

The information exposed in our Ultimate PMP Exam Prep Guide is often sufficient for you to pass your PMP Exam on the first try...without any other aids or tools.

However, since we are all interested in your success on the PMP Exam, we feel like it is imperative to remind you to read the PMBOK® Guide Fifth Edition. Throughout the Ultimate PMP Exam Prep Guide you will find references to the PMBOK.

This is an important certification and an important step in your career. We recommend that you thoroughly read ***both*** documents.

End of Lesson 53

This page intentionally blank.

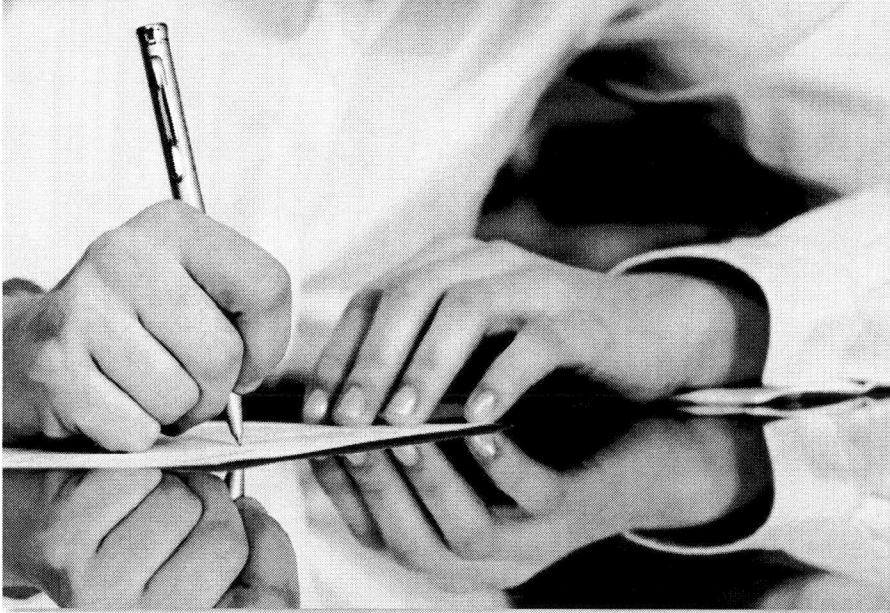

Lesson 54
Close Procurements

Objectives
At the end of this lesson, you will be able to:
- Describe the purpose of the Close Procurements process
- Describe the Inputs, Tools and Techniques, and Outputs of the Close Procurements process
- Understand how Close Procurements interacts with Close Project or Phase and other processes

Process Locator for the PMBOK® Guide

	Initiating	Planning	Executing	M&C	Closing
Integration					
Scope					
Time					
Cost					
Quality					
Human Resource					
Communications					
Risk					
Procurement					■
Stakeholder					

The Close Procurements process is used to formally validate that all of the requirements for each of the project's procurement activities have been met and are acceptable for both seller and buyer.

This process, in conjunction with the Close Project or Phase process, is often used to complete a project. This process is also used throughout the project's life cycle to bring a formal termination to a procurement or procurement contract.

This process is usually preceded by the Control Quality process and the Validate Scope process in order to verify that work was completed correctly and is accepted by the appropriate stakeholder(s).

The process of Close Procurements is similar to, but slightly different than the process of Close Project or Phase. First of all, Close Procurements is closing only a portion of the overall project, whereas Close Project or Phase is used to close the overall project or phase. In addition to that difference, there is a difference in activity flow in the process.

During Close Procurements, the majority of formal approval or acceptance flows from the project to the vendor. During Close Project or Phase, the project manager obtains or receives formal acceptance from the sponsor.

Formal Acceptance for:	Close Procurements	Close Project or Phase
Work	Given to Vendor	Received from Sponsor
Product		
Project		
Resource Release		
Documentation	Received from Vendor and archived	Provided to Sponsor and Organization; then archived

Figure 54.1 Formal Acceptance Flow

When closing any procurement, information, lessons learned, and other procurement data should be archived to aid in future projects.

Process Elements

The Close Procurements process has the following Inputs:
- Project Management Plan - The consolidated package of the subsidiary management plans and baselines
- Procurement Documents - Contract, supporting schedules, scope, quality, cost performance, contract change documentation, payment records, and inspection results

The Close Procurements process uses the following Tools & Techniques:
- Procurement Audits - Structured lessons learned-type reviews of the project's procurement process

- Procurement Negotiations - Final settlement of all outstanding issues, claims, and disputes

- Records Management System - Used by the project manager to manage contract documentation and records

The Close Procurements process has the following Output:
- Closed Procurements - Formal written notice of the closure of the procurement

- Organizational Process Assets Updates - Updates to procurement files, deliverable acceptance, lessons learned documentation

Close Procurements		
This process formally completes the project procurements		
Inputs	**Tools and Techniques**	**Outputs**
• Project Management Plan • Procurement Documents	• Procurement Audits • Procurement Negotiations • Records Management System	• Closed Procurements • Organizational Process Assets Updates

Figure 54.1 Process Elements within Close Procurements

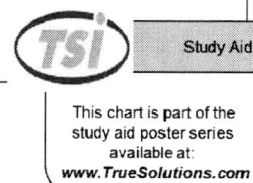

TSI Study Aid

This chart is part of the study aid poster series available at: *www.TrueSolutions.com*

Process Documents

This process focuses on providing formal acceptance to the vendor for work, for the product of the project and for the project overall. The project manger will probably use acceptance documents similar to the document shown in Validate Scope.

Process Tasks

The Close Procurements process aligns with and uses elements of several of the defined tasks that a project manager performs when managing a project:

Closing Task #1: "Obtain final acceptance of the project deliverables by working with the sponsor and/or customer, in order to confirm that project scope and deliverables were met".

Closing Task #2: "Transfer the ownership of deliverables to the assigned stakeholders in accordance with the project plan, in order to facilitate project closure".

Closing Task #3: "Obtain financial, legal, and administrative closure using generally accepted practices, in order to communicate formal project closure and ensure no further project liability".

Closing Task #6: "Archive project documents and material in order to retain organizational knowledge, comply with statutory requirements, and ensure availability of data for potential use in future projects and internal/external audits".

Think About It

Instructions: Use this exercise to compare how you practice project management to what is specified in the *PMBOK® Guide Fifth Edition.*

Best Practices suggest that the following items are used during the Close Procurements process.

Which of these items do you use when practicing project management?

☐ Verify work completion and acceptance

☐ Review vendor performance

☐ Provide formal acceptance to the vendor

☐ Use a process to make final payments

☐ Resolve any open issues before formal acceptance is provided

☐ Document lessons learned

☐ Archive all contract documents

How would you change your use of this process in your organization to resolve any gaps in application?

_____

_____

_____

Must Know Concepts

1. The Close Procurements process is used to formally validate that all of the requirements for each of the project's procurement activities have been met and are acceptable for both seller and buyer.

2. The deliverables (Outputs) of the Close Procurements process are the closed procurements and updates to the organizational process assets.

Additional Reading

- PMBOK® Guide Fifth Edition: Section 12.4   Close Procurements

Lesson Quiz

1. Close Procurements:

    A. Is the procurement process of verifying the final seller invoices have been approved and paid
    B. Is the procurement process of formally validating all the requirements for each of the project's procurement activities have been met and are acceptable
    C. Is the procurement process of documenting that the seller has been formally notified of contract end, regardless of the reason for termination
    D. Is the procurement process of formally transferring the contract to central contracting to ensure the final contract documents (including lessons learned) are properly archived

2. Among the following statements, _____ is *least* true.

    A. Close Procurements is performed by verifying that contracted work was completed correctly and contract terms and conditions were satisfied
    B. During close procurements, formal acceptance is documented and contract records area archived
    C. Close procurements is applied once, at the very end of the final project phase, like all closing processes
    D. Close procurements is applied only if services/supplies are contracted/purchases to support the project

3. Which of the following is a close procurements tool/technique?

    A. Procurement audits
    B. Closed procurements
    C. Organizational process assets updates
    D. Procurement documentation

End of Lesson 54

Lesson 55
Close Project or Phase

Objectives
At the end of this lesson, you will be able to:
- Describe the purpose of the Close Project or Phase process
- Describe the Inputs, Tools and Techniques, and Outputs of the Close Project or Phase process
- Understand the interaction with other processes that is required to close a project or phase

Process Locator for the PMBOK® Guide

	Initiating	Planning	Executing	M&C	Closing
Integration					▨
Scope					
Time					
Cost					
Quality					
Human Resource					
Communications					
Risk					
Procurement					
Stakeholder					

Close Project or Phase is the process of formally ending either the project or project phase. This process documents project results to formalize the acceptance of the product of the project or project phase.

Close Project or Phase is the process of closing either an entire project or a phase of a project. This process is also utilized when projects are terminated prior to their completion.

Close Project or Phase is performed by collecting project records, analyzing project performance, analyzing lessons learned and archiving all project information for future review and use.

This process is intended to deliver two primary outputs:

- The final product/service/result of the project (formally accepted and transitioned to an appropriate stakeholder)

- Organizational process assets updates

Process Elements

The Close Project or Phase process has the following Inputs:
- Project Management Plan - The consolidated package of the subsidiary management plans and baselines

- Accepted Deliverables - Documentation of accepted deliverables from the Validate Scope process

- Organizational Process Assets - Consideration factors such as processes, procedures and corporate knowledge base

The Close Project or Phase process uses the following Tools & Techniques:
- Expert Judgment - Expert technical and/or managerial judgment (from any qualified source)

- Analytical Techniques - Techniques used to close a project or phase

- Meetings - Meetings to conclude a project or phase

The Close Project or Phase process has the following Output:
- Final Product, Service or Result Transition - the progression of the final product, service, or result of the project or project phase.

- Organizational Process Assets Updates - Updates to corporate documents, guidelines, procedures, historical information, etc.

Close Project or Phase		
This process formally completes the project or project phase		
Inputs	**Tools and Techniques**	**Outputs**
• Project Management Plan • Accepted Deliverables • Organizational Process Assets	• Expert Judgment • Analytical Techniques • Meetings	• Final Product, Service or Result Transition • Organizational Process Assets Updates

Figure 55.1 Process Elements within Close Project or Phase

Process Documents

The main focus for this particular process is the formal acceptance of the project or the phase. A formal acceptance document similar to the one shown following will be used.

In addition to obtaining formal acceptance for the project or phase during this process, the project manager will gather (if not already collected) all of the project documentation for inclusion in the project archives. The project archives form the Organizational Process Assets that can be used in the future to assist in planning future projects in the performing organization.

Formal Acceptance of Project or Phase

Project Name:	
Prepared by:	
Date:	
Name of Product:	
Name of Phase, if applicable:	
Name of Specific Deliverable, if applicable:	
Name of Client or Sponsor:	

Statement of Formal Acceptance:

The undersigned formally accepts as complete the above identified product, project phase, or major deliverable and do hereby state that this project, project phase, or major deliverable meets or exceeds agreed upon performance standards for quality, schedule, and cost, and we state that we have seen documentation that all relevant legal and regulatory requirements have been met or exceeded.

[In the case of a Phase:] Acceptance of this Phase of the Project is conditional on the following: (e.g., satisfactory completion of all subsequent phases and meeting overall objectives of entire project)

Accepted by (name of client, sponsor, or other official)	*Date*
Accepted by (name of client, sponsor, or other official)	*Date*
Accepted by (name of client, sponsor, or other official)	*Date*

Signed form distributed to:

Stakeholder name	*Date*
Stakeholder name	*Date*
Stakeholder name	*Date*

TSI **Application Aid**

This form is available
individually or as
part of a set at:
www.TrueSolutions.com

Process Tasks

The Close Project or Phase process aligns with and uses elements of all of the defined tasks that a project manager performs when closing a project:

Closing Task #1: "Obtain final acceptance of the project deliverables by working with the sponsor and/or customer, in order to confirm that project scope and deliverables were met".

Closing Task #2: "Transfer the ownership of deliverables to the assigned stakeholders in accordance with the project plan, in order to facilitate project closure".

Closing Task #3: "Obtain financial, legal, and administrative closure using generally accepted practices, in order to communicate formal project closure and ensure no further project liability".

Closing Task #4: "Distribute the final project report including all project closure-related information, project variances, and any issues, in order to provide the final project status to all stakeholders".

Closing Task #5: "Collate lessons learned through comprehensive project review, in order to create and/or update the organization's knowledge base".

Closing Task #6: "Archive project documents and material in order to retain organizational knowledge, comply with statutory requirements, and ensure availability of data for potential use in future projects and internal/external audits".

Closing Task #7: "Measure customer satisfaction at the end of the project by capturing customer feedback, in order to assist in project evaluation and enhance customer relationships".

Think About It

Instructions: Use this exercise to compare how you practice project management to what is specified in the *PMBOK® Guide Fifth Edition.*

Think about how this process is defined, used and documented in your organization. Write a brief description of how you use this process:

_____

_____

_____

_____

What specific Inputs, Tools or Techniques do you use as part of this process in your organization?

_____

_____

_____

Are the outcomes from this process different in your organization or experiences?

_____

_____

_____

Must Know Concepts
----

1. Close Project or Phase is the process of formally ending either the project or project phase.

2. Close Project or Phase documents project results to formalize the acceptance of the product/service/result of the project (or project phase).

3. The primary deliverables (Outputs) of the Close Project or Phase process include the formally accepted product/service/result transition and organizational process assets updates.

4. Close Project or Phase is performed by collecting project records, analyzing project performance, analyzing lessons learned and archiving all project information for future review and use.

5. Celebrate!

Additional Reading

-   PMBOK® Guide Fifth Edition: Section 4.6   Close Project or Phase

Lesson Quiz

Instructions The actual PMP exam is done via computer. These questions are representative of what you will encounter. Circle the correct answer. Answer Key in Appendix A.

1. _____, best describes the Close Project or Phase process.

    A. Preparing and distributing the final project performance report
    B. Archiving the performance evaluations of project core team members
    C. Bringing an orderly end to the seller's contractual obligations
    D. Formally ending either the project or project phase

2. Close Project or Phase is intended to be applied _____.

    A. Repeatedly, upon the completion of each WBS work package.
    B. At the end of each project life cycle phase, including the very last project phase
    C. At the end of the final project life cycle phase, concluding the entire project
    D. Each time a significant project document needs to be formally archived

3. Close Project or Phase inputs include which of the following?

    A. Expert judgment
    B. Final product transition
    C. Accepted deliverables
    D. WBS

4. Which of the following is most true?

    A. You (as project manager) are responsible for performing and documenting lessons learned.
    B. Your key project stakeholders are responsible for performing and documenting lessons learned.
    C. Your sponsor is responsible for performing and documenting lessons learned.
    D. You (working with your project management team) are responsible for performing and documenting lessons learned.

5 Meetings is a Tool and Technique of Close Project or Phase. All of these are types of meetings that may be held except:

    A. Focus groups to develop Requirements Documentation
    B. Review meeting to discuss results of the last phase
    C. Closeout meeting
    D. Lessons learned discussion

End of Lesson 55

This page intentionally blank.

Lesson 56
Mastering the PMP Exam

Objectives
At the end of this lesson, you will be able to:
- Understand the fundamentals of multiple choice question (MCQ) exams, including successful test taking techniques
- Understand test anxiety and stress
- Learn the Ultimate PMP Exam Day Test Strategy to help achieve anxiety-free peak performance

Process Locator for the PMBOK® Guide

	Initiating	Planning	Executing	M&C	Closing
Integration					
Scope					
Time					
Cost					
Quality		Contains General Management Information that is applicable to all areas of the PMBOK® Guide and applies to project management in general			
Human Resource					
Communications					
Risk					
Procurement					
Stakeholder					

In this lesson, we will discuss important fundamentals in test taking, and present proven test taking strategies to help you achieve peak performance on Exam day.

To be successful in passing your PMP Exam, just knowing the material may not be enough. You must also develop some practical test taking skills. Throughout your academic experience it is likely that you have encountered many types of test question formats, such as oral questions, essay questions, fill-in-the-blank questions and true or false questions. Your PMP Exam employs a multiple choice question (MCQ) format.

MCQ exams have been proven to be highly effective for testing complex intellectual knowledge, reasoning ability and understanding. Good MCQ exams (like the PMP Exam) are both objective and reliable.

To pass, MCQ test takers must study for recall, but more importantly for understanding. Good MCQ exams require you to 1) recognize answers to problems, 2) recognize correct reasons for relationships, 3) establish causal links and 4) demonstrate an understanding of principles and standards.

Good MCQ exams make liberal use of reasonable appearing distracters. Distractors are intended to discriminate between those who truly know the correct or best answer and those who have only a cursory familiarity on the subject.

The PMP Exam presents all questions with 4 unique multiple choice answer options. There are no true/false questions and there are no combination answers where two or more answers form a correct choice. The test taker must choose the best answer from the presented choices. In some cases, one or more answer options may be correct or have some degree of correctness; the test taker must determine the best answer from his or her understanding of the subject matter.

The Science of Answering MCQ Exam Questions

Step 1: Know How to Read the MCQ

Approach each MCQ as a mutually exclusive independent event. Read the MCQ carefully, looking to determine precisely what the question is really asking for:
- Identify the correct answer?
- Identify the best answer?
- Identify the first best action?
- Identify the least best action?
- Identify the exception?
- Identify the incorrect alternative?

Many MCQ's will be straightforward, but many will include irrelevant information and other distracters. Be thankful for the straightforward questions, but expect distracters.

Be on the lookout for distinguishing terms. Directly in the wording of many MCQ's, you will find some distinguishing term or phrase. For example, *fast tracking* may appear in a question. You should recognize fast tracking as a key project management term. It may be the distinguishing term in this particular MCQ. If you focus some attention on the distinguishing term, you may be able to identify the correct answer even before reviewing the answer options.

If the MCQ is presented as double-negative (i.e. *All of the following are false, except*), then you may consider converting it to a positive before reviewing the answer options. In the example, "*All of the following statements are false, except*", logic tells us that all of the answers are false except one. The correct answer is the one *true* statement. So, instead of identifying the false statements and eliminating them, look to identify the one true statement and selecting it.

Before looking at the answer options, try to answer the question based on your recall and understanding. Many times, this will help you quickly identify the correct answer.

Step 2: Know How to Review the Answer Options and Select the Best One

- Once you feel confident that you understand what the MCQ is asking you to identify (correct, best, least, most, exception), review the answer options.

- Read *all* answer options carefully.

- If the answer doesn't come quickly, look for more clues in the question. For example; if the question indicates the answer is plural, then it may be possible to eliminate answers that are singular. Some MCQ's purposely contain awkward grammar, but most are straightforward.

- If the answer is still elusive, begin eliminating options. Use scratch paper to cross-off options that you know are wrong.

- If you are still unsure, mark the question for later review. Do not attempt an answer at this time. The general rule of thumb is to labor no more than two-minutes over a difficult question. Mark it and save it for later. (Questions can be marked with an answer, marked with an answer *and* marked for review, marked for review or simply skipped).

- When your first pass through the questions is complete, revisit unanswered questions, as well as any low-confidence questions. It is possible to encounter clues to some correct answers in other questions.

- Changing answers on an MCQ exam is neither good nor bad. If you have a sensible reason to change one or more of your answers, go ahead and make the change.

- Do not leave blanks on your completed Exam. Provide an answer for *all* of the questions. There is no added penalty for answering questions incorrectly on your PMP Exam. Correctly answered questions are tallied as one. Incorrect and unanswered questions are tallied as zero. On impossible questions, a wild guess is better than no answer at all. If you can't eliminate even one of the options, a wild guess will still give you a theoretical 25% probability of being correct.

Formal examination confrontations almost always generate significant test taking anxiety and stress. This creates a special challenge. When under extreme stress, many people do not perform well in mental recall and logical reasoning. Mastering the learning material does help to reduce test taking anxiety, but specific stress reducing techniques are needed to maintain relative calm during the exam.

MCQ exams tend to create added stress through their extensive use of distracters. These distracters force test takers to read and re-read many questions to fully understand what is being said. The level of focus and concentration needed throughout a long MCQ exam can be very draining.

Step 3: Know What to Expect on the PMP Exam

Expectation 1: Every question on your PMP Exam will be new to you. You have never seen any of them before. No matter how many practice exam questions you have mastered, these new questions will create uncertainty, anxiety and will challenge your confidence. In the extreme, you may even be somewhat shocked.

Expectation 2: Although you are fully prepared with material knowledge, there is no way to prepare for specific Exam questions. Many questions will require you to integrate several facts to derive the correct answer. This will challenge your logical reasoning.

Expectation 3: Many questions will purposely include irrelevant information and distracters. This will be somewhat disorienting.

Expectation 4: Some questions may force you to select correct answers that you fundamentally disagree with. This may generate a bit of resentment.

Expectation 5: Some questions will include alternate terminology to test your deeper understanding of a concept. This will challenge your confidence.

Expectation 6: Many questions present long situational scenarios. These questions take excessive time to read and understand. These questions can disorient your pacing, challenge your focus/concentration, add to anxiety and erode your confidence.

Expectation 7: Some questions will include obscure terms or concepts that you have never seen before. This will challenge your confidence.

Expectation 8: Your Exam may present a consecutive sequence of long difficult questions. This tends to disorient your pacing and challenge your confidence.

Expectation 9: You will face questions that have moral and cultural scenarios interwoven into the project management question. These questions test your understanding of the Project Management Institute's Code of Ethics and Professional Conduct. These questions will ask you what the "right" thing to do is, based on a cultural, ethical and project situation.

Expectation 10: Your Exam screen will feature an ever-present four-hour countdown clock, which does not stop when you take a break. This adds to anxiety.

Step 4: Know the Content Required in order to pass the Exam

This Guide has been dedicated to the content that you need to know to pass the PMP Exam. Some examples of content are:

Here are subjects you are expected to know (from the class presentation):

- ☐ Project Charter - What it is, what it does
- ☐ Project Management Plan- What makes up the plan
- ☐ Scope Statement – what it is and does
- ☐ Initiating a project – What steps to take
- ☐ Planning a project – What steps and processes are used – know how the processes flow within the planning process group
- ☐ Earned value technique to measure performance
- ☐ How to create and interpret a network diagram
- ☐ Crashing and fast tracking as a schedule compression techniques
- ☐ How to develop and manage a budget
- ☐ What the role of the project manager is
- ☐ What defines a milestone
- ☐ How to control change and the best thing to do about changes
- ☐ What a project gate or kill point is
- ☐ How to define and measure quality
- ☐ Risk Management techniques
- ☐ How to create and use the WBS – What processes does it link to
- ☐ The project management methodology – what it is and when it's used
- ☐ What are the main causes for conflict on a project
- ☐ What are the main constraints to a project
- ☐ How to define and use a communications plan
- ☐ How to use stakeholder management processes to manage stakeholders
- ☐ Team development
- ☐ How to gain formal acceptances for work, the product and the project
- ☐ Project selection methods, motivational theory, procurement and quality
- ☐ How to adhere to the PMP Code of Ethics and Professional Conduct
- ☐ General management
- ☐ Procurement methods and processes
- ☐ Customer satisfaction and management styles

Step 5: Know the PMI Code of Ethics and Professional Conduct

Project Management Institute has defined a Code of Ethics and Professional Conduct that all members of PMI are expected to adhere to when managing projects. This Code is intended to address moral, ethical and cultural competencies.

Part of your essential reading is to read the Project Management Institute Code of Ethics and Professional Conduct. This is available from PMI as a part of the "Certification Handbook" intended to prepare you for your PMP certification project. This standard governing the conduct of project managers and PMP's has been developed over the past twenty-plus years. The Code of Ethics and Professional Conduct responds to changes in the world or project management that have occurred during that time.

This Code addresses Mandatory Standards which have to be met and Aspirational Standards which are desirable.

In general, this code is intended to instill confidence in the profession of project management by providing a common frame of behavior for project managers. In general, compliance with this code should facilitate each practitioner becoming more proficient as they comply with the code.

The Code addresses the areas of responsibility, respect, fairness, honesty and cultural competence.

Responsibility
- Taking the best actions for a specific situation
- Taking actions supported by knowledge
- Fulfilling project and professional requirements
- Protecting sensitive information
- Upholding the Code
- Compliance with all applicable laws and regulations (mandatory)
- Reporting unethical or illegal behavior (mandatory)

Respect
- Keeping informed about cultural norms and customs
- Listening to stakeholders
- Addressing conflict as required
- Behaving professionally at all times
- Negotiating in good faith with customers and suppliers (mandatory)
- Refraining from personal enrichment (mandatory)
- Not acting abusively (mandatory)
- Respect others property rights (mandatory)

Fairness
- Make decisions in a transparent manner
- Act impartially

- Provide equal access to information
- Provide equal opportunity when acquiring resources
- Avoid conflicts of interest (mandatory)
- Act fairly when hiring, do not base decisions on personal considerations (mandatory)
- Do not discriminate against individuals based on social prejudices (mandatory)
- Apply rules impartially (mandatory)

Honesty
- Seek the truth
- Speak the truth
- Make commitments in good faith
- Do not engage in or condone dishonesty (mandatory)

Cultural Competence
- Be aware of cultural differences
- Respect other cultures' ways of behavior and moral interpretations
- Maintain professional sensitivity when dealing with other cultures
- Practice cultural awareness in all project situations

Many professional responsibility questions can be answered simply by using common sense. These questions will be incorporated into project scenarios. The best choice is usually to choose to do the right thing.

Step 6: Use the "Ultimate PMP Exam Day Strategy"

In order to succeed in your PMP testing, you need to have a strategy, or "Game Plan" for the testing event. This game plan might consist of Pre-Test Day and Test Day items. We suggest as the "ultimate PMP Exam Day Strategy":

Before Test Day

You have already completed your application, prepared for the exam and scheduled your PMP exam at a Prometric testing center. Now you need to address some specific items:

- Prometric allows you to use scratch paper, pencil and a four-function calculator during the PMP Exam. They provide these items for you. It is very useful, to do a *memory-dump* before you initiate the Exam. Your memory-dump is done by jotting down key equations and reminders on scratch paper as soon as you sit down to your computer station. This is perfectly legal, acceptable, even encouraged. See the diagram following for an example of a memory dump.

- As you study and prepare, practice your memory-dump immediately prior to taking a set of practice exam questions. On Exam day, it will be a quick and easy process.

- A week or so before your PMP Exam, drive to your Prometric testing center to learn the route and traffic patterns. Ask a facility representative to familiarize you with testing protocols.

- The day before your Exam, take a break. Don't study. Relax. Get a good night's sleep.

On Test Day

- Dress in layers so you can respond to whatever temperature conditions are present in the testing center.
- Eat a light nourishing meal before you go.
- Leave in time to arrive 30 minutes early.
- Once processed in and seated at your testing station, perform your memory dump
- Take the optional computer tutorial, primarily to acclimate and to relax.
- Before signaling to your test proctor that you are ready to initiate the Exam, take a minute to relax, get centered. Close your eyes, breathe easily, relax your muscles and stretch a bit.
- Begin your exam
- Treat each question as an independent event. For each question, follow the two step protocol for answering MCQ exams.
- Take periodic breaks in your seat. Sit back, close your eyes, breathe easy, relax your muscles, stretch a bit and then return to your exam.
- Maintain your focus and concentration. Don't think about anything except executing your Exam strategy. Pay attention to your exam strategy; your passing score will take care of itself.
- Take all of the time allotted.
- When you feel confident that you have answered all of the questions to the best of your ability, the computer will prompt you to end the exam.
- Your pass/fail notification will be presented in a few seconds. A printout of your result will be waiting for you as you exit the testing room.
- The PMP Exam is a stressful event, mentally and physically. Give yourself the rest of the day off to celebrate and to recover.

Sample "PMP Exam Memory Dump"

Many different elements could be included in a memory dump for your exam. You will need to choose what elements or formulas you think are important and want to write down upon entry to your testing station. Here are some suggestions:

Standard Deviation Values:
1 Sigma=± 68.26%
2 Sigma=± 95.46%
3 Sigma=± 99.73%
6 Sigma=± 99.99%

Three point estimates using Triangular Distribution: tE = (tO + tM = tP) / 3
Three point estimates using Beta Distribution: tE = (tO + 4tM = tP) / 6

Communication Channels Formula = N(N-1)/2

Earned Value Data Points:
EV = BCWP
PV = BCWS
AC = ACWP

Earned Value Formulas:
SPI = EV/PV
CPI = EV/AC

SV = EV-PV
CV = EV-AC
VAC = BAC-EAC

ETC = EAC − AC or Re-estimate based on bottom up estimate

EAC = BAC/CPI or
EAC = AC + BAC - EV or
EAC = AC + Bottom up ETC or
EAC = AC + [(BAC - EV) / CPI x SPI)]

TCPI = (BAC-EV)/(BAC-AC) or (BAC-EV)/EAC-AC)

Additional Reading
----

* PMBOK® Guide Fifth Edition: Glossary

In conclusion, we hope we have helped guide you in the right direction to prepare yourself to pass the PMP exam. Remember to keep studying for your PMP exam until you feel confident that you know the materials and can make the right decisions to guide a project using the methods defined in the PMBOK Guide Fifth Edition.

We wish you well in your studies and your endeavors.

End of Lesson 56

Appendix A
Lesson Quiz Solutions

Lesson 1 Introduction – no questions from this lesson

Lesson 2 PM Fundamentals

1. <u>B</u> Option B is the correct answer since an ongoing operation is something that has an indefinite time period and also has a flexible definition (in many cases). Options A, C and D effectively make up the definition of a project; temporary, creating a unique output and being progressively elaborated. PMBOK Guide, Chapter 1.2.

2. <u>C</u> Option C comes right from the PMBOK Guide Fifth Edition. The other answer options are less correct. Option A is incorrect since the answer is not complete. Answer B is incorrect because it indicates that the project manager would rely on intuition and feelings. (While intuition and feelings may be a useful aid for a project manager, it is not a primary definition or tool). Answer D is also incorrect due to the insertion of Art and Science into the choice. PMBOK Guide, Chapter 1.3.

3. <u>C</u> The main role of the project manager is to integrate all of the activities to achieve the project goals and objectives. Other answers are less correct. While it is true that the project manager is a manager, that does not define the overall role. It is true that the project manager is the project leader, and it is true that the project manager is a communicator. The best answer is integrator. PMBOK Guide, Chapter 1.7.

4. <u>B</u> The "triple constraint" has generally been recognized as scope, time and cost. These are respesented by answers A, C and D for this question. In addition to the traditional triple constraint, many projects and project managers often consider a wider view of project constraints to include quality, resources and risk. A previous version of the PMBOK Guide cited "customer satisfaction" as part of the constraints. PMBOK Guide, Chapter 1.3.

5. <u>B</u> The main role of the stakeholder on the project is to communicate. The PMBOK Guide describes the multiple ways that the project stakeholder is expected to participate and communicate. Answers A, C and D also each have some validity, but also define "communicating" as their intent. PMBOK Guide, Chapter 2.2.

6. <u>D</u> This question was designed to ensure you understand the definition of a project. "An ongoing work effort is generally a repetitive process that follows an organization's existing procedures." In contrast, projects create products, services, improvements, or results, such as outcomes or documents. *PMBOK® Guide Fifth Edition Section 1.2.*

7. <u>A</u> Project governance is an oversight function that provides the structure for managing the project. The governance approach should include who will be involved, escalation procedures, resources required, and general approach for completing the work. The project team is still responsible for planning, executing, controlling and closing the project. *PMBOK® Guide Fifth Edition Section 2.2.2.*

Lesson 3   Mastering the PMBOK

1. B   In the current edition of the PMBOK Guide (Fifth edition), there are 47 processes. Answer A is invalid. Answer C corresponds the the number of processes in the Third Edition. Answer D corresponds the the number of processes in the Second edition. It should be noted at this point that the student should take care to learn, understand and memorize process relationships to the Knowledge Areas and Process Groups in the PMBOK Guide. The table on page 61 of the PMBOK is an excellent place to study.

2. C   Process groups have a high level of interaction throughout the project. When you are performing the project work, there are planning, executing and monitoring and controlling processes overlapping in most cases. See the PMBOK Guide, Chapter 3, Figure 3.2. In the middle of the project, many different process groups are used.

3. A The PMBOK distinguishes between 3 different types of project information: Work Performance Data, which is raw data about the project (raw observations and measurements); Work Performance Information, which is performance data collected from controlling processes (status of deliverables); and Work Performance Reports, which is compiled project reports (physical or electronic representation of work performance, e.g. status reports). *PMBOK® Guide Fifth Edition Section 3.8.*

Lesson 4   Initiating Process Group – no questions from this lesson

Lesson 5   Develop Project Charter

1. D   Review your Develop Project Charter process illustration. You will see that expert judgment is a tool/technique, *not* an *Input*.

2. C   This is the only answer option that was discussed (and emphasized) in Lesson 5. You can derive the best answer here by eliminating the three options that received no mention in Lesson 5.

3. A   As emphasized in Lesson 3, the project charter is typically the responsibility of senior management. It may be prepared by the project manager, but is approved and authorized by senior management.

4. B   Hopefully, you found this one to be easy. The project charter is the primary *Output* (deliverable) from the Develop Project Charter process, which is one of the two processes that comprise the Initiating Processes group.

5. A Review your project charter template illustration in Lesson 3, along with your Must Know items. You will see that answer option A is the only exception, and therefore the best answer.

6. D Agreements may include, among other things, contracts, service level agreements, letters of intent, verbal agreements, and email agreements. PMBOK® Guide Fifth Edition Section 4.1.1.3.

7. <u>C</u> This question is a test of your knowledge of the Tool and Technique, Facilitation Techniques. Conflict resolution and problem solving are two types of Facilitation Techniques, which is listed as a specific Tool and Technique of Develop Project Charter. A and D are not true. B, while not necessarily untrue, does not represent the best answer. *PMBOK® Guide Fifth Edition Section 4.1.2.2.*

Lesson 6   Identify Stakeholders

1. <u>A</u>   Answer A is the best response and is the common sense answer in this group of answers. Answer B cites the function of "Plan Communications Management". Answer C is closest to a description of "Control Communications". Answer D is a combination of several processes. PMBOK Guide, Chapter 13.1

2. <u>B</u>   In this question we must choose the best group of actions that describe the process. Answer A and C describe determining communications requirements, which occurs later in project planning. Answer B shows intent to identify stakeholders in this process. PMBOK Guide, Chapter 13.1.

3. <u>B</u>   This question requires you to now your outputs from the process. Answers A, C and D are not outputs from the Identify Stakeholders process. PMBOK Guide, Chapter 13.1.

Lesson 7   Planning Process Group – no questions from this lesson

Lesson 8   Plan Stakeholder Management

1. <u>D</u>   Answer D is the best response and is the common sense answer in this group of answers. Answer B cites the function of "Plan Communications Management". Answer C is closest to a description of "Control Communications". Answer A is closest to "Identify Stakeholders". PMBOK Guide, Chapter 13.2.

2. <u>D</u>   In this question we must choose the term that best matches the question. In this case, a stakeholder can be classified like answers "A", "B", or "C". "D" is a role that is not normally used to describe stakeholder engagement. PMBOK Guide, Chapter 13.2.

3. <u>C</u>   This question requires you to now your outputs from the process. Answers A, B and D are not outputs from the Identify Stakeholders process. PMBOK Guide, Chapter 13.2.

Lesson 9   Plan Communications Management

1. <u>C</u>   This quiz question is designed to ensure you understand the intended application of the Plan Communications Management process. *ThePlan Communications Management process is applied to determine the communications needs of project stakeholders, including what information is needed, when it is needed and how it will be delivered.* Therefore,

Option C is the precise correct answer. Options A, B and D are only partially true, describing only portions of the process.

2. <u>C</u> Answer Options A and D are blatantly false statements. Option B may appear reasonable to some, but is not true. All forms of communication (formal, informal, verbal, written, non-verbal) are acceptable and encouraged when applied appropriately. Formal written communication is normally encouraged for performance reports, legal matters, contractual matters and other issues of similar importance. Option C is a true statement and therefore the correct (most correct) answer. Non-verbal communication is actually much more expressive than any type of verbal or written communication.

3. <u>B</u> This is a straightforward test of your ability to understand and apply the communication channels equation $N(N-1)/2$. Note the importance of reading the question correctly here. You are asked to determine the <u>number of additional channels</u> resulting from an increase in stakeholders. To derive the correct answer, you must perform three mathematical steps. 1) You must determine the number of communication channels with 6 stakeholders. 2) You must determine the number of communication channels with 2 more stakeholders, 8. 3) You must then determine the resulting increased number of channels. With 6 stakeholders, the number of communication channels is 15. With 8 stakeholders, the number of communication channels is 28. The increase is 13. Therefore, the correct answer is Option B. Note that answer Options C and D could represent reasonable answers if an error is made in understanding precisely what the question is asking. Option A could seem reasonable to someone who doesn't know the equation. Make a special note that the overall importance of this exercise is to reinforce the concept of communication channels growing exponentially in size and complexity with every added person in the project communications loop.

Lesson 10 Plan Scope Management

1. <u>B</u> Answer B is the best response and is the common sense answer in this group of answers. Answer A cites the ability to predict the number of scope changes to be, Answer C relies on a result that occurs in another process and answer "D" refers to Identify Stakeholders process. PMBOK Guide, Chapter 5.1.

2. <u>D</u> In this question we must know our process outputs and know that there are two important outputs to be considered. PMBOK Guide, Chapter 5.1.

3. <u>A</u> This question requires you to know your inputs and approximately when you would be performing the process. Answers B, C and D are are inputs, but answer A comes later in the project. PMBOK Guide, Chapter 5.1.

4. <u>B</u> B represents the best response for what should be included in the Scope Management Plan. Processes on how to manage changes to the Project Scope Statement and WBS are included. A is incorrect; the specific requirements that may ultimately be developed are immaterial to defining the processes for managing scope. C is a better recommendation for an item to include in the Requirements Management Plan. D cannot be the correct answer because A and C are not correct. *PMBOK® Guide Fifth Edition Section 5.1.3.1.*

5. <u>D</u> All of these items may be included in the Requirements Management Plan. Another item

that may be included is requirements prioritization process. *PMBOK® Guide Fifth Edition Section 5.1.3.2.*

Lesson 11   Collect Requirements

1. A This quiz question is designed to help ensure you understand the intended application of the Collect Requirements process. During the Collect Requirements process, stakeholder needs are defined and documented. This documentation provides the basis for defining and managing customer expectations throughout the project. Therefore, Option A is the preferred answer. Answer B is a true statement, but not fully complete. Answer C describes product requirements and Answer D describes project requirements.

2. C This quiz question is intended to ensure you understand the difference between information gathering techniques and project management methods. Answers A, B and D cite tools used in Collect Requirements; Answer C is not a tool and therefore is the correct (exception) answer.

3. C This is a straightforward test of your ability to recognize the processes contained within the Project Scope Management knowledge area. This lists five processes included in the Project Scope Management knowledge area.

4. A This quiz question provides a real-world scenario that is very commonly encountered by project managers; their boss or sponsor wants immediate results. Refusing to take immediate action is usually a career-altering experience. The choices in B, C and D offer an alternative to refusing to take immediate action and somewhat protect the project and allow definitions to take place.

5. B In Collect Requirements, three management plans are reviewed by the project team to help determine requirements that need to be collected, how to define and document requirements, and level of stakeholder participation in requirements collection activities, respectively. *PMBOK® Guide Fifth Edition Section 5.2.1.*

6. B The question is describing a stakeholder requirement, which describes what stakeholders need. Business requirements describe higher level needs of the organization. Solution requirements describe features and functions of a product that will meet the business and stakeholder requirements. Transition requirements describe temporary capabilities, such as training requirements, that move the organization into the future state being created by the project. *PMBOK® Guide Fifth Edition Section 5.2.*

7. D The question is describing Context Diagrams, which is a Tool and Technique of Collect Requirements. *PMBOK® Guide Fifth Edition Section 5.2.2.10.*

8. C The question is describing the Tool and Technique of Document Analysis in the Collect Requirements process. *PMBOK® Guide Fifth Edition Section 5.2.2.11.*

Lesson 12 Define Scope

1. <u>C</u> Review your Define Scope process illustration. You will see that the project scope statement is the intended output of the process, not an input. Therefore Option C represents the best answer.

2. <u>D</u> Each of the answer Options A, B and C are equally true. Once developed, the project scope statement serves many important functions across the entire project life cycle. Therefore Option D, all of the above, represents the best answer.

3. <u>C</u> This quiz question is designed to ensure you understand the development and intended application of the Scope Definition process. *The Define Scope process is intended to create the project scope statement.* Options A, B and D describe activities intended by processes other than Scope Definition. Therefore Option C represents the best answer.

4. <u>A</u> Answer options B, C and D are false statements. Option A represents the only true statement and is therefore the best, most correct, answer. It is important to know the difference between a Project Scope Statement and a Scope Management Plan.

Lesson 13 Create WBS

1. <u>C</u> This quiz question is intended to ensure you can differentiate the WBS from other types of breakdown structures. You can refer to *PMBOK Guide* section 5.4 for a more detailed discussion.

2. <u>C</u> This is a straightforward definition type question. Only Option C represents a reasonable choice, and is therefore the best answer.

3. <u>D</u> You will have to think a bit deeper to derive the correct answer here. Answer Option A is blatantly wrong. Options B and C could seem reasonable. Some WBS software tools will identify critical path components, but only after the project's schedule has been developed. The WBS can be used as an effective reference to help identify potential project risks, but the WBS does not automatically identify risks or single-out key risks. Option D is the best answer. The WBS can serve as an excellent communication tool, especially to create common understanding of scope among stakeholders (including project team members). Thus, it is reasonable to conclude that the WBS can enhance team buy-in, by creating better understanding.

4. <u>A</u> Answer Options B, C and D are false, leaving Option A as the only true statement. Option B is false because the WBS has no timeframe, thus no schedule information. Option C is false because the WBS defines work, not the need or justification. Option D is false because the WBS does not assign work, it identifies subdivided work elements.

5. <u>B</u> This question is defining the Scope Baseline, which is the first baseline created in the Planning Process Group. *PMBOK® Guide Fifth Edition Section 5.4.3.1.*

Lesson 14 Plan Schedule Management

1. <u>B</u> Answer B is the best response and is the common sense answer in this group of answers. Answer A cites the ability to predict the number of changes to be, Answer C relies on a result that occurs in another process and answer "D" refers to a stakeholder process. PMBOK Guide, Chapter 6.1.

2. <u>A</u> In this question we must know our process outputs and know that there is only one output to be considered. PMBOK Guide, Chapter 6.1.

3. <u>A</u> This question requires you to know your inputs and approximately when you would be performing the process. Answers B, C and D are inputs, but answer A comes from a different knowledge area of the project. PMBOK Guide, Chapter 6.1.

4. <u>B</u> This question is describing the Tool and Technique of Analytical Techniques used in Plan Schedule Management. *PMBOK® Guide Fifth Edition Section 6.1.2.2.*

Lesson 15 Define Activities

1. <u>C</u> This quiz question is intended to ensure you can differentiate *activities* from *deliverables*. The WBS is deliverables oriented. The Define Activities process essentially converts the WBS deliverables into action-oriented activities.

2. <u>A</u> Option B is false. It is the intent of the activity list to identify project activities. WBS work packages are still deliverables-oriented. Option C is false. Again, work packages should be deliverables-oriented. Define Activities is applied to further subdivide work packages into manageable sized activities. Option A is the only true statement, and therefore represents, as the exception, the best answer.

3. <u>D</u> Review your Define Activities process illustration. You will see that 'milestone list' is an intended output of the process, not an input. Option D, as the exception, is therefore the best answer.

4. <u>D</u> Answer Options A, B and C are true statements. This question is intended to help reinforce *decomposition* as a key methodology in applying both the Create WBS process (creating the WBS) and Define Activities process (creating the activity list).

5. <u>D</u> You and your team need to review the Schedule Management Plan, which includes information about the prescribed level of detail necessary to manage the work. *PMBOK® Guide Fifth Edition Section 6.2.1.1.*

Lesson 16 Sequence Activities

1. <u>D</u> *Critical path* is one of the most important terms used by project managers. It is important to know and understand its definition: *the longest path through a network diagram*. It is also important to know that the critical path defines the *shortest period of time in which a project may be completed.*

2. <u>A</u>   Although, this was not heavily discussed in Lesson 16, it is possible for a project to have more than one critical path through its network. When more than one critical path exists, it typically increases project risk. It is usually advisable for the project team to brainstorm some solution to avoid multiple critical paths. Option B is not true, by default. Option C is not true, (good judgment should dictate that it is not conventional to attempt the creation of hybrid network diagramming methods). Option D is not true; the WBS identifies all of the deliverables-oriented work within project scope, the network diagram illustrates all activities and their logical interdependencies, from project start to project finish.

3. <u>D</u>   There are three possible paths; 1) Start-A-C-D-F-Finish, 2) Start-B-E-G-Finish, 3) Start-B-D-F-Finish.

4. <u>C</u>   The critical path is the longest path through a network diagram. Option A cannot be correct because, Start-A-C-D-F-Finish is not the longest path through the network. Option B does represent one of the possible complete paths through the network and, when durations are added, requires 12 days, start to finish. Option C represents a complete path and, when added, requires 16 days. Option D is an incomplete path. Therefore, C is the correct answer.

5. <u>D</u> *The critical path defines the shortest period of time in which a project may be completed.* D represents 16 days or work periods, the longest path, the shortest time the project can be completed. If you identified the wrong path as being the critical path, then one of the other answer options may have appeared correct. In many exam question situations, you will encounter wrong answers options that appear correct if a calculation error is made.

6. <u>C</u> To answer this question, you must first construct a network diagram from the given information. Be prepared to do the same in real world project environments. The proper network diagram appears below. There are three possible paths through this network from start to finish; 1) Start-A-C-E-F-G-Finish, 2) Start-B-D-E-F-G-Finish and 3) Start-B-C-EF-G-Finish.

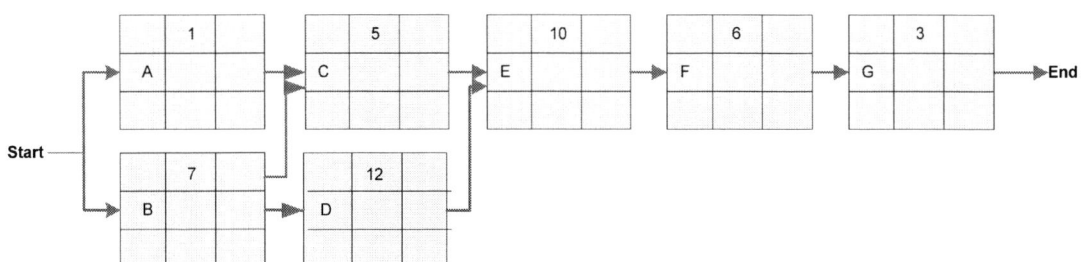

7. <u>B</u> To answer this question, you must a) construct a network diagram from the given information, b) identify each path from start to finish c) determine which path is the longest. Remember, the longest path is the critical path. We find three possible paths; 1) Start-A-C-E-F-G-Finish (25 weeks), 2) Start-B-D-E-F-G-Finish (38 weeks) and 3) Start-B-C-EF-G-Finish (31 weeks). Path 2 is the longest and therefore the correct answer.

8. <u>C</u> Once again, to answer this question, you must first construct a network diagram from the given information. Then you must identify all possible paths through the network and determine which path is longest. The longest path is the critical path, which defines the shortest period of time in which the project may be completed. In this example, Start-BD-E-F-G-Finish represents the critical path, and the shortest time to complete ... 38 weeks.

9. <u>C</u> In this question you have to know the purpose and outputs from Sequence Activities. Answer A describes a WBS, answer B describes an activity list and answer D describes the project schedule. Answer C is the only correct answer presented.

Lesson 17 Estimate Activity Resources

1. <u>B</u> *Resource* is one of the most important key terms in a project manager's vocabulary. This quiz question is intended to ensure you are familiar with the simple, yet critical, accepted definition of resource (resources).

2. <u>A</u> Each answer Option here is true. However, B, C and D are incomplete. Option A represents the most complete description of the Activity Resource Estimating process, and is therefore the best answer.

3. <u>A</u> Review your Activity Resource Estimating process illustration. Only Option A correctly identifies defined tools/ techniques associated with Estimate Activity Resource. Options B, C and D include items other than proper tools/ techniques.

4. <u>A</u> Only answer Option A is a true statement. Option B refers to role and responsibility assignments. Option C and D are also incorrect.

5. <u>A</u> In A, Schedule Management Plan, Risk Register, Activity Cost Estimates are all inputs to Estimate Activity resources, In B, the Scope Management Plan is not an Input to the Estimate Activity Resources process. In C, Activity Resource Requirements is the primary output of the process. In D, Project Documents Updates and Resource Breakdown Structure are outputs to the process. *PMBOK® Guide Fifth Edition Section 6.4.*

Lesson 18 Estimate Activity Durations

1. <u>C</u> Analogous estimating (top-down) is fast, efficient and less costly, but also less confident. It bases its estimate on the actual performance of a past similar activity. Option A, *bottom-up*, is actually a formal estimating technique that we will discuss soon, but it is the opposite of analogous. Options B and D are legitimate types of estimates, but neither satisfies the given definition.

2. <u>D</u> This question is intended to test your understanding of the term *work unit* (also termed *work period*). Most modern project management software tools need to define activity durations in terms of work units to create the project schedule. Work units are simply the defined time periods used to report duration estimates. In most projects, they are hours, shifts, days or weeks. The project team usually decides what specific work units make the most sense for their project. Answer Options A and B are boldly incorrect statements. Both

A and B confuse *work units* with *duration estimates.* Option C could appear reasonable, but the project manager should always encourage the *team* to make these types of decisions, making C not universally true. Statement D is always correct, and therefore the *most* true.

3. <u>A</u> This is a straightforward test of your ability to recognize the defined inputs, the tools & techniques and the outputs associated with the activity duration estimating process. Know that there is no need to memorize all the Inputs, Tools and Techniques and Outputs. In this question, Option B includes *three-point estimating,* which is a tool/technique, not an output. Option C includes *reserve analysis,* which is also a tool/technique. Option D includes *resource calendar,* which is an input.

4. <u>D</u> Modern project management encourages many themes. One of the most important themes dictates that estimates should be prepared by the person or people most knowledgeable about the activity, ideally by the person or people that will actually perform the work. This question is intended to reinforce that theme. Answer Options A, B and C each may appear reasonable to some extent. However, only Option D hits the mark 100%. This is a quiz question where all of the answer options appear reasonable. But generally, one will stand out as the *best* or *most correct.*

5. <u>A</u> The Triangular Distribution is used to calculate an average between estimates that represent best case, most likely, and worst case scenarios. *PMBOK® Guide Fifth Edition Section 6.5.2.4.*

6. <u>B</u> The Beta Distribution is used to calculate a weighted average between estimates that represent best case, most likely, and worst case scenarios. *PMBOK® Guide Fifth Edition Section 6.5.2.4.*

7. <u>C</u> Contingency reserves are developed to take "known-unknowns" into consideration; for identified risks that are accepted. Management reserves are allocated for "unknown-unknowns"; for unforeseen work that is within the scope of the project. *PMBOK® Guide Fifth Edition Section 6.5.2.6.*

8. <u>B</u> Contingency Reserves are included in the Schedule Baseline, but Management Reserves are not. *PMBOK® Guide Fifth Edition Section 6.5.2.6.*

Lesson 19   Develop Schedule

1. <u>D</u> This quiz question is designed to ensure you understand the intended application of the Develop Schedule process. *The Develop Schedule process is applied to determine the start/finish dates for project activities and to create the schedule management plan.* Therefore, Option D is the precise correct answer. Options A, B and C are all somewhat true, but incomplete.

2. <u>A</u> This question is intended to test your understanding of schedule compression techniques. The two most often applied techniques are *crashing* (adding resources) and *fast tracking* (performing normally sequential activities in parallel). Answer Option B identifies *resource leveling.* Resource leveling is applied to eliminate peaks and valleys in

human resource needs across a project schedule. Resource leveling actually extends the schedule in most cases. Answer Option C has nothing to do with schedule compression, but could appear reasonable to someone who's mistaken priority is to avoid schedule changes at all costs. Option D could be viewed as an application of fast tracking and therefore be somewhat correct. However, only Option A presents a complete correct statement and is therefore the best answer. Note that it is the responsibility of the project manager and team to explore the feasibility of crashing and fast tracking, then choose the lowest cost & least risk alternatives. Note that crashing and fast tracking are not always feasible.

3. <u>D</u> This is a straightforward test of your ability to recognize the defined inputs, the tools & techniques and the outputs associated with the Develop Schedule process. Option D, *activity duration estimates* represents an input to Develop Schedule, not an output. Therefore, Option D is the correct (exception) answer.

4. <u>C</u> This quiz question is intended to test your ability to identify and reinforce correct schedule development concepts. Option A is a true statement, *Completed project schedules are typically illustrated using Bar Charts (also called Gantt Charts), Milestone Charts or Dated Network Diagrams*. Option B is also a true statement; *There are two primary methods used to shorten schedules; crashing and fast tracking.* Option C is not true; *Resource leveling heuristics <u>are not</u> necessarily used to reduce the number of estimated resources, and <u>do not</u> necessarily result in lower project costs*. Option D is a true statement; *Lead time and lag time allows project teams to add realism and flexibility to their schedule. Lead time may be viewed as an overlap between tasks. Lag time is waiting time.* Therefore, Option C is the correct (least true) answer.

5. <u>D</u> D is the false statement and thus the correct answer because Modeling Techniques include What-If-Scenario Analysis and Simulation. Leads and Lags is a Tool and Technique of Develop Schedule where overlap and/or wait time is established between activities. *PMBOK® Guide Fifth Edition Section 6.6.2.*

Lesson 20 Plan Human Resource Management

1. <u>B</u>   This quiz question is designed to ensure you understand the intended application of the Plan Human Resource Management process. The Plan Human Resource Management process is applied to develop, document and assign project roles, responsibilities and reporting relationships. Therefore, Option B is the correct answer. Options A and C represent activities you may perform during organizational planning, but they do not represent the primary purpose of applying the process. Option D more closely represents the description of quality planning, not Plan Human Resource Management.

2. <u>D</u>   Answer Option A is a true statement: In matrix organizations, project managers typically share responsibility and authority with functional managers. Option B is also a true statement: In strong matrix organizations, project managers may have more authority than functional managers. Option C is another true statement: Project managers in functional organizations may have very little authority and are often termed project coordinators or project expeditors. Option D is a false statement. To make it true, it would have to be revised to read: In projectized organizations, the project manager typically assumes full

profit/loss responsibility/authority and staffs the project with human resources dedicated to the project. The question asks us to identify the least true statement. Option D is the only false statement and is therefore the correct answer.

3. <u>B</u> this is a question to test your knowledge of process tools and techniques. Answer B is the only completely correct answer. PMBOK Guide, Chapter 9.1.

Lesson 21 Plan Cost Management

1. <u>B</u> Answer B is the best response and is the common sense answer in this group of answers. Answer A cites the ability to predict the number of changes to be, Answer C relies on a result that occurs in another process and answer "D" refers to a stakeholder process. PMBOK Guide, Chapter 7.1.

2. <u>A</u> In this question we must know our process outputs and know that there is only one output to be considered. PMBOK Guide, Chapter 7.

3. <u>A</u> This question requires you to know your inputs and approximately when you would be performing the process.   Answers B, C and D are inputs, but answer A comes from a different knowledge area of the project. PMBOK Guide, Chapter 71.

4. <u>A</u> You are in the process of Plan Cost Management and are using the Tool and Technique of Analytical Techniques to consider strategic options for funding the project and financing resources, and what financial techniques will be used. *PMBOK® Guide Fifth Edition Section 7.1.2.2.*

5. <u>D</u> The Cost Management Plan describes **how** project costs will be planned, structured and controlled, and is developed during Plan Cost Management. In A, results of earned value analysis will be obtained by performing Control Costs. In B, the budget, or Cost Baseline, will be created in Determine Budget. In C, variance analysis is performed in Control Costs. *PMBOK® Guide Fifth Edition Section 7.1.3.1.*

6. <u>B</u> The Cost Management Plan describes **how** project costs will be planned, structured and controlled, and is developed during Plan Cost Management. The team needs to go back to planning and develop a detailed plan for costs. This represents the first and best next step. Once a Cost Management Plan at the appropriate level of detail is developed, the team will implement the plan. The plan **could** include refining estimates by obtaining bottom-up estimates, as described in A. Once estimates are refined, the team **could** request additional funding as described in C. D is an incorrect option; the question does not mention shortage of people resources. *PMBOK® Guide Fifth Edition Section 7.1.*

Lesson 22 Estimate Costs

1. <u>C</u> This quiz question is intended to measure you knowledge of estimate allowances. The ROM range is -25% to +75%, PMBOK® Guide, Chapter 7.2.

2. <u>C</u> This is a straightforward test of your ability to recognize the defined inputs, the tools & techniques and the outputs associated with the cost estimating process. Know that it is not necessary to memorize all inputs, tools & techniques and outputs. In this question, Options A, B and D include items that are not defined Estimate Costs inputs, tools/ techniques, or outputs.

3. <u>A</u> This question asks you identify the *least* true statement. Options B, C and D all represent clearly correct statements. Option A is false and therefore the correct answer. The cost baseline (or *budget*) is developed during the Estimate Costs process, not during Estimate Costs.

4. <u>C</u> This question is a simple test to help ensure you know *price* and *cost* are two different things. The question asks you to identify the *most* correct statement. Option A is clearly false, by definition. Option B is a misleading incorrect answer, but could appear reasonable to anyone who is not familiar with the differences. Option D is another incorrect misleading mismatch of terms.

5. <u>D</u> This is another question intended to reinforce a modern project management theme; *estimates should be developed by the person, or people, who are best qualified to prepare the estimates ... namely, the person, or people, who will be doing the actual work.* Only answer Option D can be correct.

Lesson 23 Plan Procurement Management

1. <u>C</u> This quiz question is intended to test your applied understanding of SOWs. *The Contract Statement of Work (SOW) describes, in detail, the complete scope of work expected from the supplier, along with other applicable terms.* The scenario presented in this question describes the intended application of a statement of work (SOW). Therefore, Option C is the correct answer. Options A *work package* could seem reasonable to someone who does not understand SOW, but is incorrect. Option B *contractor's project charter* may also appear reasonable to some, but is incorrect in this question's context (note that an SOW can, in fact, serve as a contractor's project charter in some cases). Option D *risk transference* is the intent of the team's *buy decision*, but does not properly describe the 'document,' as asked.

2. <u>A</u> This quiz question is designed to help ensure you understand the intended application of the Plan Procurement Management process. Answer Option A is the only true statement and therefore the best answer. Answer Option B is incorrect in that the make-or-buy decision analysis includes all costs (direct and indirect). Option C is incorrect in that the amount of risk that is shared between buyer and seller is determined by the type of contract implemented between the parties. Option D provides an incorrect definition of the procurement management plan, the selection of a seller for a particular item is accomplished in the Conduct Procurements process.

3. <u>C</u> This quiz question is intended to test your applied understanding of *source selection criteria*. Consistent source selection criteria gives the project team a fair and consistent basis from which to compare prospective suppliers. Some project teams establish numerical rating systems to evaluate bids. Many times, price is not the only consideration in selecting

a vendor. Financial stability, technical depth, management depth and understanding of scope may all be important considerations to factor. A low price bidder will not serve the project very well if they have poor financial stability and go out of business during project execution. Answer Option C is the best choice, and the best answer.

Lesson 24   Determine Budget

1. <u>B</u>   This quiz question is designed to ensure you understand the intended application of the Determine Budget process. *The Determine Budget process is applied to formally organize all activity cost estimates into a cohesive project budget.* Therefore, Option B is the precise correct answer. Options A, C and D all describe legitimate activities more closely associated with the Estimate Costs process, not Determine Budget. NOTE: You may have noticed a seeming inconsistency in the way we present processes nomenclature. Sometimes you see a process with capital letters; Estimate Costs. Other times, you may see it with small letters; estimate costs. This is by design. You should become familiar recognizing processes presented both ways, with capital letters and with small letters.

2. <u>C</u>   This question is intended to test your understanding of *cost baseline. The cost baseline is a time-phased budget, used to monitor and measure project cost performance.* Therefore, Option C is precisely the best answer. Option A is a statement that is loosely associated with the Control Costs process, not the cost baseline. Option B describes the intended purpose of the cost management plan, not the cost baseline. Option D is simply a reasonable-sounding statement that actually makes little logical sense. Note the importance of all project baselines (scope baseline, schedule baseline, cost baseline) in establishing the planned objectives by which monitoring and performance will be measured throughout project execution and controlling phases. Note also that planned baselines should remain in-tact, regardless of changes made across the project life-cycle. Only in extreme cases should a fundamental baseline change be considered.

3. <u>A</u>   This is a straightforward test of your ability to recognize the defined inputs, the tools & techniques and the outputs associated with the Determine Budget process.   Answer Options B, C and D each correctly identifies one of the Determine Budget process inputs. Option A, *cost baseline*, is the sole Determine Budget process *output* and is therefore the correct (exception) answer.

4. <u>A</u>   This quiz question is intended to further test your understanding of *cost baseline.* Option A, is exactly correct; *Cost baselines are typically illustrated using graphs. Plotted cost baselines usually form an S-Curve appearance.* Option B is blatantly incorrect. Cost baselines, like all planned baselines, should not be subject to frequent changes. Option C more accurately describes the cost management plan, not the cost baseline. Option D more accurately describes the project schedule, not the cost baseline. Therefore, Option A is the best (most true) answer.

Lesson 25   Plan Quality Management

1. <u>D</u>   This quiz question is designed to ensure you understand the intended application of the Plan Quality Management process. *The Plan Quality Management process is applied to identify which quality standards are applicable to the project, then determine how to satisfy*

them. Therefore, Option D is the correct answer. Option A is simply incorrect. Option B could appear somewhat correct if the question was referring to the Perform Quality Assurance process, but not for Plan Quality Management. *Quality improvement* is a defined output of the Plan Quality Management process. Therefore B is incorrect. Option C offers a distracting incorrect answer. While cause-and-effect diagrams are useful quality tools, there is not necessarily any such thing as a 'project cause-and-effect diagram.'

2. <u>A</u> This is a straightforward test of your ability to recognize the defined inputs, the tools & techniques and the outputs associated with the quality planning process. In this question, only Option A properly lists quality planning tools/ techniques, and is therefore the best answer. Option B includes *quality baseline*, which is not a tool/ technique. Option C includes *quality checklists*, which is an intended output, not a tool/technique. Option D includes *quality metrics*, which is also an output, not a tool/technique.

3. <u>C</u> This quiz question is intended to test your applied understanding of the term *benchmark* (or *benchmarking*). *Benchmarks are established standards and/or practices that may be used for comparison when the project team establishes its standards for measuring project performance.* Answer Options A, B and D can each appear to be reasonably correct, and arguments can be made to justify either of them as being correct. However, the given scenario describes the use of *benchmarking* much closer than *historical data, templates* or *lessons learned*. Therefore, C is the best choice, and correct answer. This quiz question requires you to select the *best* answer. Many questions will feature correct statements for all four options. In these questions, your job is to select the *best* of the four.

4. <u>A</u> This quiz question is intended to test your applied understanding of quality in project management: *In project management, quality means delivering precisely what is promised. When a project team delivers on-time, within budget and has satisfied all scope requirements, then quality has been achieved.* Answer Option A is the correct response. Options B, C and D represent possible responses in some cases, but Option A is the best.

Lesson 26 Plan Risk Management

1. <u>C</u> Project risk is formally defined as, *any uncertain event or condition that, if it occurs, has a negative or positive effect on a project objective. Uncertain* is key in this definition. If an event or condition is certain, then it is not a risk. Only answer Option C fully satisfies the definition. Options A, B and D represent partial, misleading and incorrect answers.

2. <u>D</u> This question is intended to reinforce the important concept that project risks can be positive, as well as negative. Positive risks are called *opportunities* and should be pursued. Negative risks are called *threats* and should be avoided. The question asks you to identify the most incorrect statement. Answer Option A is a correct statement. Option B is correct, reinforcing the point. Option C is also true, reinforcing the point. Option D is false (While we would certainly like to eliminate negative risks, it is not possible) and therefore the most incorrect statement.

3. <u>B</u> This is a straightforward test of your ability to recognize the defined inputs, the tools & techniques and the outputs associated with the Plan Risk Management process. In this question, you are asked to identify the exception. Answer Option A *organizational process assets* is indeed an input. Option C *the project scope statement* is also an input. Option D

the *project management plan* is another proper input. Only Option B is incorrect, and therefore, the exception. The *risk management plan* is an output, not an input.

4. <u>A</u>   The six risk management processes are, in logical application order, 1) Plan Risk Management, 2) Identify Risks, 3) Perform Qualitative Risk Analysis, 4) Perform Quantitative Risk Analysis, 5) Plan Risk Responses, 6) Control Risks.

Lesson 27   Identify Risks

1. <u>B</u>   This quiz question is designed to ensure you understand the intended application of the Identify Risks process. The Identify Risks process is applied to 1) determine which risks may affect the project and 2) to document their characteristics. Therefore, Option B is the correct answer. Options A, C and D are all legitimate objectives in project risk management, but not objectives of the Identify Risks process.

2. <u>D</u>   This is a straightforward test of your ability to recognize the defined inputs, the tools & techniques and the outputs associated with the Identify Risks process. Know that your PMP Exam will likely include only 5 or 6 questions that ask you to identify specific sets of inputs, tools & techniques and outputs. In this question, Options A, B and C all identify accepted tools and techniques. Therefore, Option D *all of the above* is the best answer.

3. <u>C</u>   This quiz question is intended to reinforce the modern project management theme: *Identifg risks is a process that should be encouraged frequently throughout the project life cycle. In many projects, new risks can surface daily.* Therefore, Option C is the best answer. Option A is directly contrary to the theme and incorrect. Option B is incorrect. Risk Identification should encourage participation by as many knowledgeable people as possible, inside and outside of the immediate project team. Option D is incorrect for the same reason Option B is incorrect.

4. <u>D</u>   This quiz question is intended to test your ability to identify diagramming techniques typically used to help identify risks. These techniques include: cause and effect diagrams (also termed *fishbone* or *Ishikawa*), systems flowcharts also termed *process maps*) and influence diagrams. Answer Options A, B and C all identify proper diagramming techniques. Therefore, D *all of the above* is the correct answer.

5. <u>B</u>   This quiz question is intended to test your ability to identify proper risk management terms. Indications that a risk has occurred, or is about to occur, are termed triggers (or *risk symptoms* or *warning signs*). Therefore, Option B is the correct answer. Options A, C and D are proper risk management terms, but not in the context of the question.

Lesson 28   Perform Qualitative Risk Analysis

1. <u>D</u>   This quiz question is designed to ensure you understand the intended application of the Perform Qualitative Risk Analysis process. *The Perform Qualitative Risk Analysis process is applied to assess the impact and likelihood of identified risks. It is intended to help prioritize identified risks and identify those risks serious enough to warrant further analysis.* Option D defines the process perfectly and is therefore the correct answer. Option A is an incorrect hodgepodge of risk management terms. Option B defines the application of the

Identify Risks process, not Perform Qualitative Risk Analysis. Option C defines a portion of Perform Quantitative Risk Analysis, not Perform Qualitative Risk Analysis.

2. <u>D</u> This quiz question is intended to test your applied understanding of a probability/impact (P-I) risk rating matrix. *A probability/impact (P-I) risk rating matrix is a tool that combines both risk probability and risk impact into a single score. It is used to help determine qualitative risk rankings.* Option A is correct. It is a defined tool/technique. Option C is incorrect. It is not a defined process output. Option C is also true. This is a proper definition for the P-I matrix. Therefore, D *A and C* is the best answer.

3. <u>A</u> This is a quiz question designed to test your practical ability to use a simple probability/impact (P-I) risk rating matrix. To derive the correct answer, a simple multiplication calculation is necessary: $(0.3)(.7) = .21$. Therefore, Option A is the best answer. Options A, B, or C could appear to be correct answers if a math error is made.

4. <u>A</u> This is another quiz question designed to test your practical ability to use a simple probability/impact (P-I) risk rating matrix. To derive the correct answer, two simple multiplication calculations are necessary: First, multiply the two highest chart values $(0.9)(0.9) = 0.81$. Second, multiply the two lowest chart values $(0.1)(0.1) = 0.01$. Answer Option A identifies the two correct values: 0.81, 0.01. Options B, C or D could appear to be correct answers if a math error is made.

Lesson 29 Perform Quantitative Risk Analysis

1. <u>D</u> This quiz question is designed to ensure you understand the intended application of the Quantitative Risk Analysis process. *The Perform Quantitative Risk Analysis process is applied to guide the additional analysis of individual risks, to determine the numerical value of its probability of occurrence and the numerical value of its consequence on project objectives, should it occur .* Option D defines the process perfectly and is therefore the correct answer. Option A describes the application of Plan Risk Management. Option B describes the application of Risk Identification. Option C describes the application of Perform Qualitative Risk Analysis.

2. <u>D</u> This quiz question is intended to test your applied understanding of sensitivity analysis. *Sensitivity analysis is a simple risk analysis technique used to help make project decisions based on the general risk sensitivity of an organization, person or group of people.* Based on the given scenario in this question, it appears that the primary rationale behind the sponsor's decision was the lower level of risk (by comparison), which satisfied her apparent risk averse policies. This certainly fits the definition of sensitivity analysis. Option A is not a recognized risk management term. Option B could be correct in some situations, but it is not directly consistent with this particular scenario. Option C could also be correct in some situations, but is not consistent with this scenario. Option D *sensitivity analysis* is a proper risk management technique, it is consistent with the scenario, and therefore the best (correct) answer.

3. <u>C</u> This is a straightforward test of your ability to recognize the defined inputs, the tools & techniques and the outputs associated with the Perform Quantitative Risk Analysis process. In this question, only Option C properly identifies tools/ techniques, as asked. You may reference them directly on your Perform Quantitative Risk Analysis process illustration.

4. C This quiz question is intended to test your practical understanding of EMV. *Expected Monetary Value Analysis (EMV) is a quantitative risk analysis tool. EMV is calculated by multiplying the value of each possible outcome by its probability of occurrence, then adding them all together. EMV= V (value $) x P (probability).* To select the correct answer to this quiz question, you must perform a series of simple calculations. Risk 1 = -$10,000 X 0.10 = -$1,000.   Risk 2 = -$8,000 X 0.70 = -$5,600. Risk 3 = +$10,000 X 0.60 = +$6,000. Risk 4 = -$800 X 0.20 = -$160. Added together, the total equals -$760. (remember to recognize the plus and minus values associated with positive and negative risks).

Lesson 30 Plan Risk Responses

1. B   This quiz question is designed to ensure you understand the intended application of the Plan Risk Responses process. *The Plan Risk Responses process is applied to develop options and determine actions to enhance opportunities (positive risks) and develop options and determine actions to reduce threats (negative risks).* Therefore, Option B is the correct answer. Options A, C and D all represent incorrect variations of the proper definition. Notice how each of these incorrect answer options use legitimate terms, but in the wrong context, to act as distracters. Options A, C or D could appear reasonable to someone who has only a cursory knowledge of the subject material.

2. D   This quiz question is intended to test your applied understanding of the risk response planning tools/ techniques: avoidance, transference, mitigation, acceptance in this scenario, the team has opted to act on the risk by handing over direct responsibility to a party outside of the organization. The team has apparently negotiated a guarantee and a fixed-price from the supplier. This indicates the supplier is willing to assume the consequence, if the risk occurs. This is all indicative of risk *transference.* Therefore, Option D is the best answer. Options A and B *active/ passive acceptance* are not correct because the team is acting now on the risk. Acceptance typically involves advance contingency planning, but no immediate action. Option C *mitigation* is not correct, because contracting does not always reduce the impact or probability of a risk, it simply assigns the consequence elsewhere. Remember, transference does not eliminate the risk, it transfers the consequence, should it occur.

3. A This is a straightforward test of your ability to recognize the defined inputs, the tools & techniques and the outputs associated with the risk response planning process. Know that it is not necessary to memorize all inputs, tools & techniques and outputs. In this question, only Option A correctly identifies process outputs, as asked. Refer to your Plan Risk Responses process illustration.

Lesson 31   Develop Project Management Plan

1. C   This quiz question is designed to ensure you understand the intended application of the Develop Project Management Plan process. *The Develop Project Management Plan process is applied to gather the outputs from all other planning processes and assemble them into a single, cohesive document, the project plan.* Therefore, Option C is the precise correct answer. Options A, B and D are all partially true, but describe only portions of the process. Option C is the only complete choice.

2. $\underline{D}$ The project management plan is used to document project planning decisions, strategies, alternatives and assumptions. It serves as the baseline for monitoring and measuring project performance during the project's execution, monitoring & controlling, and closing phases. The project management plan also serves to guide all aspects of the project through execution, monitoring &control and closing. Therefore, Options A, B and C are all equally true statements, making Option D *all of the above* the best answer.

3. $\underline{C}$ This quiz question is a straightforward choice between inputs and tools. Choices A, B and D are inputs (B is part of Organizational Process Assets, D is part of Enterprise Environmental Factors).

4. $\underline{A}$ This quiz question is intended to reinforce the modern project management concept: *Plans should be sized in sensible proportion to the size and complexity of the project.* Option A correctly communicates this concept and is therefore the best answer. Options B and C both contradict the proper concept. Based on the incorrectness of Options B and C, answer Option D *all of the above* cannot be correct.

5. $\underline{C}$ The Project Management Plan includes 1) subsidiary plans, which end in the two words "Management Plan", 2) baselines, and 3) one exception: Process Improvement Plan. All other project management documents are called Project Documents. *PMBOK® Guide Fifth Edition Section 4.2.3.1 and Table 4-1.*

Lesson 32   Executing Process Group – no questions from this lesson

Lesson 33   Direct and Manage Project Work

1. $\underline{A}$ This quiz question is designed to ensure you understand conflict resolution techniques and their impacts. Bargaining (Compromising) is the technique where each side in the conflict resolution must compromise or give up something in order to come to resolution.

2. $\underline{D}$ Answer Options A, B and C all represent perfectly true statements. Option D is not true. Work authorization systems are used primarily to manage and control scope, not to account for spending. Therefore, Option D is the preferred (least true) answer.

3. $\underline{B}$ This is a straightforward test of your ability to recognize the defined inputs, tools & techniques and the outputs associated with the Direct and Manage Project Work process. Option B is the only answer which correctly identifies two outputs and is therefore the preferred answer.

4. $\underline{A}$ This quiz question is intended to test your ability to recognize characteristics associated with different sources of leadership power. Expert power is a type of power earned when the leader is respected as a successful expert in his/ her specialty. The scenario described in this question perfectly satisfies the definition of expert power. Therefore, Option A is the correct answer. Options B, C and D are correct types of leadership power, but does not represent the type of earned power described in the scenario.

5. B The PMBOK states that "meetings are most effective when all participants can be face-to-face in the same location", thus B is the best answer. A is not a recommended practice and is, in fact, contrary to the PMBOK which states "meeting types should not be mixed". If you have to hold virtual meetings, it is best to use conferencing tools, but C does not represent the best option among those presented. D is a good practice, in general, but does not represent a technique that would probably contribute to increased participant engagement during meetings. *PMBOK® Guide Fifth Edition Section 4.3.2.3.*

6. B The Project Management Plan includes 1) subsidiary plans, which end in the two words "Management Plan", 2) baselines, and 3) one exception: Process Improvement Plan. All other project management documents are called Project Documents. *PMBOK® Guide Fifth Edition Section 4.3.3.4 and Table 4-1.*

7. B The Project Management Plan includes 1) subsidiary plans, which end in the two words "Management Plan", 2) baselines, and 3) one exception: Process Improvement Plan. All other project management documents are called Project Documents and include Requirements Documentation, Project Logs, Stakeholder Register, etc. *PMBOK® Guide Fifth Edition Section 4.3.3.5 and Table 4-1.*

Lesson 34   Acquire Project Team

1. D This quiz question is designed to ensure you understand the intended application of the Acquire Project Team process. *The Acquire Project Team process is applied to obtain and assign needed human resources (people) to the project.* Answer Options A and B are somewhat true, but not complete. Option C better describes the Plan Human Resource Management process, not Acquire Project Team. Option D is the preferred answer.

2. C Answer Option A is a true statement; *In matrix organizations, project managers may have to negotiate with functional managers to obtain needed people.* Option B is true; *In strong matrix organizations, project managers may have more authority than functional managers.* Option D is also true; *A Responsibility Assignment Matrix (RAM) illustrates assignments and levels of authority/responsibility, as a function of WBS elements. There is no time associated with a RAM.* Option C is false and therefore the preferred answer (least true); *In functional organizations, it is not necessarily the project sponsor's responsibility to assign project staff.*

3. B This is a straightforward case of choosing the correct tools for this process. Answer B cites two of the four tools used by this process. All other answers have at least one correct tool along with distracting information.

4. B This quiz question is intended to reinforce acceptable reasons why staff may be assigned early. Answer Option B is a legitimate reason; specific staff members may be proposed in competitive bids before a contract is ever awarded, thereby identifying project staff, if the bid is won. NOTE: Answer Options A, C and D represent unacceptable reasons, but more importantly they represent *unvalidated assumptions.*

Lesson 35 Develop Project Team

1. <u>C</u> In this question you are asked to choose the choice that is NOT an input to the process. Team building activities are a tool to be used in the process, not an input.

2. <u>B</u> This quiz question is designed to ensure you understand the intended application of the Develop Project Team process. *Develop Project Team is the process of enhancing the ability of individual team members to enhance overall project performance.* Therefore, Option B is the preferred answer. Options A, C and D could be correct statements in some, but not all, situations.

3. <u>C</u> This question calls on your general management knowledge to choose the correct selection. The highest level of need under Maslow's Hierarchy of Needs is self actualization. All other answers are distracters.

4. <u>C</u> This quiz question is intended to test your understanding of some of the potential challenges faced by project managers in different types of organizations. Answer Options A, B and D represent incorrect statements. In Option A, co-location *can* involve moving team members (sometimes even team members' families) to/from different parts of the world. In Option B, team development is nearly always more challenging in functional organizations, where resources are typically borrowed on a temporary basis. In Option D, team development procedures typically represent far too much detail for inclusion in the project charter. Option C is exactly true and is therefore the preferred (most true) answer

Lesson 36 Manage Project Team

1. <u>A</u> This is a straightforward test of your ability to recognize the defined inputs, the tools & techniques and the outputs associated with the Manage Project Team process. The inputs associated with the Manage Project Team process include project staff assignments, project management plan, team performance assessments, performance reports and organizational process assets. Answer Option A, best represents the inputs and therefore is the preferred answer.

2. <u>B</u> This quiz question is intended to test your knowledge of the intended application of the Manage Project Team process. Answer Options A, C and D are all false statements. Answer Option B which defines an Issue Log is true and therefore the best answer.

3. <u>C</u> This quiz question is designed to help ensure you understand the intended application of the Manage Project Team process. *The Manage Project Team process is applied to address performance, behavior, issues and conflicts associated specifically with project team members.* Therefore, Option C is the preferred answer. Options A, B, and D are more closely associated with the Develop Project Team process. Only Option C provides a complete, accurate description of the Manage Project Team process.

Lesson 37 Manage Communications

1. <u>B</u> This quiz question is designed to help ensure you understand the intended application of the Manage Communications process. *Manage Communications is the communications process of creating and making project information available to project stakeholders, as determined and documented in the communications management plan.* Therefore, Option B is the preferred answer. Option A is not complete, because it is limited to project performance reports. Option C is not complete, because it is limited to earned value reports. Option D is not complete, because it is limited to presentations.

2. <u>C</u> This is a long situational type question that is intended to test your understanding of a simple communication concept; Communication *is a two-way process. Communication is not complete until the sender verifies that the receiver has received the communication, and understood it as intended by the sender.* Based on this, Option C represents the best, most complete, answer. Options A and D, while partially true, both contradict the proper concept. Option B is much closer to the best answer, but omits the need to verify the communication being understood as intended.

3. <u>D</u> This is a simple question that asks you to choose which of the choices is incorrect. Communications Methods would be a tool for this process.

Lesson 38 Manage Stakeholder Engagement

1. <u>C</u> This quiz question is designed to help ensure you understand the intended application of the Manage Stakeholder Engagement process. *The Manage Stakeholder Engagement process is applied to satisfy the needs of project stakeholders and to resolve issues with project stakeholders.* Therefore, Option C represents the preferred answer. Options A, B and D represent remotely true statements. Only Option C provides a complete, accurate description of the Manage Stakeholder Engagement process.

2. <u>B</u> This question tests your ability to recognize that an immediate face-to-face meeting directly with the other party is always the preferred method in issue/conflict resolution situations … opposed to emails, phone calls or other less direct approaches. Therefore, Option B represents the preferred answer.

3. <u>C</u> This is a straightforward test of your ability to recognize the defined inputs, the tools & techniques and the outputs associated with the Manage Stakeholder Engagement process. Manage Stakeholder Engagement tools & techniques include 1) communications methods and 2) interpersonal skills. Only Option C correctly identifies these defined process tools/techniques and is therefore the preferred answer.

Lesson 39   Perform Quality Assurance

1. <u>A</u>   This quiz question is designed to ensure you understand the intended application of the Perform Quality Assurance process. *The Perform Quality Assurance process is applied to provide confidence that the project will satisfy relevant quality standards.* Therefore, Option A is the preferred answer. Options B and C are not correct because the Perform Quality Assurance process is not intended to *measure* any parameters. Measurement is associated more closely with the controlling process Control Quality. Option D is not correct because Perform Quality Assurance in the project management context is primarily concerned with project management processes, not the product/service of the project.

2. <u>A</u>   This question is intended to test your ability to recognize with whom the responsibility for project quality lies. While various team members and/or organizational groups may support project quality objectives, overall project quality is the responsibility of the project manager. Therefore, Option A is the preferred answer.

3. <u>B</u>   This is a straightforward test of your ability to recognize the defined inputs, the tools & techniques and the outputs associated with the Perform Quality Assurance process.   Only Option B correctly identifies one of the four defined Perform Quality Assurance outputs, and therefore represents the preferred answer.

4. <u>D</u>   This quiz question is intended to reinforce critical project quality concepts. Option A is a true statement; *Quality Assurance (QA) is the collective total of all activities intended to ensure the project satisfies recognized quality requirements.* Option B is another true statement; *Quality activities should be applied across the entire project life cycle.* Option C is also a true statement; *Process improvement is sometimes termed KAIZEN, representing the quality philosophy of achieving improvement via small incremental steps.* Option D is not true; *Process improvement is focused on improving project performance (to increase stakeholder value), not improving functionality of the product of the project.* Option D is therefore the preferred (least true) answer.

Lesson 40   Conduct Procurements

1. <u>A</u>   This is a straightforward test of your ability to recognize the defined inputs, the tools & techniques and the outputs associated with the Conduct Procurements process. The tools & techniques associated with the Conduct Procurements process include bidder conferences, proposal evaluation techniques, independent estimates, expert judgment, advertising, analytical techniques and procurement negotiations. Answer Option A, bidder conferences is the only correct tool/technique of the Conduct Procurements process and is therefore the preferred answer.

2. <u>C</u>   This quiz question is intended to reinforce the intended application of the Conduct Procurements process. The Conduct Procurements process is the process of obtaining seller responses, selecting seller(s) and awarding contracts. A key tool/technique in this process is bidder conference, which ensures that all prospective sellers are provided with the same information so procurements are made in a fair and impartial manner.

3. <u>B</u>   This quiz question is intended to reinforce the intended application of the Conduct Procurements process. The Conduct Procurements process is the process of obtaining

seller responses, selecting seller(s) and awarding contracts. Answer Option A describes the Plan Procurements Management process. Answer Options C and D are somewhat correct; however Answer Option A provides the most detailed description of the Conduct Procurements Management process and is therefore the preferred answer.

Lesson 41   Monitoring and Controlling Process Group – no questions

Lesson 42   Control Scope

1. <u>A</u>   This question is intended to test your practical judgment in recognizing legitimate reasons for scope change.   Options B, C and D each present a valid reason for considering/justifying scope change.   Option A represents a situation that has nothing to do with project scope.   Therefore, Option A is the preferred (not) answer.

2. <u>C</u>   This is a straightforward test of your ability to recognize the defined inputs, the tools & techniques and the outputs associated with the Control Scope process.   Answer Option C, change requests is actually an output of the Control Scope process.

3. <u>D</u>   This quiz question is designed to ensure you understand the intended application of the Control Scope process.   *Control Scope is the process of effectively managing changes in project scope, then integrating those changes with other control processes across the entire project.* Therefore, Option D is the preferred answer.   Option A is simply a false statement. Option B describes the scope planning process, not the scope change control process. Option C is another blatantly false statement.

4. <u>B</u>   This is an order-of-priority type question.   In these type questions, all options may represent correct actions, but only one is the best first action.   In this question, Options A, B and C all represent reasonable actions with respect to change control.   Option D is the only false statement (the sponsor review requirement, as well as your authority to approve changes, are unvalidated assumptions).   Upon closer examination of Options A, B and C, B should logically surface as the best first priority. It stands to reason that the first priority in change control is to discourage unnecessary change requests in the first place.   Placing this priority first (directly at the source) will help reduce the overall number of change requests, and the need for subsequent actions.   Therefore Option B represents the preferred answer.

Lesson 43   Control Schedule

1. <u>A</u>   This quiz question is designed to help ensure you understand the intended application of the Control Schedule process.   *Control Schedule is the process of effectively managing changes to the project schedule baseline, then integrating those changes with other control processes across the entire project.* Therefore, Option A is the preferred answer.   Options B, C and D represent remotely true statements.   Only Option A provides a complete, accurate description of schedule control.

2. <u>A</u>   This question tests your understanding of a schedule change control system. *A schedule

change control system is intended to provide the procedural guidance by which the schedule may be changed. Option A is therefore the best and preferred answer.

3. C This is a straightforward test of your ability to recognize the defined inputs, the tools & techniques and the outputs associated with the Control Schedule process. Options A, B and D each correctly identifies one of the defined Control Schedule tools/techniques. Option C, *project schedule*, is a process input, not a tool/technique. Therefore, Option C is the preferred (exception) answer.

4. B Work Performance Data refers to information about project progress such as which activities have started, their progress, and which activities have finished. *PMBOK® Guide Fifth Edition Section 6.7.1.3.*

5. B Various Project Calendars may be considered when developing schedule forecasts. A is incorrect because Crashing and Fast Tracking are schedule compression techniques. In C, Trend Analysis is used to evaluate schedule performance over time. *PMBOK® Guide Fifth Edition Section 6.7.1.4.*

6. D You are in the process of Control Schedule. The calculated SV (Schedule Variance) and SPI (Schedule Performance Index) are documented and communicated to stakeholders via the output called Work Performance Information. *PMBOK® Guide Fifth Edition Section 6.7.3.2.*

Lesson 44 Control Costs

1. A This quiz question is designed to help ensure you understand the intended application of the Control Costs process. Control Costs is the process of effectively managing changes to the cost baseline, then integrating those changes with other control processes across the entire project. Therefore Option A is the correct answer. Options B, C and D are all somewhat true, but not as complete and accurate as Option A.

2. D This is a judgment question. With respect to proper cost control, Option D represents the most reasonable statement, and is therefore the correct answer. Options A, B and C would all require validating the stated assumptions to be considered true. Remember, answer Options that include unvalidated assumptions should be rejected.

3. A This question tests your understanding of a cost change control system. *A cost change control system is intended to provide the procedural guidance by which cost change requests will be managed.* Option A is therefore the best and preferred answer.

4. B This is a straightforward test of your ability to recognize the defined inputs, the tools & techniques and the outputs associated with the Control Costs process. Options A, C and D each identify one of the six defined Control Costs tools/ techniques. Option B, *performance measurements*, is a process output, not a tool/technique. Therefore, Option B is the preferred (exception) answer.

5. D Variance at Completion (VAC) is determined by applying the equation, VAC = BAC - EAC. In this question, BAC (total planned budget) is given as $850,000. EAC is determined

by applying the equation EAC = BAC/CPI. CPI is determined by applying the equation, CPI = EV/AC. In this question, EV is $425,000 (50% of the work is complete and 50% of the total planned budget is $425,000). AC is given as $600,000 (the actual cost of work completed). Now we have all the variables necessary to complete the VAC calculation. CPI = $425,000/$600,000 = 0.708. EAC = $850,000/0.708 = $1,200,560. VAC = $850,000 - $1,200,560 = - $350,560 . Note that calculated values on the PMP Exam typically use 'rounding' for large numerical values. Option D (-$350,000) is therefore the correct answer. This answer generally indicates the project will be over budget by roughly $350,000 at completion.

6. <u>C</u>   This is another deceptively easy question. Earned value (EV or BCWP) is given directly in the question as $6,000. No calculations are necessary to identify the correct answer, Option C.

7. <u>D</u>   Schedule Performance Index (SPI) is determined by applying the equation, SPI = EV/PV. Therefore, Option D is the correct answer. Remember EV and BCWP are interchangeable terms. PV and BCWS are also interchangeable.

8. <u>D</u>   Schedule Variance (SV) is determined by applying the equation, SV = EV - PV. Cost Variance (CV) is determined by applying the equation, CV = EV - AC. In this question, EV (BCWP) is given as $650,000. PV (BCWS) is given as $750,000. AC (ACWP) is given as $800,000. Therefore, SV = $650,000 - $750,000 = -$100,000. CV = $650,000 - $800,000 = -$150,000. Option D is the correct answer. This answer generally indicates the project is behind schedule, and over budget by $150,000.

9. <u>B</u>   Estimate to Complete (ETC) is determined by applying the equation, ETC = EAC - AC. AC (ACWP) is given as $600,000. EAC was calculated earlier, in quiz question 5, as $1,200,560. Therefore, ETC = $1,200,560 - $600,000 = $600,560. Rounded, Option B presents the best correct answer. This answer generally indicates that roughly $600,000 is needed to complete the project from this point forward.

Lesson 45   Control Communications

1. <u>B</u>   The Control Communications process is intended to monitor and control project information throughout the project life cycle. A key input to this process are organizational process assets which define how control is be performed.

2. <u>C</u>   Project Forecasts are not an output from Control Communications. Answers A, B and D are correct outputs. Answer D can be inferred in "project management plan updates".

3. <u>B</u>   Answer B is the best choice for communicating information that may be sensitive. Answers A, C and D are certainly options that might be used in addition to a face to face meeting, but Answer B is the best course of action.

Lesson 46   Control Stakeholder Engagement

1. <u>B</u>   The Control Stakeholder Engagement process is intended to monitor and control stakeholder engagement and involvement throughout the project life cycle. A key input to

this process are project documents and the project management plan which defines how control is be accomplished.

2. C   Stakeholder Management Plan updates are not a named output from Control Stakeholder Engagement.   Answers A, B and D are named outputs.

3. B   Answer B is the best choice for communicating information that may be sensitive. Answers A, C and D are certainly options that might be used in addition to a face to face meeting, but Answer A is the best course of action.

Lesson 47   Control Risks

1. C   This quiz question is designed to ensure you understand the intended application of the Control Risks process.   *The Control Risks process is applied to monitor identified risks, identify new risks, ensure proper execution of the Plan Risk Responses, and evaluate overall effectiveness of the risk management plan in reducing risk.* Therefore, Option C is the correct answer. Options B and D are more descriptive of the risk response planning process, not risk monitoring and control. Option A is somewhat correct, but only partially. Only Option C describes risk monitoring and control completely and accurately.

2. C   This question tests your understanding of the term *workaround. A workaround is a response to an unanticipated risk event, typically executed after the risk event occurs.* Therefore, Option best C satisfies the proper response to the scenario presented in this question, and is the correct answer. Note that Option A describes going to your sponsor for guidance. You should begin to take note that issues, problems and challenges should be handled at the project level. Only very significant issues (that can't be resolved at the project level) should be escalated to the sponsor level.

3. A   This is a straightforward test of your ability to recognize the defined inputs, the tools & techniques and the outputs associated with the Control Risks process. Only Option A correctly identifies defined process tools/ techniques, as asked, and is therefore the preferred answer.

4. A   This quiz question is intended to help reinforce critical risk monitoring and control concepts. Option B is true*; Project team members and stakeholders should be vigilant in looking for risk symptoms, as well as for new project risks.* Option C is also true; *Risk monitoring is intended to be a daily, on-going process across the entire project life-cycle, from project start to project finish.* Option D is another true statement; *Workarounds (or workaround plans) are responses to unanticipated (surprise) risk events after they occur.* Option A (*Unanticipated risks that occur during project plan execution must be ignored, because no advance plans exist to deal with them. The project must simply accept the consequences.*) is not true. Risks can be accepted, mitigated, avoided and/or transferred, but they cannot be ignored. Therefore, Option A is the preferred (least true) answer.

Lesson 48   Control Procurements

1. C   This quiz question is designed to help ensure you understand the intended application of the Control Procurements process.   *The Control Procurements process is applied to*

ensure that the seller's performance satisfies contractual obligations. Therefore, Option C is the correct answer. Options A, B and D are all somewhat true, but not as complete and precise as Option C.

2. <u>D</u>   This question is intended to test your judgment. There is no clear, right or wrong, reference to cite here. However, proper thinking is intended to have you arrive at the conclusion that, *with a well-defined scope of work*, the need for contractual changes should be minimal. In this question scenario, the well-defined scope of work should significantly mitigate the only identified risk with this particular seller. Therefore, Option D is probably the best response. Options A and B represent unvalidated assumptions and may be rejected (remember … you can confidently reject answer options that present unvalidated assumptions). Option C represents a position of mistrust, a position that should never be knowingly entered.

3. <u>C</u>   This is a straightforward test of your ability to recognize the defined inputs, the tools & techniques and the outputs associated with the Control Procurements process. Options A, B and D each correctly identifies one of the six defined Contract Administration inputs, as asked. Option C, *change requests*, represents a process output, not an input. Therefore, Option C is the preferred (exception) answer.

4. <u>A</u>   This question is intended to reinforce critical project procurement concepts. Option B is a true statement; If *a contract is well-planned and negotiated, then the need for contract changes should be minimized.* Option C is another true statement; *Contract changes that will lead to improved project performance should be facilitated, but in accordance with the project's change control system.* Option D is also a true statement; *Unnecessary contract changes should be discouraged.* Option A (*Once negotiated and executed, a buyer/seller contract becomes a legally binding agreement and cannot be changed.*) is not true. While contracts *are* legally binding agreements, they may certainly be changed, if both parties agree. Therefore, Option A is the preferred (least true) answer.

Lesson 49   Control Quality

1. <u>D</u>   This quiz question is designed to help ensure you understand the intended application of the Control Quality process. *The Control Quality process is applied to monitor specific project results to ensure they comply with the project's quality standards.* Option D describes the process precisely this way and is therefore the preferred answer. Options A and C are somewhat true, but not as complete or accurate as D. Option B is not true. Quality Control, in the project management context, is concerned with project management processes, not the product of the project.

2. <u>D</u>   The PMP Exam will require you to understand a few statistical QC fundamentals. This question tests your understanding of certain characteristics of typical QC control charts, specifically Upper Control Limit (UCL) and Lower Control Limit (LCL). Option D correctly describes UCL and LCL and is therefore the preferred answer. Specification Limits, as alluded to in Options A, B and C, are not the same as ULC and LCL. Specification Limits are generally further away from the mean (average) than ULCs and UCLs.

3. <u>D</u>   This is a straightforward test of your ability to recognize the defined inputs, the tools & techniques and the outputs associated with the Control Quality process. Options A, B and C

each correctly identifies a defined process tool/technique. Option D, *quality metrics*, is a process input, not a tool/technique. Therefore, Option D is the preferred (exception) answer.

4. <u>B</u>   This quiz question is intended to test your general understanding of standard deviation (sigma) with respect to project quality control. *Standard deviation in project quality control is a measure of how far you are from a determined mean (average)*. Therefore, Option B is the preferred answer. Options A, C and D represent statements that may sound somewhat reasonable at first glance. But upon closer examination, each should be recognized as not accurate.

5. <u>C</u>   This is another question intended to test your understanding of certain quality control chart characteristics, specifically *out-of-control*. Generally, an out-of-control condition exists when a data point falls outside an established Upper or Lower Control Limit or when seven or more consecutive data points fall on one side of the mean (above or below) (*rule of seven*). In this question, Option C best describes an out-of-control condition and is therefore the preferred answer. Options A and B are simply not true. Option D could appear reasonable at first, but upon closer examination it describes only one data point. The rule of seven involves seven consecutive data points.

Lesson 50   Validate Scope

1. <u>A</u>   This quiz question is designed to reinforce the difference between Validate Scope and Control Quality. It is important to know the difference between the two. Validate Scope focuses on the formal acceptance of the project deliverable while Control Quality focuses on the how the deliverables meet quality requirements.

2. <u>D</u>   This is a straightforward test of your ability to recognize the defined inputs, the tools & techniques and the outputs associated with the Validate Scope process.   Answer Option D, scope management plan is not one of the inputs related to the Validate Scope process.

3. <u>C</u>   This quiz question is designed to help ensure you understand the intended application of the Validate Scope process.   *Validate Scope is the process of obtaining <u>formal acceptance</u> of project deliverables*. Therefore, Option C is the correct answer. Options B and D erroneously allude to verifying the 'correctness' of project deliverables. Scope Verification is applied to obtain *formal acceptance*, not verify correctness. It is possible to correctly complete a deliverable, but fail to obtain formal acceptance ... and vice-versa. Option A wrongly alludes to guiding parallel performance.

4. <u>A</u> Work Performance Data is an Input to Validate Scope. *PMBOK® Guide Fifth Edition Section 5.5.*

Lesson 51   Monitor & Control Project Work

1. C   This quiz question is designed to help ensure you understand the intended application of the Monitor and Control Project Work process. *The Monitor and Control Project Work*

process is applied to 1) monitor all other processes through initiating, planning, executing and closing and 2) take/make corrective/preventive actions, as needed. Therefore, Option C is the preferred answer. Options A, B and D are all somewhat true, but not as complete and precise as Option C.

2. <u>B</u>   This question is intended to test your understanding of 'preventive action.' *Preventive actions are actions required to reduce the probability of negative consequences associated with project risks.* Option B best describes the actions presented in the root question, and is therefore the preferred answer.

3. <u>C</u>   This is a straightforward test of your ability to recognize the defined inputs, the tools & techniques and the outputs associated with the Monitor and Control Project Work process. Only Option C correctly identifies process outputs, as asked, and therefore represents the preferred answer.

4. <u>A</u>   This question is a test of your knowledge of the Inputs, Tools and Techniques, and Outputs of Monitor and Control Project Work. B is wrong because it includes Work Performance Reports, which is an Output of this process. C is wrong because it includes Analytical Techniques, which is a Tool and Technique of this process. D is wrong because it includes Meetings, which is a Tool and Technique of this process, and Work Performance Reports, which is an Output of this process. *PMBOK® Guide Fifth Edition Section 4.4.*

5. <u>C</u>   This question is a test of your knowledge of the Inputs, Tools and Techniques, and Outputs of Monitor and Control Project Work, specifically the Tool and Technique of Analytical Techniques. A is wrong because it includes Work Performance Information, which is an Input of this process. B is wrong because it includes Meetings, which is a Tool and Technique of this process. D is wrong because it includes Work Performance Reports, which is an Output of this process. *PMBOK® Guide Fifth Edition Section 4.4.2.2*

Lesson 52   Perform Integrated Change Control

1. <u>C</u>   This question is designed to test your understanding of the Perform Integrated Change Control process's interrelation with the project life cycle. The Perform Integrated Change Control process is conducted from the beginning to the end of a project. Answer Option C, project life cycle best reflects this timeframe and therefore is the preferred answer.

2. <u>D</u>   This is a straightforward test of your ability to recognize the defined inputs, the tools & techniques and the outputs associated with the Perform Integrated Change Control process. Answer Options A, B and C each correctly identify defined process outputs. Option D, change control meetings, is a tool & technique associated with Perform Integrated Change Control. Therefore, Option D is the exception (correct) answer.

3. <u>B</u>   This quiz question is designed to help ensure you understand the intended applications of the Perform Integrated Change Control process. Perform Integrated Change Control is the process of effectively managing changes and integrating them appropriately across the entire project. Option B describes the process precisely this way and is therefore the preferred answer. Options A, C and D are all somewhat true, but incomplete compared to

Option B.

4. <u>C</u> In Perform Integrated Change Control, the Tool and Technique of Meetings refers to Change Control meetings. A Change Control Board (CCB) may be established to meet and review Change Requests and approve, reject or make other dispositions of the Change Requests. The CCB may also review configuration management activities. *PMBOK® Guide Fifth Edition Section 4.5.2.2.*

5. <u>D</u> Only D, Change Control Tools, is a Tool and Technique within Perform Integrated change Control. A and B are Inputs. C is out Output. *PMBOK® Guide Fifth Edition Section 4.5.2.3.*

Lesson 53 Closing Process Group – no questions from this lesson

Lesson 54 Close Procurements

1. <u>B</u> This quiz question is designed to help ensure you understand the intended application of the Close Procurements process. *Close Procurements is the procurement process of formally accepting and closing contracted work.* Therefore, Option B is the preferred answer. Options A, C and D could all be somewhat correct statements in some situations, but certainly not universally. Only Option B provides a complete and accurate description of the contract closeout process.

2. <u>C</u> This question further tests your understanding of activities typically associated with the contract closeout process. Option A is true; *Procurement closeout is performed by verifying that contracted work was completed correctly and contract terms and conditions were satisfied.* Option B is true; *During procurement closing, formal acceptance is documented and contract records are archived.* Option D is true; *Close Procurements is applied only if services/supplies are contracted/ purchased to support the project.* Option C (*Close Procurements is applied once, at the very end of the final project phase, like all closing processes.*) is not true. Close Procurements must be applied to formally end every project contract, regardless of the number of contracts or the point in time when each ends. Therefore, Option C is the preferred (least true) answer.

3. <u>A</u> This is a straightforward test of your ability to recognize the defined inputs, the tools & techniques and the outputs associated with the Close Procurements process. Only Option A identifies one of the defined tools/ techniques, and therefore represents the correct answer.

Lesson 55 Close Project or Phase

1. <u>D</u> This quiz question is designed to help ensure you understand the intended application of the Close Project or Phase process. *The Close Project or Phase process is applied to formally end either the project or project phase.* Therefore, Option D is the preferred answer. Options A and B are true statements, but not complete descriptions. Option C better

describes the Close Procurements process, not the Close Project process.

2. <u>B</u>   This question is intended to reinforce the concept that administrative closure is applied to formally end *each* phase in the project life cycle, not just the end of the entire project. Based on this, Option B best describes the concept, and is therefore the preferred answer. Options A and D are blatantly false. Option C is true, but not complete.

3. <u>C</u>   This is a straightforward test of your ability to recognize the defined inputs associated with the Close Project or Phase process. Only Option C identifies one of the defined inputs, and therefore represents the preferred answer.

4. <u>D</u>   This quiz question is intended to reinforce the concept that lessons learned should be performed by the project manager and project management team, not by any one individual. Option D best describes this concept, and is therefore the preferred (most true) answer. Options A and C contradict the concept and can be eliminated quickly. Option B is somewhat true, in that you and your team members are key stakeholders. However, Option D is the best, most accurate and complete answer.

5. <u>A</u> All of these are meetings that may be held if a phase or entire project is being closed during the Closing Process Group, with the exception of the Requirements Documentation focus groups, which would be held during the Planning Process group. *PMBOK® Guide Fifth Edition Section 4.6.2.3.*

Lesson 56   Mastering the PMP Exam – no questions from this lesson

Appendix B
Rapid Review Sheets

Lesson 2 – Fundamentals

In this chapter, we will explore some basic information about project management. We will provide basic definitions of projects and project management, discuss organizations and cultural affect on projects and their chances for success.

How the PMBOK® Guide Applies Processes

The PMBOK® Guide defines material and processes that are "Generally recognized as good practices" for project management. In the PMBOK® Guide, 47 processes have been defined. Will the project manager use each and every one of these processes on every project? The answer to this question is a resounding "maybe".

PMBOK® Guide stresses that there is no specific fixed way that a project must be managed. The project manager must choose which processes, and in what order the processes are performed, based on the needs of the specific project.

Many companies' project life cycles define specific subsets of processes that should be performed based on the size and complexity of the project. PMI specifies that the project manager must choose which processes are appropriate for the project, but each of the 5 process groups must be performed in each project phase.

We encourage the project manager to look at the 47 processes as a checklist. As we delve further into this information, we will discuss the concept that each of the 5 process groups must be performed in each phase of the project. Since we are using all of the process groups, it provides some logic that each of the 47 processes might be addressed in each phase of the project as well. While the project manager and project team may not fully perform and address each process in each phase, if the project manager uses the processes as a checklist, then there is a lesser chance that items will be missed on the project. Refer to your TSI Project Management Process Poster #1; reference the Process Knowledge Areas Table.

Must Know Concepts
----

1. A project is a temporary endeavor undertaken to create a unique product, service or result. A project has a beginning and an end and is progressively elaborated.

2. Project management is the application of knowledge, skills, tools and techniques to project activities in order to meet project requirements.

3. A project manager must have several areas of skill and knowledge in order to manage projects successfully. These skills and knowledge are grouped into three categories: project management knowledge, performance ability and personal skills.

4. Portfolios are collections of projects, programs and other work in the organization.

5. Programs are made up of related projects that are managed in a unified manner to achieve planned benefits for the organization.

6. Projects should be organized in terms of phases or stages to form an overall project life cycle.

7. A stakeholder is anyone or any group that is actively involved in the project or whose interests may be affected (positively or negatively) by the project activities or outcome.

Lesson 3 – Mastering the PMBOK® Guide

The PMBOK® Guide (A Guide to the Project Management Body of Knowledge; published by the Project Management Institute, PMI®) is the de-facto global standard for managing projects. In September 1999, the PMBOK® Guide was formally adopted as an ANSI Standard. The PMBOK® Guide has been updated multiple times since being adopted; the current version is the *PMBOK® Guide Fifth Edition*.

Many exam questions are designed specifically to test your content knowledge of the PMBOK® Guide. However, the PMBOK® Guide is a reference standard, not a learning text. Therefore, the PMBOK® Guide can be difficult to quickly master. The PMBOK Guide® is not a methodology.

In this lesson, we will begin to master the PMBOK® Guide by developing a high level understanding of the intent, content and presentation structure. If you have purchased TSI's companion Project Management Process Poster Set, you can see the many processes, process groups and process flows illustrated in a full color graphics format.

Must Know Concepts

---

1. The PMBOK® Guide identifies and describes generally recognized best practices that are applicable to most projects most of the time.

2. The level of project management effort should be sensibly proportional to the size and complexity of the project.

3. The PMBOK® Guide organizes its content as an interrelated set of 47 well defined processes, further grouped into 5 process groups and 10 knowledge areas.

4. The Process Groups are: Initiating, Planning, Executing, Monitoring & Controlling and Closing.

5. The 10 Knowledge Areas are: Project Integration Management, Project Scope Management, Project Time Management, Project Cost Management, Project Quality Management, Project Human Resource Management, Project Communications Management, Project Risk Management, Project Procurement Management and Project Stakeholder Management.

6. The relationship of project processes to specific project management knowledge areas and process groups is an important element to learn for the PMP Exam.

Lesson 4 – Initiating Process Group

The primary purpose that these Initiating processes are performed is to authorize the project (or phase) and to indentify the stakeholders that will be involved and interested in the project as it progresses. Initiating processes occur in the Integration Management knowledge area and the Stakeholder Management knowledge area of the *PMBOK® Guide Fifth Edition*.

An important part of the Initiating process group is the assignment of the project manager to the project and the PM's authority. This usually occurs during the authorization process of Develop Project Charter.

If there was a "keyword" that would characterize the Initiating Process Group, it might be "high-level". When a project is started, the sponsor, project manager and stakeholders have a high level view of the project; a vision of what is about to happen. There are usually not specific details available to define the complete project.

At the beginning of subsequent project phases, Initiating processes are used to confirm that the vision for the project is sound and that identified stakeholders still have a role on the project. In subsequent project phases, the Initiating processes will work in conjunction with the Closing processes as part of the Project Life Cycle review, stage gate or kill point decision. The Closing processes are used to review what happened in the phase that is ending; the Initiating processes will confirm that the project vision is sound, the business case is viable and the project manager who has been assigned can perform effectively on the subsequent phase.

Initiating Tasks

On your PMP Exam, you will encounter approximately many questions that will test your understanding of Initiating processes. These questions will generally focus on Initiating tasks. As a PMP or project manager initiating a project (or project phase), you may be required to:

1. Perform project assessment based on available information and meetings with the sponsor, customer, and other subject matter experts, in order to evaluate the feasibility of new products or services with the given assumptions and/or constraints.

2. Define the high-level scope of the project based on the business and compliance requirements, in order to meet the customer's project expectations.

3. Perform key stakeholder analysis using brainstorming, interviewing, and other data gathering techniques, in order to endure expectation alignment and gain support for the project.

4. Identify and document high level risks, assumptions and constraints based on current environment, historical data and/or expert judgment, in order to identify project limitations and propose an implementation approach.

5. Develop the project charter by further gathering and analyzing stakeholder requirements, in order to document project scope, milestones and deliverables.

6. Obtain approval for the project charter from the sponsor and customer (if required), in order to formalize the authority assigned to the project manager and gain commitment and acceptance for the project.

Lesson 5 – Develop Project Charter

The Develop Project Charter process is intended to ensure that any project chartered and authorized by management is well thought-through and justified. With a solid beginning, any project has a greater probability of ultimate success. The process suggests that management employ expert judgment and facilitations techniques to make good decisions and choose the "right" project. Typical facilitation techniques used to gather information could include: brainstorming, Delphi technique, problem solving techniques, meetings and facilitation.

The Develop Project Charter process suggests management prepare and issue a formal Project Charter that:

- Documents the preliminary characteristics of the project or a phase

- Authorizes the project

- Identifies/authorizes the project manager

A project sponsor or initiator authorizes the project by approving the Project Charter. The project initiator may be the Project Management Office (PMO) or Portfolio Steering Committee.

Develop Project Charter		
This process formally sanctions a new project or authorizes a project to continue into the next phase		
Inputs	**Tools and Techniques**	**Outputs**
• Project Statement of Work (SOW) • Business Case • Agreements • Enterprise Environmental Factors • Organizational Process Assets	• Expert Judgment • Facilitation Techniques	• Project Charter

Must Know Concepts

1. The Develop Project Charter process is intended to formally authorize a new project.

2. The primary deliverable (Output) of the Develop Project Charter process is the Project Charter.

3. The Project Charter is a high-level document that communicates preliminary project characteristics, authorizes the project, and identifies and authorizes the project manager.

4. The Project Charter is typically issued by a project initiator or sponsor, external to the immediate project organization, at a funds-providing management level.

5. The project's business need, and product or service description should be clearly defined and documented.

6. Chartering a project links the project to the ongoing work of the performing organization.

7. The project manager should be assigned as early as possible, preferably during Project Charter development.

8. The Project Charter should be relatively brief (broad, not deep), perhaps 1-5 pages in length.

Lesson 6 – Identify Stakeholders

A "Stakeholder" is any person or organization that is actively involved in a project, or whose interests may be affected positively or negatively by execution of a project. Stakeholders can be internal to the organization or external. In many projects the public at large will become a stakeholder to be considered on the project. The challenge for the project manager when the public is a stakeholder will be to act while considering public needs. Often there is no direct representative of the public to be consulted during project planning and execution. A project manager must be sure to identify and list all potential stakeholders for a project.

The project manager must document relevant information for all identified stakeholders. This information may include the stakeholder's interests, involvement, expectations, importance, influence, and impact on the projects execution as well as any specific communications requirements that may be required. It is important to note that although some identified stakeholders may not actually require any communications, those stakeholders should be identified.

When identifying stakeholders and rating their level of interest and involvement in the project it will become important to use some sort of a tool, a rating scale an influence diagram or some chart form to identify the level of power, influence, interest or impact that the stakeholder may have on the project.

Identify Stakeholders		
This process identifies all persons/organizations impacted by a project and documents their interests, involvement, and impact on the project		
Inputs	**Tools and Techniques**	**Outputs**
• Project Charter • Procurement Documents • Enterprise Environmental Factors • Organizational Process Assets	• Stakeholder Analysis • Expert Judgment • Meetings	• Stakeholder Register

Must Know Concepts

---

1. A "stakeholder" is any person or organization that is actively involved in a project, or whose interests may be affected positively or negatively by execution of a project.

2. The Identify Stakeholders process is used to identify all people or organizations that maybe impacted or have an impact on a project.

3. A key output of the Identify Stakeholders process is the Stakeholder Register which lists the projects stakeholders and relevant information for each stakeholder or stakeholder group.

4. Stakeholder Analysis is a technique used to determine stakeholder interests, influence, participation and expectations for a project.

Lesson 7 – Planning Process Group

The primary purpose that these Planning processes are performed is to define the elements and work for a project (or phase). Planning processes cover all ten knowledge areas of the *PMBOK® Guide Fifth Edition*.

During the Planning processes, the project is fully defined. At the end of the Planning processes, the Project Management Plan and all related documentation is completed and accepted by the project stakeholders. Usually, after the Project Management Plan and all defining documents are accepted, then change control processes are employed to manage all subsequent changes to the project baseline.

Of particular importance are the project baselines for project scope, schedule and budget.

In general, when a change is made to the project baseline while the project is in the executing phases of the project, the project manager returns to the Planning processes in order to update the affected documentation.

Planning Tasks

On your PMP Exam, you will encounter many questions that will test your understanding of planning processes. These questions will generally focus on the following tasks, that are in turn, related to specific processes and process actions in planning. As a PMP or project manager planning a project (or project phase) you may be required to:

1. Assess detailed project requirements, constraints, and assumptions with stakeholders based on the project charter, lessons learned from previous projects, and the use of requirement-gathering techniques (e.g., planning sessions, brainstorming, focus groups), in order to establish the project deliverables.

2. Create the work breakdown structure with the team by deconstructing the scope, in order to manage the scope of the project.

3. Develop a budget plan based on the project scope using estimating techniques, in order to manage project cost.

4. Develop a project schedule based on the project timelines, scope, and resource plan, in order to manage timely completion of the project.

5. Develop a human resource management plan by defining the roles and responsibilities of the project team members in order to create an effective project organization structure and provide guidance regarding how resources will be utilized and managed.

6. Develop a communications plan based on the project organization structure and external stakeholder requirements, in order to manage the flow of project information.

7. Develop a procurement management plan based on the project scope and schedule, in order to ensure that the required project resources will be available.

8. Develop a quality management plan based on the project scope and requirements, in order to prevent the occurrence of defects and reduce the cost of quality.

9. Develop a Change Management Plan by defining how changes will be handled, in order to track and make changes.

10. Develop a risk management plan by identifying, analyzing, and prioritizing project risks and defining risk response strategies, in order to manage uncertainty throughout the project life cycle.

11. Present the project plan to the key stakeholders, in order to obtain approval to execute the project.

12. Conduct a kick-off meeting with all key stakeholders, in order to announce the start of the project, communicate the project milestones, and share other relevant information.

Lesson 8 – Plan Stakeholder Management

Once stakeholders have been identified, it is imperative to develop management strategies for ensuring that the stakeholders are engaged and participating throughout the life of the project. This can be done by creating an actionable plan showing the intent of the project manager and team for interaction levels based on individual stakeholder needs.

Plan Stakeholder Management identifies how the project will affect individual stakeholders. From this information, the project manager can tailor a plan to keep each stakeholder engaged and participating in the project by addressing specific interests and elements which affect that stakeholder.

The project manager may use analytical techniques to compare actual stakeholder involvement and engagement to planned involvement. This is usually done using a five-point scale ranging from an "Unaware" condition to a "Leading" condition.

Plan Stakeholder Management		
This process develops management strategies to engage stakeholders throughout the project life cycle		
Inputs	**Tools and Techniques**	**Outputs**
• Project Management Plan • Stakeholder Register • Enterprise Environmental Factors • Organizational Process Assets	• Expert Judgment • Meetings • Analytical Techniques	• Stakeholder Management Plan • Project Documents Updates

Must Know Concepts

1. The Plan Stakeholder Management process is performed to develop appropriate management strategies to engage stakeholders throughout the project.

2. A key output of the Plan Stakeholder Management process is the Stakeholder Management Plan which lists the project's stakeholders and relevant information for each stakeholder or stakeholder group, their communications needs and expectations.

3. The project team should determine the desired level of engagement by each stakeholder for the current phase of the project. Using the five levels of stakeholder engagement (PMBOK 13.2.2.3) project teams must analyze current and desired state of stakeholder engagement.

Lesson 9 – Plan Communications Management

Communication provides the vital connections between people, concepts and information throughout the project environment. Good communication management ensures that important information is generated, collected, distributed and stored in an appropriate and effective manner. Effective communications can facilitate success and enable the project to succeed. The lack of effective communications almost always contributes to project confusion, deficiencies and failure.

The Plan Communications process is applied to determine the communication needs of project stakeholders. This includes determining:

- What information is needed
- When it is needed
- How it will be delivered

Communications needs for the project are typically determined by first engaging identified project stakeholders (communication requirements analysis), to determine their detailed information needs, then documenting the details in a Communications Management Plan. The Plan Communications process will be executed at the beginning of planning processes. The fact that this process is performed so early in the project attests to the overall importance of having an effective communications plan.

Plan Communications Management		
This process determines who needs what information, when, and how they get it		
Inputs	**Tools and Techniques**	**Outputs**
• Project Management Plan • Stakeholder Register • Enterprise Environmental Factors • Organizational Process Assets	• Communication Requirements Analysis • Communication Technology • Communication Models • Communication Methods • Meetings	• Communications Management Plan • Project Documents Updates

Must Know Concepts

1. The Plan Communications Management process is applied to determine the communications needs of project stakeholders. This includes what information is needed, when it is needed and how it will be delivered.

2. The primary deliverable (Output) of the Plan Communications process is the Communications Management Plan.

3. Effective communications in project management is a critical success factor; it is an accepted heuristic that good project managers spend up to 90% of their time communicating.

4. Communication is a two-way activity. Communication is not complete until the sender confirms the receiver has understood the intended message.

5. The number of communication channels within a project increases exponentially as the number of stakeholders increases. The equation used to calculate communications channels is $N(N-1)/2$.

Lesson 10 – Plan Scope Management

Plan Scope Management is the process of creating a scope management plan that will document how project scope will be defined, documented, validated and controlled throughout the project life cycle. Using the very simplest definition, the Scope Management Plan might say something like: "Any changes to project scope must be approved by these key stakeholders".

The Scope Management Plan will document how scope is to be developed. This implies that the level of detail required and the format for the project scope statement will be defined here. This also includes development of the scope baseline which occurs in Create WBS. The Scope Management Plan should define what level of detail will go into the work breakdown structure/scope baseline. The level of detail defined will then dictate how scope will be tracked and managed throughout the project.

The Plan Scope Management process creates the Scope Management Plan and Requirements Management Plan, both which are considered part of the overall Project Management Plan.

Plan Scope Management		
This process documents how project scope is defined, validated and controlled		
Inputs	**Tools and Techniques**	**Outputs**
• Project Management Plan	• Expert Judgment	• Scope Management Plan
• Project Charter	• Meetings	• Requirements Management Plan
• Enterprise Environmental Factors		
• Organizational Process Assets		

Must Know Concepts

1. The Plan Scope Management process is applied to create a Scope Management Plan that documents how project scope will be defined, controlled and validated.

2. The primary deliverable (Output) of the Plan Scope Management process is the Scope Management Plan. A secondary, companion output from this process is the Requirements Management Plan.

3. Scope Management is part of the overall Project Management Plan.

Lesson 11 – Collect Requirements

Project "requirements" are the conditions and capabilities that must be achieved through the projects' execution. Requirements must be documented in sufficient detail to allow measurement in determining the status of project completion and in determining whether or not the documented requirements have been met.

There are many tools and techniques than can used to help facilitate identifying requirements, such as; focus groups, workshops, brainstorming, mind mapping, surveys, observation, and others.

A key output of this process is the Requirements Documentation. Requirements Documentation describes how the identified requirements fulfill the business needs of the project. This documentation is normally progressively elaborated as a project progresses. In addition, a Requirements Traceability Matrix links each requirement to the business objectives to ensure that each requirement is adding value to the project and organization.

Additional attributes to ensure that the requirement has met stakeholders' satisfaction may include stability, complexity and acceptance criteria. A project's success is directly influenced by the accuracy and completeness in identifying all of the requirements and expectations through this process.

Collect Requirements		
This process defines and documents the project and product features and functions needed to fill stakeholder's needs and expectations		
Inputs	**Tools and Techniques**	**Outputs**
• Scope Management Plan	• Interviews	• Requirements Documentation
• Requirements Management Plan	• Focus Groups	• Requirements Traceability Matrix
• Stakeholder Management Plan	• Facilitated Workshops	
• Project Charter	• Group Creativity Techniques	
• Stakeholder Register	• Group Decision Making Techniques	
	• Questionnaires and Surveys	
	• Observation	
	• Prototypes	
	• Benchmarking	
	• Context Diagrams	
	• Document Analysis	

Must Know Concepts

1. The Collect Requirements process defines and documents the product and project features that are required to meet the expectations and requirements of the projects stakeholders.

2. A key output of the Collect Requirements process is the Requirements Documentation.

3. A Requirements Traceability Matrix links requirements to business objectives to ensure each requirement is adding value to the project and organization.

4. A project's success is directly influenced by the accuracy and completeness in identifying all of the requirements and expectations through this process.

Lesson 12 – Define Scope

The Project Scope Statement defines the projects deliverables and the work required to create those deliverables. During scope definition, you and your team create the major deliverables, assumptions and constraints by progressively elaborating on data that was defined during project initiation. Stakeholders' needs and desires, as defined in the Requirements Document, are analyzed and developed into firm work requirements. Assumptions and constraints can be further analyzed and the opinions of domain experts can be solicited.

It is important to understand that your Project Scope Statement will serve to provide a common understanding of the project scope among stakeholders. The process of Define Scope creates a detailed Project Scope Statement. The Project Scope Statement is required to complete detailed project planning. The Work Breakdown Structure, Activity List and Project Schedule will derive from key information that is documented in this process.

During project execution the Project Scope Statement will be used to guide decisions. When changes to the project scope are approved, the Project Scope Statement will be updated.

A detailed and thorough Project Scope Statement is critical to the success of a project.

Define Scope		
This process defines and documents the project and product features and functions needed to fill stakeholder's needs and expectations		
Inputs	**Tools and Techniques**	**Outputs**
• Scope Management Plan	• Expert Judgment	• Project Scope Statement
• Project Charter	• Product Analysis	• Project Documents Updates
• Requirements Documentation	• Alternatives Generation	
• Organizational Process Assets	• Facilitated Workshops	

Must Know Concepts

1. The Define Scope process is intended to create the Project Scope Statement.

2. The Project Scope Statement defines the projects deliverables and the work required to create those deliverables. It defines what is and what is not, part of the project.

3. The Project Scope Statement serves as a documented basis for common understanding of project scope among stakeholders.

4. Alternatives generation that is used during Define Scope is a key technique for generating different approaches for defining and performing project work.

Lesson 13 – Create WBS

The Create Work Breakdown Structure process decomposes (subdivides) major project deliverables into smaller, more manageable components. This process is typically the first process applied after the Project Scope Statement has been developed.

The primary deliverable from the Create Work Breakdown Structure process is the Work Breakdown Structure (WBS). The WBS may be the most important tool for management of a project. When properly developed, the WBS illustrates all of the work elements that define the project and serves as the basis for most planning activities from this point forward.

The WBS documents all the work required to successfully complete the project. The WBS must identify **all of the work required, and only the work required**, to successfully complete the project. "Scope Creep" or continual changes in a project's work requirements can be eliminated by carefully defining scope and managing it using the WBS.

The completed Project Scope Statement, WBS, and WBS Dictionary form the Scope Baseline for the project.

Create WBS		
This process subdivides major deliverables into manageable components		
Inputs	**Tools and Techniques**	**Outputs**
• Scope Management Plan • Project Scope Statement • Requirements Documentation • Enterprise Environmental Factors • Organizational Process Assets	• Decomposition • Expert Judgment	• Scope Baseline • Project Documents Updates

Must Know Concepts

1. The Create Work Breakdown Structure process is intended to decompose (subdivide) major project deliverables into manageable sized components.

2. The primary deliverable from the Create Work Breakdown Structure process is the Scope Baseline, which is made up of the Scope Statement, WBS and WBS Dictionary.

3. The Scope Baseline describes all of the work to be performed on the project. This is described graphically in the WBS.

4. There is no predefined limit to the number of sublevels in a WBS. The lowest level in a WBS is a "Work Package". Activities represent the work effort of work packages.

5. Work Packages in the WBS should be decomposed to a level where adequate cost and duration estimates are possible and where acceptance criteria can be easily defined.

6. The WBS has no time frame. In its purest form, the WBS defines work only.

Lesson 14 – Plan Schedule Management

Plan Schedule Management is the process of creating a schedule management plan that will document how the project schedule will be defined, documented, validated and controlled throughout the project life cycle. Using the very simplest definition, the Schedule Management Plan might say something like: "Any changes to project schedule must be approved by these key stakeholders".

The Schedule Management Plan will document how the schedule is to be developed. This implies that the level of detail required and the format for the project schedule will be defined here. This also includes development of the schedule baseline which occurs in Develop Schedule. The Schedule Management Plan should define what level of detail will go into the schedule; whether you are tracking at the task or activity level, or tracking at a higher work package, deliverable or milestone level.

The Plan Schedule Management process creates the Schedule Management Plan which is considered part of the overall Project Management Plan.

Plan Schedule Management		
This process determines how the project schedule will be developed and managed		
Inputs	**Tools and Techniques**	**Outputs**
• Project Management Plan • Project Charter • Enterprise Environmental Factors • Organizational Process Assets	• Expert Judgment • Analytical Techniques • Meetings	• Schedule Management Plan

Must Know Concepts

1. The Plan Schedule Management process is applied to create a Schedule Management Plan that documents how the schedule will be defined, controlled and validated.

2. The primary deliverable (Output) of the Plan Schedule Management process is the Schedule Management Plan.

3. The Schedule Management Plan is part of the overall Project Management Plan.

Lesson 15 – Define Activities

The process of Define Activities logically follows closely after the Create WBS process. The WBS identifies the total of all project work in terms of deliverables. The WBS is deliverables-oriented. To adhere to this definition, our WBS should identify work using descriptive nouns, as opposed to action-oriented verbs. We apply the Define Activities process to convert our WBS work packages (lowest level elements) into action-oriented activities.

The primary deliverable from the Define Activities process is the project's Activity List; the Activity List becomes an extension of the WBS.

The primary Tool & Technique used to create the Activity List is "decomposition." This is basically the same decomposition method used to create the WBS. The difference is that, in Define Activities, decomposition is used to further subdivide work packages into manageable sized activities, and the final output is described in terms of activities, rather than deliverables.

Ideally, Define Activities is applied immediately following Create WBS. In real-world practice, however, the two processes are many times applied in parallel. In many projects, Rolling Wave Planning can be an effective tool to support activity definition. In Rolling Wave Planning, only near-term work is planned in detail, leaving future work summarized with less detail. As future work draws nearer, detailed planning is performed.

Define Activities		
This process specifically identifies all schedule activities		
Inputs	**Tools and Techniques**	**Outputs**
• Scope Management Plan	• Decomposition	• Activity List
• Scope Baseline	• Rolling Wave Planning	• Activity Attributes
• Enterprise Environmental Factors	• Expert Judgment	• Milestone List
• Organizational Process Assets		

Must Know Concepts

1. The Define Activities process identifies the specific activities necessary to complete the project deliverables.

2. The Define Activities process is intended to decompose or subdivide WBS work packages into manageable sized activities.

3. The primary deliverable (Output) from the Define Activities process is the Activity List.

4. The Activity List may be viewed as an extension of the WBS.

5. Decomposition is the primary methodology (Tool/Technique) used to create the Activity List.

6. In some projects, Rolling Wave Planning can be an effective tool to support activity definition. In Rolling Wave Planning, only near-term work is planned in detail, leaving future work summarized with less detail. As future work draws nearer, detailed planning is performed.

Lesson 16 – Sequence Activities

Sequence Activities is an essential step that must be performed accurately prior to the development of a realistic and achievable schedule. The output from this process is a Project Network Logic Diagram, aka, Project Schedule Network Diagram. Project Diagrams are often, though not correctly, referred to as PERT Charts.

When sequencing activities, activity dependencies must be identified. Dependencies can be categorized as mandatory, discretionary or external. When planning sequences, certain activities must start before others can finish. There are four possible inter activity logical relationships:

- Finish-to-Start – One activity must finish before the next activity may start. F-S is the most common type of interdependency.

- Finish-to-Finish – The completion of the successor activity depends upon the completion of the predecessor activity.

- Start-to-Start – One activity must start before the next activity may start.

- Start-to-Finish – One activity must finish before the next activity may finish. S-F is the least common type of interdependency.

These relationships must be identified and documented in some form of Network Diagram. This is what activity sequencing is all about.

Because there is a lot of important information in the Sequence Activities process (compared to other processes), expect to devote a little more time learning this process.

Sequence Activities		
This process indentifies and documents dependencies among schedule activities		
Inputs	**Tools and Techniques**	**Outputs**
• Schedule Management Plan • Activity List • Activity Attributes • Milestone List • Project Scope Statement • Enterprise Environmental Factors • Organizational Process Assets	• Precedence Diagramming Method (PDM) • Dependency Determination • Leads and Lags	• Project Schedule Network Diagrams • Project Documents Updates

Must Know Concepts

---

1. The Sequence Activities process is intended to identify and document interactivity logical relationships.

2. The primary deliverable (Output) of the Sequence Activities process is the project schedule network diagram.

3. The project schedule network diagram illustrates all project activities and their predecessor/successor relationships/interdependencies. It also identifies the project's Critical Path and all of the activities on the Critical Path.

4. The Critical Path is the longest path through a network diagram. It defines the shortest period of time in which the project may be completed. A project may have more than one critical path, or dual critical paths at certain times in the project.

5. Project schedule network diagrams are typically created and documented using the Precedence Diagramming Method (PDM) technique.

6. PDM is also referred to as Activity-on-Node (AON). In AON diagrams, activities are represented by nodes which are connected by arrowed lines to illustrate their interdependencies.

7. AON diagrams can show four types of interdependencies (F-S), (S-F), (F-F) and (S-S). Dummies are not needed to illustrate network logic in AON diagrams.

8. A Forward Pass (left-right through the network) may be performed to determine Earliest Start times (ES) and Earliest Finish times (EF) for each project activity.

9. A Backward Pass (right-left through the network) may be performed to determine Latest Start times (LS) and Latest Finish times (LF) for each project activity.

10. Slack (also referred to as float, reserve, path float or total float) for any given activity may be determined by subtracting ES from LS. Activities on the Critical Path typically have zero slack.

11. Subnet (or fragnet or subnetwork) is a subdivision of a network diagram.

12. Hammock is group of related activities illustrated as a single summary activity.

13. Lead time and Lag time allows project teams to add realism and flexibility to their schedule. Lead time may be viewed as an overlap between tasks. Lag time is waiting time.

Lesson 17 – Estimate Activity Resources

Ideally, resource needs are determined at the lowest level components, then rolled-up to higher levels (major deliverables).

The primary deliverable of the Estimate Activity Resources process is a documented description of Activity Resource Requirements. Typically, the resource needs identified here will be obtained by later applying the Acquire Project Team process and/or Procurement processes.

The Activity Attributes provide the primary data input for Estimate Activity Resources. The Estimate Activity Resource process is closely coordinated with several processes, including Estimate Costs, Acquire Project Team, Estimate Activity Duration and Plan Procurements processes.

Estimate Activity Resources		
This process determines the physical resources needed for each activity		
Inputs	**Tools and Techniques**	**Outputs**
• Schedule Management Plan	• Expert Judgment	• Activity Resource Requirements
• Activity List	• Alternatives Analysis	
• Activity Attributes	• Published Estimating Data	• Resource Breakdown Structure (RBS)
• Resource Calendars	• Bottom-up Estimating	
• Risk Register	• Project Management Software	• Project Documents Updates
• Activity Cost Estimates		
• Enterprise Environmental Factors		
• Organizational Process Assets		

Must Know Concepts

1. The Estimate Activity Resources process is intended to estimate the type and quantities of material, people, equipment or supplies required to perform each activity (physical resources).

2. The primary deliverable (Output) from the Estimate Activity Resources process is the documented description of Activity Resource Requirements.

3. Bottom-up estimating is often used in this process. It generally produces the most confident estimates, but is more costly and time consuming than it's opposite, analogous estimating. Typically, bottom-up estimating is performed by developing detailed estimates for each activity at the work package level of the WBS. They are then rolled-up to derive a project total.

4. Identified resource requirements will typically be obtained later by applying the Acquire Project Team process and the Procurement processes.

Lesson 18 – Estimate Activity Durations

In simpler projects, estimates are typically documented as deterministic, single-point values (one number). Single point estimates are generally less confident. Using expert judgment or an analogous estimate (also known as top-down estimate) is simple and quick, and usually produces a single point estimate.

In more complex projects, it is common to use sophisticated mathematics to determine probabilistic distributions for each activity, resulting in a time range estimate instead of a single time estimate. For example, a probabilistic estimate may be documented as a graphical curve indicating the probability of an activity finishing at any given time on the curve. Probabilistic estimates generally provide for more confident expectations. Probabilistic estimates usually use a method like three-point estimating to predict a range of outcomes. Duration estimates do not include any lags.

Three point estimates are sometimes called "PERT" estimates (Program Evaluation Review Technique). Three-point or PERT estimates can be determined using triangular or beta distributions. The formulas are:

Three point estimates using Triangular Distribution: $tE = (tO + tM = tP) / 3$

Three point estimates using Beta Distribution: $tE = (tO + 4tM = tP) / 6$

This Beta Distribution formula is equivalent to the most common PERT formula: $E = (O + 4ML + P)/6$

O = Optimistic estimate
ML (or M) = Most Likely estimate
P = Pessimistic estimate

Estimates should from the person or group of people who have expert familiarity with the activity.

Estimate Activity Durations
This process estimates the number of work periods for each schedule activity

Inputs	Tools and Techniques	Outputs
• Schedule Management Plan	• Expert Judgment	• Activity Duration Estimates
• Activity List	• Analogous Estimating	
• Activity Attributes	• Parametric Estimating	• Project Documents Updates
• Activity Resource Requirements	• Three-Point Estimating	
• Resource Calendars	• Group Decision Making Techniques	
• Project Scope Statement	• Reserve Analysis	
• Risk Register		
• Resource Breakdown Structure		
• Enterprise Environmental Factors		
• Organizational Process Assets		

Must Know Concepts

1. The Estimate Activity Durations process is estimating time durations for each defined activity resource. These estimates will ultimately be used to create the project schedule.

2. The primary deliverable (Output) from the Estimate Activity Durations process is the Activity Duration Estimates.

3. Deterministic (single-point) estimates are typically documented with only one value. Probabilistic (range) estimates typically report estimates in terms of probabilities, instead of hard numbers.

4. Estimating should originate from the person, or group of people, who are most knowledgeable about the activity, ideally by the person or people who will be doing the work.

5. Analogous estimating (also termed top-down estimating) typically involves basing an estimate on a known previous activity performed in the past. Analogous estimates are relatively quick to perform and inexpensive, because no detailed estimating protocols are necessary. Analogous estimates are also the least confident, typically proving to have a significant margin of error.

6. Three-Point Estimates uses the three estimates (Pessimistic, Most Probable and Optimistic) and may be used as a tool to help determine an approximate range for an activity's duration. PERT analysis calculates an expected activity duration using a weighted average of these estimates. A triangular [tE = (tO + 4tM = tP) / 3] or Beta Distribution formula [tE = (tO + 4tM = tP) / 6] may be used.

7. Estimators may choose to include reserve time (also termed time buffers) to proportionately compensate for the level of risk associated with the activity.

8. Duration estimates are typically documented in terms of work periods. Work periods are determined by the project team and are typically defined as shifts, hours, days or weeks.

9. Ideally, estimates should be reported with ranges of possible results such as; 8 days ±2 (indicating 6-10 days).

Lesson 19 – Develop Schedule

Scheduling software has become an essential tool to help create the schedule. Most scheduling software today will allow project teams to input raw data, and then automate the process of maneuvering it to create the schedule baseline. Once the schedule has been baselined, then software can automate changes and tracking throughout the project's remaining phases.

Developing and maintaining a project schedule file can be quite time consuming and require expert support. In large projects, it is not unusual to assign one full-time scheduler for every thousand lines in the schedule.

The Develop Schedule process is applied to determine the start/finish dates for project activities.

Creating a Project Schedule

There are four primary methods used to calculate theoretical early/late start/finish dates for project activities:

- **Critical Path Method (CPM)** CPM determines start/finish dates using a one-time duration estimate for each activity by performing forward and backward passes. The Critical Path Method is the "most probable" time duration estimate.
- **Critical Chain Method** This method may be used to modify a project schedule to account for limited resources and project uncertainty. Critical chain methodology is characterized by a focus on the use and management of duration buffers. Durations used do not include safety buffers for risk, logical relationships or resource availability; time buffers are added to compensate for project characteristics. The resource-constrained critical path is known as the critical chain.
- **Resource Optimization Techniques** Resource Leveling and Resource Smoothing are resource management tools sometimes used to adjust resource utilization across the project schedule, to minimize exaggerated peaks and valleys.
- **Modeling Techniques** What-if-Scenario Analysis and Simulation tools compute different scenarios to derive the schedule. Typically, this is done using Monte Carlo simulations to support this method.

Completed project schedules are typically illustrated using a Bar Chart (Gantt Chart), Milestone Chart or Dated Network Diagram.

Tools to Compress a Project Schedule

- **Crashing** This is the process of adding more resources to the activity. Crashing typically adds cost and potentially increases risk. The key to using this is to choose the most efficient and effective alternative. It is not always a feasible alternative.
- **Fast Tracking** The project schedule can sometimes be shortened by 'fast tracking' activities on the critical path. Fast tracking is the process of realigning normally sequential activities to be performed in parallel. Fast tracking typically increases risk and can cause rework. Like crashing, fast tracking is not always a feasible alternative.

Develop Schedule		
This process analyzes activities and constraints to create the project schedule		
Inputs	**Tools and Techniques**	**Outputs**
• Schedule Management Plan • Activity List • Activity Attributes • Project Schedule Network Diagrams • Activity Resource Requirements • Resource Calendars • Activity Duration Estimates • Project Scope Statement • Risk Register • Project Staff Assignments • Resource Breakdown Structure • Enterprise Environmental Factors • Organizational Process Assets	• Schedule Network Analysis • Critical Path Method • Critical Chain Method • Resource Optimization Techniques • Modeling Techniques • Leads and Lags • Schedule Compression • Scheduling Tool	• Schedule Baseline • Project Schedule • Schedule Data • Project Calendars • Project Management Plan Updates • Project Documents Updates

Must Know Concepts

----

1. The Develop Schedule process is applied to create the project schedule based on activity sequences, durations, resource requirements and schedule constraints.

2. There are four primary methods used to calculate theoretical early/late start/finish dates for project activities; Critical Path Method (CPM), Critical Chain Method, Resource Optimization Techniques and Modeling Techniques.

3. Care must be taken to differentiate the actual effort-time (performance-time) required to perform the activity work and the calendar-time (elapsed-time) required to completed the activity. Some activities may have non-work waiting time involved.

4. The primary deliverables (Outputs) of the Develop Schedule process include the Schedule Baseline and the Project Schedule.

5. There are two primary methods used to shorten schedules; Crashing and Fast Tracking.

6. Completed project schedules are typically illustrated using Bar Charts (also called Gantt Charts), Milestone Charts or Project Schedule Network Diagrams.

7. Resource Optimization Techniques include Resource Leveling and Resource Smoothing which are tools to 'level' resources across the project schedule, to minimize exaggerated peaks and valleys.

8. Schedule Modeling Tools include "What-if-Scenario Analysis" and Monte Carlo simulations; both are used to factor in uncertainties into the project schedule.

Lesson 20 – Plan Human Resource Management

Plan Human Resource Management typically involves creating a project organization chart, a Human Resource Management Plan, defining team policies/procedures and creating a Staffing Management Plan.

Projects can be staffed by people external to the organization, internal to the organization, or by a mix of both. As you may imagine, a project team comprised of staff members who are temporarily borrowed from various groups within an organization will be quite different from a project team comprised of members who are all hired from the outside..

Develop Human Resource Plan		
This process documents project roles, responsibilities and reporting relationships		
Inputs	**Tools and Techniques**	**Outputs**
• Project Management Plan • Activity Resource Requirements • Enterprise Environmental Factors • Organizational Process Assets	• Organizational Charts and Position Descriptions • Networking • Organizational Theory • Expert Judgment • Meetings	• Human Resource Management Plan

Must Know Concepts

1. The Plan Human Resource Management process is applied to develop, document and assign project roles, responsibilities and reporting relationships.

2. The primary output of this process is the project's Human Resource Management Plan.

3. The Human Resource Management Plan describes how/when human resources will be brought into the project and how/when human resources will leave the project. A Resource Histogram is often used.

4. Roles (who does what) and responsibilities (who decides what) are often illustrated using a Responsibility Assignment Matrix (RAM).

5. A Responsibility Assignment Matrix (RAM) illustrates assignments and levels of authority/responsibility, as a function of WBS elements. There is no time associated with a RAM.

6. A RACI Chart (Responsible, Accountable, Consult, Inform) is a type of RAM. In the RACI chart, there can be only one person accountable.

7. Functional organizations typically do not perform much work as cross-functional projects. When they do, projects are usually the full responsibility of a functional manager. Project managers have very little authority..

8. In matrix organizations, projects are performed using human resources borrowed from functional areas within the organization. In matrix organizations, project managers share responsibility & authority with functional managers.

9. In projectized organizations, most work is performed as projects. In projectized organizations, the project manager typically assumes full profit/loss responsibility and authority and staffs the project with dedicated (not borrowed) human resources.

Lesson 21 – Plan Cost Management

Plan Cost Management is a simple process in terms of change control, and can be compared to the similar processes of Plan Scope Management and Plan Schedule Management. In this process a Cost Management Plan that will document how the project budget will be defined, documented, validated and controlled throughout the project life cycle. Using the very simplest definition, the Cost Management Plan might say something like: "Any changes to the project budget must be approved by key stakeholders".

The Cost Management Plan will document how the budget is to be developed. This implies that the level of detail required and the format for the project budget will be defined here.

The Cost Management Plan will also define what level of detail will go into the tracking the budget as the project is executed. An important part of the Cost Management Plan is the definition of accuracy levels, thresholds for reporting and earned value rules for performance measurement.

The Plan Cost Management process creates the Cost Management Plan which is considered part of the overall Project Management Plan.

Plan Cost Management		
This process determines how the project Cost will be developed and managed		
Inputs	**Tools and Techniques**	**Outputs**
• Project Management Plan • Project Charter • Enterprise Environmental Factors • Organizational Process Assets	• Expert Judgment • Analytical Techniques • Meetings	• Cost Management Plan

Must Know Concepts

1. The Plan Cost Management process is applied to create a Cost Management Plan that documents how the cost will be defined, controlled and validated.

2. The primary deliverable (Output) of the Plan Cost Management process is the Cost Management Plan.

3. The Cost Management Plan is part of the overall Project Management Plan.

Lesson 22 – Estimate Costs

The purpose of this process is to produce preliminary cost estimates for the project. The first estimate used is typically a "Order of Magnitude" (aka: Rough Order of Magnitude) estimate. The ROM is in a range of - 25%, to +75%. A Definitive estimate is used later in planning and defines the confidence of an estimate to be: - 5%, to +10%. Cost estimates should be prepared and documented by the person or group most familiar with the project element.

One tool or technique that is mentioned in this process is the Three-Point Estimate. The PMBOK® Guide uses a new formula with new designations for the values. Most Likely value = Cm, Optimistic = Co, Pessimistic = Cp. The Three-Point Estimate can use a Triangular Distribution formula: $cE = (cO + cM = cP)/3$, or a Beta Distribution formula: $cE = (cO + 4cM + cP) / 6$.

Many organizations use an established chart of accounts for financial tracking and reporting.

Estimate Costs		
This process approximating the costs of resources needed to complete project activities		
Inputs	**Tools and Techniques**	**Outputs**
• Cost Management Plan	• Expert Judgment	• Activity Cost Estimate
• Human Resource Management Plan	• Analogous Estimating	• Basis of Estimates
	• Parametric Estimating	• Project Documents Updates
• Scope Baseline	• Bottom-up Estimating	
• Project Schedule	• Three-Point Estimating	
• Risk Register	• Reserve Analysis	
• Enterprise Environmental Factors	• Cost of Quality	
	• Project Management Software	
• Organizational Process Assets	• Vendor Bid Analysis	
	• Group Decision Making Techniques	

Must Know Concepts

----

1. The Estimate Costs process is applied to develop cost estimates for each identified project activity. Costs include direct costs plus indirect costs and contingency reserves.

2. Estimating should be performed by the person, or group of people, who are most knowledgeable about the activity, ideally by the person or people who will be doing the work.

3. Cost estimates should be prepared and documented with ranges of possible outcomes, instead of inflexible single-point values. For example, $9,300 -10% +25%.

4. An Order of Magnitude (or Rough Order of Magnitude ROM) estimate is in a range of: - 25%, to +75%.

5. A Definitive estimate defines the confidence of an estimate to be: - 5%, to +10%.

6. Tools used to Estimate Costs include Analogous estimating, Bottom-up Estimating, and Three-Point Estimating.

7. It is helpful to document cost estimates using a coding structure aligned with some selected chart of accounts.

Lesson 23 – Plan Procurement Management

Plan Procurement Management process documents approaches, procurement decisions and identifies potential sellers for required project resources. Required resources include more than just physical materials or components, and can include services and labor from outside the immediate project organization. For example, construction projects may require special permits. This process would be used to specify who and how those permits will be obtained.

There are several actions taken during the Plan Procurement Management Process:

- Make-or-buy decision making
- Identifying approaches and potential sellers
- Creating the Procurement Management Plan and the Procurement Statement of Work

Plan Procurement Management		
This process documents purchasing decisions, the procurement approach, and identifies potential sellers		
Inputs	**Tools and Techniques**	**Outputs**
• Project Management Plan	• Make or Buy Analysis	• Procurement Management Plan
• Requirements Documentation	• Expert Judgment	• Procurement Statement of Work
• Risk Register	• Market Research	
• Activity Resource Requirements	• Meetings	• Procurement Documents
• Project Schedule		• Source Selection Criteria
• Activity Cost Estimates		• Make-or-Buy Decisions
• Stakeholder Register		• Change Requests
• Enterprise Environmental Factors		• Project Documents Updates
• Organizational Process Assets		

Must Know Concepts

1. The Plan Procurement Management process is the planning process used to document decisions regarding the purchase and acquisition of required project resources.

2. Primary outputs of the Plan Procurement Management process are the Procurement Management Plan, Procurement Statements of Work, Procurement Documents and Source Selection Criteria.

3. If it is determined during Plan Procurement Management that there are no products or services that need to be acquired or developed outside of the project team, then other Procurement processes are not used.

4. There are three primary activities during the Plan Procurement Management Process: Make-or-buy decision making, identifying approaches to procurement and potential sellers and creating the Procurement Management Plan and Statement of Work.

5. There are the three broad categories of contract types: Fixed Price, Cost Reimbursable and Time and Materials (T&M).

Lesson 24 – Determine Budget

Determine Budget is the process of aggregating cost estimates into a final project budget. The project budget is sometimes termed the "Project Cost Baseline" or "Performance Measurement Baseline (PMB). Formally, the cost performance baseline is the time-phased budget. It is used to monitor and measure project cost performance across remaining project phases. When measuring the project using Earned Value Techniques, the Cost Baseline is represented by the Budget at Completion (BAC) value. Cost baselines are typically illustrated using graphs. Plotted cost baselines usually form an S-Curve appearance.

Contingency reserves and management reserves are established in the Determine Budget Process or reevaluated if developed in Estimate Costs. However, management reserves are excluded from the cost baseline. Management reserves can become part of the cost baseline if approved as a result of change control during project execution.

.

Determine Budget		
This process aggregates individual activity costs to establish the project's Cost Performance Baseline		
Inputs	**Tools and Techniques**	**Outputs**
• Cost Management Plan • Scope Baseline • Activity Cost Estimates • Basis of Estimates • Project Schedule • Resource Calendars • Risk Register • Agreements • Organizational Process Assets	• Cost Aggregation • Reserve Analysis • Expert Judgment • Historical Relationships • Funding Limit Reconciliation	• Cost Baseline • Project Funding Requirements • Project Documents Updates

Must Know Concepts

1. The Determine Budget process is applied to formally aggregate all activity cost estimates into a cohesive project budget, also known as the Cost Baseline.

2. The primary deliverable (Output) of the Determine Budget process is the cost baseline.

3. The Cost Baseline is the project's time-phased budget.

4. The Cost Baseline is used to monitor and measure project cost performance across project phases.

5. Cost Performance baselines are typically illustrated using graphs. Plotted cost performance baselines usually form an S-Curve appearance.

6. Management Reserves are excluded from the Cost Baseline, but are part of the overall Project Budget

Lesson 25 – Plan Quality Management

Quality planning is often applied in parallel with other processes during project planning.

The term quality means different things to different people, depending on their specific orientation and application environment. For our purposes in project management, quality means delivering precisely what is promised. When a project team delivers on-time, within budget and has satisfied all scope requirements, then quality has been achieved.

It is important to understand, quality must be "planned-in" to the project, not "inspected-in".

It is also helpful to understand that the terms quality and grade are not identical. Quality is the totality of characteristics to satisfy requirements. Grade is a measurement of technical characteristics. For instance, a high-grade product would be characterized by having many complex features. A low-grade product would have few features. Both could be of high-quality. When speaking of quality and grade, low-quality is a problem, low-grade is not.

.

Plan Quality Management		
This process indentifies project quality standards and defines how they will be satisfied		
Inputs	**Tools and Techniques**	**Outputs**
• Project Management Plan	• Cost-Benefit Analysis	• Quality Management Plan
• Stakeholder Register	• Cost of Quality	• Process Imrovement Plan
• Risk Register	• Seven Basic Quality Tools	• Quality Metrics
• Requirements Documentation	• Benchmarking	• Quality Checklists
	• Design of Experiments	• Project Documents Updates
• Enterprise Environmental Factors	• Statistical Sampling	
• Organizational Process Assets	• Additional Quality Planning Tools	
	• Meetings	

Must Know Concepts

1. The Plan Quality Management process is applied to identify which quality standards are applicable to the project then determine how to satisfy them.

2. The primary outputs of the Plan Quality Management process are the project's Quality Management Plan and the Process Improvement Plan.

3. In project management, quality means delivering precisely what is promised. When a project team delivers on-time, within budget and has satisfied all scope requirements, then quality has been achieved.

4. Quality must be planned-in to a project, not inspected-in.

5. Quality and grade are not the same. Low-quality is a problem, low-grade is not.

6. Cost of quality includes all costs expended to achieve product/service quality objectives.

Lesson 26 – Plan Risk Management

There are six closely associated processes in project risk management. In this lesson, we will discuss the first process, which is Plan Risk Management. In Plan Risk Management, we decide how to approach and plan our risk management activities for a particular project. Definitions of risk and how to quantify risk are developed in this process. The Plan Risk management process is intended and used to develop the project's Risk Management Plan.

There are several important things to understand concerning risk: *Project risk is any uncertain event or condition that, if it occurs, has a positive or negative effect on a project objective.* Therefore, project risks can be positive or negative! Negative risks are Threats and should be avoided. Positive risks are Opportunities and should be pursued.

When planning risk management for the project, the project manager must ascertain the stakeholder levels of risk tolerance. This can be expressed in terms of: risk appetite, risk tolerance, risk thresholds.

Plan Risk Management		
This process is intended and used to develop the project's Risk management Plan		
Inputs	**Tools and Techniques**	**Outputs**
• Project Management Plan • Project Charter • Stakeholder Register • Enterprise Environmental Factors • Organizational Process Assets	• Analytical Techniques • Expert Judgment • Meetings	• Risk Management Plan

Must Know Concepts

----

1. Project risk is any uncertain event or condition that, if it occurs, has a positive or negative effect on a project objective.

2. Project risks can be positive or negative.

3. Negative risks are Threats and should be avoided.

4. Positive risks are Opportunities and should be pursued.

5. Project risk management is comprised of six closely associated processes.

6. Plan Risk Management is applied to decide and document how project risk will be approached and planned.

7. There are four generally accepted categories of risk in project environments: project management risks, organizational risks, external risks. technical risks (technical, quality, performance),

8. The primary deliverable (Output) of the Plan Risk Management process is the Risk Management Plan.

9. Part of the Risk Management Plan may include the risk categories to be considered, documented as a Risk Breakdown Structure.

10. There are three types of risk attitudes: risk appetite, risk tolerance, and risk threshold.

Lesson 27 – Identify Risks

The primary objective of Identify Risk is to create a list of identified risks, along with the indications that the risk has occurred or is about to occur. These indications are termed triggers or risk symptoms or warning signs. Each identified risk will be analyzed during the application of subsequent risk management processes. To help identify as many risks as possible, many knowledgeable people should participate in the process.

While most risk identification is done during planning, identifying risks is a process that should be encouraged frequently throughout the project life cycle. In many projects, new risks can surface daily and others dissipate.

Identify Risks		
This process formally sanctions a new project or authorizes a project to continue into the next phase		
Inputs	**Tools and Techniques**	**Outputs**
• Risk Management Plan	• Documentation Reviews	• Risk Register
• Cost Management Plan	• Information Gathering Techniques	
• Schedule Management Plan		
• Quality Management Plan	• Checklist Analysis	
• Human Resource Management Plan	• Assumptions Analysis	
• Scope Baseline	• Diagramming Techniques	
• Activity Cost Estimates	• SWOT Analysis	
• Activity Duration Estimates	• Expert Judgment	
• Stakeholder Register		
• Project Documents		
• Procurement Documents		
• Enterprise Environmental Factors		
• Organizational Process Assets		

Must Know Concepts

1. Project risk is an uncertain event or condition that, if it occurs, has a positive or negative effect on a project objective. A risk has a cause, and if it occurs, a consequence.

2. The Identify Risks process determines which risks may affect the project and to document their characteristics.

3. Identifying risks is a process that should be encouraged frequently throughout the project life cycle.

4. Information gathering techniques include: brainstorming, Delphi technique, interviewing, root cause identification,

5. Diagramming techniques include: cause and effect diagrams (also termed fishbone or Ishikawa), systems flowcharts (also termed process maps), influence diagrams.

6. SWOT Analysis is another technique to identify Strengths, Weaknesses, Opportunities and Threats.

7. Indications that a risk has occurred, or is about to occur, are termed triggers (or risk symptoms or warning signs).

8. The primary output of the Identify Risks process is the Risk Register. The Risk Register is created during risk identification and then used to capture the outputs of all subsequent risk processes.

Lesson 28 – Perform Qualitative Risk Analysis

Perform Qualitative Risk Analysis is intended to help prioritize identified risks and identify those risks serious enough to warrant further analysis. A probability/impact (P-I) risk rating matrix is used as the primary tool in Qualitative Risk Analysis to determine the impact and likelihood of identified risks. The probability/impact (P-I) matrix is a tool that combines both risk probability and risk impact into a single score. It is used to help determine risk rankings.

Probability/Impact Matrix						
		Multiply P x I = Risk Score				
Risk Probability →High Low	.9					
	.7					
	.5					
	.3					
	.1					
	Risk Impact→	.1	.3	.5	.7	.9
		Very Low	Low	Moderate	High	Very High

Using this P-I matrix type of qualitative assessment, each identified risk may be assigned a score by plotting it appropriately in the matrix. In this simple P-I matrix example, risks that are assessed with scores in the lower left portion of the matrix indicate low-probability with low-impact. Risks scored in the upper right indicate high-probability with high impact. Typically, these high-high risks would receive priority for either analysis or for action.

Perform Qualitative Risk Analysis
This process prioritizes risks by analyzing their combined probability and impact

Inputs	Tools and Techniques	Outputs
• Risk Management Plan	• Risk Probability and Impact Assessment	• Project Documents Updates
• Scope Baseline		
• Risk Register	• Probability and Impact Matrix	
• Enterprise Environmental Factors	• Risk Data Quality Assessment	
	• Risk Categorization	
• Organizational Process Assets	• Risk Urgency Assessment	
	• Expert Judgment	

Must Know Concepts

---

1. The Perform Qualitative Risk Analysis process is applied to assess the impact and likelihood of identified risks. It is intended to help prioritize identified risks and identify those risks serious enough to warrant further analysis.

2. A risk probability/impact (P-I) matrix is a tool that combines both risk probability and risk impact into a single score. It is used to help determine qualitative risk rankings.

3. The primary output of the Perform Qualitative Risk Analysis process is updates to project documents, which are new inputs to the Risk Register, including a list of risks for additional analysis, a list of prioritized risks, a list of risks requiring near-term response, risks grouped by category, and more.

Lesson 29 – Perform Quantitative Risk Analysis

The Perform Quantitative Risk Analysis process is applied to guide the additional analysis of individual risks, to determine the numerical value of its probability of occurrence and the numerical value of its consequence on project objectives, should it occur. Perform Quantitative Risk Analysis is the fourth of five risk planning processes and is normally applied as the logical next step following perform qualitative risk analysis.

Today's powerful desktop computers and application software allows project teams to perform sophisticated quantitative risk analyses, which contributes to higher confidence in schedule estimates, cost estimates and overall quality. Monte Carlo simulation and Expected Monetary Value (EMV) analysis are commonly used tools to apply perform quantitative risk analysis. (Reference PMBOK® 5th Edition p. 339.)

Perform Quantitative Risk Analysis
This process numerically analyzes the effect of risks on overall project objectives

Inputs	Tools and Techniques	Outputs
• Risk Management Plan	• Data gathering and representation techniques	• Project documents udpates
• Cost management plan		
• Schedule management plan	• Quantitative risk analysis and modeling techniques	
• Risk register	• Expert judgment	
• Enterprise environmental factors		
• Organizational process assets		

TSI Study Aid

This chart is part of the study aid poster series available at: www.TrueSolutions.com

Must Know Concepts

1. The Perform Quantitative Risk Analysis process is applied to guide the additional analysis of individual risks, to determine the numerical value of its probability of occurrence and the numerical value of its consequence on project objectives, should it occur. This process is also applied to determine a numerical value for overall project risk.

2. Data gathering and representation techniques used include interviewing and probability distributions.

3. Quantitative risk analysis and modeling techniques used include sensitivity analysis, expected monetary value analysis and modeling and simulation tools.

4. Expected Monetary Value Analysis (EMV) is calculated by multiplying the value of each possible outcome by its probability of occurrence, then adding them all together. EMV= V (value $) x P (probability). Decision tree analysis uses EMV to illustrate the decision being considered, along with all the implications of choosing various alternatives. Solving a decision tree yields the path with the greatest expected monetary value.

5. The primary output of the Perform Quantitative Risk Analysis process is Project Documents Updates represented by new input information to the Risk Register including, probabilistic analysis of the project, probability of achieving cost and time objectives, a prioritized list of quantified risks, and more.

Lesson 30 – Plan Risk Responses

The Plan Risk Responses process is applied to develop options and determine actions to enhance opportunities (positive risks), and to develop options and determine actions to reduce threats (negative risks).

Once a risk has been identified and analyzed a decision must be made on what to do about the risk. It is the intent of Plan Risk Responses to guide that decision, by planning an appropriate response to the risk.

Risk responses for negative risk include: Avoid, Accept, Transfer or Mitigate. Risk responses for positive risk include: Enhance, Exploit, Share or Accept.

Plan Risk Responses		
This process develops options & actions to reduce threats and enhance opportunities		
Inputs	**Tools and Techniques**	**Outputs**
• Risk Management Plan • Risk Register	• Strategies for Negative Risks or Threats • Strategies for Positive Risks or Opportunities • Contingent Response Strategies • Expert Judgment	• Project Management Plan Updates • Project Documents Updates

Must Know Concepts

1. The Plan Risk Responses process is applied to develop options and determine actions to enhance opportunities (positive risks), or to reduce threats (negative risks).

2. The primary output of the Plan Risk Responses process is the project's completed Risk Register, characterized as Project Documents Updates.

3. Avoidance is one of the strategies for negative risks or threats. Avoidance involves changing the project plan, or condition within the plan, to eliminate the risk.

4. Transference is one of the strategies for negative risks or threats. Risk transfer involves shifting the consequence and ownership of a risk to a third party.

5. Mitigation is one of the strategies for negative risks or threats. Mitigation involves reducing the probability and/or impact of a negative risk to an acceptable threshold.

6. Acceptance is a strategy for both threats and opportunities. With active acceptance, a contingency plan is developed in advance to respond to the risk, should it occur. With passive acceptance, a response action is developed only if and when the risk event occurs.

7. Exploit, Share and Enhance are strategies for positive risks or opportunities.

8. Contingency action is any planned response action to a risk, should it occur.

9. Contingency allowance (or contingency reserve) is a cost buffer or time buffer included in the project plan to compensate for risk and to help reduce the probability of overruns.

Lesson 31 – Develop Project Management Plan

The Develop Project Management Plan process represents both the first step and the final step in project planning.

As the Planning Process Group starts, the Project Charter is a key output from Initiating. The Project Charter becomes a key input to the Develop Project Management Plan process. This signifies that the Develop Project Management Plan process actually starts as soon as the Planning processes are begun and continues concurrently with the other planning processes throughout planning.

Once approved and authorized, the Project Management Plan is used to:

- Serve as the baseline for monitoring and measuring project performance during execution
- Facilitate stakeholder communications during execution and control
- Guide all aspects of the project through execution, monitoring & control, and closing
- Document project planning decisions, strategies, alternatives and assumptions

The Project Management Plan consists of two categories of documents: baselines and subsidiary plans. All of these are part of the inputs to this process and are developed during project planning.

Develop Project Management Plan		
This process documents all actions required to define, prepare, integrate, and coordinate all subsidiary plans		
Inputs	**Tools and Techniques**	**Outputs**
• Project Charter • Outputs from Other Processes • Enterprise Environmental Factors • Organizational Process Assets	• Expert Judgment • Facilitation Techniques	• Project Management Plan

Must Know Concepts

1. The Develop Project Management Plan process represents the first process started during planning and the final step in project planning.

2. The Develop Project Management Plan process is applied to gather the outputs from all other planning processes, all subsidiary plans, then assemble them into a single, cohesive document; the Project Management Plan.

3. The primary deliverable (Output) of this process is the Project Management Plan.

4. The Project Management Plan documents planning decisions, strategies, alternatives and assumptions.

5. The Project Management Plan serves as the baseline for monitoring and measuring project performance during executing, monitoring & controlling and closing.

6. The Project Management Plan facilitates stakeholder communications during executing, monitoring & controlling and closing.

7. The Project Management Plan guides all aspects of the project through executing, monitoring & controlling and closing.

Lesson 32 – Executing Process Group

The primary purpose that these Executing processes are performed is to manage the work so that the intended deliverables of the project or phase are created as planned. Executing processes occur in Project Integration Management, Project Quality Management, Project Human Resource Management, Project Communications Management, Project Procurement Management and Project Stakeholder Management knowledge areas in the *PMBOK® Guide Fifth Edition*.

If there was a "keyword" to characterize the Executing Process Group, it might be "deliverables". The most important output of the entire process group is the deliverables created for the project.

The Executing processes work very closely and have a high degree of interaction with each other. In addition, these Executing processes also work very closely with the processes in the Monitoring and Controlling process group. Executing processes focus on producing deliverables, the Monitoring and Controlling processes concentrate on confirming that the planned deliverables are created and that these outputs meet the planned specifications and requirements.

Executing Tasks

On your PMP Exam, you will encounter many questions that will test your understanding of Executing processes. These questions will generally focus on Executing tasks. As a PMP or project manager executing a project (or project phase), you may be required to:

1. Obtain and manage project resources including out-sourced deliverables by following the procurement plan, in order to ensure successful project execution.

2. Execute the tasks as defined in the project management plan, in order to achieve the project deliverables within budget, schedule and defined quality.

3. Implement the quality management plan using the appropriate tools and techniques, in order to ensure that work is being performed according to required quality standards.

4. Implement approved changes according to the change management plan, in order to meet project requirements.

5. Implement approved actions (e.g. workarounds) by following the risk management plan, in order to minimize the impact of the risks on the project.

6. Maximize team performance through leading, mentoring, training, and motivating team members.

Lesson 33 – Direct & Manage Project Work

Direct and Manage Project Work is performed in order to successfully execute the Project Management Plan. The project manager and team must constantly monitor and measure performance against baselines, so that timely corrective action can be taken, as appropriate. Changes must be incorporated into the project as approved and, cost and schedule forecasts must be updated periodically, as appropriate.

During project execution, it is typical that most project costs are expended during this period.

The understanding and appropriate use of general management skills is most important during project execution.

Direct and Manage Project Work		
This process executes the work defined in the project management plan		
Inputs	**Tools and Techniques**	**Outputs**
• Project Management Plan • Approved Change Requests • Enterprise Environmental Factors • Organizational Process Assets	• Expert Judgment • Project Management Information System • Meetings	• Deliverables • Work Performance Data • Change Requests • Project Management Plan Updates • Project Documents Updates

Must Know Concepts

1. The Direct and Manage Project Work process is applied by the project manager and project team to coordinate and direct all the resources to carry out the Project Management Plan.

2. When using the Direct and Manage Project Work process, the project manager and team must monitor and measure performance against baselines, so corrective action can be taken.

3. The primary deliverable (Outputs) of the Direct and Manage Project Work process are work results (deliverables).

4. Approved change requests become a key input to Direct and Manage Project Work in order to incorporate changes into the project.

5. The effective use of people skills is essential to achieve success during project execution.

6. Formal work authorization systems are helpful to control project work, especially with respect to minimizing unnecessary scope expansion (scope creep).

Lesson 34 – Acquire Project Team

When considering people to support the project, the project team should factor things such as experience, availability, competencies, personal characteristics and whether or not the potential resource has an interest in working on the project. Many times, especially in matrix organizations, you as project manager may need to use your best negotiating skills to get the people you want from their functional manager(s).

Best practice guidelines would suggest that a core project team will be acquired early in the project – immediately after the project charter is issued. Other human resources will be brought on throughout the project as needed. It will be important that the project manager plan carefully and not acquire resources without first considering the Develop Human Resource Plan process and its outcomes: the Staffing Management Plan and Roles and Responsibilities for the project.

An important consideration for the project manager will be to negotiate for and acquire resources which have the needed levels of competency that are required to execute the project. If the available resources do not have the required competencies and experience, if there are not sufficient resources available to perform project activities or if resources cannot be acquired in a timely manner, the project manager will return to the planning processes and re-plan portions of the project that are affected by differences in planned human resources.

The Acquire Project Team process is complete when the project is reliably staffed with appropriate people. Many project teams publish a formal team directory when staffing is complete.

Acquire Project Team		
This process obtains needed project human resources		
Inputs	**Tools and Techniques**	**Outputs**
• Human Resource Management Plan • Enterprise Environmental Factors • Organizational Process Assets	• Pre-Assignment • Negotiation • Acquisition • Virtual Teams • Multi-Criteria Decision Analysis	• Project Staff Assignments • Resource Calendars • Project Management Plan Updates

Must Know Concepts

1. The Acquire Project Team process is applied to obtain and assign needed human resources (people) to the project.

2. The project manager will negotiate with functional managers and other sources of possible project team members as necessary to obtain the people a project manager desires.

3. The project manager will use procurement processes to acquire staff if external staff are used for the project

4. The primary deliverable (Output) of the Acquire Project Team process is project staff assignments.

Lesson 35 – Develop Project Team

In practice, team development is a continuous process applied from the time the project team comes together until the team disbands. In concept, stronger individuals will naturally create a stronger team.

Generally, Develop Project Team tools include:

- training
- team-building activities
- recognition and rewards
- co-location

Some project managers like to establish a project war room where core team members can be co-located to work in close proximity during the project.

In some matrix organizations, team development can be extra challenging when team members report to both the project manager and to their functional manager. In most organizations, the resource will be more closely aligned with their functional manager and will minimize input from the project manager on any organizational issues other than those directly relating to the project. Successful team development requires a practical understanding of the dynamics of human behavior to create a project environment in which team members feel motivated to excel.

Develop Project Team		
This process documents project roles, responsibilities and reporting relationships		
Inputs	**Tools and Techniques**	**Outputs**
• Human Resource Management Plan • Project Staff Assignments • Resource Calendar	• Interpersonal Skills • Training • Team-Building Activities • Ground Rules • Co-Location • Recognition and Rewards • Personal Assessment Tools	• Team Performance Assessments • Enterprise Environmental Factors Updates

Must Know Concepts

1. Develop Project Team is the process of enhancing the ability of individual team members (skills and team cohesiveness) to enhance overall project performance.

2. In some matrix organizations, team development can be extra challenging when team members report to both the project manager and to their functional manager.

3. The primary deliverable (Output) of the Develop Project Team process is team performance assessments.

4. Important content theories of motivation include Maslow's Hierarchy of Needs and Herzberg's Motivator/Hygiene Theory.

5. Important process theories of motivation include McGregor's Theory X - Theory Y.

Lesson 36 – Manage Project Team

Manage Project Team process involves tracking and appraising team member performance, resolving issues, observing team behavior, managing conflicts and providing feedback. In matrix organizations, dual reporting roles of team members typically create complications that must be managed properly by the project manager. Effectively managing these dual reporting situations is often a critical success factor in project environments.

Of course, the intended outcome of the Manage Project Team process is enhanced overall project performance.

Manage Project Team		
This process documents project roles, responsibilities and reporting relationships		
Inputs	**Tools and Techniques**	**Outputs**
• Human Resource Management Plan	• Observation and Conversation	• Change Requests
• Project Staff Assignments	• Project Performance Appraisals	• Project Management Plan Updates
• Team Performance Assessments	• Conflict Management	• Project Documents Updates
• Issue Log	• Interpersonal Skills	• Enterprise Environmental Factor Updates
• Work Performance Reports		• Organizational Process Assets Updates
• Organizational Process Assets		

Must Know Concepts

1. The Manage Project Team process is applied to address performance, behavior, issues and conflicts associated specifically with project team members.

2. Observation and conversation are key methods to stay in touch with the work and attitudes of project team members.

3. Successful conflict management results in greater productivity and positive working relationships.

Lesson 37 – Manage Communications

Manage Communications process involves the activities that are necessary to create, distribute, receive, acknowledge and understand project information. Communications methods should be appropriate to the project, the timeliness required and the culture of the organization that you are working in.

Communications can be done most effectively if there are effective retrieval systems available and put into use. And, in order to effectively communicate information, we have to remember that the project manager must possess good general communications skills. Information is often communicated to stakeholders that is clouded with technical terms or acronyms which are not readily understandable by managers or customers.

Effective communications techniques include:

- Sender-receiver models – understanding feedback and barriers to communication
- Choice of media - written, verbal or electronic based; based on needs of project
- Writing styles – using active vs. passive
- Meeting management - agendas and effective means for addressing conflict
- Presentation - body language and presentation aids
- Facilitation - obtaining consensus and overcoming obstacles

It is important to be mindful that communication is not complete until the sender is confident that the receiver understands the information, as intended. In a later process, Manage Stakeholder Engagement, the project manager will address any issues that arise from the distribution of information. Project success is most likely when all stakeholders have a shared understanding of the current condition of the project.

Manage Communications		
This process provides needed information to stakeholders in a timely fashion		
Inputs	**Tools and Techniques**	**Outputs**
• Communications Management Plan • Work Performance Reports • Enterprise Environmental Factors • Organizational Process Assets	• Communication Technology • Communications Models • Communication Methods • Information Management Systems • Performance Reporting	• Project Communications • Project Management Plan Updates • Project Documents Updates • Organizational Process Assets Updates

Must Know Concepts

1. Manage Communications is the process of making project information available to project stakeholders, as determined and documented in the communications management plan.

2. Communication is not complete until the sender is confident that the receiver understands the information, as intended.

3. Orderly record keeping, effective distribution methods (meetings, project intranet, presentations, email), effective retrieval systems, and good general communication skills facilitate information distribution.

Lesson 38 – Manage Stakeholder Engagement

Manage Stakeholder Engagement process deals with communicating and working closely with stakeholders, resolving issues and keeping stakeholders interested and active throughout the project.

There is often a great deal of communications between the project management team and the project stakeholders. For the project to be managed effectively and efficiently the project manager should ensure that the stakeholder communications needs/desires are being met and that stakeholders are not being flooded with excessive and unnecessary communications.

Stakeholder engagement includes involving stakeholders at appropriate points in the project, negotiating and communicating with stakeholders, addressing stakeholder concerns before they become issues, then resolving issues that have been identified.

Manage Stakeholder Engagement		
This process manages communications to satisfy stakeholders requirement		
Inputs	**Tools and Techniques**	**Outputs**
• Stakeholder Management Plan • Communications Management Plan • Change Log • Organizational Process Assets	• Communication Methods • Interpersonal Skills • Management Skills	• Issues Log • Change Requests • Project Management Plan Updates • Project Documents Updates • Organizational Process Assets Updates

Must Know Concepts

1. The Manage Stakeholder Engagement process is applied to ensure that communications with project stakeholders is productive and meets the needs and desires of those stakeholders.

2. Actively managing project stakeholders increases the likelihood that the project will not be negatively impacted by unresolved stakeholder issues.

3. An issue log (or action-item log) is used to document and monitor the resolution of issues.

Lesson 39 – Perform Quality Assurance

Quality activities should be applied across the entire project life cycle. An intended outcome of applying the Perform Quality Assurance process is continuous process improvement. This is accomplished through the audit of quality requirements and quality control measurements to ensure that quality standards and metrics or operational definitions have been met for the project. Continuous process improvement includes all actions to reduce waste and non-value-added activities, to increase project efficiency and effectiveness. Continuous process improvement is sometimes termed KAIZEN, representing the quality philosophy of achieving improvement via small incremental steps. ("Kaizen" is Japanese for improvement.) Note that process improvement is focused on improved project performance, not improved functionality of the product of the project.

While many organizations support quality assurance with dedicated departments, it is important to understand that project quality management is the responsibility of the project manager.

Perform Quality Assurance		
This process ensures the project employs all processes needed to meet requirements		
Inputs	**Tools and Techniques**	**Outputs**
• Quality Management Plan • Process Improvement Plan • Quality Metrics • Quality Control Measurements • Project Documents	• Quality Management and Control Tools • Quality Audits • Process Analysis	• Change Requests • Project Management Plan Updates • Project Documents Updates • Organizational Process Assets Updates

Must Know Concepts

1. Perform Quality Assurance is the application of the Quality Management Plan to ensure the project will employ all processes necessary to satisfy recognized quality requirements.

2. The primary deliverable (output) from this process is change requests.

3. Quality activities should be applied across the entire project life cycle.

4. An intended outcome of applying the Perform Quality Assurance process is continuous process improvement.

5. Continuous process improvement (quality improvement) is sometimes termed KAIZEN, representing the quality philosophy of achieving improvement via small incremental steps.

6. Continuous process improvement is focused on improved project performance, not improved functionality of the product of the project.

7. Remember that project quality management is the responsibility of the project manager.

Lesson 40 – Conduct Procurements

During the process of Conduct Procurements, the project manager (or purchasing department) will notify sellers of the potential need by providing appropriate procurement documents to the sellers. In response, the project manager (or purchasing department) will receive proposals from the seller on how the need can be satisfied by the vendor. The project manager or purchasing department will select a seller, negotiate and award a contract and ensure availability of the procured resources. Statements of work and evaluation criteria developed during Plan Procurements may be used in conjunction with notifying the vendor and evaluating their response or proposal.

This process is often repeated many times within the life-cycle of the project. In its simplest form, this may include searching for parts via the internet (for example) and placing an order from the cheapest source, or it can be a more complicated process of submitting procurement packages, reviewing seller bids, seller evaluations, negotiations, and contract award.

Successful procurement is often very critical to project success and can greatly impact the project's expenses.

Conduct Procurements		
This process obtains seller responses, selecting sellers, and awarding contract		
Inputs	**Tools and Techniques**	**Outputs**
• Procurement Management Plan	• Bidder Conferences	• Selected Sellers
• Procurement Documents	• Proposal Evaluation Techniques	• Agreements
• Source Selection Criteria		• Resource Calendars
• Seller Proposals	• Independent Estimates	• Change Requests
• Project Documents	• Expert Judgment	• Project Management Plan Updates
• Make-or-Buy Decisions	• Advertising	
• Procurement Statement of Work	• Analytical Techniques	• Project Documents Updates
• Organizational Process Assets	• Procurement Negotiations	

Must Know Concepts

1. Conduct Procurements is the process of obtaining bids and proposals from sellers and selecting a seller to provide resources for the project.

2. The primary deliverable from this process is selected sellers and agreements.

3. Source selection criteria should be performed to determine the successful bidders.

4. The project manager should play an integral role throughout the contracting process.

5. Contracts are legally binding agreements between buyer and seller and may be simple or complex, proportional to the size and complexity of the procurement.

6. A purchase order is a contract.

Lesson 41 – Monitoring and Controlling Process Group

The primary purpose that these Monitoring and Controlling processes are performed is to ensure that the work that is performed is the planned work or is changed to meet the requirements of the project in a controlled manner. Monitoring and Controlling processes occur in all knowledge areas except the Human Resource Management area in the *PMBOK Guide® Fifth Edition*.

A "key-word" that might characterize the Monitoring and Controlling Process Group could be "check". The most important element of Monitoring and Controlling is to check against the plan and the execution to ensure that the project is on track.

The Monitoring and Controlling processes work very closely and have a high degree of interaction with each other. In addition, these processes also work very closely with the processes in the Executing process group. Executing processes focus on producing deliverables, the Monitoring and Controlling processes concentrate on confirming that the planned deliverables are created and that these outputs meet the planned specifications and requirements.

When a change occurs on the project, the project manager will return to the Planning processes to update affected project documents to ensure that the entire project is constantly and properly documented.

Monitoring and Controlling Tasks

On your PMP Exam, you will encounter many questions that will test your understanding of Monitoring and Controlling processes. When studying, remember to focus on Earned Value topics, since many Monitoring and Controlling processes depend on Earned Value formulas for data measurement and forecasting. Other questions will generally focus on the following Monitoring and Controlling tasks. As a PMP or project manager monitoring and controlling a project or project phase, you may be required to:

1. Measure project performance using appropriate tools and techniques in order to identify and quantify any variances, perform approved corrective actions, and communicate with relevant stakeholders.

2. Manage changes to the project scope, schedule and costs by updating the project plan and communicating approved changes to the team, in order to ensure that revised project goals are met.

3. Ensure that project deliverables conform to quality standards established in the quality management plan by using appropriate tools and techniques (e.g., testing, inspection, control charts) in order to satisfy customer requirements.

4. Update the risk register and risk response plan by identifying any new risks, assessing old risks, and determining and implementing appropriate risk response strategies, in order to manage the impact of risks on the project.

5. Assess corrective actions on the issue register and determine next steps for unresolved issues by using appropriate tools and techniques in order to minimize the impact on project schedule, cost and resources.

6. As a PMP or project manager monitoring and controlling a project (or phase), you may be required to communicate project status to stakeholders for their feedback, in order to ensure the project aligns with business needs.

Lesson 42 – Control Scope

In Control Scope, scope changes are identified by utilizing the variance analysis tool. After a scope change has been identified it becomes an output from this process (as a change request), which becomes an input to perform Integrated Change Control.

It is important to understand that it is the project manager's responsibility to discourage unnecessary scope changes. It is also important to understand that when changes are warranted, that they be made in strict accordance with the project's scope change control process, and that the established scope baseline remains intact. Scope changes are inevitable, but controlling scope minimizes uncontrolled "scope creep".

Some organizations utilize a change control board (CCB) to evaluate and approve/disapprove scope change requests.

Control Scope		
This process controls changes to project scope		
Inputs	**Tools and Techniques**	**Outputs**
• Project Management Plan • Requirements Documentation • Requirements Traceability Matrix • Work Performance Data • Organizational Process Assets	• Variance Analysis	• Work Performance Information • Change Requests • Project Management Plan Updates • Project Documents Updates • Organizational Process Assets Updates

Must Know Concepts

1. Control Scope is the process of effectively managing changes in project scope, then integrating those changes across the entire project through the Perform Integrated Change Control process.

2. The primary deliverables (Outputs) of the Control Scope process include change requests which, if approved, result in updates to all associated project plans and documents.

3. It is the project manager's responsibility to discourage unnecessary scope changes.

4. When legitimate scope changes are warranted, they should be made in accordance with the project's scope change control system.

Lesson 43 – Control Schedule

In the process of Control Schedule, schedule changes are indentified using various tools, including variance analysis. When a schedule change has been identified it becomes an output from this process in the form of a change request, which then becomes an input to Perform Integrated Change Control.

It is important to understand that it is the project manager's responsibility to discourage unnecessary schedule changes. It is also important to understand that when changes are warranted, that they be made in strict accordance with the project's schedule change control process that is defined in the Schedule Management Plan. In most methodologies, performance measurement is usually performed using the original baseline schedule as the measurement point.

Performance measurement formulas used in Control Schedule include Schedule Variance (SV) and Schedule Performance Index (SPI). We will discuss these in detail in Lesson 44 – Control Costs.

Control Schedule		
This process controls changes to the project schedule		
Inputs	**Tools and Techniques**	**Outputs**
• Project Management Plan • Project Schedule • Work Performance data • Project calendars • Schedule data • Organizational Process Assets	• Performance Reviews • Project Management Software • Resource Optimization Techniques • Modeling Techniques • Leads and Lags • Schedule Compression • Scheduling Tool	• Work Performance Information • Schedule Forecasts • Change Requests • Project Management Plan Updates • Project Documents Updates • Organizational Process Assets Updates

Must Know Concepts

1.   Control Schedule is the process of effectively monitoring the project progress and managing project schedule baseline changes, then integrating those changes across the entire project through the Perform Integrated Change Control process.

2.   The primary deliverables (Outputs) of the Control Schedule process include change requests that, if they are approved, result in updates to all associated project plans and documents.

3.   Control Schedule uses earned value to calculate SV and SPI values for the project schedule.

4.   It is the project manager's responsibility to discourage unnecessary schedule changes.

5.   When legitimate schedule changes are warranted, they should be made in accordance with the project's schedule change control system.

Lesson 44 – Control Costs

Control Costs is first of all a change control process. In this process, the project manager will monitor for changes that are occurring or need to occur, and if a change is warranted, a change request will be generated and sent as an input to Perform Integrated Change Control. In addition, in Control Costs, the application of earned value measurement (EVM) is a key tool used to measure project performance. Earned value analysis integrates cost, scope and schedule to derive measurement values that accurately assess project progress to date, as well as forecast future performance.

Earned value measurement relies on four key data points:

Planned Value (PV) - (also termed Budgeted Cost of Work Scheduled BCWS) Planned value is the established baseline that indicates the amount of money planned for spending to date, at any particular point in time (regardless of what actual work has been performed). *Simplified: "what you intend to do, the value of the work planned".*

Earned Value (EV) - (also termed Budgeted Cost of Work Performed BCWP) Earned value is the established baseline that indicates the amount of money planned for spending on the actual work performed to date, at any particular point in time (regardless of other planned objectives). *Simplified: "what was accomplished and the value of the work accomplished – compared to Planned Value".*

Actual Cost (AC) - (also termed Actual Cost of Work Performed ACWP) Actual cost is the amount of money spent on the actual work performed to date, at any particular point in time (regardless of other planned objectives). *Simplified: "what was spent to achieve the earned value?"*

Budget at Completion (BAC) - Budget at completion is simply the amount of money planned for spending on the entire project.

Based on these data points, EVM Performance Analysis and Forecasting can be accomplished. Measurements occur at a specific point in the project.

Variance Formulas	Index Formulas	Forecast Formulas
• SV – Schedule Variance • CV – Cost Variance • VAC – Variance at Completion	• SPI – Schedule Performance Index • CPI – Cost Performance Index	• EAC – Estimate at Completion • ETC – Estimate to Complete • TCPI – To Complete Performance Index

Control Costs		
This process controls changes to project costs		
Inputs	**Tools and Techniques**	**Outputs**
• Project Management Plan • Project Funding Requirements • Work Performance Data • Organizational Process Assets	• Earned Value Management • Forecasting • To-Complete Performance Index • Performance Reviews • Project Management Software • Reserve Analysis	• Work Performance Information • Cost Forecasts • Change Requests • Project Management Plan Updates • Project Documents Updates • Organizational Process Assets Updates

Must Know Concepts

----

1. Control Cost is the process of effectively managing changes to the project budget, then integrating those changes across the entire project through the Perform Integrated Change Control process.

2. The primary deliverables (outputs) from Control Costs are work performance information, forecasts and change requests. Approved change requests will result in project management plan updates.

3. Earned value measurement (EVM) is a key tool used to measure project performance. Earned value analysis integrates cost, scope and schedule to derive measurement values that accurately assess project progress to date, as well as forecasted future performance.

4. Planned Value PV (also termed Budgeted Cost of Work Scheduled BCWS) is the established baseline that indicates the amount of money planned for spending to date, at any particular point in time (regardless of what actual work has been performed).

5. Earned Value EV (also termed Budgeted Cost of Work Performed BCWP) is the established baseline that indicates the amount of money planned for spending on the actual work performed to date, at any particular point in time (regardless of other planned objectives).

6. Actual Cost AC (also termed Actual Cost of Work Performed ACWP) is the amount of money spent on the actual work performed to date, at any particular point in time (regardless of other planned objectives).

7. Budget at Completion BAC is simply the amount of money planned for spending on the entire project.

8. Schedule Variance (SV) SV = EV - PV SV>0 = ahead of schedule. SV<0 = behind schedule.

9. Cost Variance (CV) CV = EV - AC CV>0 = under budget. CV <0 = over budget.

10. Variance at Completion (VAC) VAC = BAC - EAC VAC>0 = under budget. VAC<0 = over budget.

11. Schedule Performance Index (SPI) SPI = EV/PV SPI>1 = ahead of schedule. SPI<1 = behind schedule.

12. Cost Performance Index (CPI) CPI = EV/AC CPI>1 = under budget. CPI<1 = over budget.

13. Estimate to Complete (ETC) forecasts remaining project costs. Two formulas are available: ETC = EAC – AC, or ETC = new bottom up estimate.

14. Estimate at Completion (EAC) forecasts final project cost total. Four formulas can be used: EAC = BAC/CPI, EAC = AC + BAC - EV, EAC = AC + Bottom up ETC or EAC = AC + [(BAC – EV) / (CPI x SPI)]. Formula use is based on project circumstances.

15. To Complete Performance Index (TCPI) forecasts how efficient the performance for the remainder of the project must be in order to achieve BAC or EAC. Two formulas are available: TCPI = (BAC – EV) / (BAC – AC) or TCPI = (BAC – EV) / (EAC – AC)

Lesson 45 – Control Communications

Control Communications is the process of monitoring and controlling project communications throughout the entire project life cycle. This implies that this process begins early in the project, immediately after the project is initiated and a Communications Management Plan is determined and documented.

An important part of Control Communications is to ensure that the level and detail of information reporting should be appropriate to the intended audience. Providing an excessive amount of performance data where it is unneeded or desired should be avoided.

Throughout the project life cycle, work performance information such as performance reports, status reports and forecasts will be communicated and controlled.

Control Communications		
This process monitors and controls communications throughout the project life cycle		
Inputs	**Tools and Techniques**	**Outputs**
• Project Management Plan • Project Communications • Issue Log • Work Performance Data • Organizational Process Assets	• Information Management Systems • Expert Judgment • Meetings	• Work Performance Information • Change Requests • Project Management Plan Updates • Project Documents Updates • Organizational Process Assets Updates

Must Know Concepts

1. Control Communications is the communications process of monitoring and controlling the communications for the project throughout the project life cycle.

2. Communicated information should meet the needs and desire of stakeholders by providing them with performance information, through the use of status reporting, progress reporting and forecasting.

3. The primary deliverable (output) from this process is work performance information.

Lesson 46 – Control Stakeholder Engagement

Control Stakeholder Engagement is the process of monitoring and controlling overall project stakeholder relationships throughout the entire project life cycle. This implies that this process begins early in the project, immediately after the project is initiated and a Stakeholder Management Plan is determined and documented.

An important part of Control Stakeholder Engagement is to ensure that stakeholder interest and effectiveness is maintained during the project. As the project evolves and the project environment changes, the project manager may be required to adjust stakeholder management strategies in order to facilitate continued performance.

Control Stakeholder Engagement		
This process monitors and controls stakeholder relationships throughout the project life cycle		
Inputs	**Tools and Techniques**	**Outputs**
• Project Management Plan • Issue Log • Work Performance Data • Project Documents	• Information Management Systems • Expert Judgment • Meetings	• Work Performance Information • Change Requests • Project Management Plan Updates • Project Documents Updates • Organizational Process Assets Updates

Must Know Concepts

1. Control Stakeholder Engagement is the process of monitoring and controlling stakeholder relationships throughout the project life cycle.

2. As project conditions change during the project life cycle, it may be necessary to adjust stakeholder management strategies.

3. The primary deliverable (output) from this process is work performance information.

Lesson 47 – Control Risks

The Control Risks process is applied to monitor identified risks, identify new risks, ensure the proper execution of planned risk responses and, evaluate the overall effectiveness of the risk management plan in reducing risk.

If a risk event occurs during project execution, there is a likelihood it was identified sometime earlier, it was analyzed and an appropriate response action was planned to deal with it (captured in the Risk Register). For the most part, Control Risks is the process of putting into action all of the risk planning done earlier in the project life-cycle.

It is important to understand that risk monitoring is intended to be a daily, on-going process across the entire project life-cycle. Project team members and stakeholders should be encouraged to be vigilant in looking for risk symptoms, as well as for new project risks. It is suggested that project risk always be an agenda item for all team meetings. Newly identified risks and symptoms of previously identified risks should be communicated immediately for evaluation and/or action.

Control Risks		
Executes risk response plans and evaluates their effectiveness		
Inputs	**Tools and Techniques**	**Outputs**
• Project Management Plan • Risk Register • Work Performance Data • Work Performance Reports	• Risk Reassessment • Risk Audits • Variance and Trend Analysis • Technical Performance Measurement • Reserve Analysis • Meetings	• Work Performance Information • Change Requests • Project Management Plan Updates • Project Documents Updates • Organizational Process Assets Updates

Must Know Concepts

1. The Control Risks process is applied to monitor identified risks, identify new risks, ensure proper execution of planned risk responses and evaluate overall effectiveness of the Risk Management Plan in reducing risk.

2. The primary outputs from Control Risks are work performance information and change requests.

3. Workarounds (or workaround plans) are responses to unanticipated (surprise) risk events after they occur. Workarounds are for risk events that were not previously identified, and have no advance planned response action. Workaround plans should be documented and incorporated into the Risk Register as soon as they are developed.

4. Risk monitoring is intended to be a daily, on-going process across the entire project life-cycle, from project start to project finish.

5. Project team members and stakeholders should be vigilant in looking for risk symptoms, as well as for new project risks.

Lesson 48 – Control Procurements

Control Procurements includes validating that the seller's performance is meeting requirements and contract obligations. In many organizations, the role of contract monitoring and control is performed by a specialized contracts department. This is often done because of the legalities associated with contracts. Regardless of who is performing contract administration, project team members should be aware of the legal obligations and impact of their actions in regard to contracts.

During the application of this process, each seller's performance should be recorded and documented. A performance review of sellers can lead to identification of issues to be resolved, and provides additional data for similar future projects in regards to contracts and purchases with sellers.

When applying this process the project manager will have a high degree of interaction with several other processes. It is important to integrate the vendor project team into the overall project team and stakeholder organization. Project management elements for managing work, for verifying work and deliverable conformance, for managing change and for developing the team are important during this process.

Control Procurements		
This process manages procurement relationships and contract performance		
Inputs	**Tools and Techniques**	**Outputs**
• Project Management Plan • Procurement Documents • Agreements • Approved Change Requests • Work Performance Reports • Work Performance Data	• Contract Change Control • Procurement Performance Reviews • Inspections and Audits • Performance Reporting • Payment Systems • Claims Administration • Records Management System	• Work Performance Information • Change Requests • Project Management Plan Updates • Project Documents Updates • Organizational Process Assets Updates

Must Know Concepts

1. The Control Procurements process is used to manage procurement relationships, monitor contract performance, and make changes and corrections to procurements.

2. The primary outputs from Control Procurements are work performance information and change requests.

3. Many organizations utilize a contract administration department or office to administer procurement contracting due to the amount of legality involved in formal contracting.

4. Seller performance should be formally documented for use in future decisions and in evaluation of sellers.

5. Contract changes can be kept to a minimum by proper and thorough procurement planning but can be used to reduce risk, or when such amendments are beneficial for the buyer, the seller, or both.

Lesson 49 – Control Quality

Control Quality (QC) is the process of monitoring specific project results to ensure they comply with the project quality standards. Like quality assurance (QA), Control Quality should be applied across the entire project life cycle. The quality control process is also intended to identify ways to eliminate quality problems such as causes of weak processes or poor product quality. Process improvement is a natural adjunct of the Control Quality process.

Quality control monitors both product-related deliverables (work packages) and project management deliverables (cost/schedule/scope performance). This process focuses on outputs and uses tools that measure these outputs.

Control Quality		
Monitors project results against relevant quality standards to assess results and recommend changes		
Inputs	**Tools and Techniques**	**Outputs**
• Project Management Plan • Quality Metrics • Quality Checklists • Work Performance Data • Approved Change Requests • Deliverables • Project Documents • Organizational Process Assets	• Seven Basic Quality Tools • Statistical Sampling • Inspection • Approved Change Requests Review	• Quality Control Measurements • Validated Changes • Verified Deliverables • Work Performance Information • Change Requests • Project Management Plan Updates • Project Documents Updates • Organizational Process Assets Updates

Must Know Concepts

1. Control Quality monitors project results to ensure they comply with quality standards.

2. The primary deliverable (Output) of the Control Quality process is verified deliverables.

3. Perform Control Quality monitors both product-related deliverables (work packages) and project management deliverables (cost/schedule/scope performance).

4. Statistical sampling is used as a QC technique to test a sample number of items from a larger population of items. Statistical sampling can be effective and it can reduce overall QC costs.

5. A Pareto diagram is a histogram, applied as a QC analysis tool to help illustrate the frequency of occurrences by category of causes. Pareto diagrams typically identify quality root causes.

6. Standard deviation (sigma) is a measure indicating the distance from the mean (average). 1 sigma = 1 standard deviation = ± 68.26%. 2 sigma = 2 standard deviations = ± 95.46%. 3 sigma = 3 standard deviations = ± 99.73%. 6 sigma = 6 standard deviations = ± 99.99%.

7. Control Charts are graphic displays of process results over time. They are used to monitor a process, to verify its continued stability.

8. Scatter Diagrams, Flowcharts, Cause and Effect Diagrams, Check-sheets and Histograms are commonly used quality control tools.

Lesson 50 – Validate Scope

Validate Scope is the process of accepting completed project deliverables. Scope validation differs from quality control. Quality control focuses on the correctness of work. Scope validation focuses on formal acceptance of the work. In practice, both are normally performed in parallel.

Formal acceptance must be documented. Scope verification can occur at any level of the project; it can be done for work, for a specific deliverable, for a milestone, for a phase or for the project overall. Validate Scope is often a predecessor to the closure of a project phase or when closing the overall project.

Validate Scope		
Formalizes acceptance of complete project deliverables		
Inputs	**Tools and Techniques**	**Outputs**
• Project Management Plan • Requirements Documentation • Requirements Traceability Matrix • Verified Deliverables • Work Performance Data	• Inspection • Group Decision Making Techniques	• Accepted Deliverables • Change Requests • Work Performance Information • Project Documents Updates

Must Know Concepts

1. Validate Scope is the process of obtaining formal acceptance of project deliverables.

2. The primary deliverable (Output) of the Validate Scope process is accepted deliverables.

3. A project deliverable is not complete until it has been formally accepted, in writing by the individual or group authorized to accept it.

4. Validate Scope differs from quality control because Validate Scope focuses on formal acceptance of the work; whereas Control Quality focuses on correctness of work.

Lesson 51 – Monitor and Control Project Work

Monitor and Control Project Work is performed to track project work performance and take action when performance is different than planned.

As project managers, it is our responsibility to continuously monitor project work, and when we detect some aspect is heading off-course, we make controlling adjustments, as necessary, to bring the project back in alignment, to ultimately achieve our defined objectives.

Monitor and Control Project Work		
This process monitors and controls the processes used by the team		
Inputs	**Tools and Techniques**	**Outputs**
• Project Management Plan	• Expert Judgment	• Change Requests
• Schedule Forecasts	• Analytical Techniques	• Work Performance Reports
• Cost Forecasts		
• Validated Changes	• Project Management Information System	• Project Management Plan Updates
• Work Performance Information		
• Enterprise Environmental Factors	• Meetings	• Project Documents Updates
• Organizational Process Assets		

Must Know Concepts

1. The Monitor and Control Project Work process is applied to monitor all project work through initiating, planning, executing and closing in order to identify exceptions and take corrective or preventive actions, as needed.

2. The primary deliverable (output) from Monitor & Control Project Work is change requests.

3. Corrective actions are actions required to bring expected future project performance into conformance with the project management plan.

4. Preventive actions are actions required to reduce the probability of negative consequences associated with project risks.

Lesson 52 – Perform Integrated Change Control

Perform Integrated Change Control is the process of controlling changes for the project. The general goal of the project manager is to discourage unnecessary changes and focus on the project scope that is tied directly to requirements and strategic business needs. When changes are warranted, they must be made in strict accordance with the project's change control system, and established project baselines normally remain intact. Re-baselining the project and measuring performance against a new baseline is appropriate only in rare project situations when major changes in scope have occurred.

Configuration management, kept in the Enterprise Environmental Factors, is applied in conjunction with change control processes to control changes to the project baselines and product specifications. Configuration management is focused on specifications surrounding the deliverables and the specifications for processes that are used on the project. Change control works with configuration control.

Change control documents and controls changes to the project baseline, scope, schedule, cost and product deliverables baseline. To oversimplify the description, configuration management applies mostly to the framework or specifications for the product and project processes. Change control deals with the deliverables planned for the project.

Project changes, although often initiated verbally, should always be documented to allow tracking and control. Additionally, all project changes should be formally approved or rejected.

Change Requests that are used as inputs to the Perform Integrated Change Control process come from many sources. Some organizations utilize a change control board (CCB) to evaluate and approve/disapprove project change requests.

Perform Integrated Change Control		
This process reviews, approves and controls changes to project deliverables		
Inputs	**Tools and Techniques**	**Outputs**
• Project Management Plan	• Expert Judgment	• Approved Change Requests
• Work Performance Reports	• Meetings	• Change Log
• Change Requests	• Change Control Tools	• Project Management Plan Updates
• Enterprise Environmental Factors		• Project Documents Updates
• Organizational Process Assets		

Must Know Concepts

1. Perform Integrated Change Control is the process of effectively managing changes and integrating them appropriately across the entire project.

2. The primary deliverables (Outputs) of the Perform Integrated Change Control process include Approved Change Requests, Project Management Plan Updates and Project Document Updates.

3. Configuration management applies mostly to the framework or specifications for the product and project processes. Configuration management is an especially useful tool when the product of the project is very complex.

4. It is the project manager's responsibility to discourage unnecessary changes. When legitimate changes are warranted, they should be made in accordance with the project's change control system.

Lesson 53 – Closing Process Group

The primary purpose that these Closing processes are performed is to authorize the project (or phase) to end. End of phase reviews will be held as part of Closing processes. Closing processes occur in the Integration Management knowledge area and the Procurement Management knowledge area of the *PMBOK® Guide Fifth Edition*.

An important part of the Closing process group is the authorization for the vendor to terminate activities and for the overall project (or phase) to terminate.

When a project is closed, the sponsor, project manager and stakeholders have the final view of the project. Approvals for work, the product that was created and the project overall are obtained prior to closing the project or phase.

Once the project team and/or vendor team is released from the project, unless there is some form of warranty verbiage in contracts, then the team is done and the project is officially closed.

The PMBOK® Guide is very certain that the project ends when final approval for work, for the product and the project are obtained.

Closing Tasks

On your PMP Exam, you will encounter approximately several questions that will test your understanding of Initiating processes. These questions will generally focus on Closing tasks. As a PMP or project manager closing a project (or project phase), you may be required to:

1. Obtain final acceptance of the project deliverables by working with the sponsor and/or customer, in order to confirm that project scope and deliverables were met.

2. Transfer the ownership or deliverables to the assigned stakeholders in accordance with the project plan, in order to facilitate project closure.

3. Obtain financial, legal and administrative closure using generally accepted practices, in order to communicate formal project closure and ensure no further liability.

4. Distribute the final project report including all project closure related information, project variances, and any issues, in order to provide the final project status to all stakeholders

5. Collate lessons learned through comprehensive project review, in order to create and/or update the organization's knowledge base.

6. Archive project documents and materials in order to retain organizational knowledge, comply with statutory requirements and ensure availability of data for potential use in future projects and internal or external audits.

7. Measure customer satisfaction at the end of the project by capturing customer feedback, in order to assist in project evaluations and enhance customer relationships.

Lesson 54 – Close Procurements

This process, in conjunction with the Close Project or Phase process, is often used to complete a project. This process is also used throughout the project's life cycle to bring a formal termination to a procurement or procurement contract.

This process is usually preceded by the Control Quality process and the Validate Scope process in order to verify that work was completed correctly and is accepted by the appropriate stakeholder(s).

The process of Close Procurements is similar to, but slightly different than the process of Close Project or Phase. First of all, Close Procurements is closing only a portion of the overall project, whereas Close Project or Phase is used to close the overall project or phase. In addition to that difference, there is a difference in activity flow in the process.

During Close Procurements, the majority of formal approval or acceptance flows from the project to the vendor. During Close Project or Phase, the project manager obtains or receives formal acceptance from the sponsor.

Close Procurements		
This process formally completes the project procurements		
Inputs	**Tools and Techniques**	**Outputs**
• Project Management Plan • Procurement Documents	• Procurement Audits • Procurement Negotiations • Records Management System	• Closed Procurements • Organizational Process Assets Updates

Must Know Concepts

1. The Close Procurements process is used to formally validate that all of the requirements for each of the project's procurement activities have been met and are acceptable for both seller and buyer.

2. The deliverables (Outputs) of the Close Procurements process are the closed procurements and updates to the organizational process assets.

Lesson 55 – Close Project or Phase

Close Project or Phase is the process of closing either an entire project or a phase of a project. This process is also utilized when projects are terminated prior to their completion.

Close Project or Phase is performed by collecting project records, analyzing project performance, analyzing lessons learned and archiving all project information for future review and use.

This process is intended to deliver two primary outputs:

- The final product/service/result of the project (formally accepted and transitioned to an appropriate stakeholder)
- Organizational process updates

Close Project or Phase		
This process formally completes the project or project phase		
Inputs	**Tools and Techniques**	**Outputs**
• Project Management Plan • Accept Deliverables • Organizational Process Assets	• Expert Judgment • Analytical Techniques • Meetings	• Final Product, Service or Result Transition • Organizational Process Assets Updates

Must Know Concepts

1. Close Project or Phase is the process of formally ending either the project or project phase.

2. Close Project or Phase documents project results to formalize the acceptance of the product/service/result of the project (or project phase).

3. The primary deliverables (Outputs) of the Close Project or Phase process include the formally accepted product/service/result transition and organizational process assets updates.

4. Close Project or Phase is performed by collecting project records, analyzing project performance, analyzing lessons learned and archiving all project information for future review and use.

Appendix C
Additional Examples & Supplemental Materials

CONTROL QUALITY

Fishbone Diagram

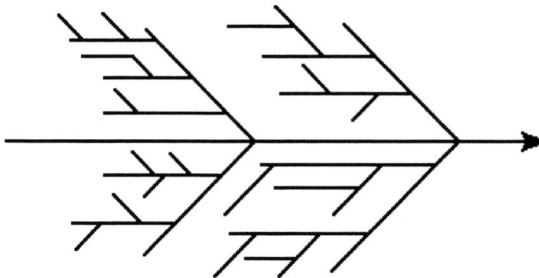

Also referred to as Cause & Effect Diagrams that illustrate how various factors might be linked to potential or effects.

Benefit: Helps uncover root causes

Control Chart

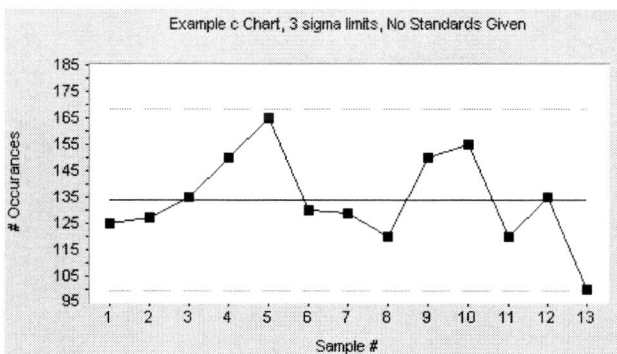

Determines whether or not a process is stable or has predictable performance.

Benefit: Validates the process is within acceptable limits

Flowcharting/Flowcharts

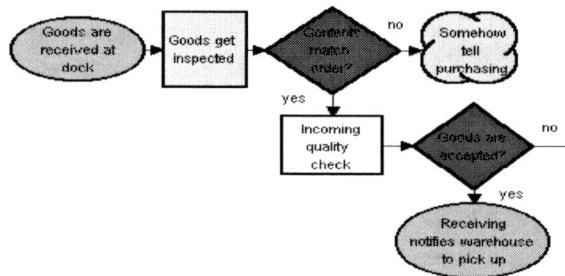

Show activities, decision points & order of processing determine a failing process step

Benefit: Helps PM anticipate quality problems & potential process improvement opportunities.

Histogram

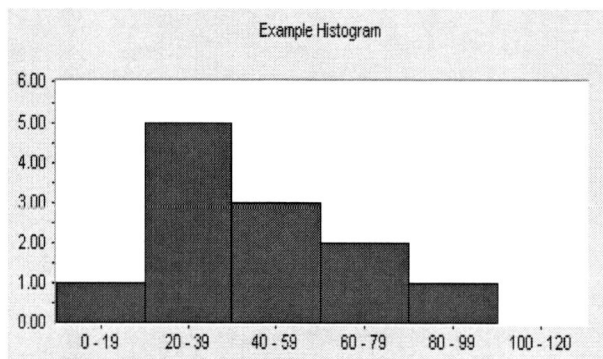

Vertical bar charts shows how often a particular variable state occurred (represents an attribute or characteristic of a problem/situation).

Benefit: Illustrates the most common cause of problems in a process

Pareto Chart

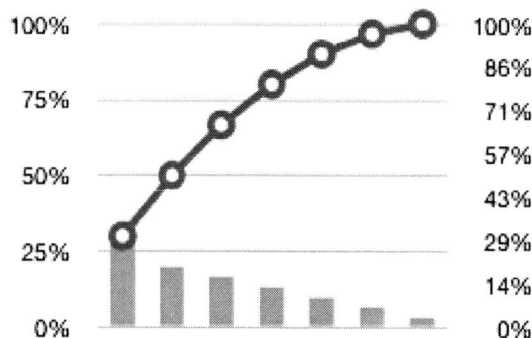

Shows how many car defects were generated by type or category of identified cause (type of histogram).

Benefit: Helps project team address the causes creating the greatest number of defects first (80/20 principle)

Scatter Diagram

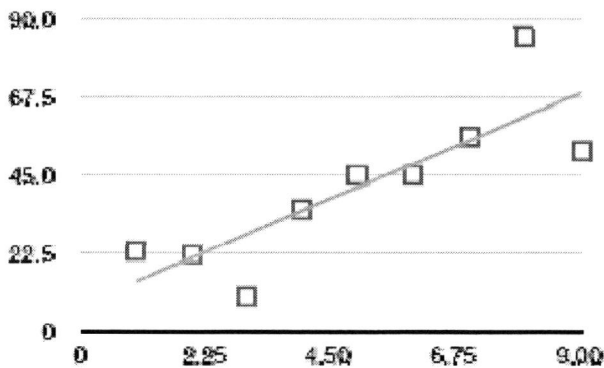

Shows relationship between 2 variables.

Benefit: Allows quality team to identify possible relationships between changes. Tthe closer the points are to the diagonal line, the more closely they are related, i.e. $18,000 & $29,000 cars may be experiencing the same type of defect.

Run Chart

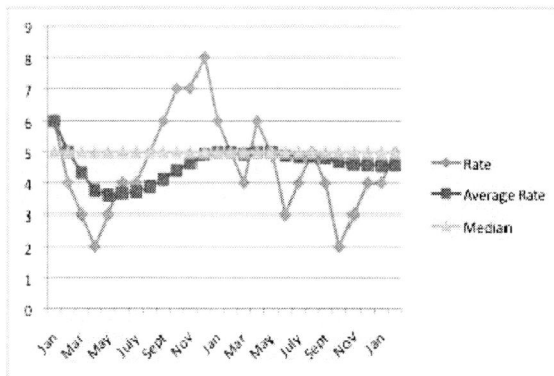

Shows history and pattern of variable (line graph, similar to control chart without displayed limits.)

Benefit: Reflects trends to forecast future outcomes based on historical results. (Used in technical and cost/schedule performances.)

PMI® PMP® Application
Project Description Examples (500 character limit)

Experience 1:
I: Developed Feasibility Study & Scoping Requirements

P: Identified risks / risk management plan / long lead procurement req's; developed schedules & contracts; conducted stakeholder meetings

E: Managed field implementation; Managed contract results; Conducted Implementation/ schedule meetings

M&C: Reported project results / Performed self-assessments / Managed scope changes

C: Facilitated Lessons Learned meetings; Closed contracts

Experience 2:

I: Developed Feasibility Study & Scoping Requirements

P: Identified risks; developed schedule & costs; conducted stakeholder meetings

E: Acquired & managed field resources; Conducted schedule review meetings

M&C: Measured project baselines; Resolved Issues / implemented risk responses

C: Archived project docs; Conducted post mortem

Experience 3:

I: Project was in planning phase when I started

P: Identified risks; developed schedules & contracts; documented stakeholder req's

E: Managed field implementation; Managed contract results; Conducted implementation/ schedule review meetings;

M&C: Reported project results; Performed self-assessments / Facilitated CCB meetings

C: Facilitated Lessons Learned meetings; Closed contracts

Estimate Costs
Financial Accounting Terms and Examples

Straight Line Depreciation

Straight line depreciation is considered to be the most common method of depreciating assets. To compute the amount of annual depreciation expense using the straight line method requires two numbers: the initial cost of the asset and its estimated useful life.

> Straight line depreciation =
> original cost of asset / estimated asset life

Example A:
You purchase a truck for $20,000 and expect to use it in your business for 10 years. Using the straight line depreciation method, you would divide the initial cost of the truck by its useful life.
= $20,000 / 10 = $2,000, i.e., the truck depreciates $2,000 every year.

However, if there is an estimated value of the asset at the end of its life (salvage value), then straight line depreciation is calculated as below:

> Straight line depreciation =
> (Original costs of asset − salvage value) /
> estimated asset life

Example B with known salvage value:
A company purchased a new system for $200,000. The company estimates that the system will have a value of $50,000 at the end of its 15 year life. Using the straight line depreciation method, the company's depreciation expense would be calculated as follows:
= ($200,000 - $50,000) / 15 = $10,000, i.e., the system depreciates $10,000 every year.

Accelerated Depreciation

The accelerated depreciation method allows faster write-offs than the straight line method. A popular method is 'double declining balance' that essentially doubles the rate of depreciation of the straight line method.

> Double declining depreciation = 2 x straight line rate.

Example:
Using example A above,
= 2 x $2,000 = $4,000, i.e., the truck depreciates $4,000 each year for the first five years

Opportunity Cost

Opportunity Cost is the cost of passing up an alternative choice when making a decision, i.e., opportunity lost.

Example:
Project A has potential revenue of $30, 000 and project B has potential revenue of $55,000. What is the opportunity cost of selecting project B?

> Answer: $30,000

Benefit Cost Ratio (BCR)

BCR is the ratio of benefits to costs that depicts the total financial return for each dollar invested.

> BCR = benefits / costs
>
> BCR < 1 = costs are greater than benefits
> BCR > 1 = benefits are greater than costs
> BCR = 1 means costs equal benefits

Example:
You expect a construction project to cost $1,000,000, and you expect to be able to sell the completed office building for $1,750,000. Then your BCR is $1,750.000 / $1,000,000 = 1.75. Thus, you get $1.75 of benefit for every $1.00 of cost.

Question:
If the BCR of project A is 1.3 and the BCR of project B is 1.1, which project would you select?

> Answer: Project A with the higher BCR. A BCR of 1.3 means the benefit is 1.3 times the cost.

Internal Rate of Return (IRR)

IRR is viewed as the interest rate an organization will realize on the money invested in a project. It measures the average yield on an investment.

Question:
If project A has an IRR of 24% and project B has an IRR of 13%, which project would you invest in?

> Answer: Project A with the higher IRR – just like you want the highest interest rate on your saving account.

Payback Period

Payback period is the time to recover/recoup an initial investment in a project through cash flows generated by the investments.

Example:
Project A will cost $10,000 and will generate an income of $2,500 every year after it is complete, The payback period can be calculated by dividing the initial cost by the annual income = $10,000 / 2,500 = 4 years, i.e., in 4 years the costs of the project will be recovered.

Question:
If project A has a payback period of 14 months and project B has a payback period of 6 months, which would you chose?

> Answer: Project B since it needs less time to recoup its investment.

Estimate Costs
Financial Accounting Terms and Examples

Present Value (PV)

PV is the value today of cash flows in the future. PV can be used to take time out of the equation and evaluate how much a project is worth right now. With PV, bigger is better.

$$\text{Present Value} = \frac{FV}{(1 + r)^n}$$

FV = Future Value
r = interest rate, n = number of time periods

Example:
Assume you need $20,000 in three years for a down payment on a house. If the simple interest rate is 5%, how much would you have to invest today to accumulate the $20,000 in three years?

FV = $20,000
r = 5%
n = 3 years

$$PV = \frac{\$20,000}{(1 + 0.05)^3}$$
= $20,000 / 1.157625
= $17,276.75

Therefore, if you invest $17,276.75 today at 5% interest, you will have $20,000 in 3 years.

Net Present Value (NPV)

The NPV of a project is defined as the sum of all present values of the annual cash flow produced by an investment during its lifetime, less the initial cost of the investment. Thus, it is the same as PV except that you also factor in your costs.

NPV = sum of all PV - cost

An investment should be given further consideration if the net present value is positive and rejected if it is negative.

Example:
A company has decided to start a project with projected cash flows of $1,000 in the first year, $2,000 in the next 2 years and $1,000 in the fourth year. The project will cost $5,000 to start up the project and requires a 10% return.

NPV = [($1,000 / (1.1)) + ($2,000 / 1.1$)^2$) + (2,000 / 1.1$)^3$) + ($1,000 / 1.1$)^4$)] - $5,000
= [($1,000 / 1.1) + ($2,000 / 1.21) + (2,000 / 1.331) + ($1,000 / 1.4641)] - $5,000
= [$909 + $1,653 +$1,503 + $683] - $5,000
= - $252

Return on Investment (ROI)

ROI is a percentage that shows what return you make by investing in something. Remember that the bigger the ROI, the better.

$$ROI = \frac{(\text{benefit} - \text{cost})}{\text{cost}}$$

Example:
Your project will cost $300,000 and has projected benefits to save the company $360,000 in the first year alone. The ROI would be calculated as
= ($360,000 - $300,000) / $300,000
= $60,000 / $300,000
= 20%

Putting It All Together

Look at the table below and decide which project you would pick.

	Project A	Project B	Pick a project
BCR	2.11	1.22	
IRR	12%	13%	
Payback Period	2 months	8 months	
NPV	$35,000	$27,000	

Weighing all of these factors, which project would you choose?

TEST TIPS

Here are subjects you are expected to know (from the class presentation):

- Project Charter - What it is, what it does
- Stakeholders – Definition & examples, How and when to identify them, How to analyze
- Project Management Plan - What makes up the plan
- Requirements – When to collect, How to categorize
- Scope Statement – What it is and does
- Initiating a project – What steps to take
- Planning a project – What steps and processes – know how the processes flow within the planning process group
- Financial accounting terms – Definitions, How to calculate, How to interpret results
- Earned value technique to measure performance
- How to create and interpret a network diagram, What are the types of dependency relationships, What are the type of dependency determinations
- Schedule Compression: Crashing and fast tracking
- Critical Path – What is it, How to determine and calculate
- How to develop and manage a budget
- What the primary role of the project manager is, What is a critical skill
- What defines a milestone
- How to control change and the best thing to do about changes
- What a project gate or kill point is
- How to define and measure quality, What is the difference between quality vs. grade, and precision vs. accuracy
- Quality philosophies by their proponents
- Risk Management – What are the techniques, How to use a probability and impact matrix
- How to create and use the WBS – What processes does it link to
- What is included in Enterprise Environmental Factors and Organizational Process Assets, and what is needed from each process
- What are the main causes for conflict on a project, What are techniques to manage conflict
- What are the main constraints to a project
- How to define and use a communications plan, What is a basic communication model
- Interpersonal skills (10)
- Leadership styles and types of power
- Team development
- How to gain formal acceptances for work, the product and the project
- Organization Structures – What are they, What is the project manager's authority and role
- Motivational theories
- Procurement methods and processes – What are contract types and associated risks, What are procurement documents
- How to adhere to the PMP Code of Professional Conduct
- General management expertise
- Know the tools and techniques – What they are, How to use them, When and why to use them
- Customer satisfaction (understanding and meeting stakeholder expectations)

SAMPLE DUMP SHEET

Earned Value

Key Data Points	Variances	Indices
PV or BCWS	CV = EV – AC	CPI = EV / AC
EV or BCWP	SV = EV – PV	SPI = EV / PV
AC or ACWP	VAC = BAC - EAC	
BAC		

Forecasting

Variances Continue	Variances Corrected
ETC = (BAC – EV) / CPI	ETC = BAC – EV
EAC = AC + ETC	EAC = AC + ETC

EAC for ETC work considering both SPI & CPI =
AC + (BAC-EV)/(CPI x SPI)

TCPI (To-Complete Performance Index

(BAC – EV) / (BAC – AC)   (based on BAC–with original budget/variances continue)

(BAC – EV) / (EAC – AC)   (based on EAC–new budget/variances corrected)

Other Equations

Present Value $PV = \dfrac{FV}{(1+r)^n}$

Communication Channels $\dfrac{(n * (n-1))}{2}$

Cost Estimating
ROM = -25% to +75%
Definitive = -5% to +10%

EMV = Probability * Impact (value, $)
Negative Risk = Negative Results
Positive Risk = Positive Results

3 Point Estimate

Triangular Distribution
$\dfrac{P + M + O}{3}$

Beta Distribution
$\dfrac{P + 4M + 0}{6}$

c = Cost
t = Time

Standard Deviation
1 Sigma = +/- 68.26%
2 Sigma = +/- 95.46%
3 Sigma = +/- 99.73%
6 Sigma = +/- 99.99%

EARNED VALUE FORMULAS

	FORMULAS	USE FOR DUMP SHEET
	Variances Continue	
ETC	(BAC - EV) / CPI	**(BAC - EV) / CPI**
	EAC - AC	
EAC	ETC + AC	**ETC + AC**
	BAC / CPI	
	AC + ((BAC - EV) / CPI)	
VAC	BAC - EAC	**BAC - EAC**
TCPI (Based on BAC) with original budget		**(BAC-EV)/(BAC-AC)**
	Variances Corrected	
ETC	BAC - EV	**BAC - EV**
	EAC - AC	
	(using new EAC)	
EAC	AC+BAC-EV	
	ETC + AC (using new ETC)	**ETC + AC**
VAC	BAC - EAC (using new EAC)	**BAC - EAC**
TCPI (Based on EAC) new estimates		**(BAC-EV)/(EAC-AC)**

PLAN PROCUREMENTS

Common Procurement Documents for Soliciting Proposals from Prospective Sellers

	RFP (Request for Proposal)	RFQ (Request for Quote)	RFI (Request for Information)	IFB or ITB (Invitation for/to Bid)
Brief Description of Solicitation Document	Requests price and other information such as approach, product information, company financial information and/or technical capabilities. The RFP is usually business requirements-based and typically includes the buyer's strategy and short/long-term business objectives.	Requests a price quote for commodity type items with specific known requirements that require minimal customization. The RFQ includes specifications for the product/service and relevant parameters, e.g., quantities/volumes, skills, quality metrics, terms and conditions, etc.	Requests information regarding seller's capabilities, qualifications, and/or products/services. Note: If pricing is requested, it is used for estimating or comparative purposes.	Requests price and other information such as approach, product information, company financial information and/or technical capabilities. The IFB/ITB is usually business requirements-based and typically includes the buyer's strategy and short/long-term business objectives.
Typical Purpose & Usage	• Solicit proposals for bigger, higher priced, customized services or products. • Buyer uses Source Selection Criteria and Proposal Evaluation Techniques (weighted criteria) to award the contract based on best value and other factors, not just price. • Conduct Procurements is usually lengthier when RFPs are used. • May lead to a creative relationship or partnership.	• Solicit price quote for a small dollar amount or commodity type items (products or services) that do not require a great degree of customization. • Buyer awards contract based on lowest price. • RFQ is sometimes used to develop a list of qualified sellers for a subsequent RFP. • RFQ can be used to Estimate Costs using Vendor Bid Analysis.	• Solicit information from broad base of sellers to learn more about qualifications and/or products/services for comparative or estimating purposes and to determine next steps. • RFI is often used to develop a list of qualified sellers preceding an RFP or RFQ. • RFI can be used to help with make-or-buy analysis. • RFI can be used to Estimate Costs using Vendor Bid Analysis. • RFI may also be used to develop strategies or build seller databases.	• Used for government sealed bidding processes with characteristics similar to those for a RFP.
Negotiations	Yes	No	No	Yes
Legally Binding	Yes	Yes	No	Yes
Associated Contract Type	Fixed-price or Cost-reimbursable	Time & material	n/a – usually followed up with an RFP, RFQ or IFB/ITB	Fixed-price or Cost-reimbursable

Note: Typically, US companies have policies and standards regarding usage of procurement documents and contract types. Thereby, refer to Enterprise Environmental Factors and Organizational Process Assets.

This page intentionally blank.